MORALS
FOR THE 21ST
CENTURY

D1257477

John Baines

MORALS FOR THE 21ST CENTURY
(Originally published as "Moral Para el Siglo XXI")
By John Baines
Translated from the Spanish by Josephine Bregazzi

Copyright 2000 by John Baines

ISBN 1-882692-03-9
Library of Congress Control Number: 00-091908

1st Edition 2000

Published by John Baines Institute, Inc
Printed in the United States of America

MORALS FOR THE 21ST CENTURY

BY

John Baines

Edited by the Editorial
Staff of the John Baines Institute, Inc.

2000
Published by

JOHN BAINES INSTITUTE, INC.

P.O. Box 8556 • F.D.R. Station • New York, NY • 10150
Jbi@bway.net

CONTENTS

Preface ix

Chapter I   **Basic Tenets of Moral Physics**   **1**

Chapter II   **The Difficulties of Acting Morally**   **17**

1. The Fact That We Live in an Era of Masses   21

2. The Alienation of Our Time   30

3. The Erroneous Educational System   39

4. The Subjective Nature of Values   48

5. Man's Low Level of Evolution   57

6. The Weakness of People's Character   64

   Causes That Weaken People's Character and Will   66

     (a) The Compulsive Quest for Pleasure   66

     (b) Overprotection   70

     (c) Idleness and Decadence   72

     (d) Sexual Ambiguity   74

     (e) Sedentariness   75

     (f) Lack of Self-Worth   76

7. Environmental Hypnosis   81

8. Lack of a Consensual Morality   90

Chapter III   **Norms Pertaining to the True Human Being**   **99**

Chapter IV   **The Values of the Average Man**   **109**

Chapter V   **Sin and Moral Faults**   **121**

Marriage Without Love   121

The Shirking of One's Self-Control and Responsibility   127

False Friendship   130

Mental and Emotional Manipulation   135

The Manipulation of the Image   142

Dishonesty   148

The Abuse of Power   156

The Financial System   164

Envy   181

Egoism   198

Corruption   214

Mediocrity   227

Parasitical Vampirism   234

Self-Indulgence and Self-Pity   242

Living for One's Image   247

Lack of Individual Merit   256

Ignorance of Good and Evil   269

Swindling   279

Abortion   289

Masturbation   320

Relations Against Nature   336

Adultery   345

Divorce   355

Sadomasochism   365

The Weakening of the Family   378

Comfort   395

Hate   408

Drug Abuse   419

Not Keeping One's Word   433

Deceiving the Eye and the Ear   441

Alcoholism   451

Materialism   462

To Expect Without Deserving   475

Ten Moral Rules   **487**

To Prioritize Personal Objectives   488

To Commit Oneself to Good and Swear Loyalty
   to One's Own Spirit   497

To Confront One's Own Dishonesty   506

To Put Oneself Emotionally in the Place of Others   514

To Have Dominion Over Oneself   520

To Come Out of One's Own Mental Burrow   527

Developing Will and Tempering the Character   533

Living in Harmony with Nature   541

Acting in Accordance with the Law of Egalitarian

Equivalence   550

Seeking More Profound Truths   557

Carefully Examining the Legality of Nature   569

Appendix   **Experimental Proof of the Negative Physical**

Effect of Certain Moral Violations   589

Measuring the Electromagnetic Energy of the Body

in Different Physiological Processes   591

Introduction   591

1. Bases of the Experiment   593

2. Experimental Variables   606

3. Experimental Procedures   606

   (a) *Measurement of Menstrual Blood*   609

   (b) *Measurement of Energy Loss with Masturbation*   610

   (c) *Measurement of Electromagnetic Energy of the Anus*   611

   (d) *Measurement of Seeds Magnetized with Feelings of*

   Rage   611

4. Results of the Experiment   612

5. Discussion of the Results   619

Bibliography   623

PREFACE

Why be good? What does it mean?

What do I gain by being good?

Are good people better than corrupt ones?

Will I be happier if I am good?

I can guarantee the reader that if he complies with the proposed moral norms of this work, not only will he be happier but also truly successful in life. I am talking about a kind of SUCCESS (written in capital letters), which far surpasses people's common expectations; the triumph that really matters, namely, to be in harmony with life and with the designs for which we were created; to triumph on the path of evolution which also includes success in our daily affairs.

One cannot have imagined morality to be a powerful tool for attaining success in life, but it is, because one whose behavior conforms with a higher moral code, enters into harmony with Nature. At this precise moment in world history, we need more than ever to arrive at a moral consensus, something which has never before been achieved. This accord is possible only through the existence of moral norms that emanate from a type of undeniable and self-evident supreme good; a real virtue, rather than a merely apparent good; a good that equally benefits people of every condition, epoch, and place, and that can be experienced every day by everyone; a good that is so very illuminating that every individual would have the profoundest interest in adopting it. Supreme bounty, the source of genuine happiness, is revealed to a man only when he practices proper rules, and by experiencing positive effects, he will be able to create the necessary motivation to adopt those norms in general. No one invented these norms of conduct. They are inscribed upon the memory of Nature, to which one has access while in a state of higher consciousness.

The type of morality I propose is a straightforward description of transcendental values which are the building blocks of the Universe, archetypal forms of Nature that constitute the basis for sustaining life. It is necessary to adapt oneself internally to these values in order to experience life differently—in a more productive, fuller, fairer, and happier manner. I think that the majority of people's behavioral problems derive from an erroneous and deficient mental attitude *vis a vis* the nature of good in contrast to the nature of evil— and beyond simple belief, benefit, or personal convenience.

In this work, I hope to define, in a technical way, what is goodness and what is malice, and what it means to ally oneself with one or the other. Having been born with this intuitive faculty that has manifested itself from my very beginnings, I have not needed to extract this knowledge from books. I have been guided by this intuition since childhood to seek confirmation of Nature's Wisdom in the School of Life. My definitions are "portraits of Nature"; photographic descriptions of the form in which certain unknown life forces interrelate with man and other life forms, influencing their destiny. This process of feedback describes well-defined codes that have existed since long before the human being appeared on the planet. There is no other way to be abundantly successful than by complying with these principles, which are virtually "the path of heaven and earth."

Man does not possess a stable morality, and his norms of conduct are typically subordinated to egotistic interests, passions, desires, and the apparent good of the moment. In his search for happiness and good, he confuses the apparent with the real, and is diverted all too frequently towards vice and corruption. Neither religious nor moral precepts can prevent such alterations because men have no knowledge of real good in life, nor do they know what is licit as opposed to what is questionable. The individual lives in submission to an infinite number of morally conflictive situations in which he is completely unaware of what decisions to make, since he cannot clearly and precisely perceive which is the right path. There is general confusion on this matter. People no longer distinguish between "the good ones" and "the bad ones," and so moral boundaries are disappearing and rules of conduct are becoming vague, whimsical, and easy to manipulate.

My intention is for this work to help dispel the prejudice and ignorance that exists on this theme, and to initiate the reader into the knowledge of what real morality is, beyond recommendations or personal interpretations, providing at the same time a personal guide to the path to higher virtue. Nevertheless, I expect that hypocrites will resist this book. A dictionary definition for "hypocrisy" is: "pretense of qualities or feelings contrary to those one truly feels or experiences."

By "hypocrites" I refer to those whose primary, fundamental tendencies are dissimulation and deceit. They are insincere people who try to erect an acceptable façade in order to conceal their defects, sentiments, and inner designs. They are individuals who present themselves with an image of straightness and authenticity but who conceal personalities that are, in reality, covert and untrustworthy. These are the same people who, on certain occasions, would be exaggeratedly dramatic in the face of an evident reality, not because they feel offended or affected, but in order to disguise their own guilt or true state.

Why do they make a pretense of virtue or devotion?

The person needs to feel valued, respected, accepted, and loved by others. He thinks and feels that others will accept him only if he seems "good." He believes that if he shows his weaknesses, he will not be accepted or respected. This is just how he treats himself, incapable as he is of accepting his own weaknesses. More profoundly, this need to feel respected and accepted is related to the need to be confirmed as an individual. The person's individuality is pathologically conferred only if someone else confirms it, since that person is incapable of independently being an individual and experiencing himself as an individual. His inner world is not sufficiently stable, potent, and autonomous to provide him with a feeling of security, based on his own emotions and capacities. The person reproduces in the adult world his childhood memories of feeling helpless and defenseless when others (his parents) had not accepted his weaknesses; when he felt the intense fear that if his parents did not love him he could have died, since in the first years of life one is effectively and completely dependent on one's adult caretakers. This model is reproduced in the social context and can be seen by the way public personages are assessed. In order to be esteemed, they hypocritically present themselves as being "good," to confirm themselves as worthwhile people, unable to feel a sense of self-worth on their own. They exist only psychologically through other people. This happens to all people, to differing degrees.

—In collaboration with the psychologist
Juan Pablo Villanueva

Alas, our society is afflicted with hypocrisy and priggishness, and these patterns are deeply ingrained in people's minds, preventing them from accepting obvious truths, albeit truths that clash with the great social masquerade. Hypocrisy is the mother of all prejudices, clouding the comprehension of any unconventional wisdom. It allows for people who are immoral, to seem to be puritanical; people who never remember God in a sincere way, to be considered as religious; people who are disgraceful, to underrate those who see right through them; people who are immoral, to maintain devout and charitable external behavior; white-collar delinquents, to remain camouflaged in respectable institutions; and for sexual morbidity to be disguised behind a cloak of purity and chastity.

If we comprehend authentic morality, we can overcome our defects and shortcomings instead of wasting our energies on hiding them, serving them, and protecting them, thus learning a sense of self-worth. A rational conviction of the way to act correctly will permit us to lose the fear of being neither loved nor accepted by others, since we will have attained our own development, in accordance with higher moral norms. I would advise the reader that this work does not constitute a "moral recipe" or a set of predigested concepts in a format that requires no effort in thought for them to be accepted. There is nothing worse than sugar-coated morality, or morality with a vested interest that theorizes on idealized situations which are disconnected from the reality of life.

This work conforms to a different paradigm—one that goes beyond the purely informational level, thus it permits one to practice or recover the marvelous art of deep thinking in order to gain access to a true level of significance, a skill which is most certainly in the process of extinction.

Finally, I must point out that I am not responsible for statements that are taken out of the context of this book, such being the exclusive liability of those who wish to attribute a biased or capricious meaning that does not correspond to my intention, nor to that which was really expressed in the entirety of this work which I call *Moral Physics*.

The Author

CHAPTER I

BASIC TENETS OF MORAL PHYSICS

The science that enables one within the Universe to interact voluntarily and consciously with Nature, with the aim of attaining transcendental bounty, is what I refer to as *moral physics,* in which ethical and human excellence must also be included. Unlike traditional morality, it is not based upon faith, and this is a huge obstacle for nonbelievers. Rather, it is founded upon man's comprehension and volitive handling of the level of his mental posture within the Universe as a whole. He arrives at this condition by developing and handling uncommonly high states of consciousness, as well as by adopting higher values and inner discipline, all of which lead to supreme success and happiness.

The approach taken by *moral physics* is of necessity technical, centered as it is on a personal understanding and testing of the mechanics of energetic processes that characterize the relationship between Nature and the human being. Traditional morality is based upon religious or ideological foundations and is inculcated in an automatic and passive way. This leads inexorably to the repression of impulses so that, in cases where actions run counter to moral norms, they also lead to destructive emotions, such as guilt. Repression is not a healthy process to be recommended, and over time, it inevitably gives rise to a sort of "devil's cauldron" in the unconscious mind. Therefore, the sublimation of the instincts would seem to be a preferable alternative. Because traditional morality is clearly and inherently repressive, it is a mechanism through which the individual will try to reject or maintain thoughts, images, or memories in his unconscious. All of these are linked to instinctive pulsions that arise from his "id." (*The term "id" is used in in-depth psychology and psychoanalysis to denote that aspect of the personality that lies outside the "I." It is the unconscious, the most profound part of the psyche, the realm of the instincts, as contrasted to the conscious part of the psyche which is called the "I."*) However, this suppression is not perceived, since such pulsions take place outside the individual's conscious control, while still residing within the individual. Even though repressed impulses are unknown to the conscious mind, it does not mean they do not exist. Therefore, they become gradually archived and accumulated within the unconscious mind until they become functional. This creates collaterally a chain of undesirable effects:

1. If repression is unsuccessful, the individual will give in to his impulses, and this will give rise to self-blame, self-punishment, self-depreciation, and inevitably self-destruction.

2. If the repressive mechanism is successful, it will serve only to stoke the passional boiler of the unconscious mind, resulting in overfeeding the repressed impulses. This results in deterioration of the individual's conscious behavior. I should point out here that repression generally has only a transitory success, for the force of the pulsions increases by virtue of their very restriction. This, at some point, brings about a violent,

instinctive outburst, which once more gives rise to feelings of guilt.

According to some psychoanalysts, most mental and emotional disorders are caused by repression and it is quite logical that they should be, for this mechanism, in practice, entails a sort of corruption of that which is repressed. For example, cases are common of devout people who, in a desire to maintain a higher code of ethics, make vows of chastity without being able to prevent genital containment from reaching their imagination. When given over to its uncontrollable arbiter, this containment unleashes all manner of prurient images that give rise to morbidity, perversion, and ultimately to an inevitable sexual promiscuity. At the same time, it gives rise to a sense of guilt which is equivalent in magnitude to the sin committed.

Moral physics, as contrasted with traditional morality, requires a technical, conscious, and reflective apprenticeship, so that the individual can become conscious of his impulses instead of repressing them. He maintains them in his conscious "I," confronting them, taking full charge of them and accepting them as his own, even though they are unsuitable for higher ethical behavior. He should work on the simultaneous purging of these impulses by means of inner reflection, for the more they come to light, the more diminished will be their power over him. On the other hand, they attain a disproportionate influence over his behavior if they are repressed in his unconscious mind.

Let us suppose, for example, that he managed to confront a desire he may have felt for maternal incest, and by doing so, realizes that previously, his behavior had been dominated by the unconscious impulse to possess his mother sexually, a pulsion that emanates from his most primordial and animal aspect. By understanding that this desire correlates with his animal identity, he will no longer give it the importance it once seemed to have—simply by accepting that he has no further need to satisfy his baser impulses, which are only the primitive urges that await their subsequent sublimation by his higher aspect. He should also realize that despite retaining an animal part, he also possesses a developed brain, and he suspects the transcendental fact that he is a bearer of the divine spark and is therefore dramatically different from beasts, however much he tends to ignore this from time to time when he behaves badly.

On the one hand, it is the denial and repression of unconscious impulses that upsets the human being's mind and emotions; on the other hand, it is unbridled passion that corrupts and degenerates them. The only solution to this dilemma is *moral physics,* the path of psychic training that guides one to confront one's base nature, which one is obliged to cleanse, cultivate, and sublimate from the position of one's luminous "I." One must transform himself into a truly clean, transparent human being without guilt or sin, and unrestrictedly comply with the Creator's design for him to become an architect of his own destiny, free from the fear of divine wrath.

This great work is the finest and most beautiful thing that an individual can undertake, for its aim is not only one's own evolution, but is also to offer oneself as a contribution to society, as an example of spiritual value worthy of imitation. If one continues to flee from one's own defects by mechanically denying and repressing one's animal pulsions, he will become increasingly sickened in his soul with an incurable illness for which science knows no prescription. The application of *moral physics* is notably different from what is usually known as "training," whether this be mental or psychological, and which usually consists of applying repetitive, mechanical techniques. Initial work in *moral physics* is comprised of the practical understanding of oneself and the type of relationship one has with Nature. For this, one has to make a series of cognitive premises, some of which are based on quantum physics. One has also to make proposals of provable procedures that are consonant with the universal repercussion of a person's actions according to his ethical quality.

Whoever is sincerely interested can verify what I am saying through self-observation by the simple expedient of establishing, over the course of a year, a cause–effect relationship between the morality of his own actions and everyday events. Thus, in time he will discover that what he has reaped always corresponds in its moral quality to what he had sown, although at times, in the short or middle run, it might seem otherwise.

What are the tenets to which I refer here?

1. We live in a conscious, intelligent Universe with a holographic structure, in which there is only one type of essential energy that by multi-dimensionally interpenetrating with the Cosmos, comes into absolute unity at the most profound level of life. Whatever happens to the tiniest particle simultaneously affects the complete structure, since there is an inseparable relationship between all parts of the Universe.

2. In accordance with the holographic principle, "each part contains the whole," which can be verified by the discoveries of cellular biology where it has been seen that each cell contains a replica of the original DNA, which is sufficient to create a clone and reconstitute the whole body.

3. Therefore, the whole is "The Creator," the omnipotent and omniscient primary energy from which all forms of existence emanate—the spiritual essence or vital substance that sustains all forms of energy and matter.

4. Nature is eminently sensitive to the vital actions and energies that emanate from the human being, inevitably conceiving them in its own womb.

5. We are hybrid beings who have evolved from animals, but have attained certain qualities that distinguish us from them, qualities we call *human*—capacities that, through a moral imperative, we have to develop to their maximum expression.

6. Each individual is essentially sacred because he bears within himself the divine spark, the emanation of the Creator.

7. We were created incomplete, so that each of us has to fulfill the task, during his material incarnation, of completing himself. Each must decode his own vital circumstances to attain the wisdom and values that accompany them.

8. The purpose of our life is the evolution of individual consciousness, which consists in developing and enlarging truly human qualities, as opposed to those of the animal, although this goal has been forgotten in the indiscriminate pursuit of sensorial pleasure as a primary aim.

9. We are creative beings, for the psychic energies that originate in our thoughts, feelings, and actions are biophotonic pulses that are projected into space to interact with the forces of cosmic Nature insomuch as they *influence them and in turn are influenced.*

10. Each human particle modifies Nature with its biophotonic projections, while Nature at the same time, receives back the energy that it requires to reestablish cosmic equilibrium through our action.

11. "Like attracts like" once it has been conceived in the womb of Nature, so that if an individual's emanations have been constructive, positive, and harmonious, he will be rewarded with an equivalent disposition.

12. Natural equilibrium will bring to a perpetrator an equally negative reaction if his energetic projection has been destructive, filthy, unharmonious, or criminal. This reaction will be considerably increased in power, and this can be interpreted as being fair punishment for moral violation.

13. Space is holographically interconnected, and the individual unwittingly and constantly interacts with Nature, thus maintaining a continuous feedback of energy, with the aforementioned consequences.

14. The "cosmic egg" irreversibly conceives our photonic projections which, analogous to the energetic sperm, moves around the Universe at the speed of human thought.

15. We shall inevitably pay for our sins and be rewarded for our virtue, regardless of our opinion on the matter. You do not have to believe this to obtain either the reward or the punishment appropriate to the quality of your personal emanations.

16. "He who sins, pays" regardless of his good or bad intentions.

The concept of universal unity is not new, for according to Aristotle, the Universe is organized in such a way that all its parts interact as if it were a living organism. This is currently confirmed in the works of the Professor Emeritus of Physics, David Bohm[1] on "the structural totality of the Universe." Likewise, the premises mentioned above can be tested practically in the fray of everyday existence by witnessing the law of cause and effect and how it inexorably conditions people's destinies.

An important part of the application of this knowledge consists in mastering the vibrations of one's own energies, a control that has nothing to do with repression but with the sublimation of the libido and the elevation of the level of individual consciousness. It is obvious that when a person sees, from his own life, that "virtue pays" and that "moral offensiveness does not pay," he will learn to love virtuous conduct by the mere fact that it is beneficial for himself and the rest of the world. By realizing that success and happiness largely depend on irreproachable moral conduct, one becomes inspired to comply with a higher code of ethics. Each man or woman who acts in accordance with the norms of "moral physics" will experience the benefits of inner harmony brought about by a heart without wrath, envy, or resentment and the renewed joy of living in perfect harmony with Nature.

The model of what constitutes success can no longer be represented exclusively by mere economic affluence, but also in attaining a transcendental dimension through the fulfillment of the true purpose of our lives: the evolution of individual consciousness. There is nothing in life more beneficial than the conscious virtue that we propose here, for the individual's inner space is the only thing over which he can attain lasting control. Evidence of its decisive importance is that it is in the inner world that whatever type of material experiences we might have are finally interpreted and elaborated. An untrained person lives an unconscious, clumsy, and uncontrolled life; therefore, he will more than likely find pain, failure, and sickness. He who practices *moral physics* will be able to consciously and actively live out his everyday experience—to build on this foundation an existence of undying plenitude and happiness, one free of guilt and resentment. Each of us reaps what we sow, and Nature will give back a thousandfold what is planted in it. Sow winds and you will generate storms; sow wheat and you will produce food.

Someone who has not disciplined his libido will remain a slave to his passions, to degrading and overwhelming animalistic impulses that enslave the "I" to spurious stimuli, such as jealousy, envy, and resentment, among others. These are passions that poison the blood and make the heart heavy. They sicken both body and soul. Feelings of guilt are derived from the unconscious need for punishment, which is often translated into failure in one's profession or in love. Therefore, if one can avoid this burden, one can experience a happiness known to only few people. Guilt makes us easy prey of those who seek to victimize us through this feeling, whereas if we are convinced that we are acting rightly, ethically, and impeccably, then we become steadfast and strong.

When someone commits a repugnant deed, he generates a destructive photonic pulse that disrupts universal harmony and equilibrium. He thereby exposes himself to a defensive reaction from Nature that gives birth to an offspring of energy. This offspring is a corrupt magnetic nucleus that will accompany him for the rest of his life, feeding on his energies and upsetting his physical and mental health. It is a negative presence that we can intuitively perceive in people who have bad habits.

Any constructive or destructive action, feeling, thought, or impulse that takes place at the instinctive level will materialize, so that we will inevitably receive the natural backfire of its effects whether positive or negative, according to the nature of the seed we had sown. Thus, man is the child of his works in the broadest sense of the word. He who can understand, confirm for himself, and accept this, will need no compulsive moral prohibitions because he will always act on the conviction that in order to receive the best, he has first to give the optimum.

Ethical disorientation makes far too many people adopt immoral attitudes, whatever their culture or social station. This often happens through a slackening of their principles, or through mere ignorance—at other times through the mere fact that they slip into faulty behavior that, through habit, come to be accepted as "normal."

For example, there are sexual habits that were, in the past, classified as aberrations, but which today have come to be euphemistically called "variations in sexual conduct." These types of conduct, despite what some might say, not only alienate and debase, but also seriously undermine and deteriorate one's mental and physical health.

Thus, we have selected certain moral faults which are conducive to experimentation, in order to test their negative effects. I refer to masturbation, sexual relations during the woman's menstruation, anal sex, and the destructive irradiation people acquire when they are under the influence of rage and hate. The result of these experiments clearly demonstrates how there comes about a sudden drop in the individual's vital energies—how visible electromagnetic waves appear that are similar to those that produce toxic substances in the human organism, such as chlorine, for example. This proves the antinatural character of such practices, which by contravening universal harmony generate a destructive organic state. Envy, hate, jealousy, pessimism, and resentment are also contagious, destructive forces which, having once produced their effect, turn back on the person who had caused them and bring about a negative impact.

We can see how an individual's moral behavior influences his whole environment, both near and far, modifying the holographic equilibrium of the Universe. We live in a perfectly interrelated cosmic environment in which our thoughts and feelings influence even the furthest corners of space. We are transmitters of vibratory energies that saturate our energetic environment. If we become pessimistic, *we vibrate pessimism, sending out such vibrations that sensitize ourselves to other forces of the same type.* If we send out waves of pessimism, we will attract unlucky events, but if we irradiate happiness and optimism, we sympathize with similar vibrations, which then affect our lives as they reach us. By irradiating love, harmony, tolerance, happiness, or purity, we will attract vibrations of a similar type.

Not taking the seventh point of the principal tenets of *moral physics* into account, in that we are creative beings in the fullest sense of the word, makes many people fail, because they are like unpolished stones insomuch as they have not taught their animalistic nature the discipline that is necessary for consciously transmitting higher photonic pulses—the emanations that create transcendental values—as opposed to those that create passional freaks. Thus, they usually reap anguish from the widest variety of painful or destructive circumstances.

Superlative success is spiritual rather than social in character and represents the individual success of our being along its path of evolution, which is the supreme virtue to which the human being can aspire. However, do not believe that this option can be freely chosen, for from the very moment we're born as human beings, we have no alternative but either "to repeat the school year indefinitely" or to evolve spiritually, for this is the purpose of the "school of life." The problem is that people suppose that this *aula magna* was created for their own pleasure, without realizing that it is really a path for perfection. There are also people who erroneously believe, when they hear about this subject, that it is the species and not the individual that has to evolve, so they take no personal responsibility with respect to their own evolution. What is certain is that the apparent slowness with which we age and approach death keeps us complacent within our own dreams and fantasies, and only exceptional individuals manage to achieve evolutive success.

In this Universe of fully interpenetrating processes, the success or failure of a single being produces cosmic repercussions that ultimately affect every form of life (even those on other planets, constellations, and galaxies; even the Creator Himself). However, no matter how removed from the path of perfection we may be, it nonetheless depends on our own will and freedom of choice to take this path even though the ways of the Supreme Being may seem mysterious. The majority are thus lost by the wayside when they follow paths that seem attractive but which merely serve to distract them (for their illusory or fantastic nature generally leads to a narcissistic subjectivism that is totally divorced from Nature rather than leading to genuine evolution).

Unless we can find the right path to evolution, we will remain as lost wanderers in a wilderness of mirages, possessed by a sense of dissatisfaction and an inner void; we will be afflicted by an eternal and unquenchable thirst because the spring we seek on the outside in fact lies within our own spirit.

Moral physics enables us to find the doorway that leads to the source of eternal life that lies within us. But as the Bible cautions: "many are called, but few are chosen," for there are countless false doors designed to fool the pilgrim (which we all are) in one way or another.

Yet who is it that chooses? It is the individual himself who qualifies or disqualifies himself, depending on the clarity of his consciousness, which is a product of his previous evolution. The greater his inner content, the greater his capacity to objectively contemplate reality. What I call "inner content" corresponds to the chronological aggregate of lucid moments of insight which contribute substantially to one's being, as contrasted with mechanical learning carried out in a state of "drowsiness" (between sleep and wakening) which results only in cerebral training.

It is important to understand that the concept of evolution by which I abide bears no relation to the Darwinian concept *vis-à-vis* the species. What I mean is *individual* evolution, which can take place only at the level of "being," and not at the level either of the emotions or cerebral information. Thus, the human being's normal activity is merely *pre-evolutive,* insomuch as his habitual cognitive experience lacks the necessary depth to attain levels where the "being" is. Only an *individual* who earnestly sets himself to it can emerge from this larva-like state to develop a higher consciousness that will enable him to enlarge his "being," which is nothing less than his *spirit* or *divine spark.* Genuine evolution, therefore, can take place only at the level of "being," from where its beneficial effects to the material body emanate. It is to this type of success that *moral physics* leads, and whoever attains it will find that *the rest is smooth sailing.*

Mankind has deviated from his path of evolution, and it is of the greatest urgency that he gets back on course, otherwise he will languish in the swamp of moral, emotional, and cognitive desolation. However, there is nothing more intimidating to the seeker who is accustomed to dealing with illusory fantasies than to be suddenly confronted with a sure, rational opportunity that can be proven on the personal level. The infernal mechanism of self-deceit may well lead him to immediately disqualify or evade such an intimidating prospect, for it threatens an end to chasing after his fleeting dreams and requires a new commitment to true reality by getting down to work.

The luminous quality of the truth may blind those who are addicted to self-deceit or to flimsy utopias, thereby bringing about a mental and emotional blockage. This may end in a rejection of the greatest opportunity a person can have in this life: *to unite with the Creator through fusion with his own spirit.* An indispensable technical requisite for evolutive progress without "repeating the course" is to demolish one's personal mirages about the imagined qualities and capacities one believes one possesses, but which one in fact lacks, for it is not possible to apply effective remedies without realizing the magnitude of one's own limitations.

Inescapable reality reveals to us, at each moment, that only a thin veneer of civilization distinguishes the common man of today from primitive man. All too often this veneer is swept away by the influence of the passions, which lead people to commit deeds that contradict their higher ethical values. The currently fashionable belief is that man *possesses free will, a capacity for freedom of choice and freedom of conscience, competence to perceive reality as it really is, and the ability to behave in a civilized way.* But even a cursory perusal of the daily press would tend to refute these assumptions, for they project instead a picture of "barbarous civilization" or "civilized barbarism."

The fear one has of self-knowledge and of accepting one's own faults and failings generally makes him create an idealized opinion of himself as well as a fanciful overestimation of his capacities. Likewise, one rationalizes the problems he faces when he attributes them to causes outside and separate from his own will. One cannot attain human excellence without having first undergone the ordeal of acknowledging oneself as one truly is, with all one's defects, failings, and blemishes—stripped of the artificial image so often used to deceive oneself and to seduce one's fellows.

To become conscious of one's own weaknesses and limitations, in contrast with one's potential, makes one better disposed to understand the need for the work of spiritual self-fulfillment, for the spirit does not recognize any boundary between the human and the divine. It is the latter which can, with one fell swoop, dispense with social distinctions, thereby rendering all people equal in terms of the essence of their divine spark. If one wishes to develop, one must first recognize one's own smallness, an improbable feat for one who clings to the mask of the image. It is a fundamental requisite, when embarking upon the path of wisdom, for one to first discover the magnitude of one's own ignorance and imperfection. Those who are oblivious to this are unprepared to attempt the task of completing the Creator's great work on themselves. They must be content with indefinitely "repeating the school year," having not learned the lessons of life but remaining instead at the larval state.

Humans overestimate their capacity, believing that by the mere fact of possessing a brain with its popularly known attributes, they can attain knowledge and wisdom. This attitude completely ignores the fact that the most important faculties a man may have access to remain in a latent state, waiting to be developed so that he can become perfectly and completely human—once he has been stripped of the psychic traces of his animal heritage. The aim of *moral physics* is to rediscover the path to evolution, so that one can attain supreme good and lasting happiness in a world that is serene, peaceful, unified, and virtuous, with no marginalized members of any type whatsoever. Thus, it gives back to man his honor, nobility, dignity, and higher ethics.

---

1. David Bohm, *The Wholeness and the Implicate Order* (London: Routledge, 1980.)

CHAPTER II

THE DIFFICULTIES OF ACTING MORALLY

Society expects and needs everybody to adequately comply with the norms it considers appropriate, but this moral code is being violated at each moment either by commission or omission. When they occur, various explanations are usually proffered to justify these errors which range from small misdemeanors to serious offenses that are punishable by law. Also, when very humble people commit offenses, they are usually explained away as having stemmed from a "lack of opportunities," but when the offenders belong to the upper classes, their offense is typically called "corruption."

One might wonder what leads people to unethical or immoral behavior. This invariably originates in a misguided search for, and failed attempts at, happiness. As Aristotle said, "all humans seek happiness through doing good." Unfortunately, they confuse supreme good with circumstantial and apparent virtue, which they in turn identify with pleasure, while pain is viewed negatively. This is how people who begin with a laudable intention usually end by doing wrong, for they allow themselves to be seduced by what gives them pleasure and, as we know, the senses are normally submissive to pleasure. Correct behavior demands far more than good intentions. One can be well intended at heart yet immoral in deeds, but on the other hand, one cannot be moral if one has bad intentions.

To be good at the level of mere desire does not require any pains at all, for this is the spontaneous behavior of most people. On the other hand, to be virtuous demands painstaking work and entails sustained effort over a long period of time. Expectations of apparent or immediate virtue usually stun the senses and perturb one's point of view, thus leading to truly primitive behavior.

While it is true that most people have good as their ultimate aim, vice and corruption are far more commonplace than might be expected, because in his normal state, man is not an ethical being and he will generally seek the path of least resistance. Unfortunately, it is easier for ordinary people to ignore the golden rule, "do unto others, as you would have done unto you," in their lunge for easy gain and immediate profit, and this often displaces prudence and rectitude.

Society is fully aware of this dilemma and this is why it punishes immoral and antisocial conduct in various ways. On extreme occasions the punishments of ostracism and imprisonment might deter offenders, but in general practice this does not happen because people are just not moral by nature, and so ethical norms become a mere social implant that are unrelated to anything intrinsic. We should also recall that these rules of conduct are no more than the norms considered to be correct by a certain society and that they vary greatly from one place to another, or continually change with time. During the Spanish Inquisition, for example, it was perfectly normal for the law to cruelly torture the accused, and in another milieu the Greek moralists referred quite naturally in their writings to the necessity of "not possessing too many slaves" without, however, condemning slavery as a general practice.

In reality, morality is neither a genetic capacity nor a voluntary individual acquisition. It has unfortunately become simply a "veneer" issued by civilization whose rules are a mere convenience for the contemporary culture. If a certain society considers it suitable to exterminate elderly people, all will do so without scruples. If, in another place, theft, murder, fraud, and pillaging were considered laudable, then honest people would be punished for being bad citizens. In such a case, we would be faced with the contradiction of witnessing evil rewarded and virtue penalized, in the name of morality, by society and its agencies.

This would become an ethical anomaly but is, in fact, actually getting more and more prevalent, albeit inadvertently. Therefore, one must think that true morality cannot conform to mechanistic environmental conditioning, but must be based on individual ethical development of a reflective nature in which the individual, by his own free choice, adopts the highest transcendental values. While it is true that society wages constant moral campaigns via its usual resources, it is rare to find an individual who can assimilate such concepts comprehensively without external pressure or compulsion.

Most people find morality to be a burden or a bothersome duty with which one is obliged to coexist, and which does not require great attention if one is not to spoil one's favorite entertainment. What is certain is that beyond environmental pressures, each person can choose either to give free rein to his passions or to sublimate them, thus becoming committed to either vice or virtue. This is a voluntary choice. Unfortunately, at the cultural level there is no knowledge that genuinely enables one to make decisions of conscience, for the procedure to confront reality objectively has not been divulged. Neither can people recognize, by virtue of their feedback from Nature, how an individual is affected by his good or bad deeds. They also cannot recognize specific incentives for them to behave virtuously, bearing in mind the persistent effort this requires. They ignore the immense practical advantages of committing themselves to virtue and thus succumb to the line of least resistance. The cultural concept of morality concerns only what a certain society considers suitable at a given moment in its history, but this does not mean that this code has any real basis in Nature.

Authentic morality, at present unknown, is based on the structure of Nature, and its code consists of observing cosmic laws that predate the history of man and which are the supreme mechanism that sustains all of Creation. Because of the quality of the commonly held cultural and religious concept of morality, it is quite understandable that man should show no interest in it and consider it bothersome, boring, rigid, authoritarian, or a mere expression of personal preference.

I am sure that if people could only understand the magnitude of what they would gain by always acting *justly* and *perfectly*, there would be few immoral individuals; we would have no need for judges or police other than in exceptional cases. The morality with which we are familiar is lax and accommodating because it excludes the ethical norms of Universal Nature, and therefore lacks any higher significance. It is my aim in this book to offer glimpses of natural and divine justice and the way in which each person can verify this for himself in his everyday life. However, in order to be able to appreciate the light, one must first know darkness and the ignorance and the harm that it brings. This is why I shall first discuss the causes that limit or hinder higher ethical behavior in the human being.

1. The Fact That We Live in an Era of Masses

The Spanish thinker, Jose Ortega y Gasset, pointed out that the most significant fact of his time was the "rebellion of the masses." This is today even truer than ever. He alluded to the phenomenon of the sudden upsurge of "agglomerations," of which he wrote, "we see the mass per se, possessed by the places and tools created by civilization." He added that "the individuals who make up these masses had existed before, albeit not as a mass. Scattered over the world in small groups or alone, they apparently had led a divergent, dissociated, and distant way of living. Each one, each individual, or small group occupied a space, perhaps his own [property], in the country, in the village, in the town, in the district of a large city. And suddenly they appeared under the label of an agglomeration and our eyes see masses everywhere."

Later on, he added, "The mass is average man. In fact the mass can be defined as a psychological phenomenon, which has no need to wait for individuals in order for the agglomeration to appear. The mass represents everything that has no self-esteem—either for better or for worse—because of unique reasons, but *it feels the same as everybody* and yet feels no anxiety but feels at ease by feeling identical to everybody else." (Jose Ortega y Gasset, *The Rebellion of the Masses*)

At the close of the 20th century we have reached the mental and psychological homogenization of man, and in all truth we have surpassed the rebellion of the masses and are now living through "the tyranny of the masses," which celebrates the most deplorable mediocrity. The mob is like a brainless monster that devours all before it, for it lacks any intelligence or will of its own. We are obliged to obey this anonymous mass in compliance with the concept of "majority rule." The tyrannical, absurd principle that the will of the majority is invariably correct sprang from the philosophy of Jean Jacques Rousseau. According to him, we are obliged to obey the general will, which is always right. However, as Cardinal Ratzinger also said, "the truth never lies with the majorities."

With the phenomenon of massification, the individual as such, has become a nuisance for state bureaucracy, which relishes dealing with numbers and statistics. The mass media has had a very powerful homogenizing effect on people's minds and individual existence has become more of a corporeal reality than a mental or psychological phenomenon. We act, think, and feel as a mass. We depend on the opinions of others insomuch as we convert the mass into a judge and arbiter of our own conduct and would make any sacrifice to be considered "alike." We seek acceptance as our reward and fear dissimilarity because of the social stigmas of mistrust, questioning, and rejection that it entails. In short, we come to irrevocably form part of a homogeneous mass, which gives us feelings of acceptance, security, and affection, but also a lack of identity, loneliness, and internal anguish.

The material crowding of big cities in this case becomes a "psychic agglomeration" that brings on anxiety through the feeling of a loss of one's "I." People fail when they seek their individual identity because they do just the opposite of what they should—they imitate one another. One basic reason for popular mediocrity is that people prematurely renounce the development of their own individuality because they find it easier and more agreeable to fuse with the masses, thereby artificially expanding their "I" as it is dissolved into the collective soul.

Instead of acknowledging the seriousness of this phenomenon, society encourages it, to increase the number of compliant citizens that feed the system, citizens who are oblivious to the fact that the ultimate cost is the underdevelopment or even the death of individuality. This is a sort of psychic handicap that stunts a maturing of the "I" by encouraging irresponsibility and a lack of ethics. When the individual's brain and heart belong to the mass, he will never be able to behave in a truly moral way, for he ignores this virtue. Neither will he be aware of the need for any kind of higher conduct. The mass has no morality because it has no thought of its own, no discrimination, and no judgment; its intrinsic mediocrity governs the behavior of its members.

In his work *The Crowd*, Gustave Le Bon[1] masterfully described the behavior of the mob as summarized below:

> The strangest phenomenon displayed by the psychological mass is the following: whatever the nature of the individuals comprising the mass may be, and however diverse and dissimilar their lifestyles, their professions, their character, or intelligence, the mere fact that they are turned into a mass endows them with a sort of collective soul. This soul makes them feel, think, and act in a completely different manner to that in which each of them in isolation would feel, think, and act.
>
> The individual who becomes part of a mob places himself in a situation that will enable him to suppress the repressions of his unconscious tendencies. The apparently new characteristics he will then display are precise exteriorizations of the individual unconscious, a system in which the seed of all that is evil in the human soul is contained.
>
> If we wish to get an accurate idea of the morality of the mass, we have to bear in mind that all individual inhibitions disappear in a group of individuals who are integrated into a mass, while all cruel, brutal, and destructive instincts, as well as latent atavisms, become awakened within the individual and seek free expression . . .

The most characteristic thing about the mass is the disappearance of the singular nature of those who belong to it. A flock of sheep clearly display these same characteristics because sheep also have a gregarious instinct that makes them go wherever the others go . . . it is a delicate matter to give examples that might seem to indict, but it is obvious that our society is one of the masses. A football stadium with a hundred thousand spectators, a subway station full of people, a tourist bus driven by the leader of a group, twenty million people sitting in front of a TV seeing the same quiz-show, twenty thousand young people at a rock concert, twenty thousand runners who start out in the New York Marathon on the Verazzano Bridge, a six mile line of cars trying to enter or leave a big city, a beach crowded with sunbathers . . . the list could be interminable . . .

. . . but the real danger of the mass is its alienating and depersonalizing effect on the individual.

The average or mediocre man is no more than a faithful copy of a single model, who indefinitely repeats his behavior according to societal norms.

There is nothing valuable in vulgarity—only imitation, an absence of creativity, a lack of any critical sense and will power.

It is interesting to have a clear idea of why the individual demonstrates such a desire to be "vulgar," melding easily into the mass. The appeal lies in the fact that the mass offers the individual a series of possibilities that gratify his animal impulses:

1. It removes moral brakes and repressions without a feeling of guilt.

2. It melds his anemic, underdeveloped "I" into a larger "I," the collective soul, formed by the accumulation of

countless other individuals, and enables him to feel important and to ignore his own mediocrity.

3. By killing his "I" and dissolving it into the anonymous mass, he effectively makes himself irresponsible. Moral norms vanish with this sort of psychic suicide and the individual no longer feels submitted to social reprisal.

4. There is a regression toward the womb. The mass is a substitute for the mother's uterus, which beckons the individual to the primary stages of his existence, when he had lived in the nirvana of uterine life, with no dilemmas or responsibilities whatsoever.

5. He gives himself up to ease and sloth, without having to make any individual effort to attain higher objectives.

The proliferation of youth gangs in developed societies can be readily explained by means of this analysis. These youngsters acquire a feeling of omnipotence when they join a gang. Whatever they do in it, however bad or dangerous this might be, loses significance for them. They feel authorized to do whatever they want, thus annulling any moral criterion or norm. They think they can steal, kill, or murder without guilt, because the group takes on the role of the family and the government, meting out its absolution in advance.

Whatever form this phenomenon of the psychological mass takes, it is certain that it will provoke an alienation of such magnitude that the individual "I" is easily swept along to be subsumed into the collective soul of the group. This does not mean that there cannot be organized groups of people who do not make up a psychological mass. A good example would be a union of people who, in full knowledge of this mechanism, decide from the outset how to free themselves from the harmful effects of a vulgar form of grouping.

Television is another powerful element that has contributed to the homogenization of the mass. All TV audiences share together a sort of subculture that derives from TV soap operas, news programs, shows, and films. For instance, at a certain moment CNN held the mental control of millions of people throughout the world in its hands—avid TV spectators who wanted information about what was going on in the Gulf War. While it is true that there might not be proximity or physical contact between TV audiences, there is an equivalence of received messages, which must also bring about some form of mental union and diminish conscious rationality. We should not forget that the TV or computer screen is the best-known hypnotist to date, and it is hard to believe that a child who goes through this experience will be able to escape unaffected by its fascination and control.

Ironically, everything in the world today is conceived with the aim of massifying people, "demoralizing" them, or eliminating morality through fusing them into masses. Demoralization leads directly to the loss of the meaning of existence and to a subsequent relaxation of ethics. It does not matter what a person's level of intelligence might be, by the fact of joining a psychological mass, his higher rationality will be annulled and will reappear only if he leaves the group. This partly explains the human being's infinite idiocy and enables us to understand the causes for the incredible mistakes in decision making at certain moments in large companies, when the executives themselves, in that precise moment, form part of a psychological mass.

We shall also understand the genesis of famous political or strategic blunders in the history of nations. Because of the sheer power that society gives him, a statesman should always be independent of, and not alienated by, any political party or psychological mass that might taint his higher rationality—at least as long as there is no "vaccine" to counteract or neutralize the social "virus" we are discussing here.

Any parliamentary assembly in which members could free themselves of the phenomenon of the psychological mass would notably raise their level of efficiency, impartiality, and justice and so become both a true guide to people's collective consciousness, and a model of virtue as well.

To return to Le Bon, he states that when it comes to deliberating on some very important and nontechnical but emotional matter, an assembly of wise men would not reach conclusions different from those reached by an assembly of fools. Whoever doubts this should earnestly verify these affirmations in practice. A council of doctors, jurists, or professionals of any type, for instance, is prone to making very serious errors of judgment if for any reason there arose among them the phenomenon of the "psychological mass." No one, regardless of his status, is immune to falling under the unsettling influence of this obscure mechanism. That is why I defined it as an important obstacle to ethical conduct and to the adoption of new and better ways of behaving—it clouds the mind, befuddles understanding, and so elicits the worst qualities of the species. The result, then, is just the opposite of what we aim to achieve through morality. The deeper we delve into the behavior of a psychological mass, the more convinced we shall become of its dreadful devastating power that is inimical to good judgment, and the declared adversary of individual consciousness.

Beyond external appearances, there is no great difference between the savage hordes and the contemporary masses. It is really quite surprising and suspect that our civilization has not investigated this very special type of human behavior to develop some discipline which would allow for the recovery of the individual's total freedom. Initiative and talent—and the liberty to exercise and develop these freely—are smothered by the most tyrannical of all tyrannies: the totalitarianism of the masses. This pressure is a direct assault on ethics and higher spiritual values, for authentic morality is conscious and not mechanical. Although the individual may become conscious, the masses never will. The nature of man at this point in time is that of a being in a state of lethargy, which is put to sleep through his fusion with the masses, stripped of an individual "I," and directed by a collective "I" or collective soul. Individual morality, with few exceptions, cannot surmount the ethical standards of behavior of the masses.

2. The Alienation of Our Time

A dictionary definition of *alienation* is that it is "the process by which the individual or a collectivity transforms its consciousness to thus make itself contradictory to what might be expected from its inherent condition."

I am firmly convinced that the species as a whole "does not behave as it ought to" in view of its assumed level of civilization. Obviously, the idealized cultural portrait of the human being is far removed from reality. We are less civilized and less conscious than we pretend to be, and similarly, less fair and less virtuous. We demand justice while we act unjustly and we seek equality without being egalitarian in our social dealings. In reality, we are barely beginning to evolve, and our sensation of splendor and power emanates from the scientific conquests by mankind which, for certain, does nothing to improve the internal nature of men.

From this perspective we are "civilized savages," children who scamper through life, playing with space stations and nuclear warheads. The deceptive feeling of power engendered by science and technology cripples and clouds the individual's capacity for self-criticism. It thus prevents him from realizing the enormous contradiction between the commonly accepted version of a civilized race and the harsh reality of a world constantly at war and in conflict—a place in which death by starvation or by criminal violence is the order of the day in many parts of the planet. Man's alienation has stripped him of the necessary will and lucidity to act consciously. Mechanical and stereotypical conduct has become the norm, damaging his higher faculties and preventing him from perceiving the true value of things. His sleepy state also prevents him from realizing the magnitude of his own alienation.

Alienation is an invasive process in which the individual's brain is penetrated by alien or foreign information, which, in a very real way, takes possession of his neurons in the form of autonomous information that is not subordinated to the "I." From that point forward, this invasive process wields power over the conduct of the individual, leaving him without the possibility to rid himself of its effects. In such cases, we could speak of a subliminal penetration of the mind, which is indeed what happens. This is made possible via an erroneous learning process in which the "I" is split off from the consciousness while the brain processes information passively. This means that instead of taking in information voluntarily, the mind is possessed and penetrated and therefore absorbs information indiscriminately. We then become filled with "informational garbage," subliminal information that remains in our unconscious mind as meaningless material, which disrupts and weakens the conscious "I," resulting in disorientation and emotional and psychological conflicts.

It is quite possible that the unconscious mind can "gorge" itself to the detriment of consciousness, and this is precisely what happens. The greater the informational saturation, the lesser the discrimination and hence the progressive weakening of the conscious "I." In this respect, common man is a mere servant, the passive tool of powerful informational mandates that are stored in his brain. This is the alienating force that gradually strips him of his own intrinsic condition, and turns him into a stranger to himself, even to the extent that his desires and ideals are usually not his own but that of the informational nucleus that has become the uninvited guest of his neurons and captor of his mind. This alienating force inhibits conscious behavior because it rigidly conditions the individual's conduct. The more information a person absorbs, the greater will be his dependency on such parameters, and the fewer possibilities he will have to practice higher ethical conduct.

Any activity, any training, whether the "training ground" happens to be the workplace, a social event, a sporting event, or leisure activity, has the potential to reinforce the process of alienation. It was recently published in the Chilean press how the KGB had created veritable "human robots," soldiers whose personalities were annulled with high frequency radio waves, electromagnetic fields surrounding the brain, and hypnotic messages induced by computer. This exposé was thanks to the research carried out over three years by the Russian journalist Yuri Vorobiovski.[3] He adds that an association of the "victims of psychotropic experimentation" has recently been organized in Moscow to demand pensions and compensation from the government for the psychic injuries suffered during those years.

This is nothing new for modern man, for he lives submerged in an ocean of high frequency radio waves, various magnetic fields, and environmental hypnotic inducements. It is certain that common man is no less a robot than the subjects of the aforementioned KGB, except that in the case of the common man, it is not noticeable at first glance, because his conditioning drives him to participate compulsively in activities which society considers normal, such as consumerism, compliance in the defense of mediocrity, and passive submission to various forms of totalitarian government. In all likelihood, the influence of present-day television far surpasses the Soviet experiments. The latter had as their goal the training of invincible soldiers who would be absolutely fearless. On the other hand, current communications media has trained a huge mass of obedient consumers, leveling all people in the world to the same consumption patterns. In the absence of a consensus on morality, there nonetheless exists an implicit agreement to consume similar merchandise.

One of the greatest threats confronting the modern mind is "informational congestion" through saturation of its neural pathways. This congestion is due to the disproportionate growth of scientific and cultural information; to the continual sensorial bombardment, especially audiovisual, of the senses; and to the grandiose, sensationalist, and overwhelming style of advertising messages. All these factors saturate the gateways to one's brain, successfully blocking its higher centers, so that most messages and stimuli take on a subliminal quality, passing—uncensored and unimpeded—directly to the unconscious mind. This is, in fact, precisely what advertising wants to accomplish in order to achieve its objectives. Millions of humans act as automatons—buying and acquiring certain products because they have been scientifically persuaded by the autonomous messages flooding their brains with this type of advertising. Many others become immoral or delinquent by mimicking models from the cinema, television, or the offenses repeatedly divulged by the media. There are films that graphically illustrate how to efficiently steal, embezzle, and attack. Others, of an erotic or sexual nature, promote various forms of sadomasochism or perversion. Newspapers generally abstain from publishing good news; melodramas, tragedies, and morbid stories invariably predominate. The visual and auditory stimuli of the press, the cinema, and television keep people amused, while robbing their most valuable and yet most vulnerable possession: their own "I."

I should point out that this is only possible because there is a cerebral, psychological, and cultural deficiency that affects the species as a whole, a subject we shall discuss later. For the moment, I would say only that everybody possesses two "I's": a "superior I," which is his intrinsic identity, and an "inferior I," which is a pseudo-identity coming from the collective psyche of mankind. It is a sort of "informational graft" that corresponds to the aggregate of autonomous subliminal information stored in people's brains. This "I" is the part of the individual psyche that is most vulnerable to cultural alienation.

Our world is an alienating one, but if we were to possess a higher level of mind control, we would be free of this scourge of cultural alienation. Unfortunately, this technique for mind control is not part of the cultural agenda. Therefore, every day, countless millions of people throughout the world regress in terms of their individual potential for consciousness, which is continuously diminished due to the extreme difficulty entailed in developing the noblest material of the human psyche: its superior consciousness.

This world does not have authentic ethics, nor can one find any morally adequate behavior because people's conduct is usually mechanical and compulsive, and such programming does not include any solid, consistent, or authentic ethical norms. Man's gregarious nature not only drives him to merge with the masses, but also encourages him to allow his mental individuality to be subsumed into a common mind or "collective soul." On account of this, freedom of thought and idea is becoming increasingly rare, and in general, one can only internalize certain ideologies by melding into the respective current of thought, much as a drop of water falls into the sea.

Mankind's mental deterioration is progressive, albeit subtle, well concealed beneath the erroneous and arbitrary parameters which are used to measure individual intelligence. Mechanical cerebral agility is often mistaken for higher intelligence, and blind imitation is mistaken for creativity. Humanity does not give sufficient importance to mental health because there is no authority whose purpose is to prevent alienating information from perturbing or disrupting the integrity of the mind. Either there is insufficient knowledge of the effect of alienating information, or else such knowledge is cleverly and carefully hidden. An enormous current of images, news, and sounds flows uninterruptedly from the television, with no control at all over the negative impact all of this has on people's mental health.

Perhaps there has not been a serious study in this area because no one has realized the benefit of such a study. Or perhaps this investigation has been intentionally avoided because of the magnitude of the deterioration that could occur in the consumer market if the real level of damage caused in the health and mental integrity of people as a consequence of the media saturation and excesses in forms of communication is proven. Such knowledge would make it necessary to limit advertising and create strict regulations on audiovisual communications.

The vulnerability of the individual's brain to the audacious intrusion of mental privacy and the functional harm suffered by his higher capacities through informational congestion and saturation are quite alarming. This harm is manifested through the deterioration of his higher rationality and a decrease in his capacity for attention. The hypertrophy of his unconscious mind, coupled with the consequent atrophy of the ability to behave consciously, accounts for a weakening of his character and a consequent disempowering of his conscious will. This results in deteriorated moral conduct.

Unwittingly controlled by, rather than in control of, vulgar communications, people lose sight of the true stature that the human being deserves. They focus instead on the image of physical appearance and possessions. This attitude of judging people for what they possess rather than for what they really are leads to a most-egregious confusion of values. The overwhelming majority equates happiness with good, making themselves believe that good is equal to pleasure.

There is no doubt as to the consumer alienation that the world is experiencing. The pleasure people derive from the act of purchasing and acquiring things is a pleasure that convinces them for that moment that they are happy. The supreme achievement of the marketers is to create an international group of homogeneous consumers who lack any real will or higher criteria, who are obsessed like drug addicts, driven by an addiction to continually replenish a transitory illusion of happiness, and who are always ready to accommodate or to warp moral norms to achieve their goals. What can morality matter to such people in the face of their vicious necessity? Where can they find time and energy for ethical deliberations when the exhausting voraciousness of their addiction consumes all their resources?

A lack of the necessary economic means for satisfying consumerism adds another dimension to this problem. The multiplicity of product offerings and the omnipresent gap between desire and restrictions imposed by economic reality results in chronic depression. This is occurring in Chile, where 90 percent of suicide cases are derived from that kind of depression. Now, 33.8 percent of the population has psychiatric problems that require specialized attention. This is attributed to poverty by some authorities, and is certainly true in a high percentage of cases. However, one has to make the very important distinction between a paucity of the essential means of subsistence and poverty as a sense of deprivation aroused by the overwhelming temptations of consumer offerings. When one compares the full extent of these offerings with one's own scant resources (which will always seem scant relative to one's consumer appetites), there are invariably devastating feelings of deprivation and insignificance, resulting in depression. *The more extensive the worldwide shop-window for consumer offerings is, the more anguished and depressed people will be.*

Alienation also appears as a mental epidemic, which will, at a given moment, attack almost everybody. Clear examples of this are world wars, during which a sort of collective madness arises and the normal level of alienation becomes unbearably exacerbated, so as to collapse the mental sanity and stability of the general population, individually and collectively.

Fashion is another and different form of alienation that shows just how contagious this phenomenon is. In fact, those who are not "infected" by it feel unhappy and struggle desperately to catch its symptoms.

The cult of money, social climbing, political trafficking, a love of luxury, gambling, drug consumption, aggression and violence, terrorism, the quest for power, envy, resentment, narcissism, sex as a consumer product, pornography, perversions of all kinds, are all diverse forms of alienation in which we invariably find the human masses possessed and directed by outside forces which have overwhelmed and thus overcome their will and rationality.

The masses avoid any higher morality, not because they are "evil" but because they lack the capacity to be "good." However, the most powerful alienation is that which gratifies those people who become addicted to strong feelings of pleasure. They will forget any moral boundary or limit as long as they can satisfy their impulses, without pausing to evaluate their virtue or vice, and without previously deliberating on the consequences of their proposed acts. These people are unable to fulfill their desires in the absence of money, and when they lack a sufficient amount of money to obtain what they desire, they are prone to theft or delinquency. Thus amorality (a total absence of all moral consideration) prevails. The main attribute of sensorial pleasure is that it is transient, and so it has to be continually indulged. Neither is an abundance of money a moral safeguard, but often a source of corruption which will pervert one's character and one's will insomuch as excess, in any form, is a vice.

The tyranny exercised by majorities over the individual makes him worthless as himself, being accepted only in accordance with the social level he is able to reach. Individual self-esteem is popularly based on looking at the expression or gestures in the faces of one's neighbors in order to gauge one's level of acceptance or rejection, and thereafter to accommodate one's own behavior to the demands of the group. Yet, the individual condemns himself to his own destruction by his social mimicry insomuch as it is precisely in the masses where mediocrity and a lack of ethics reside.

3. The Erroneous Educational System

The current approach to education does not turn out better human beings but fictitious characters with scant human content, "electronic men" whose memory chips direct their conduct. When I observe people who are paragons of etiquette, I cannot help but picture them as holographic projections of some stereotyped smile or empty gaze, victims of a civilization that alienates their minds and vanquishes their souls. There are times when, in a desire to know what lies within such an individual, one tries to plumb the depths of his soul. These attempts are in vain because one finds only a sort of giant onion whose countless layers of skin one keeps peeling off without ever managing to discover the inner essence sought.

These automatons are not an exception, but are the legitimate and logical children of present-day society, ignorant of higher values and incapable of elevated moral conduct. Far from being evil, they seek only good. However, their cerebral programming prevents them from distinguishing between actual and apparent value. They wander through life like ghosts, without any transcendental goal, in perpetual pursuit of an illusory happiness which they never manage to attain because they confuse what is good with a succession of new fantasies that feed on their good intentions.

The basic problem with education is that it is not directed to promoting the student's human excellence, since its fundamental aim is to enforce social and cultural concord. It is concerned only with socializing people to comply faithfully with indigenous prohibitions and mandates, and with creating professionals who will be useful to society in their respective specialties—good doctors, architects, engineers, and lawyers, who will maintain and ensure the smooth running of the system. From a technical perspective, they will be deficient human beings because, like everyone else, they will have received a memoristic, circumscribed education that does not develop their consciousness—an education that is centered on the concept of "having," and that totally neglects the concept of "being." Indeed, a profession is something that the individual "has."

The individual is not, for example, an engineer. Rather, he performs the profession of engineer, which is not part of his being but an autonomous cerebral capacity, that is, one that is not hierarchically subordinate to his "I." Yet, just the opposite occurs: the individual is essentially forced into a state of mechanical servitude by the cerebral information that he receives from the exterior by virtue of his professional and human conditioning. At the same time, he is at a generally deficient level of awakening, because cerebral information is internalized only when it is subordinated to the "I," and not the reverse. It goes without saying that the same thing happens to the "normal" man in terms of all professions, skills, and knowledge, that is, *those skills which are not subordinated to the "I," but instead become superimposed identities which ultimately encompass the entire psyche of the individual.*

Education begins with parents who obviously cannot teach or pass on what they themselves lack. The legacy an alienated parent leaves to his offspring will be his own perturbation, thereby creating a vicious circle that is hard to break, since that legacy will be passed on to successive generations. All too often, parents turn out to be "bad parents," not because they do not love their children but because they do not know how to educate them properly. Generally, they tend to be either too authoritarian or too permissive, and they most often feel that they have been subjugated by their offspring. It is known that the home and the family are the child's model of the world. The child will perceive the truth in the world in the same light as he perceives it in the home and family. It is the nuclear family that shapes the moral habits of the child, whether good or bad, according to the parents' behavior. It is obvious that the child of a thief will find nothing wrong or out of the ordinary with larceny.

In any case, our parents were themselves victims of an aberrant educational system that prioritizes blind imitation and memoristic learning, so that their fault for our erroneous education is only relative. We start in school as small, scared children awed by giants who have absolute power over our minds in the classroom, and we have little or no power to question or evaluate what they teach us. We take what they say as gospel, and in doing so we are obliged to accept, study, memorize, and execute what they tell us to do. These mentors also possess the power to set us against our parents, for low grades will immediately disrupt the affective inflow and outflow between children and parents.

The reality is that we go to school only to please our parents, since during that time of our lives, we do not have the discrimination necessary to realize that we need to study. The most serious defect of education lies with learning techniques that emphasize understanding by glib memorization. Current pedagogy unwittingly promotes the student's mental passivity in the sense that it completely opens his mind to the indiscriminate entry of obligatory information from an authoritarian source, most of which penetrates his brain subliminally. Traditional brainwashing techniques employ a bombardment of the mind with subliminal stimuli. Such stimuli encounter no rational opposition for they directly enter the unconscious. This, precisely, is the modus operandi of current education: to produce a citizen in such a way that he becomes an extension of the dominant culture or a faithful copy of those who influenced his brain.

There is a huge contradiction between the requirements of professional training and training that pursues human excellence in the sense of "higher consciousness." The university is usually a sort of "assembly line" of professionals in various specialties in which the most agile, ductile, permeable brain is lauded. Totally disregarded is the need to develop the human being's higher consciousness, which is his most uniquely individual mental possession. Without it, knowledge loses the moral and spiritual objective that is the transcendental goal for which man must aim in order to attain his total self-fulfillment.

The entire educational system is imitative, inducive, manipulative, and hypnotically mesmerizing. The greater the prestige of a professor or the university in which he teaches, the greater will be the students' passivity and suggestibility, and so they will never question what they are told and what they are taught. Even though questioning is not a requisite for learning, discerning what one hears in class indeed is. Inner deliberation leads to true comprehension. Unfortunately, this does not normally occur because the excess of information contained in normal syllabuses confounds and saturates the mind. It is quite common for a student to wonder in astonishment after a class, as to what it was really about. To this dilemma, one should add the students' own psychological problems, such as various complexes, fears, insecurities, shyness, and low self-esteem, all of which paralyze thought and impede comprehension. Notwithstanding these obstacles, it is a well-known fact that there are excellent professionals in most fields of knowledge, but not because they have an in-depth understanding of what they are doing. Simply put, their brains have been skillfully programmed.

What's the problem then? It lies precisely in the fact that education transforms people into *mere informational containers*, filling their heads with autonomous information that certainly results in a profound level of alienation, with the aforemen-tioned dangers. The alienated individual becomes increas-ingly like a machine and less and less human, drifting towards the anguished solitude of someone who has lost his true direction in life. He has distanced himself from his own inner nature and is thus compelled to do what his memory chips dictate rather than what he desires within his soul.

When we wish to know what a person is, it is customary for us to ask for his "degrees" or references, and the more prestigious his alma mater, the greater will be our esteem for him. What would seem normal is not really so at all. It merely reflects our mental shortcoming when we highly esteem anything that comes from a prestigious source without considering that this opinion is of no value if the capacities it is supposed to guarantee cannot function effectively and effi-ciently in real life. It is possible to test this opinion only with the passing of time. Likewise, professional excellence does not necessarily equate with human excellence, and indeed these two areas are generally considered—and often are—entirely unrelated to each other.

If Aristotle could reincarnate in such a form that every-body would recognize him, and, being bored with human smallness, he decided to trick people by spouting nonsense in a "profound discourse," everyone would be convinced of the undeniable virtue and truth of his words, without suspecting

information that is not subordinate to the "I," and which manages to control certain areas of conduct without the individual being able to rid himself of its influence.

11. To educate in the usual way is to *map out a mental boundary* and restrict the student's possibilities to what is contained within this boundary.

12. Not enough attention is paid to the psychological problems that may hinder learning. There are many students with serious problems that are carefully concealed to avoid mockery or censure. People with the most sensitive temperaments are often forced to sacrifice their gifts in order to adapt themselves through obligation to the coarseness of the group.

Audiovisual education is, in my opinion, the most nefarious type of education, insomuch as it can lead to a world of illiterate robots. Of all forms of training it is the one in which the student participates least consciously, as there exists no control of the "I" over the messages being inculcated—to the contrary, these latter come to master the "I."

It should be understood that any information that penetrates one's mind without one's "I" being able to discern, in this respect has the quality of a hypnotic induction. The consequent deterioration in his conscious behavior makes it difficult to maintain adequate moral conduct. This can be explained by the fact that authentic morality cannot be involuntary, for it requires the individual's *intention* and *volition*. Any form of hypnotic induction brings about a shrinking of the individual's conscious mind, with a consequent weakening of his character and will. This is a serious matter in that weak characters easily succumb to vice and corruption. However, let us be optimistic and hope that in the next century both teachers and leaders alike will no longer be *hypnotized hypnotists.*

I should point out the important mental difference in the self-taught person, an individual who learns and cultivates himself by his own free decision, without the aid of a teacher, so that the sheer magnitude of his effort forces him to raise his level of awareness. This is how he unwittingly develops greater human content, which can be perceived when one observes such a person.

Perhaps certain readers will not see clearly just why these educational faults hamper people's moral behavior, yet the explanation is quite simple. Any authentic morality must be free, voluntary, and conscious, whereas our education and culture neither teach nor encourage the development of consciousness. Instead, consciousness is ignored, and in such a barren environment, the importance of it cannot be realized.

The moralistic utopia of a truly civilized world in which everybody is governed by higher ethics could be realized only with an aggregation of such individuals who, by means of a personal, voluntary decision, underwent many years of training with the aim of achieving genuinely conscious behavior. If people only understood the huge advantage of invariably acting with absolute adherence to the highest moral norms, delinquency, wars, and conflicts would all be terminated, for the law of egalitarian equivalence would be the yardstick for interpersonal relationships. However, in order to achieve this, we would have to radically change the educational system, so that morality would become an individual ethical conquest, a set of rules accepted freely and comprehensively by each person. The highest fundamental achievement of education must be to train and develop human beings to have greater humanity and inner content, not merely turn out mechanically efficient subjects.

Society prefers to look for people who suit the system and this means adding more sheep to the flock by increasing quantity rather than quality. Unless there is an awareness of the need for individual higher spiritual self-fulfillment, the world can hardly be improved upon, for it will continue to subject the individual to the bondage of collective mediocrity. The school and the university are definitely not temples in which the humanity of the species is forged. Only the school of life offers the opportunity to encounter for oneself the straight path marked out by the Creator. Unfortunately, too many have lost their way in the attempt.

4. The Subjective Nature of Values

It is necessary to face the fact that most people practice a kind of moral subjectivism, a doctrine that holds that the aim of moral action is the fulfillment of a subjective state of pleasure or happiness. This means that the individual labels as "good" any act that gives him pleasure, and as "bad" the pain that suffering provokes. It is clear that in this way the sense of morality, understood as superior ethical behavior, has been abolished. Subjectivism becomes a pretext to give free rein to one's most primitive or animalistic desires and impulses without feelings of discomfort, embarrassment, or culpability—for as long as they produce a sense of pleasure, those impulses would be considered acceptable. Thus, it would be okay for an individual to habitually get drunk just because he enjoys drinking, even though in his state of inebriation he is liable to provoke episodes of domestic violence or child abuse. Many fathers have raped their daughters in such a state and felt not the slightest remorse. If Jack the Ripper had enjoyed dismembering prostitutes, we could not, according to the theory of moral subjectivism, classify his actions as immoral. Nor could we do so for the terrorist who carries out an atrocious bombing, for as long as this act makes him feel important, subjectivism sustains that he would perceive it as virtuous. Unfortunately, despite continual efforts by moralizing campaigns, moral subjectivism is the most widespread attitude among people, thanks to the contribution of all those moralists who see morality as a matter of personal preference or personal desire.

Bertrand Russell with his *theory of the subjectivity of values* states, for instance, that "if two men differ about values, there is no disagreement on any type of truth but only a difference in taste. The chief basis for adopting this opinion is the total impossibility of finding arguments to prove that this or that has any intrinsic value." It is clear that with this type of thinking "sin" disappears.

"An act which is sinful for one man," writes Russell, "may be virtuous for another," adding that "Hell, as a place of punishment for sinners, becomes irrational." The immoral consequences of these concepts are obvious, but this is precisely the moral cancer we are afflicted with at present: the absence of any higher values.

Respect for the elderly is becoming less and less valued; romantic love that ends in marriage has been replaced by sex as "pleasure consumerism"; honor is almost a matter of the past; patriotism is no longer valued as it used to be; the grotesque has invaded the world of art; dueling as a means of settling offenses has been replaced by nuclear genocide. The medical apostleship is getting rarer and rarer. The family doctor, who was once also a sort of spiritual adviser for the family, is facing extinction. Friendly relations between neighbors in the same district are getting rarer, despite the explosive increase in city agglomerations. Drugs that could cure many diseases in less-developed countries are not manufactured, because there is no money in such countries to buy them. Food is abundant in the world (only money is needed to buy it), yet thousands of people die of hunger each day.

In many countries access to justice is a cruel mockery for those who lack the necessary economic means. The same occurs with health and education. There are occasions when it is almost a bad joke to speak of "civilization" in a world that is continually at war. It would seem that what we term "progress" is amoral and without ethics. We can, therefore, hardly expect people to behave correctly. When they do so, it is only through fear of punishment and not through *any inner moral impulse.*

For example, if a law of the land were passed that would grant amnesty beforehand to all offenses that might be committed on the first of January, the result would be total catastrophe. Most people would just give free rein to their basest instincts, assured that they would not be punished. There are numerous examples of this. There are countless "bleached sepulchres" of the type Jesus Christ mentioned. Oftentimes we hear about the president of some country who stole vast sums of money; of politicians who grew rich through insider dealing; of corrupt civil servants; of mercenary police at the service of those who can pay; of a certain judge who sells himself to the highest bidder. Currently, I am reading a book written by a Venezuelan Journalist entitled: *How Much Does a Judge Cost?*[4] This book reveals the irregularities of judicial power in that country, shedding light on that high authority. Whether we agree or not with this author's point of view, it is very likely that the book will eventually contribute to making public service more transparent to the public, which is a praiseworthy aim. If only there were the freedom in other democracies to carry out similar investigations without being silenced by a secret political inquisition. Through their position as public figures, those who are in the various spheres of power have a duty to make things perfectly transparent, and refusing to do so is a deplorable moral example.

Certainly, none of the people who violate ethics feel that they are "evil," for in all certainty the only thing they intend is to seek happiness and virtue, albeit in a dramatically misguided way. One of the greatest problems of morality is that at the cultural level there are no clearly defined, immutable, and consensual rules of the game. Each person interprets the question according to his own personal interests. Therefore, the only valid course is to work individually on the raising of consciousness to gain access to more-profound, more-transcendental realities and thus to attain a spiritual condition, wherein lies supreme truth. As long as men remain in a deficient state of consciousness, they will continue fruitlessly seeking a consensual morality, losing themselves in obscure, complex discussions and mystifying the matter even more rather than clarifying it.

The truth is that if we expect to survive and genuinely progress, morals should be of the purest steel, not of elastic, for when one falls into the temptation of beginning to dodge certain ethical imperatives or to accommodate others, there is no knowing when and where one will stop. This means a return to humanity's traditional values, such as *hard work, perseverance, honesty, virtue, sacrifice, family unity, tolerance, individual merit, goodness, love, justice, friendship, altruism,* and *solidarity.*

Mankind is currently taking "the easy path," since all vice, corruption, or immorality is a downhill path, which does not require the minimum effort to traverse. Moral degradation is nothing more than a senseless lowering of oneself along the human scale, without realizing it. By following this course,

man" so as to approach the state of superman. It is essential that the concept of "higher man" be stripped of any racist or elitist connotations in the conventional sense, for the path of evolution is freely accessible to all. There are those who would rend their garments if it were asserted, for example, that Jesus Christ was black. What would that matter? As far as I am concerned, he could have been black, white, or yellow and this would change nothing at all, for the life of the spirit transcends any human distinction. Which role models are imitated by most young people today? Do they admire Pythagoras, Socrates, Confucius, Michelangelo, Leonardo da Vinci, St. Augustine, Shakespeare, Cervantes, or others like them? Certainly not. The role models they imitate are generally weak, asexual, anguished, and insecure individuals who lack any of the higher values—social parasites who have contributed nothing of value to the community.

Are there modern examples worthy of being held up as role models of spirituality and morality? Very few, for in our system, the only thing that is valued is that which makes money or profit for specific interests, so that the few individuals who attain spiritual excellence generally remain unknown. It seems as if honor, chivalry, and inner nobility have been extinguished or have gone out of fashion. In the Middle Ages, the ideal of nobility was the "knight" (he who mounts a horse; he who controls his animal side). In the 14th century, when this ideal was on the decline, an author of the time described it as follows:

> Thou, who desires to reach the order of chivalry, must lead a
> new life; thou must devoutly persevere in thy prayers, flee from
> sin, from pride, and from vileness; thou must defend the church
> and help the widow and the orphan; thou must be valiant and
> protect the people; thou must be loyal and willing and never
> take anything from anybody; this is how a knight should

behave. The knight must be humble at heart and always try to carry out chivalrous actions; be loyal in war, he must be ready to set out on long voyages; he must attend tournaments and joustings for his beautiful lady's sake; he must always think of honor, so that he will never be blamed for ignominious deeds nor be accused of cowardice; and he must consider himself to be the last of all men; this is how a knight must behave.

I should add here that in the ancient orders of knighthood, horsemanship was a spiritual exercise in which a transfer between the beast and the animal aspect of the rider was provoked, to thus indirectly attain greater control over his baser nature. Just as I am certain that the truly important men of the world are completely unknown, I also believe that there are many spiritually admirable people, whose thoughts, because of the conceptual elevation of their minds, do not appeal to those who are interested in keeping man in his condition of obedient consumer. In fact, it is improbable that they may ever become known.

Socrates was condemned for speaking too much; Nero murdered Seneca because he found the truth intolerable; Jesus Christ revealed himself to the world and was crucified. It would seem that the truth has at all times been unbearable for dark consciences, so that genuine prophets at times have ended up as sacrifices or have been stigmatized by the corrupt beings who disguise themselves as good men. Indeed, it should be made known that it is not easy to either follow or imitate the virtues of the best moral models, for this entails painful individual work possible only for those who truly thirst after human and spiritual excellence. Most of Jesus Christ's followers, for instance, merely imitated him externally, but were not able to emulate him internally. Only very few "turn the other cheek" when they are offended. Even fewer practice the golden rule of *"do unto others, as you would have done unto you."* It is essential to understand that the path of virtue is the only course possible. When people fail to set out on this course, or when they swerve off it, life punishes them by making them go round in circles. They go round and round a thousand times along torturous paths, each time further removed from what they really desire, without having any access to supreme virtue and desired happiness. Their only hope is to someday do what they had failed to do before—to go quickly straight to the path of highest human virtue.

Before this point, there must be many who repeatedly bang their heads against the wall of lamentations, full of skepticism and resentment. It is ironic that people who are exceptions actually follow a type of secularly spiritual course, for they are regarded with suspicion by a society that cannot understand activities in which economic gain or selfish ambition are no longer the main objective. I think it would be relevant to mention here an ancient society of builders who have traditionally used the bricklayer's tools as symbols of moral perfection. I refer to the Freemasons, who in their beginnings were operative but who today are merely symbolic. The square, the hammer, the level, the compass, and the plumb line were all tools that had to be used to work "rough stone," a symbol of human imperfection, so as to carve it into a perfect cube. The aforementioned tools symbolize moral and spiritual instruments for bringing about the individual's spiritual transformation. They show us that morality cannot be arbitrary or manipulated but has to adjust to a norm or a perfect measure that emanates from the natural and divine order of the Universe. In another context, the spiritual practices of St. Ignatius of Loyola are also an example of inner work intended to master the passions and the practice of virtue.

5. Man's Low Level of Evolution

If we consider that the estimated age of the planet Earth is about 4.5 billion years, and that man's "conscious" behavior goes back no further than 30,000 years at most, we shall understand that we have hardly begun to walk upright. Therefore, man's level of evolution is almost nonexistent.

To return to Aristotle's concept that *morality should be a morality for man*, it should be understood that this is just what happens and the results are plain to see. Moral rules are "for the man of today" and he is hardly more than a child, which is why he confuses rules with toys that he can use to satisfy his continuous whims, or to justify his temper tantrums. The way man behaves at present coincides with his evolutive age, and what he does is all that he knows how to do or is able to do according to his level. At barely 30,000 years of age, we cannot demand that the species behave as if it had lived for 200,000 years.

Why then, has mankind known better eras? This is due to the fact that evolution is not continuous, that there are halts, regressions, and failures. I have no doubt that man has had greater moral stature during certain past epochs, and that we are today rapidly declining. The cause for this interruption is quite simple: schools today center their work on programming people's brains to function socially and professionally and stress the transmission of the greatest possible amount of information, whereas they neglect any type of moral training. The grossest scientific error was made by sustaining the view that "intelligence is the human being's most prized faculty," thus detaching it from consciousness, without which the intellect is no more than a ship adrift. Also concealed is the fact that consciousness not only conditions creative intelligence but also possesses a myriad of possibilities according to higher or lower levels of awakening. We only make use of the most meager levels of awakening.

Recall here the words of Sir Arthur Eddington when he stated that "the mind is the first and most direct object of our experience, and all that we can study is the content of our own consciousness." I am convinced that, just as there is a supreme good, there must also be an absolute evil, and I believe that this latter is a cosmic force of an involutive nature. It is an intelligence that manipulates language over time to alter its semantic content and remove the real meaning of words and transcendental concepts, which, if understood, would lead too many people onto the path of virtue. I do not believe, for example, that the mythical Tower of Babel referred to different languages but rather to a consciously partial, manipulated, obfuscated, and superficial semantic. So much so that the human being's most important faculty no longer exists as a cultural concept within his reach. This supreme faculty is "higher consciousness" in the sense of *being more conscious or supremely conscious*. The scant cultural importance given to the word consciousness is demonstrated by the fact that its most profound and valuable semantic significance for man does not appear in dictionaries. People are thus deprived of any concept of the possibility of evolution by means of certain disciplines that would enable them to gain access to higher states of consciousness. Really, man can evolve only by using the cognitive tools which are higher than the usual ones, because culture employs only ordinary and common tools. This can be verified by the fact that, if exceptional knowledge were to be included in culture, then anybody could find the path to evolution. There are also important words whose true meaning remains obscure, for example, *spirit, "I," being, consciousness, honor, love, liberty, good, evil*, etc. It is as if there were a silent conspiracy that took charge of hiding the most profound meaning behind certain expressions. It is very likely that similar things occur in all languages. Some dictionaries have given the following definitions of consciousness:

1. Property of the human spirit for recognizing itself in its essential attributes and in the modifications that it experiences in itself.

2. Inner knowledge of good and evil.

In psychology, consciousness is spoken of as "the feature that differentiates psychic life, diversely characterized as: (a) general awareness; (b) central effect of nervous reception; (c) capacity to have experiences; (d) subjective aspect of cerebral activity; (e) relationship of the 'I' to the environment."

While all these definitions are indeed accurate, they have nothing to say about the most important meaning of the word *consciousness*, which refers to "the capacity to be conscious in a higher manner" as compared to the common state of consciousness. This latter is innate, but *higher consciousness* can only be attained through a strict spiritual discipline that is not known in the cultural sphere. Higher consciousness implies a prior condition of "intensified awakening," for the normal state of human consciousness has been defined as one of "drowsiness" (between sleep and waking). This means that, although we are awake, there is at all times a significant remnant of sleep in our brains. This is different from nocturnal sleep, in that it corresponds to a sort of hypnotic stupor. One has to counteract this remnant of sleep if one wishes to attain the highest states of consciousness. It is true that this hypnotic phenomenon remains a somewhat mysterious area of research, for it has not been studied from the point of view of "cosmic energy that in some way influences

For some reason, man *imagines himself to be complete* and this makes it difficult for him to acknowledge his own problems. The feeling of being complete perhaps came from contemplation of the normal physical body, of which there is nothing missing, so that we do not feel a need to have another head or a third hand. At the mental and spiritual level, it is quite a different matter, for man is born without having even hardly begun the work with his *raw material,* the chief purpose of his life being *to complete himself,* and he who fails to do this ought to consider himself a failure on the path of evolution.

We shall avoid many problems in life if we accept that our human condition is innate only as far as latent possibilities are concerned, but that our higher homineity has to be wrested with our own bare hands, at great sacrifice and with much effort. This is what distinguishes the inner quality among people. We are born equal but we become different from each other through individual refining, when we seek perfection. If we are all born incomplete, and we remain at this level, this should not be a reason for shame or resentment. On the contrary, just the opposite is true. Personal self-fulfillment should be presented as a challenge and should be solidly supported by the entire society, since it is society that reaps the rewards from the labors of men who become higher beings through their own efforts. Special schools for the development of higher consciousness should be the most important subject of study and practice for those who wish to attain their full spiritual and moral rights. Such a training should not be compulsory but absolutely voluntary, for without a shadow of a doubt all would in time struggle to attain such knowledge when they see the fruits obtained by those who went before them.

The world greatly admires and reveres intellectual geniuses, yet ignores the geniuses of consciousness. Such people are not in abundance and would prefer to live in absolute or relative anonymity, their attributes being more of a spiritual than physical type. At this point, many might wonder whether this type of "more conscious" person will necessarily be "more moral." To answer this, you must understand that the state of consciousness I am discussing here, of necessity excludes the possibility of causing harm to other people or acting unethically. This can be appreciated when one understands that higher consciousness is the most elevated form of spirituality possible, for it does not exclude higher rationality. A high spiritual level invariably corresponds to an elevated moral and evolutive stature.

The more a person's spiritual stature grows, the greater the demands on one's self that this entails, with a concomitant increase in the person's level of voluntary self-control. The moral problem of mankind is a matter of the absence of individual spirituality and a lack of an impulse to evolve because of culturally based conceptual omissions. I should insist on the fact that there is no concept within our common knowledge of the possibility of setting out on a secular path to spirituality. Yet to do this is really within everyone's reach if so desired. However, we have no appreciation for the magnitude of the benefits this may bring to mankind. It is ironic that a brand of refreshment, clothing, or cigarettes should be well-known throughout the world and yet man is totally ignorant that a more-meaningful lifestyle exists than is currently experienced—one that is more valuable and profound; one that is within his reach if he so wants it; one that can bring him new, extraordinary possibilities for attaining happiness and supreme virtue.

The moral conduct of common man is unacceptable, because the evolutive level of the species is scant, and the moral standard is equally scant. Therefore, moralizing campaigns based on simple recommendation as to what one should or should not do are not very effective. When morality is unconscious, it is no longer genuine because it becomes an ethical impossibility. Unfortunately, people are more inclined to complaining and proclaiming, but when the moment comes to shoulder one's evolutive duties, only a few are ready to do so.

6. The Weakness of People's Character

One connotation of the word character is ethical value, and this is attributed to those individuals whose volitive attitude and way of thinking are organized so as to reveal two fundamental qualities: full responsibility and consequentiality in their way of doing things—and by extension, consistency in their conduct. Faithfulness to one's self, firmness, and an univocal guideline in life are the main characteristics—considered as ethical values— which we infer when speaking of training and educating the character.

—*Philipp Lersch*[5]

A well developed character includes qualities such as *will power, responsibility, and consistent conduct.* In light of these parameters, and being realistic, there are not many people who conform to this description because a weak character is today's practiced disease. Young people who are in search of their own identity are the ones most affected by this problem. Their dependency on their elders, the insecurity typical of their age group, their lack of self-discipline, uncertainty as to the nature of good and evil, tendency to daydream, permissive or excessively authoritarian education, psychological complexes, overprotection, the undefined quality of male or female roles, poor social adaptation, and rebellious temperament are some of the causes that hinder adequate development of their character. Drug abuse requires particular concern, not only because it corrupts the character and weakens the will, but also because it drives the abuser to immorality and delinquency. With adults, defects of character also result from wrong lifestyles that prioritize leisure over work, easy gain over strenuous effort, minimal physical activity, the fear to confront new challenges, and the fear to defend one's own rights, overprotection in childhood, shyness, the ambiguity of the masculine role, and drug abuse. Television, as a portal to people's unconscious, allows people's minds to be colonized by false values such as materialism, hedonism, and permissiveness.

One should add to this the fact that the entire machinery of publicity and marketing is founded upon devising deceptively easy offers to tantalize the individual into unconsciously envisioning the world as a fantastic tree from which goods and services can be effortlessly plucked. The individual dissolution that occurs in the masses creates the illusion of navigating through life in a huge ship piloted by an unknown captain, with the sensation of "being carried" towards a destiny that does not depend on oneself.

City life offers few opportunities for the type of heroic confrontation, which would oblige someone to develop his character when he does not want to. Only those who make special demands on themselves to attain higher goals will succeed in developing strength of character as a result of the continuous practice of self-control. But what most debilitates and destroys character and will power is self-indulgence, as can be seen in the case of alcoholics and drug addicts who customarily demand from their fellows what they would never demand of themselves. Such self-indulgence is a noxious mixture of inertia, self-pity, and resistance to methodical labor; it is a form of licentious permissiveness that dodges duty, good habits, and moral rules. Reluctance to put forth effort induces the individual to search for the easy path, forgetting that the value of things is very often measured by the difficulty in obtaining them. The individual with vices needs make no effort of will to live as he does. He does indeed live effortlessly. Correct moral behavior always requires a vigilant attitude and moderate character that includes sustained will power and effort throughout time. Ethical behavior does not appear automatically; we have to achieve it through work and discipline. On the other hand, vices are like weeds insomuch as they surface spontaneously and need no care to survive.

CAUSES THAT WEAKEN PEOPLE'S CHARACTER AND WILL

(a) The Compulsive Quest for Pleasure

Hedonism is perhaps the contemporary human being's most prominent feature. It is the enthronement of pleasure as the greatest of kings. It is the compulsive quest for sensorial gratification, beyond any other consideration, no matter what the price. The masses are so alienated that they perceive the world as a marketplace of entertainment and pleasure, as if they had come into the world merely to endlessly enjoy themselves, and not to perfect themselves morally and spiritually. Life is seen as a circus and it is believed that it is not worthwhile living unless the levels of pleasurable entertainment meet their expectations.

We are marked by the sign of Thanatos, attempting with anguish to return to the womb to recover the unlimited nirvana of uterine existence. It is there that the fetus experiences pleasure uninterrupted by any kind of obligation. The fetus needs make no effort to be fed; it is not disturbed by noise or anything else; it has boundless love and the exclusive dedication from the whole world towards him *(the world being its mother)*. Actually, the fetus "is" the world, since it forms a unity with its mother. It is, therefore, impossible for it to experience loneliness, as loneliness assumes that the individual is a being separate from the material world, and such separation does not occur until several months after birth. After birth, he will never again in life, experience a happiness of this kind.

Hedonism is an irrational attempt to, in some way, recover prenatal nirvana. All the pleasure that had come from "his world" *(his unity with his mother)*, he now seeks in the outside world. The prospect of this pleasure is presented by the unlimited power that marketing offers. As is quite obvious, the demand for this is doomed to inevitable failure, for the individual seeks something that exists only in his own unconscious mind, and not in the material world. Thus, the pleasure he may find *will never satisfy him* for it will only be a fleeting joy. On the other hand, what is likely to happen will be something similar to what happens when we eat. At what point is hunger really satisfied? Experience shows us that this never happens, for once digestion occurs, prolonged emptiness of the stomach provokes in us the anguish to continue being fed.

However, there is a very important difference between feeding the stomach and feeding the senses. Food nourishes the organism and is indispensable for maintaining it. Its effect is "cumulative" since the nutrients turn into integral parts of the cells. This is why the act of eating "fills up" bodily needs. Conversely, pleasure never satisfies the hunger of the senses, and it has to be continually replenished so as to combat the void and anguish. Furthermore, pleasure *is not cumulative*. The individual cannot store pleasure for a later occasion. It then happens that rather than contributing valuable elements to a person, pleasure *drains him*. This is the pathetic case of narcissism which ultimately depletes the heart and soul of the narcissist, thereby leading him to mental and emotional frigidity. Narcissistic pleasure has quite rightly been compared to a "bottomless well," which is never full, no matter how much water flows into it. In a more general context, material *concupiscence* is the type of animal pleasure people most often seek. It is directly pertinent to sex, the stomach, and the taking of stimulating drugs.

Marketing exploits these appetites by indiscriminately offering an artificial paradise of satisfaction: comfort, luxury, travel, and adventure. The bombardment by publicity to this end is such that people come to conceive of existence as a form of opportunity for unlimited enjoyment. When this does not pan out, they fall into a profound depression, arguing that "life has no meaning" for them. It is quite logical that, for those who set pleasure as their goal in life, the incentive for life should disappear once the paradoxical frustration of happiness occurs. The existential void is no more than the sensation of "having been swindled" in some way. It is as if the promised land was not the promised land, after all. Uninterrupted happiness is what is expected and it is identified with pleasurable experiences, but when the desired expectations are not fulfilled, disillusionment and boredom prevail. Material pleasure empties people, and leaves them dry and infertile within their souls. Such is the inevitable destiny of the worldwide confederation of consumers.

There are of course a great number of people who, on an individual basis, lack any significant consumer purchasing power. Their almost unavoidable destiny is to fall into depression, experiencing envy and resentment, and unconsciously suspecting that they are "being deprived of something." According to their reasoning, those who deprive them of this are the more affluent segments of the general population. The person who is possessed by envy stops living in terms of self-reference and his existence revolves around the ones who caused his passion, remaining emotionally "enchained" forever. This person is unable to recuperate his libido, ending up in a situation totally opposite to the pole or extreme of falling in love. Whereas the positive pole generates love, the negative pole generates rage.

Consumerism stems from the offerings of massive advertising, which incessantly multiplies the number of objects or situations that tempt our need to possess. This obsession becomes so compelling that it leads people into a moral laxness without their knowledge, and ultimately to a loss of honor and personal dignity. He who at first has scruples in regard to smoking marijuana, for instance, once having crossed this threshold and having smoked the marijuana, will want to cross other such thresholds, and will end up by trying out cocaine or other more-powerful substances. The woman who becomes promiscuous may, without realizing it, flout the norms of morality that had hitherto governed her conduct and may finally lose any ability to exercise discrimination concerning the moral quality of her lover or her partner. Something similar happens with certain men who pass with ease from smoking marijuana or cocaine to homosexual experiences, which are usually called "variations in sexual conduct." An indiscriminate attitude implies that "anything goes," and thus results in objectifying people, redefining them as useful or pleasurable "objects" instead of persons.

The permissive person becomes progressively weakened, because he has no need to exert his will or control his character so as to overcome temptations. He who yields to temptation is a fool of the kind that the English moralist David Hume spoke of when he said that "the villain is the greatest fool of all, for in exchange for a few worthless material pleasures, he will sacrifice the higher pleasure of becoming a fully developed person."

By their behavior, the consumer addict and the permissive individual sacrifice the possibility for spiritual perfection that could lead them to supreme virtue and true happiness. "Giving in" weakens and atrophies the muscle of the will which, it goes without saying, has yet to be born in mediocre men. A man of untarnished morality is an athlete of the will. He is like a disciplined Spartan who knows how to make a sacrifice or postpone the pleasure of the moment in order to obtain some future good of a more elevated type. This is the case with virtue: when it is well administered, it leads to happiness.

(b) Overprotection

Overprotected children become weak and cowardly, and when they grow into adults they generally lack the minimal assertiveness to make their way in life and to command respect. Once grown, they will often seek the protection of a paternalistic State as surrogate parent. Such people have inadequately developed personalities, and in extreme cases, they are emotionally handicapped and find it very difficult to adapt to normal conditions. Excessive protection by their parents or family failed to give them sufficient personal space to develop normally. Most likely some relative had habitually taken charge of solving all their childhood problems without giving the child either enough space or enough time to try to do so himself. When an overprotected child attends school, he usually has significant problems with his peers and teachers and may even fail in his studies. However, it is difficult to set parameters to determine when protection becomes excessive in its aims. It is quite likely that in some Latin American countries young people are more protected than in the U.S.A., for instance, particularly in the case of women.

What is important here is to realize that this mechanism prevents a harmonious development of the character and the will by creating a tendency to try to achieve things in life by emotionally manipulating other people instead of organizing one's life through personal merit and effort.

Such individuals often see themselves as victims and easily slip into self-indulgence and self-pity. All this makes them avoid effort which is perceived as painful, and prevents them from developing the habit of striving for what they want. Burdened by such problems, they have no energy left for moral struggles and none of the force necessary to reject temptation and postpone immediate pleasure for the sake of a less immediate good of greater value. This moral listlessness makes them ambiguous and aimless in their choice of ethical values, for they have no profound convictions and do not know how to firmly defend the convictions they do have. They shun important challenges because of the fear these challenges arouse in them. One must understand that the overprotected individual's weakness of character leads him directly to permissiveness, for in order to abide by sound rules and principles, one needs discipline and will power.

"To give oneself permission," in its more negative sense, means to gradually increase the "normal doses" of pleasure, entertainment, and consumerism, thus making it increasingly difficult to shape good moral habits. Gastronomical delights, an affection for sweet things, and the consumption of alcohol, are all forms of self pampering that can lead to addiction and disorders like obesity and low self-esteem. Permissiveness is just another expression referring to "self-indulgence," a habit that brings about a low level of self-demand, with the subsequent moral deterioration that this entails.

(c) Idleness and Decadence

Lack of activity and the tendency for sybaritic behavior are significant obstacles to the normal development of character. Idleness leads one to imagine nonsense because of a lack of anything better to do, or as a mental diversion to withdraw from tedium and boredom. If a person has no work or special activity, he will sleep a great deal and wake up late. He will lack family responsibilities and will not face significant challenges. He will also lack opportunities to shape his character.

A cushy, easy life leads to a lack of energy, yet work involving sacrifice can also lead to this absence of energy if it is not rewarded by the necessary recognition. A lack of incentives and opportunities brings on apathy and indifference, even in cases in which the problem is purely subjective.

The mediocrity of the environment may also act as a disincentive to creativity and personal drive. To be more precise, character is tempered by the overcoming of significant obstacles, but when there are no obstacles, or when the individual refuses to confront them, this brings about a softening of the will.

One should recall that ethical behavior is possible only when there is a strong determined will that knows how to withstand vice and temptation. This type of energy appears only occasionally for it is not a general norm. Similarly, the individual who feels unsuccessful in life tends to become disheartened and depressed—exhausting sentiments that lead him to rebel against the world in a nonconstructive way.

Life in the big cities centers on ease and comfort. Only very few people walk several miles to get to work. With few exceptions, there are no opportunities for tough physical effort. Everything centers on mechanical accommodations—buses, subways, cars, elevators, consumer electronics, electronic banking, faxes, computing, and telecommunications, not to mention luxuries and sophistication. It is indeed a world of external things that make life easier. Everything points to the fact that we are approaching a materially "easier" existence at high speed, one requiring less effort, with more leisure and comfort. With man's dependence on machinery becoming ever greater—if he fails to grow internally—the 21st century may be the era in which the tyranny of the masses is succeeded by the tyranny of the machine. Science and technology are continually developing, but man's inner evolutionary status is unchanged; he is no more human than men 20 or 30 centuries ago. Mankind and all that it represents is shrinking. "Progress" is maximized, and while everyone applauds continuing technological advances, moral values become obsolete. The culture of luxury, pleasure, and ease is rapidly alienating the human being's spiritual world, while materialism and violence multiply. Opportunism and consumerism ultimately "steal" people's souls, usurping the functions traditionally attributed to the devil.

It is ironic, albeit not strange, that people have the impression that the level of our civilization is rapidly improving in the sense that they believe we are growing more and more civilized, which becomes an exercise for feeling that "all is well" and that there is no real reason to worry. Such "triumphalism" and consumer alienation cause people to conveniently forget certain realities and to ignore questions that they avoid asking themselves. One such question, for instance, is: why does spiritual progress fail to go forward in tandem with material advances, when in actuality, regression has occurred, with the external becoming more highly valued than the internal? Sometimes it would seem that these two worlds are inversely related to each other—the strengthening of one implying the diminishing of the other.

(d) Sexual Ambiguity

Until a few years ago, man and woman were polarized in sexual extremes with well-defined characteristics. However, at the moment, "men want to have babies." There are numerous movies in which men dress up as women, and ads in which a man appears pregnant. Pants are no longer the prerogative of men, nor are long hair, earrings, necklaces, and bracelets the prerogatives of women. Males wear makeup and go to beauty parlors, and there are women who box and smoke cigars. Sexual ambiguity fills TV advertising. Video clips are full of strange asexual beings whose gender, as female or male, is left to the spectator's imagination. Many male stars of modern music wear feminine attire and become models to be emulated by young people who have not yet come to terms with their own sexual identity. Meanwhile, feeling disqualified by male chauvinism, women strive to compete with men as equals, which often leads them to adopt clearly masculine styles in attempts to surpass men and thereby to make themselves respected. Unisex attire fulfills many people's expectations, so that men and women are similar in appearance. Thus, she will feel less discriminated against, while he, in this way, will overcome his unconscious fear of castration.

However, this gender and sexual ambiguity goes beyond the mere image, and is not constrained to physical appearance. It resides in the cerebral information that comes from the cultural environment, and which as a result of its subliminal nature, penetrates the mind, infiltrating mandates of behavior. Those affected are generally individuals who have not managed to define their own identity, and who are insecure with who they are in themselves and what they desire. By dressing and behaving in such a nontraditional way, they derive a feeling of a more clearly defined identity. A man with long hair makes himself the center of attention, and by doing so, cannot avoid an intensification of his feeling of identity at the level of "being" *("being" in the social sense or in relation to someone or something else).*

The search for identity can be too time consuming; it preoccupies much of a person's life in the form of an unresolved problem. A continuous state of inner ambiguity perturbs the normal development of the personality and brings about a lack of interest in anything that goes beyond the limits of the psychological conflict. An androgynous individual will hardly be able to strengthen his character and will power, for the solution to the conflict from which he suffers will not leave him enough time to do anything superfluous to obtaining an external identity that will endow him with value in the eyes of his peers. If he is successful in his quest for such an external identity, he will resort more and more to the outside world. It is unlikely that he will question himself in a way, as that would encourage analysis of his own character and conduct. A person's frivolity blinds him to the value of the most-profound and important matters of the human condition. Alas, the world of external appearances is, per se, a frivolous consideration, and whoever attempts to base his value on such criteria has to pay the price by experiencing an unbearable inner void.

(e) Sedentariness

People who lead sedentary lives are more than normally vulnerable to weakness, pessimism, sadness, and melancholy and hence to a somewhat negative approach to life. On the other hand, sportsmen are usually far more optimistic, well-balanced individuals in better physical and mental health. After running four or five miles, it is hardly likely that a person would feel the desire to commit an offense, harm anyone, act immorally, or become depressed. The Eskimos, whose lives depend upon hunting and fishing, are usually obliged to walk long distances, and so their daily routine entails a considerable effort. As a result, they have the lowest levels of cholesterol in the world, despite the fact that their diet is based almost exclusively on animal fat. Neither are there many examples of delinquency in such cultures; it is as though intense physical activity is a catharsis for people's baser passions and instincts. This is the reason that young men in ancient Sparta were submitted to painful physical efforts to temper their character and will. Only if they were successful in this could they attain full civil rights at the age of 30. The person who keeps his body in good condition is blessed with joy and optimism. It would seem as if the sweat of physical exercise purges rage and tension.

Sedentariness is also a form of permissiveness in which the individual avoids any sustained or intense effort, thus losing a valuable opportunity to strengthen his will. Sedentariness is, in fact, debilitating as can be seen in excessive sleep or in languishing in bed.

The baser passions flourish because of weak wills in those people who feel aversion to great effort, ignorant as they are of the fact that there can be no development or self-fulfillment without challenges. An austere, active life is a good aid to optimum moral training.

(f) Lack of Self-Worth

According to Max Scheler, one cannot lead a truly moral life without a sense of one's own value, and the more this feeling of one's own value deteriorates, the more this person will depend on what others say of him.

In reality, most people measure their own worth through the approval of others, so they continually strive to inflate their images to elicit from others the admiration and respect upon which their own sense of self-worth depends. This is the reason for the anxious quest for symbols of power and status. Luxury cars, jewels, and furs are all mere means of arousing admiration and respect under the philosophy of "the more you have, the more you are."

It is necessary to point out that the individual's true "I" weakens and deteriorates to the same degree as his ego is engorged by his image, and so he becomes less and less able to accept higher values or make arduous efforts. His center of gravity is no longer within himself; it now lies in his fellowman. However, this is not an act of kindness or detachment but one of supreme egotism. He lives through others because he uses them as mirrors of his image—mere instruments to feed his ego.

It is obvious that an individual's true worth can lie only in the very selfness of his being and not be defined by the approval of others. If such opinion did in fact add any value to a person, all that would be required to grow morally would be the sympathy of other people.

However, it is certain that one cannot grow through the approval of others, but only through one's own work. The image only increases the social projection of the individual. Instead of enlarging the value of the being, the image reduces it because it is like a parasite feeding off of him. There are famous members of the "jet set," or high society, who are nothing more than sad, empty phantoms, and like balloons they are kept inflated by their admirers; they lack any significant essential content.

When people have no sense of their own worth, their ethics are usually of a low caliber. Failures and resentful people are so possessed by passions which tear them apart that there is no room in their lives for them to aim towards more elevated matters. There is no room either in their heads or hearts to be more receptive to higher forms of conduct. Their existential anguish stems from feelings of perceived injustice that torment them, for they do not realize that morality is supreme justice.

The occult mechanics of Nature are very simply stated in the expression "give and ye shall receive," for Nature as an omnipresent energy returns what it receives from an individual. It is ironic that people should seek to raise their self-esteem through the approval of others, thus projecting their "I" outside themselves and burying it in the masses. However, what they are really doing is invalidating their own beings, which cannot survive because they assume false, capricious identities in order to attain general approval.

As if this were not enough, the masses depend on fashion, and since fashion is constantly changing, the fickle mob will reject the models which it had formerly applauded. The individual is thus obliged to continually seek new outlets for social acceptance.

The quest for, and assertion of, one's own identity through the approval of other people is the most efficient way to be subsumed into the masses and thus lose one's own essence and differentiation. This is indeed the easiest way to reach the state of nonbeing, which is the hidden goal of those who dare not confront the challenge of being on *higher levels.* It is most likely that the individual will raise his self-esteem if he feels accepted, but the true worth of his own selfness that emanates from his being, will be minimized a little more each day.

One needs to understand the insanity of seeking the approval of others, for regardless of what one does, some will agree and others will not, so that there will never be a consensus. The best way to raise one's self-esteem in a healthy, prudent way is by doing so on the strength of the moral values that emanate from transcendental spiritual parameters. These parameters are, have been, and always will be inscribed in the memory of Nature and, therefore, lie in our depths like our divine spark, the simple emanation of the Supreme Being.

By pleasing God and not the masses, by understanding that if we follow the path marked out by the Creator, we shall attain integral success in reference to our true human goal. To this end, it is not necessary for someone to believe in God, for skepticism does not eliminate Him or abolish His laws.

Frequently, agnostics or atheists are self-devalued people who do not believe in themselves. Through their rebellion they seek to attain identity or gain attention in order to raise their self-esteem. Materialism is nothing more than an expression of the thinking of those who have never had an internal experience emanating from a state of consciousness that can be called "an evaluation of the being in its fullness." (This is what some people define as a mystical experience), a state in which one is convinced of the existence of divinity by getting a glimpse of its reflection in one's own soul.

Materialism is the expression of a low level of consciousness, a consciousness whose knowledge is limited to the body and physical matter, and that has never managed to elevate itself to the world of the spirit. Matter has such a certainty that it excludes anything that transcends it. In contrast, the goal of evolution of the consciousness is *absolute certainty.*

True morality is much more than rules of behavior for a given society, for such rules may be entirely different for different groups. *Morality requires respect for the cosmic order imposed by the Logos, the divine emanation that maintains the structure and order of the Universe.* As nothing can exist outside the Logos, we are also part of it, so that we must respect its code, which is the same for all forms of life and even for inanimate objects. I refer here to *cosmic law,* one of whose most-important mandates was beautifully expressed by Greek philosophers under the concept of *egalitarian equivalence,* which is the continuous point of equilibrium sought by the intelligent Universe.

People are accustomed to visualizing themselves as beings separate from the Universe—inhabitants of a cosmic island. However, according to the holographic concept of Doctor Karl Pribram: "the part is in the whole and the whole is in each part." Pribram's research on memory and the functioning of the brain lead to the conclusion that the brain functions as a hologram in many aspects. A hologram is a special type of optical storage with characteristics that can be illustrated by the following example: if you take a photograph of a person and cut off a piece of it, the head for example, and then enlarge it to it's original size, you will not have a large head but an image of the whole person. Each individual part of the photo contains the total image in condensed form. Thus, the part leads to the whole.

This coincides with ancient philosophical aphorisms as, for instance, the one which says "the microcosm is similar to the macrocosm" (man is similar to the Universe, and potentially contains the whole within himself). When we carry out any action, its repercussions reach the furthest corner of the Cosmos, which will *give back to us the equivalent* of what it received from us. The phrase "he who does it, pays for it," thus takes on an unsuspected cosmic dimension.

A physicist will argue, of course, that if this were true, a person's actions could not travel through the Universe at a greater speed than light, but according to the teachings of ancient cultures, such as in ancient Egypt, "thought can reach all corners of the Universe." The Creator does not bother to punish our misdeeds. It is we who punish ourselves for the violation of His laws. Thus, true morality and true justice totally transcend *Homo sapiens,* and in no way depend on the codes designed by him. At the level of Nature, *the guilty person is invariably and ultimately punished, and the just and the innocent are ultimately rewarded.*

Since man's justice cannot reach as far as divine justice, it seems that one is incapable of perceiving the effects of this latter, and it is easy to deny its existence. What really happens is that cosmic punishment usually surpasses our human comprehension—so much so, that if we could perceive it, we might even confuse it with a reward. Furthermore, it is totally private, operating exclusively in and on the guilty person's private world.

7. Environmental Hypnosis

Hypnosis has been defined in its simplest form as "a state similar to sleep that is characterized by great susceptibility to suggestion and also by a loss of will."

"Suggestive influence" has been defined as:

1. For one person to inspire in another hypnotized person involuntary speech or actions.

2. To dominate a person's will, leading him to act in a certain way.

3. To experience with suggestion.

The meaning of the term "hetero suggestion," which has been defined as, "a suggestion in which the inductive phenomenon is external to the individual thus influenced," is also of interest.

What we chiefly know of hypnosis are theatrical shows in which a hypnotized person is made to believe he is in the Arctic and starts to shiver with cold; or he is made to feel hot or to imitate some animal. Environmental hypnosis is not in our repertoire, but it does exist. I refer to a process in which the traditional hypnotist is replaced by an external medium of a mechanical type, which produces stimuli similar to those used by the hypnotist. The methods used to produce hypnosis can be divided into three groups:

1. Visual stimulation by means of the use of a moving object that attracts and maintains the individual's attention, such as a twinkling light.

2. Tactile stimulation by means of taps on the forehead and face, touching the eyelids to force them closed, or tapping the extremities (mesmeric passes).

3. Auditory stimulation through the monotonous repetition of phrases such as "you feel sleepy," "you are going to be hypnotized," etc.

During hypnotic sleep, the person normally closes his eyes, but he may also keep them open, stand up, move about, and answer questions. We should not confuse it with our nightly sleep in which we renew our strength. Hypnosis is an altered state of consciousness that has nothing to do with the normal process of sleep. It has been defined as a "magnetic sleep" brought on by fascination through personal influence or the appropriate apparatus. It is of two main types:

1. That which is produced by a hypnotist. The individual falls into a state of sleep in which his eyes are closed and he ostensibly loses control of his own rationality.

2. That which is produced by stimuli generated by an external medium without the presence of the hypnotist.

In this latter type the individual enters a state of altered consciousness in which his level of awakening notably decreases. Although he does not actually fall asleep in the way we are used to defining sleep, his level of perception becomes mainly subliminal and his capacity for suggestibility ostensibly increases. There comes about a duality in which he, on the one hand, preserves his rationality and, on the other, becomes as gullible as a child—rapidly accepting that the most absurd situations are, in fact, real.

One can see an individual who looks normal in every external sense, for the alteration is kept hidden within him. However, what is true is that this individual will be in a semi-hypnotic trance, even though his eyes are open. Higher discernment will be dramatically diminished, so that his inner disposition will be to immediately believe in the most absurd, outrageous things, because his capacity to judge is partially annulled. If this were otherwise, there would be no place for advertising, for no one would be so simple-minded as to become addicted to a certain fizzy drink merely because it is offered on television by a pretty girl. In fact, the individual "buys" the girl and not the drink, although he does not realize it. Products that nobody in their right mind would think of acquiring are submitted to a marketing process to decide which are the right hypnotic stimuli to squeeze through the cracks of the consumer's mind, below his level of consciousness.

In any case, it is quite clear that what we call consciousness is really "sub-consciousness," and what is termed subconscious is really a form of infra-consciousness. When we believe that we are fully awake, we are really in a state of "drowsiness," a state of semi-sleepwalking in which we accumulate a high oneiric-hypnotic content.

The more repetitive the act of penetrating a person's mind through subliminal messages, the greater will be his tendency to suggestibility. That is, he will become considerably more influenced and manipulated, which is precisely the aim of advertising and propaganda campaigns.

Our unconscious mind is like a huge sponge absorbing everything indiscriminately, and then giving vent to this content by means of instinctive pulsions that incite the individual to consume a certain product, or to obey without protest, or to show preference for a certain political candidate. The unconscious mind is like a child without discernment, who accepts everything he is told without questioning, so that the stimuli that penetrate his mind are stored as autonomous information, not subordinated to the "I," and which condition and oblige him to behave in certain ways. To speak of brainwashing as an episode close to fiction is to show total ignorance of the irrefutable fact that most of our mind no longer belongs to us, for it has been colonized by alienating subliminal information, information that is alien to our intrinsic individual condition.

Television is the most powerful and complete hypnotic agent. According to Karl Popper, "television has become a power too strong for democracy. No democracy can survive unless we put a stop to the abuse of power practiced by television. Currently, this abuse is obvious. A democracy cannot exist if television is not put under control, or to be more precise, it cannot exist for long unless the power of television has been unmasked."

The distinguished philosopher refers to the harm caused by television through its messages, but he does not analyze what it is that brings about such a level of influence on people. Undoubtedly, television makes use of two of the three means used to provoke hypnosis that were mentioned earlier:

1. Visual stimulation through moving objects and twinkling lights.

2. Auditory stimulation through the monotonous repetition of phrases.

The TV screen constantly flickers and ceaselessly transmits myriad repetitive messages of a suggestive nature that take possession of the spectator, hypnotizing him in a highly efficient way. Nobody could seriously say that people in a state of magnetic stupor are capable of behaving in a morally superior way. On the contrary, the unconscious is amoral in itself, so that when it is dominant, it strongly influences a person to serious ethical deterioration.

Likewise, if this hypnotic television induction were used to inculcate moral principles, these would be of no ethical value whatsoever, for if morality is to be valid, it has to obey a voluntary, conscious choice. It is mere tomfoolery to speak of "individual liberty" in a world in which children are hypnotized from infancy by television with the aim of creating obedient, docile consumers—members of the flock, who reach their majority being totally programmed. Life in the big cities is a continuous succession of hypnotizing stimuli, as if everything had been organized for this purpose. Let us examine what Professor L. Von Bertalanffy says in his book *Robots, Men, and Minds:*[6]

> Elementary learning, teaching, and human life in general are essentially reactions to external conditions. They begin in early childhood with the imposition of elementary norms of hygiene and other interferences that lead to socially acceptable behavior

and restrain conduct that is not. They continue with teaching, made more effective with B.F. Skinner's principles of positive reinforcement and also with the aid of teaching machines. They end with an adult person incorporated into an opulent society that promises prosperity for everyone; a person who is conditioned in a rigorously scientific way via the public media of mass communication, to turn him into the perfect consumer. In other words, he has become an automaton who responds adequately when he reacts in accordance with what the predominant industrial-military-political powers prescribe.

He is man as a machine, that can be programmed; all these identical machines, like cars off an assembly line, with equilibrium or comfort as the *desideratum;* behavior as a commercial transaction with minimum expense and maximum profit.

The effects of such manipulations can be seen all around us: in the unspeakable vulgarity of popular culture; in the unbearable children and teenagers who do not even know how to speak their own language when they reach college, but who will sit bewitched in front of the television for five hours a day and then find no better relief than drugs, premature pregnancies, or delinquency.

. . . a society in which senselessness and ruthless competition fills thousands of mental asylums; a society whose politics have transmuted Jefferson's democracy into an easily managed flock.

Bertalanffy gives a good description of the robotization of man, a process that progressively dehumanizes man to turn him into a puppet useful to certain interested parties; an "electronic man" with an integrally programmed brain, prevented from practicing any inner deliberation to acquire genuinely solid moral and spiritual values, interested only in consuming pleasure and entertainment, ever further removed from an individual possibility of evolution.

Unless man can discover a way to immunize himself against environmental hypnosis, he will be doomed to wander through life pursuing new and varied mirages without attaining the mental independence that would enable him to achieve a freedom of thought and conduct, governed by a higher moral consciousness. This is the only path to finding oneself and valuing oneself in terms of the virtue of one's being rather than one's image.

Only through the dominion of passions and the frequent practice of introspection can one encounter the moral paths that lead to the heaven of virtue and happiness. These qualities are born and develop only within the inner silence, and not in the noisy bustle of social happenings. Any process of transforming oneself into a genuinely ethical being must take the course of encountering oneself enough to submit oneself freely and voluntarily to forms of moral purification and discipline. Otherwise, the individual will always be a mere "container" of mandates and prohibitions that he neither understands nor shares in his heart and soul.

However, one should bear in mind that without an awakening of consciousness, none of this will be possible, and such an elevation in the state of awakening can be attained only through the education of our faculty of attention. This is the only means to do away with environmental hypnosis.

In order to better understand the problem of hypnotic stupor, let us recall that sleep and awakeness are opposite extremes of one and the same phenomenon, which is the human being's psychic consciousness. As occurs with a thermometer, *awakeness* is equivalent to the higher levels above zero, while *sleep* is below zero, with the zero representing the point at which "one loses consciousness." When we say that the environmental temperature is 30 degrees, for instance, we only mean a degree of expansion of the mercury. What I mean

death. Human beings are not insects, but we long ago digressed from our intended evolutionary path. We have ceased behaving in the terms for which we were created. Instead, we direct our efforts towards the quest for comfort, pleasure, and luxury—a behavioral pattern that has distanced us from Nature, misleading us into a progressively false, frivolous, and artificial existence.

8. Lack of a Consensual Morality

The Manichaeans, a Christian Gnostic sect of the third century, believed in the existence of two eternal, absolute principles—good and evil—in perpetual conflict with each other. The founder of this movement was Mani, who was born in Babylon in 216 A.D. The Manichaean sect had a huge influence in both the East and the West, the most illustrious of its adepts being St. Augustine.

According to Mani, there were two substances in the beginning, or two roots, sources, or principles. Light was equivalent to virtue and at times to God; darkness was equivalent to evil and at times to matter.

Progress is visualized as a movement of the constant shedding of evil. Evil is an extant substance that can neither be absorbed by virtue nor be conceived by analogy with nonbeing. Triumph over evil does not require that it be exterminated, but that it be relegated to the place in which it belongs. Once it is firmly confined to its proper place, there can be no fear that it will once more invade the realm of light.[7]

I mention Manichaeism for two reasons: the first reason is because it often happens that when someone mentions the conflict between good and evil, he is usually called a Manichaeist in a pejorative sense with no accompanying analysis of Manichaeist concepts; secondly, because of the interest that a concept of good has, which is no longer subjective, but acquires a substantiality which is previous to man. The same occurs with evil; it will consistently endeavor to penetrate people who have to continually struggle to rid themselves of it.

What are good and evil really?

According to the transcendental parameters of Nature, absolute good for the human being is: *Everything that makes man awaken from environmental hypnosis, thus enabling him to have access to progressively more and more elevated states of consciousness, which will lead him to a vertically ascendant evolution.*

In contrast, *evil is everything that prevents man's higher consciousness from awakening; everything that directly or indirectly contributes to maintaining it in a state of hypnosis, thus preventing him from evolving or otherwise bringing about his involution.*

The evolution of consciousness is the highest aim of our lives, the goal that once achieved brings uninterrupted happiness and supreme good. There is no other way to find genuine happiness. The quest for apparent good leads us only to disillusionment and frustration.

Man's first moral duty is to the evolution of his consciousness, for only when he has attained this goal will he stop being a *bridge* and become a *true man*. *Bridge*, in this case, is the incomplete man, the massified mediocre person. The *superman* is he who by evolving outgrows his *hybrid* state to become completely and totally humanized. He is in fact *complete man*, who by following the path mapped by the Creator, transforms his own rough draft into a *perfectly completed work*. God brings us into the world incomplete; therefore, our work is to reach the peak. Yet we, his children, having lost the path, not only do not work to perfect ourselves, but rather insist on stubbornly "incompleting" ourselves even further.

It is not, therefore, surprising that people suffer from an existential anguish, saying that they have lost all meaning in life—and they certainly have. However, it is in their hands to regain it at any moment. Any complaint about the possible lack of meaning or purpose in life is unfounded and to lament about it is a great hypocrisy. We all have the means within our grasp to find the meaning of existence, and if we do not realize this, it is only because of hedonism, idleness, or sloth. We have two ways of defending this: one part of us moans pitifully for a life with more meaning and purpose, while the other part looks for any possible subterfuge, in order to justify the way things are, to continue acting as we always have so that we don't lose the animal gratification that pleases us so much.

It is terrifying to one day discover evidence that there is a superior way of existence, with a totally different style than the one we know—one more human, beautiful, happy, full, and harmonious. We are scared to open our eyes and suddenly discover this new reality, which is so irrefutable and overwhelming as to oblige us to put our hands to work immediately, and by doing so, start to lose the semi-animal lifestyle to which we are so accustomed.

This means having to abandon the little, mediocre world with which we are familiar. It means shedding self-complacency and permissiveness; it means leaving behind our justifications for our wrong actions; it means throwing irresponsibility out the window; it means to stop being hypocrites and liars; it means no longer accommodating reality but confronting it as it is; it means communicating genuinely with other people; it means loving the truth and not just pretending to love it; it means being joyful, creative, and harmonious; it means expelling any feeling of envy in order for us to be able to rejoice at the good fortune of others; it means practicing *egalitarian equivalence* with all human beings; it means ridding ourselves of all of our vices; it means not to have room for evil in our hearts; it means no longer complaining and pitying ourselves; it means to be happy and virtuous. If it were in our power to choose this lifestyle, at the cost of the effort and discipline that it entails, would we have the integrity necessary to make that decision?

Well, the decision is in your hands, because the opportunity is within your reach; it depends only on your desire and your will. Once and for all let it be stated loud and clear that *all* persons in this world, regardless of race, color, class, social status, or cultural level, can find the path of happiness and supreme good. So far, people have been cruelly deceived into believing that their prosperity and happiness depends on the State or on divine blessing. The State only administers for the people, and the Creator already blessed us sufficiently by giving us life. It is we, who now from the point of our infinite smallness, have to return what we owe for this gift by *completing* our own being, to thus fulfill the task which we were assigned. Each person possesses within himself the power to break his chains through moral and spiritual improvement.

The development of higher consciousness is not a frivolous choice of the human being, since life offers us only the alternatives of *evolution or involution,* and he who fails to rise, will *fall and become petrified.* Really, it is the noblest and most praiseworthy goal an individual can pursue, for only by perfecting himself can he offer Mankind the same values he has developed in himself. Nobody, however well meaning, can give that which he does not possess within himself. There is only one serious, profound, and coherent way that the human being can come to behave in accordance with a higher morality: that is by first discovering his own worth. He must understand that he possesses, in a latent state, the same material from which great men have been shaped—and realize that he is no less than the most valuable person who has ever existed. He only has to realize that this precious state lies latent within him, and he only needs a straightforward, decisive character, and a strong, conscious will under the service of the discipline required for the work of self-realization.

Once a man discovers his own value, he will no longer be puny, and will learn to raise his eyes from the ground to gaze at the sky. A famous axiom says: "hitch your wagon to a star." Do just this. The star is within you. Stop plodding at the speed of an ox. Nobody could deny that good can reign in the world only when it has been achieved at the *individual* level, and this is only feasible through personal spiritual work. It is not the mass which has to change, since it has no individuality, consciousness, or will.

I formally propose that supreme good should be defined as *the vertically ascending evolution of individual consciousness.* Nobody can refute this fact. Nobody can say that this may suit some people and not others. It is impossible to argue that it is bad for the individual consciousness to be raised to higher levels, for this means the consciousness of all individuals: white, black, westerner, easterner, uncivilized, or civilized. If there were at any moment a consensus that supreme good is inherent to the evolution of the individual consciousness, this could become a widespread cultural concept that would motivate people to follow this path. The good I propose is not *my opinion,* nor does it merely express *my preferences.* I am speaking of an imperative of Nature, which will not tolerate the petrification of evolution and which will gradually destroy all that will not progress in accordance with the rhythm of the Universe. Such was what possibly occurred with many animal species that are today extinct because they failed to adapt to change.

Man's progress has been mainly scientific and technological. Like the development of the human brain which has tripled its volume since the beginnings of the species, science and technology have experienced great growth. Intelligence, as in the common concept that already exists, has also increased greatly as a consequence of the pressure of external changes. We could say however, that whereas intelligence and the brain evolved, consciousness remained static. The semantic content of the word *consciousness* transcends dictionary definitions, and we could define it as *the sum of conscious learning carried out in states of higher awareness.* Common consciousness has not evolved towards vigilic consciousness because man has never awakened from environmental hypnosis. There have always been powerful external stimuli which mesmerized his senses and induced him to sleep.

Humans possess a static consciousness and a dynamic intelligence, and this is what leads us to create many things without anticipating the collateral effects of this process. Intelligence and consciousness are absolutely different faculties. One is of the brain and the other emanates from the being. Intelligence is formed through memoristic learning and moves in the world of information. It is an innate capacity. Vigilic consciousness is developed through learning in optimum states of awakening, and it is linked to the world of meaning. It is not an innate capacity and exists only in a latent state.

The intelligent person is equal to the ignoramus or simpleton in that he lacks an evolved consciousness, but he who manages to possess consciousness will never be a simpleton or a fool. The *significant capacity* of the higher consciousness enables him to visualize with absolute clarity the positive effects of acting always by adjusting his own actions to the highest ethical norms. We shall never meet a conscious individual who intentionally harms another person, since the highest moral code is inherent to the one who possesses higher consciousness.

If the majority of Mankind could attain the evolution of consciousness, then the violence would stop, putting an end to war, delinquency, and terrorism. Delinquents would become convinced that "the cosmic law" cannot be violated, and that "crime does not pay." No one would abuse drugs and people would be peaceful, stable, harmonious, and profound. No one would rob or harm others. The most perfect understanding would reign over the state of male–female relationships and the family would be the perfect model of moral actions. There would be no juvenile delinquency and no wayward youth. There would be no court cases because people would come to agreements in an amicable way over any differences of opinion. Without wars, the armies of the world would only fulfill functions of peace. There would be no more addiction to drugs because people would regain the higher meaning of existence. With the end of drug abuse, one of the most important sources of corruption would be eliminated.

The most important leaders would be those with the most elevated level of higher consciousness, which could be scientifically determined by means of sensitive devices which could register this type of energy.

In the absence of wars, the armies of the world would perform only peaceful tasks and under the leadership of "conscious sages," they would carry out the mission of spreading the highest moral norms, acting as "crusaders" for a new civilization.

I have, in a few lines, imagined a utopia, by showing what the world might be like once we had carried out a moral crusade of a technical character aimed at convincing people to set out on the path of the ascendant change in their consciousness by their own free will.

This is not merely a chimera. All that it requires is a return to the individual of his own "I" that has been snatched from him by the brainwashing campaigns of advertising and propaganda, and to teach him how he can transmute his meaningless, low level of consciousness into a meaningful consciousness of incalculable value. Like the fabulous *Excalibur*, this would enable him to overcome the obstacles to his progress and allow him to gain access to happiness and the supreme good. I should point out that although it is most likely that there will never be a consensus on this subject, anybody could at this very moment, set out on the path for himself, without waiting for others to reach an agreement. He needs only discard mediocrity and conformity to come a little nearer to what right now seems a mere chimera, but which in the 21st century may not be just a chimera anymore.

---

1. Gustave Le Bon, The Crowd (New Brunswick, N.J.: Transaction Publishers, 1995).
2. Ricardo Yepes, *Las claves del consumismo (The Keys to Consumerism)*, (Stork: Libros MC).
3. Yuri Vorobiovski, *La Tercera* (Chile: July 13, 1995).
4. William Ojeda, *¿Cuánto vale un juez? (How Much Does a Judge Cost?)*, (Caracas: Vadel Hermanos Publishers, 1995).
5. Philipp Lersch, *La estructura de la personalidad (The Structure of Personality)*, Barcelona: Editorial Scientia, 1981).
6. L. Von Bertalanffy, *Robots, Men and Minds* (New York: ed. George Braziller).
7. José Ferrater Mora, *Diccionario de filosofía (Dictionary of Philosophy)*, (Buenos Aires: Editorial Sudamericana, 1969).

CHAPTER III

NORMS PERTAINING TO THE TRUE HUMAN BEING

The word *norm* means: "a rule that must be observed or to which conduct, tasks, activities, etc., must be adjusted." *Normal* means:

1. "Whatever is in its natural state."

2. "That which serves as a norm or rule."

3. "Whatever by its nature, form, or magnitude is adjusted to certain prior fixed norms."

We feel reassured when the word *normal* is used to describe someone, and we are inclined to feel that this connotes the best possible condition. In fact, it really expresses only the concept that the biological or psychic conduct of that individual fits into the general parameters of the species. Because we allow ourselves to be so impressed by majorities, they would seem to represent the model of human perfection.

When a person is sick, one speaks of a *pathological* state which represents an abnormality in his health. This state of health is detected through symptoms and disorders that are perfectly classified. Psychological or psychiatric disorders are less easily defined and are of a more diffuse nature, in which several pathologies are at times mingled, so that they are hard for the nonexpert to recognize. Gastroenteritis is easily diagnosed, but such is not the case for example with *narcissistic neurosis.* I have often wondered with regard to the case of mental pathologies, because they may have appeared hundreds or thousands of years ago and might have been affecting the whole of Mankind for centuries. What chance would we have to detect them if, after having affected the whole species for thousands of years, they had become the norm and not the exception?

We would be living in a state that is mentally and psychologically "deficient" without any ability to perceive it. Without having contact with other intelligent extraterrestrial beings with which to compare ourselves, we would have no other point of reference.

I am absolutely certain that a state of deficiency prevails and that we are "retarded" or "handicapped" in relation to the concept of the optimum normality of Nature. What we consider as "normal" is really "deficient," and what we lack is *a higher vigilic consciousness,* the elevation of the self to the higher levels of the brain; the conscious manifestation of the self through the brain; *total consciousness* that includes both subject and object. The being of the individual is an integral part of the being of the Universe; it is *the part that contains the whole.* From a holographic perspective, the photo of God is printed on our interior, but we are incapable of perceiving it. It is man's immortal spirit, the divine spark that emanates from the Creator, that contains all his attributes on a small scale.

Throughout the history of Mankind, there have been men who have in all truth been considered "Super-Men": Confucius, Jesus in his human aspect, Appolonius of Thiana,

Socrates, Buddha, Krishna, Orpheus, Zoroaster, Hermes, and Mohammed. By "Super-Men," I mean *more than men;* more than incomplete men but similar in essence to Cosmic Man, the archetypal model for complete, evolved man. It is enough to glance at the state of the present world and the world of the past to concede that this state is the result of the behavior of civilized, albeit incomplete men. They are "half-men" who, having perfected part of their brains, nevertheless remain deprived of their own higher half, analagous to unfinished buildings.

Existential anguish is only the intuitive feeling of being incomplete. It is the perception that one is disconnected from the most important part of what one is. Indeed, the meaning of life is consubstantial to the fact of *completing oneself.*

What are the norms that pertain to a true human being?

The Complete Man:

1. He controls his *consciousness,* keeping it at a gradually ascending level of awareness.

2. He is immune to hypnotic sopor.

3. He can transcend the psychoanalytical defense mechanisms of the "I"—repression, projection, reactive formation, fixation, and regression.

4. He has an objective view of himself.

5. He manages to overcome self-deceit and rationalization.

6. He is honest, through both morality and logic, for he is convinced that Nature gives back to an equal extent what it receives from man's actions.

7. He is incapable of intentionally harming anyone.

8. He retains the highest traditional values.

9. His self-esteem is based on the level of "humanity" he has managed to develop, and not on the approval of others.

10. He is tolerant, good-natured, and compassionate.

11. He does not hate anyone.

12. As a basic norm of conduct, he embodies the famous golden rule: "do not do unto others as you would not have others do unto you."

13. He practices the highest virtues and can perfectly master his passions.

14. He sees reality for what it is and not in accordance with his own projection.

15. He is profoundly human and possesses a noble heart.

16. He honors God, the family, and his homeland.

17. He fights tirelessly for truth and justice.

18. He manifests his being through his own brain.

19. He knows and practices true love.

20. He has "significative" capacity and not only informative.

21. The information he possesses in his brain is subordinate to his "I."

22. He has a fully developed, adult "I."

23. He is immune to the effects of the phenomenon of the "psychological mass."

These are just some of the ideals of a true human being who has completed himself through the long process of spiritual perfectioning. These qualities represent a transcendental value of cosmic proportions, which shows *what man should be like. As long as our conduct does not adjust to these parameters, we shall forever be deficient imitations of real human beings; "bridgemen" who have not managed to gain access to a meaningful level of evolution.* Indeed, we are really talking about almost the whole species, which for thousands of years has merely remained in a state of "hominal apprenticeship," despite the fact that man was placed on this planet to learn and to evolve, by studying in the toughest and most real academy: the school of life.

Success or failure in this endeavor is not of a local character, and has nothing to do with the individual's limited physical existence, but rather it acquires a cosmic dimension. *It has holographic connotations, for it refers to the success or failure of **the particle** in the great work of materializing in oneself the archetypal model of cosmic man that emanates from **the whole**.*

It is a victory of particle-man in the task of materializing within his own microcosmos, the qualitative equivalent of the attributes of the father who created him. He thus allows the tiny divine spark that dwells within him to become the beacon that enlightens his *consciousness.* By learning how to act in accordance with the Creator's laws, he will be able to transcend erratic existence that is devoid of any purpose, like those who are manipulated by their passions and blinded by egoism, violence, and ambition.

The absurdity and contradictions of human actions disappear when we accept that it is normal for us to behave in this way, because *we are less than men,* and our behavior is closer to that of animals. In spite of this, we try to act as we suppose true human beings would. It is impossible to demand higher ethics of animal-man. One can only expect this of man-man. That is the harsh reality of our condition and we must accept it. *We are very little, yet we possess much.* The lack of ethics is just one of the inherent characteristics of our condition as incomplete men—children at a level of scant evolution who possess the intelligence of adults but the judgment of babies. Therefore, we should not be astonished by war, famine, corruption, delinquency, immorality, or destruction. What would be amazing would be for such scourges not to exist.

The world has always been thus and will continue to be, unless the *individual* changes. It might be argued that if man changes positively, that would have little effect on Humanity, but, in reality, Humanity is only a sum of individuals. Besides, we do not know the true dimension of the fruits of *complete men,* so that it is impossible for us to foresee the magnitude of their actions in the world.

However, we do know that the sacrifice on the cross of a single perfect man washed away the sins of the Earth. What must have been the caliber of this being to achieve this? May there not also be humbler levels of the same essence? This is precisely what I maintain: the feasibility of "bridge-man" raising his level of consciousness by means of a spiritual life until achieving the level of a "super man," who is nothing other than a *true man.* I can already feel the fear and mistrust of certain "bleached sepulchres," who will obstinately deny this possibility or will try to discredit it, for it represents a threat to their immoral, passional, or materialistic lifestyle.

There are many vested interests that quake before the word *freedom* when they intuit that it could refer to a genuine possibility, beyond a mere slogan. They are afraid that *robot man* may awaken and free himself, and no longer be an obedient consumer. They fear that the individual may think for himself and freely choose his own destiny without any external pressure whatsoever. They are afraid that he may attain mental individuality and full freedom of thought, so that he no longer bows to the mandate of advertising and propaganda. They are alarmed by the possibility that any citizen may sit in front of his television and miraculously not become hypnotized by its images, or that he may read the press without experiencing any informational alienation. They are uneasy about the possible coming of a new order that *would offer total equality of opportunities to all.* Race, the color of one's skin, religion, wealth, sex, or any other consideration would no longer be of interest and only the level of higher consciousness that people reached would matter. Those with greater human content would be more valuable, and those with less human potential would assume humbler roles. However, the opportunity to become humanized at higher levels would be within everyone's reach, so that individual merit would determine peoples' destinies.

The most important discovery in the history of Humanity will take place when one can scientifically measure a person's level of individual consciousness. Much like what happens today with IQ tests, the one who measures the level of consciousness would set the rules as to the kinds of responsibilities a person would be prepared to assume, and the importance of the positions he would be capable of handling. This would provoke a total revolution in the world, since this would be the moment when "each would be given his own" in accordance with egalitarian equivalence, which is one of the most important rules of cosmic justice.

Wealth, social status, academic degrees, or political power would no longer matter. There would of course be intellectuals, learned or erudite fools *(with an insignificant or very low level of consciousness)* but also, on the other hand, there would be very humble folk who, on the merit of their inner content, would attain the highest spiritual peaks. Many of the most important leaders or statesmen who have aroused general admiration to date, could not continue in their posts because there would be technical proof of their deficient human condition. It would be discovered that highly intelligent or cultured people, in the conventional sense, could also simultaneously possess an underdeveloped or atrophied consciousness.

True sages would also surface—those who, more than educated men of letters, possess an alive wisdom that transcends the place and the moment. Discrimination against women would disappear because they would be treated as "people with an X level of consciousness," according to their individual analysis. Therefore, it would not be possible to discriminate unfairly between a man and a woman of the same level; this would be the ultimate measure beyond any other consideration. The truth is that the real worth of the human being lies in his being, and not in his intelligence or feelings. Unfortunately, intelligence is at the service of the personality, and personality obeys the passions. At the level of being, we are all intrinsically equal as far as our own essence is concerned, but we differ in accordance to individual evolution, when this exists. This means *we can have a greater accumulation of value in our being,* when we learn the lessons of life and we are able to have a virtuous and conscious way of existence. At bottom, there is neither equality nor inequality between people, just different degrees in the expansion of the self. What is it that leads some to progress and others to remain paralyzed? The answer lies in the way a person processes each daily experience and the reality that surrounds him. What we do in our daily life may help us either to develop and enlarge our consciousness, or it may only mean "to live with our eyes shut."

An individual manages to "fulfill himself" through a careful elaboration of what he experiences—a process of reflection or introspective deliberation that is possible only for the being whose states of consciousness are at increased levels of awakening. This entails daily distilling of the moral and spiritual lessons of the school of life, a process which leads to growth of the being with a corresponding increase in essential value. The person who can achieve this comes to be worth more because he earns this value through his own efforts, while he who remains static and with an exiguous value can only reap the fruits of his laziness, indolence, and permissiveness. It is not society that really values an individual; it is Nature herself that approves his works because she finds that they coincide with the transcendental rules of spiritual perfection.

He who attempts to arbitrarily establish his own parameters, without respect for *universal justice,* will ultimately be disqualified by it, and will have a life of constant confrontation with legality.

CHAPTER IV

THE VALUES OF THE AVERAGE MAN

The conceptual world of the average man is usually so small that what he believes to be valuable does not generally extend beyond the sphere of his bodily needs, and is limited to what certain philosophers have called the "infra-spiritual life," that is, a purely biological existence.

Each day there are more people whose chief existential value resides in the body and in the senses, and who only aim to be consumers and to enjoy themselves, with the remainder of their time devoted to earning the money necessary to fund these pursuits. They also wish for health, to have a family, a good job, a home, and of course, a TV, a car, a good stereo, and to be able to go on vacation when they so wish.

Their aim is to "live in peace," "not to have any problems," and to be loved and accepted. Mediocre people, who are the majority, were accurately described by José Ingenieros[1]: "the mediocre man is a shadow projected by society; he is essentially imitative and is perfectly adapted to living in a flock, reflecting the routines, prejudices, and dogmatism recognized as useful to domesticity. His chief characteristic is to imitate all those around him: to think with the head of others and be incapable of shaping his own ideals."

Mediocrity is the norm; what is exceptional is to be other-wise. Most people's thought generally centers on the preoccu-pations of the moment, and they never give themselves time to think in order to understand their neighbor better, but, at the same time, they expect to be accepted by him. One of the great obstacles for common man to better himself morally and spiritually is his mental myopia that prevents him from perceiving his own smallness, for he feels so at ease with it that he lacks any self-criticism at all. He is so mimical to millions of copies of his own person that he thinks it impos-sible that so many people could be wrong in their lifestyle or way of being. He does not compare himself to his superiors but rather to his peers. He values those who are a reflection of his own image and he envies "great men"—better or complete men. Mediocre man does not wish to listen to the truth about himself or to accept his own insignificance, an attitude that brings his possibilities of evolution to a premature end.

The comparison between the common individual's char-acteristics and the capacities of the person who completes himself opens up an immeasurable abyss of differences that consist, simply, of the different qualities between a "raw man" and a "refined man."

It goes without saying that common men have all the right in the world to be as they are, and they should under no circumstances be disqualified for their mediocrity. A child is also small and nobody would dream of reproaching him for it, because we know that he will grow. However, it is a fact that the great majority of the human race fits the pattern of "defi-cient man," who is not interested in "fulfilling himself" but prefers instead to indefinitely and fruitlessly pursue his own mirages, fantasies, and illusions, a pursuit that only changes when he is faced with death.

This results in a huge ethical and moral deadweight for Humanity, because few of those people who behave in the manner described above have any firmly defined ethical principles; higher values can be accepted only by those who, having recognized their own imperfections and limitations, decide to fight to improve themselves, and this is not possible without first properly tempering one's character and will.

Any process of self-fulfillment necessarily begins with a differentiation of individual identity, but this is impossible if one remains fused with the mass. Only exceptional men can do this, but it should be stated that anybody who sets out to do so with determination and perseverance can become an exceptional person. The moral reservoir of Humanity is not in the mass but in those special individuals who, having triumphed in the process of natural selection, manage to develop spiritually and become models worth emulating. However, it is necessary to state that anyone who dares to grow as a human being, to surpass the common level, risks the disdain with which the flock will punish those who become different in the higher sense of the word. Because of this very difference he will arouse the suspicions of the common people and will only be "reinstated" once the passing of time has proved his true worth, which usually occurs after he is dead. One has to add to this the deaf, but hateful, disqualification from all those who, in one way or another, feel that this superior person puts them in the shadows. It often happens that those who were not accepted as superior human beings in life end up being idolized as gods after they have departed.

It is deplorable that our culture should so completely ignore what the lifestyle and possibilities of a more spiritual, conscious, alive, and awake individual can be. Ignorance of this existential option means a limitation of the desires of those who, in seeking a higher expression for their vitality, squander it on things of little worth, without having the opportunity to discern that human self-fulfillment is possible. It would seem that the more cultural or scientific information an individual possesses, the thicker will be the veils that cloud his perception of natural reality, and this is quite consistent with the fact that an excess of cerebral information injected while one is in a state of deficient awakening or a state of "fogginess," totally subordinates the "I" to autonomous cerebral information. This limits the individual to that model by narrowing and fixing the boundaries of his conceptual paradigms. This can be better understood by realizing that the common model of learning is memoristic–subliminal and not cognitive–conscious, and thus, no educated person is free from this limitation. On the other hand, those who are less cerebrally programmed display a lesser level of alienation.

That factor which is of most importance and significance for a man's life, that is, the spiritual path leading him to fulfill Nature's cosmic mandate of evolution, currently has no place in our culture. It is, therefore, improbable that anyone who seeks to perfect himself will find the doorway leading to this priceless opportunity that remains concealed or cut off by scientific and cultural discrimination. Because all that is worthwhile is scant, and usually remains hidden, there will not be many people, who will want to change their current lifestyle for something better, but less known. Until this opportunity is clearly defined and properly divulged, humanity will indefinitely display the same moral flaws it now has. Similarly, the possibility for moral and spiritual evolution is threatening to those who refuse to rid themselves of their vices and inadequate behavior. It threatens the mediocrity of insignificant people and it threatens those who profit from the deficient limitations of the human mind. People are seriously disoriented with regard to what they value, and this is caused by a confusion between their goals and the means, or mere tools, needed to achieve these goals. People then turn means into goals, and lead a life that is totally lacking in higher aims. Their greatest wish is to enjoy themselves to the maximum, to be loved and respected, to enjoy consumerism, to reach old age peacefully, to die tranquilly, and to leave a sizable family behind them. And what happens after all this enjoying, consuming, having children, and growing old? What comes then? What goals has the individual attained in his life?

He is never aware of the fact that he remained within the "means," converting them arbitrarily into the "goal," or purpose of his life. Intending to truly live, he only reached the most rudimentary beginnings of existence. The values of common people are fixed on entertainment, the sensorial pleasures, and on obtaining certain material goods that will bring them certain comforts. Additionally, they yearn to start a family, to be happy in love, and have many children.

All these are the goals of their life and rarely are they seen as the tools or means to attain spiritual perfection. In other words, they seek to "have," and only exceptionally to "be."

This is why people neither grow nor place any value on the level of *being*, and why the experiences of a lifetime have as their destination the cerebral memory and not the *being*. There are people who earn a great deal of money and put themselves to the service of this money; they become enslaved to material pleasures which take control of their conduct; they are servants of the television or the automobile; they are captives of their image and of the opinion of others, enchaining the last little remnant of the self that still remains in them to any type of vulgarity or frivolity that they encounter.

It comes therefore, as no surprise that so many people in the world experience the anguish of a permanent crisis of identity and purpose, navigating through life randomly twisting the helm, without a compass or sextant, and without a polestar to guide them.

The compulsion to travel is, at heart, due to these reasons. Millions of people who travel with the secret hope of encountering themselves in distant lands, are fleeing continually from their own reality, so as not to confront it, under the pretext of rest and entertainment.

Yet, where are they really going? Nowhere of course, and they will never really arrive anywhere unless they set out on the path of their individual evolution. They are like ants who tirelessly come and go but remain in the same place. Each trip is a new fantasy, an unconscious desire to encounter something special without knowing what this special something is. What really happens is that, in their hearts, each individual yearns to return to his roots but cannot consciously visualize this intuitive urge. He is not able to realize that what he really wants is to reintegrate with his being, with the essential "I am" from which he has become more and more distanced since birth.

An excess of pleasure and entertainment empties and withers the individual's soul, so that he will, with growing desperation, need to renew his existential merrymaking in order to appease his inner void. When he understands that the apparent good he has taken as a goal neither fills nor satisfies him, he is obliged to seek something different which, when the moment comes, will also be insufficient; this is a cycle that he will repeat time and again with different mirages. This distances him further and further from the possibilities of "being," for far from seeking things within himself, he seeks them instead from the outside. Normal people generally reach the end of their lives with their memories filled with thousands of "life experiences" at the level of the body, the senses, and the brain. Yet their being is empty and frustrated because it has been denied the chance to confront the game of life in a direct and honest way.

Common man is incomplete, but at least he possesses half of his own totality, and from this foundation may construct his higher part. However, he remains apathetic, inert, and ignorant—shirking this task which should be a priority for him—seduced, stunned, and hypnotized by the multiplicity and intensity of environmental stimuli.

It usually happens that people confuse "being" with "having things" for the more things they have, the greater is their subjective sensation of "being," because external things become an extension of their "I." This occurs with any external thing with which the "I" identifies, provoking an artificial extension of the limits of the "I." This extension inflates until it reaches the limits in terms of degrees or honors and because those degrees or honors are given by society, those titles become a substitute for that society.

A professional person confuses his diploma with the social power embodied in that degree, and he expands his "social I" to the very limits of society, without realizing that he is merely "in the function of"—which means, in the function of the social group that patronizes him. A car is like an extension of the "I," as with any other type of material possession that intensifies the sensation of being. This is because the "I" becomes part of those possessions due to our instinct to possess.

Parties or other social gatherings for pleasure are of great importance to common man, for they represent an occasion to tangibly multiply his own insignificance through the temporary acquisition of a vast and important common "I," thereby having for a few hours the sensation of living intensively. It is mostly in such gatherings that he experiences feelings of being normal, and that "everything goes well"—fusing with similar people in moments of pleasure and happiness. The influence of the group stimulates the feeling of being happy and important, so that it often becomes an experience that is necessary to repeat time and again in order to scare away the ghosts of loneliness and anguish.

The world of "non-being" has its own non-values, and anyone who falls into this game finds it is very difficult to get out of it. Compulsive frivolity and joy reign supreme in this place, but so too do mechanical suffering and self-provoked moral pain. This latter is the psychological suffering of those who become frustrated when they make disproportionate demands on the world, demands that the world cannot meet. These demands originate in artificial characteristics enlarged by narcissism and self-worship. A repugnance of being alone is explained by the fact that, in this situation, the individual looks at himself and is not pleased with what he sees. Due to this, he needs to turn on the television immediately, or the stereo system or to start to talk on the phone with someone. He cannot bear external silence because it brings an equivalent silence to his inner world, which in turn brings out the perception of his own insignificance. The crowd, the hustle and bustle, and the multiple visual stimuli serve the defense mechanisms, for they dull the inner intuition that could lead to true self-criticism, thus representing an ominous threat to his narcissistic image.

To remain within the realm of the known and hide one's head in the sand as the ostrich is said to do, is the strategy most often deployed in order to continue doing what one has always done. This is to turn a deaf ear to the demands of higher values that call one to action. Fear of the unknown, another characteristic of *Homo sapiens*, invites him to stay within the bounds of his mental burrow, to become deaf and blind to anything that does not form part of his own cerebral program. The mediocre individual tends to remain static, refusing to make the effort for the change which is requisite to attaining excellence. His moral tepidity makes him meekly follow the flock, which lacks any clearly defined ethical principles, limiting himself to giving in to his own impulses. In spite of this, he follows an obligated respect for law and order, though not because its norms are an integral part of his conduct, but merely to avoid punishment. He accepts whatever others approve of and rejects whatever the majority rejects; he prefers what is in fashion and imitates popular personalities. He is generally haughty to his inferiors, cruel to those fallen, and servile to his superiors. He needs many friends, but rarely offers true friendship. He demands love, but does not know how to give it. He speaks of humanity yet often acts inhumanly. He makes demands on his fellows but not on himself. He talks too much but does little. He "has a lot" and yet he "is little."

Nevertheless, at the level of being, he carries the same essence as complete man, albeit in tiny amounts. He possesses the precious pearl of the spirit but prefers to squander his energies on consuming diverse illusions and fantasies rather than on perfecting himself. He earns his bread with the sweat of his brow but does not struggle to return to his roots and attain *consciousness* of the being.

Like the Nibelungs, the children of the mist, he possesses a treasure that he cannot use and that only Siegfried managed to conquer with the sword of his will. This hero is a symbol of the man who, weary of being a "bridge," makes the unbreakable decision to evolve in order to unify with his own essence.

Those who cling to their condition as "bridges" feel not the slightest curiosity for knowing what is false versus what is true. The concepts of good and evil have become such lamentable ambiguities that nobody rightly knows what is good and what is bad. They simply allow themselves to be easily swept along by the habits of the majority through fashion and public opinion.

Through ignorance, many upright and virtuous people end up falling into situations wherein they act wrongly. Conversely, corrupt individuals often appear to be benefactors of Humanity, without common people being able to perceive this.

From this perspective, it would seem that there is no justice in the world. Heroes and innocents alike are at times unjustly punished, while certain disguised delinquents are rewarded. This happens because only a tiny minority has the necessary individual criteria to perceive the truth.

The blind mass applauds, punishes, or opines mechanically, totally lacking any cognitive capacity to do so properly. Their dictates are deified and end up being adored as if they were manifestations of a higher truth. For the mass, good and evil are no more than "visceral incidents," instinctive pulsions that are discharged one way or the other merely to release the inner pressure of the collective. A soccer match, for example, may have a highly therapeutic effect on the mass of fans who attend the match, for it enables that mass to release its collective aggression, violence, or repressed impulses in a healthy way, thus projecting its own problems onto what is happening on the field. The fans yell, get excited, suffer, become furious or enthusiastic, and so their tensions, frustrations, aggressions, and unsatisfied desires are dissolved. A referee who makes a mistake could be vilified in an instant, and attract the wrath of the whole stadium, thus attaining a dimension that transcends his own person. The precise facts themselves become extremely enlarged through the sum of the instinctive pulsions of the spectators. They leave the stadium satisfied because they had participated in a "grandiose collective I," which gives them the chance to fuse themselves into a single soul, and to thereby exalt the sensation of existing to the maximum.

If we place ourselves within the parameters of social normality and aspire to be "mere men" in the Aristotelian sense, popular sport could be one of the healthiest ways of correctly channeling young people towards significant moral rules. However, if we look further upwards and seek an "optimal normality" of a higher nature, everything that entails fusion with the mass will also entail a loss of individuality, with the subsequent weakening of the will, and an inevitable moral difficulty.

The art of this matter consists in participating without letting oneself be absorbed, retaining one's individuality and inner freedom. This can be achieved only by those who, through previous spiritual work, have created a powerful, stable inner identity of an individual nature.

---

1. José Ingenieros, El hombre mediocre (The Mediocre Man), (Argentina: Losada Publishers, 1992).

CHAPTER V

SINS AND MORAL FAULTS

Marriage Without Love

What I shall term "sin" is the transgression of the cosmic moral rules of Nature, in the sense used by the ancient Greeks, who considered sin to be the attitude, usually attributed to ignorance, that rendered a person unfit to attain full self-expression and unable to form adequate relations with the rest of the Universe. One must understand that the human acts that constitute a "sin" for Nature (a breaking of fundamental laws) are perhaps not of particular interest to people, and they might even totally ignore that they are acting badly. Of course, this does not mean that they are not punished for it. The opposite situation also occurs with respect to supposed "sins" that are not such in the eyes of Nature. We should speak then, of "open sins," that are wrong types of behavior for a great majority. An example would be to break any of the Ten Commandments. There are also "hidden sins" in which there is not the slightest suspicion that the person is acting incorrectly. We all know about the open type of infractions, so I will preferably refer to all that constitutes a violation of the universal harmony of Nature, which in some cases can also represent a moral fault.

To clarify this matter, I shall begin by discussing marriage, which is the union of a man and a woman according to law, and which, from the religious point of view, is a sacrament that unites them. Matrimony normalizes their union in accordance with social morality, but not with regard to "the optimal moral of Nature." In this description of marriage, taken from the dictionary, a most important element is missing, and this is love—the only link that can make the marriage union licit before Nature.

A couple may get married according to civil and religious law, but if there is no true love between them, they will not have a genuine marriage as per the universal law of Nature. There is a social truth, a judicial truth, and a reality that is evident from Nature. The latter is the only one that corresponds to the laws of the Creator and has neither beginning nor end because it is the projection of the universal, ageless mother, who has always existed and who will continue to exist eternally, the same one that took man and all other living beings to her bosom. The human being, in his infinite smallness, interprets laws, rules, and norms in the way he finds most fitting for felicitous cohabitation and development. Such norms, however, are not transcendental and are of a merely circumscribed origin and effect—limited to a specific historical moment and to the scant understanding and evolution of the misnamed *Homo sapiens*, who has nothing adult about him at all, since he is only a child. Man accepts what Nature disapproves of, or vice versa ad infinitum. Man's vision is so poor that he cannot penetrate profoundly into the process of evolution, and for that reason, he cannot recognize the cosmic mother, but only perceives the limits of his narrow and tiny reality.

For cosmic law, "marriage" means a couple united in true love, which is what legalizes and sanctifies this union even though it may not have been validated by the laws of man. On the contrary, those who have a marriage certificate without being "a loving couple" live in concubinage before Nature. It should be pointed out that because he is so mechanical, what the human being takes for love is usually a mere substitute or imitation of genuine love, and this is the root cause of marital crises. The breakdown comes when this supposed love fails the test of reality and the partners employ all manner of arguments to justify the split, without daring to accept that they had never really loved each other.

Love, like morality, is really an expression of the individual's level of evolution, and not a mere imitation of the models popularized by the cinema and television. True love is a science like any other, and cannot be learned mechanically. One has to discover it through states of increased *consciousness* and through full maturity of the "I." True love is the result of one's level of evolution and not of the sensation of feeling "in love," which is often the furthest removed from true love; it is only a gratifying emotional and erotic flight of fantasy that bears absolutely no relation to genuine love.

It is inevitable that two people often believe themselves to be in love without really being so, but it is illicit to marry for mere convenience, to use the other party as an instrument of personal satisfaction. The motivations for marriage are not generally based on a union of true love, so that they are often the source of a violation of cosmic law. It is immoral to marry without love. It is not an extenuating circumstance that the couple was not consciously aware of this, for there is always a factor of "unconscious intent" that plans these matters in such a way as to achieve something desirable but not perfectly ethical, so that one does not feel obliged to accept the corresponding blame.

Pythagoras believed that celestial bodies were separated into vibratory tones equivalent to the melodic scale, and that when they moved they produced music, which he called "the music of the spheres." Musical sound responds to a vibration that becomes audible or perceptible in some way, and different sounds that occur together or combine with each other can make up a concerto. The human body may, in certain ways, be similar to certain celestial bodies for everything in the Universe has a certain level of equivalence or similarity. It has physical form, weight, and vibration. It is a living being that feeds and breathes, moves in space, is nourished by the sun, is bombarded by cosmic rays, and has gravitation in the sense of its gregarious instinct and its taste for being a part of the crowd. Someday we shall discover how to make audible the music produced by two human bodies, male and female, when they enter an erotic relationship with each other, make love, or express their mutual feelings.

In Greek mythology, Orpheus was a poet and musician, the son of the muse Calliope and Apollo, the god of music. Having been given a lyre by his father, he became such an excellent musician that he had no rival among mortal men. When Orpheus played and sang, he moved both the animate and the inanimate worlds. His music charmed trees and rocks, tamed wild beasts, and rivers even changed their course to follow him.

I am fully convinced that the mythology and mysteries of ancient Greece conceal more profound truths than those known to common man, although what they reveal has to be properly interpreted. Orpheus' lyre obviously represents the human body, which, when it experiences certain feelings, states of mind, or levels of consciousness, sends out harmonious or discordant musical vibrations, which set out on a voyage to the depths of the Universe—positively or negatively mingling and interacting with the music of the spheres. According to the holographic paradigm, the part influences the whole and receives an equivalent impact from the whole. Such an energetic, vibratory projection of that couple's bodies attracts a reaction from Nature to themselves, which we could consider equivalent to either a reward or a punishment.

The story of Adam and Eve, expelled from Paradise on account of their original sin, is curiously similar to this subject. They had interpreted some sort of corporeal music, forbidden by the Creator (one which came into conflict with the laws of Nature), for they were most likely guided by concupiscence rather than by love. Therefore, the intelligence of the Cosmos returned to them an equivalent discordant musical vibration that stripped them of the tranquility in which they had previously lived, thus offering a perfect lesson in morality. A couple who is united by true love generates the most harmonious, perfect musical concert, a harmony that is projected into the womb of Nature, which will give back the equivalent of the beauty it has received.

No marriage certificate can bring about this type of union, which shows that human legality is limited, fallible, and circumscribed, as is to be expected from any creation by the *"child sapiens."* The lack of true love generates repulsive, discordant music that will, at a given moment, turn back on its creators with an equivalent retribution. Of course, at the level of higher values, a loveless marriage is a grave moral fault, but even more serious is the procreation of children in such circumstances, for they will physically incarnate the disharmony of their parents, thus fulfilling the biblical prophecy that "the sins of the fathers shall be visited upon the children." It signifies that the uniting of two lyres in a discordant cacophony of vibrations will incarnate this discord in the offspring's psyche.

This is an assault on "optimally normal life," insomuch as it condemns the child to the bland mediocre social normality of the embittered, the depressed, or the maladapted person, who can find no meaning in his own life because he bears in his genes the inheritance of the vibration of his parents' discordant music. This will drive him to resentment, selfishness, and vulgarity. It means condemning a human being to perpetual imprisonment by snatching him from the harmonious womb of Nature and shackling him to a corrupt, twisted, and alienated lifestyle. It means an aggression on human dignity which is expressed by the Creator in the cosmic archetype of normal man. It means to offend and devaluate this ideal value by bringing to life a being who cannot be properly educated because he is the incarnate manifestation of the passions of the parents and not of their true love. To have a child by accident or without love is indeed an assault on Nature, because the parents cannot assume responsibility for the type of life they will give to this offspring who will have to shoulder the sins of his parents.

Little by little, we shall see that a class in authentic morality is more like one in physics than a course in friendly recommendations for behavior. It is said that if you throw a stone up into the earth's atmosphere it will fall back because of a natural law and not because we have offended God or that he wishes to punish us in this way.

Genuine morality is like a survival course in which one learns not to put one's fingers in the fire to avoid getting burned, and not to do to others what one would not want to be done to oneself, in any marked or repeated way. This implies that the respect and harmony we are obliged to observe for purposes of cosmic ordering will decisively influence our lives.

Doubtless, if we lower our sights to the level of the common "social basis," it is of no importance whatsoever that two people should marry without love, for this is what usually happens every day. However, if we remain steadfast to the morality that is "only for man" (for the individual of average behavior), we shall remain indefinitely at the same ethically ambiguous level that we are at in this moment. If there is no demand for higher values, mankind will not be able to progress morally and spiritually, and a gradual moral decline will be the most likely result. The future is in the hands of young people, but they need to discover their own inner values in order not to fall into the multiple temptations of apparent good, which in due time reveals itself to be "evil," or absence of good. The high percentage of failed marriages is regrettable, and is evidence of the lack of rational, spiritual culture. Normally we are only aware of religious spirituality, which is fine for believers, but there have to be other options for people to be able to freely choose the path that will most effectively lead them to be good and virtuous. No religious group should feel threatened by a moral crusade that does not stem from its own precepts and that has as the sole objective for people to morally and spiritually perfect themselves and evolve at the individual level. To this end, one has to demonstrate transcendental value of an ideal character, in order for people to walk in ascendance, rather than descendance, or simply horizontally.

The Shirking of One's Self-Control and Responsibility

A lack of concern for the bettering of oneself, and being content with remaining incomplete, is perhaps a human being's most egregious sin, inasmuch as it is an indirect insult to both the Creator and to one's fellowman. It is an insult to God because one is here on earth to fulfill a path of evolution, that necessarily, must take place at the individual level. One evades this duty when one remains inert and ignorant in the face of the opportunity for perfection.

It is an insult to one's fellowman, because we will be continually throwing our own imperfection and negligence in his face, assaulting him with our unbearable irresponsibility, dishonesty, unconsciousness, hypocrisy, envy, violence, and insensitivity, denying him help in his time of need; also, by offending him on countless occasions, by cutting him off from communication; by being intolerant; and by obliging our fellowman to bear our lack of human quality.

A person lacks dignity when he does not care about the self-discipline that will lead to a state of ethical and moral perfection. The individual's fundamental duty is to fulfill the purpose for which he was created, and which is the supreme good: vertically ascendant evolution. If he fails in this, he is breaking the most important commandment of life, and this is equivalent to evolutive suicide.

I should mention here that the world is in a state of degradation because of the individual's scant or nonexistent interest in training, perfecting, and fulfilling his potential. Ironically though, the intellectual arrogance of those who believe that they are already complete or perfect encourages in them an attitude of disdain and disqualification, since they surrender themselves entirely to the worship of the false values of a materialistic society that is oriented only towards entertainment and consumerism.

He who will not believe in nor embrace higher values is merely projecting his skepticism onto himself, in that, knowing himself to be puny and impoverished, he bases the judgment of others on his own condition. Unless an individual understands the pressing need to get down to work on saving himself from the solitude and anguish of "non-being," he will live permanently possessed by the existential pain of knowing that he is empty and purposeless, without having the strength of taking the reins of his own life in hand. Having received the priceless gift of life, he squanders his existence by pursuing mirages and chimeras, forever searching on the outside for what actually lies within the depths of his being, and wasting the precious opportunity of growing internally towards superior levels of moral and spiritual perfection. Possessed by an arrogant selfishness, he denies his "higher I" the most elevated gifts offered by life, thus, also depriving the world of all the good he might have done for others had he perfected himself. It is, indeed, a great hypocrisy for all those who, having received the gift of the divine spark, roam through life complaining that it has no purpose or meaning, and argue that nobody understands them, and that the only purpose of life is amusement and pleasure. This reveals a colossal contempt for their own spirits, which languish in waiting for the awakening to higher *consciousness* that would enable them to manifest fully through the physical body and thereby attain total access to the concrete reality of the present moment.

Although they do not realize it, those people suffer inconceivable spiritual anguish by being separated from their selves. It is thus that they aim to desensitize themselves with material pleasures and stimulants, hoping that such measures will cushion the terrible solitude and despair that pervades their hearts and prevents them from attaining the happiness and the good they pursue so avidly. There are others who, with the same aim in mind, abandon themselves to unceasing professional activity, struggling continuously to multiply and replace the material goods they possess, hoping to attain happiness from these assets. But happiness escapes their grasp, because, as soon as they think they have gotten it, frustration and emptiness comes over them once more. As I mentioned before, people's material success covers only one aspect of their lives, while the rest of their totality remains inert or underdeveloped. Neither can they find any correspondence in Nature, for they exist only in the material world of mankind.

The total success of the individual resides in the process of elevating oneself through the path of vertical ascendant evolution, thereby conforming to the Creator's design and to the demands of Nature. This is the greatest reward to which a human being can aspire, and he who fails to achieve it, in however small a measure, must consider himself a failure in the school of life, and must merge himself into the ranks of the cynical legions who have lost faith in everything, including themselves.

One cannot progress spiritually without knowing oneself; by ignoring one's own faults, defects, and shortcomings; by refusing to accept one's known and hidden vices; or without tempering one's character and strengthening one's will. This is the work of a whole lifetime, not a mere pastime or hobby that serves to dispel existential tedium.

False Friendship

According to Aristotle, "the primary, true friendship is that of good, virtuous men, who love each other for being good and virtuous." According to him, there are three types of friendship. The first one is the one already mentioned, the second is that which is developed for the sake of pleasure, and the third is that which is started for utilitarian aims or vested interests. In regard to this matter, I wish to discuss only those people who, in their friendships with someone, unwittingly damage that person. These are the well-intentioned individuals who, in a desire to support their friend in all things, avoid criticizing him in a way that would make him see the errors he commits in his life. This can be done by showing him what he might be doing wrongly, which, as is well known, can be perceived quite clearly from the outside, but very dimly from the inside. While they feel affection for their friend, they try to please him and avoid showing him the realities he is unable to perceive. They succeed in making him feel good, even though he might not be quite so good. He could even be bad as seen from the outside, but a friend who loves him despite all this will seldom make him aware of that reality. It seems as though the popular approach to friendship is "to stick up for your friend through thick and thin," even if this means condemning him to remain enslaved by his vices and defects.

False friendship does not mean having a friend who does not love you, but who by wanting to support you, ends up hurting you. This is the case, for instance, when someone asks an important favor of a friend, who quickly agrees to comply with the good intention of doing him a favor. Yet, when the moment for performance arrives, he fails to keep his promise, perhaps because he has doubts about it and no longer wishes to help, or maybe because the matter is complex and will demand great effort. This is the case of the naïve one who requested the favor and ended up in a bad situation because he expected to obtain what he asked for.

Let us illustrate by using an example dealing with money transactions. John needs to pay a pending debt and thought of asking for a bank loan, but his friend Charles told him not to worry because he, Charles, will personally lend him the money. When the moment comes, Charles fails to come through and John is left in debt on account of that broken promise. There are thousands of variations on that example and all of us have at some time suffered from them in life. Many people go to prison because of a "friend." Others end up being ruined. Most often, all this occurs with the best of intentions, with no malice from either party.

It is often the case that good friends are really harmful friends, because they do not understand that true friendship does not entail the cover-up of vices, defects, or misdeeds, but rather, consists of desiring good for one's friend and helping him to achieve it, even though that means making him perceive his own defects and irresponsibilities by showing him what he is really like, as seen from the outside. In this way, if he comes to know himself better, he will be able to take advantage of this knowledge for his own self-fulfillment. It means helping him to not take flight on fantastical projects that may be unattainable, to not justify his failures to himself, and to confront his subjective reality as this reality is being perceived from his surroundings.

This is what the so-called "good friend" usually fails to do. Instead, he will devote his efforts to reinforcing his friend's misguided conduct, patting him on the back and emotionally "caressing" him to make him feel what a good friend he is in the hope that his friend will do the same for him.

The easiest way to lose your path in life is to be surrounded by friends or colleagues who are incapable of telling you the truth about your own deeds, friends who are not willing to be faithful mirrors that enable one to better know one's own failures and weaknesses. It seems that the slightest criticism will threaten to damage that friendship, which is what actually occurs on many occasions. It is evident that there are many individuals who are unable to accept criticism because their level of narcissism keeps them detached from objective reality.

Friendships so influence a person's moral life that friends who we might love as brothers can be our virtual executioners when, by trying to please us, they do not give us a true opinion about ourselves, thus leading us to reinforce our defects, vices, or bad habits. For a friendship to be genuine, it ought to wear no mask, for well-meaning hypocrisy ultimately weakens or destroys the person we refuse to criticize. Therefore, we must learn to differentiate between so-called "friendship" and friendship if we wish it to yield its most precious fruits and not lead us to frustration and despair. There are people who, because they were let down by a beloved friend, have become disillusioned with the sentiment of friendship. They argue that "loyalty does not exist and all is for the sake of self interest." This, although obvious in certain cases, is not true in the case where one is firmly reproached for one's misdeed by a true friend.

We should differentiate between the three types of friendship as defined by Aristotle:

1. The perfect friendship of virtuous men who, because they are virtuous, resemble one another in their virtue and mutually want the best for each other.

2. The friendship which is based on the self-interest of friends, and for the use they can make of one another. They do not love one another for who they are, but for the profit to be gained from their mutual relationship. At the end they are only looking for their own personal profit.

3. The friendship which is based on pleasure, as is the case with individuals who share pleasurable activities.

According to Aristotle:

> . . . pleasure seems to be the only thing that inspires friendship among young people; they are dominated by passion and only seek pleasure, and moreover, the pleasure of the moment. With time, pleasures change and become different. Thus, young people rapidly make friendships and break them off with the same speed. The friendship is over once the pleasure that gave rise to it is over, and the change in this pleasure is very fast. Young people are swept off their feet by love, and love is most often born under the dominion of the passions and of pleasure.
>
> ***Morals: to Nichomachus.***

The most harmful type of friendship is that which gives rise to teenage gangs and delinquent groups, for their true purpose is illicit personal gain, for which all must unite in the absolute conviction that they're acting rightly, thereby squashing any attempt to criticize what they are doing, mimicking and shielding one another in a collective soul that drowns out any individual responsibility. Each one hides the corruption of the others so that they will, in turn, hide his own. In this way he reinforces the group's delinquent conduct. "Tell me who you surround yourself with, and I will tell you who you are," in this case, becomes an aphorism of unsuspected accuracy.

A young man's group of friends forms his character and personality—sometimes having even more influence over him than his familial collective. This group, then, becomes his "true family," according to what young boys who have gone through this experience have said.

Friendship that excludes healthy criticism under the guise of "understanding and supporting one's friend," ultimately becomes more harmful to him and is hence a serious moral fault. It is not ethical to help a person maintain a wrong view of reality, thereby preventing him from properly integrating into society or being able to comply with the pertinent norms of morality. If we reinforce this lack of contact with reality, we will ultimately do serious harm to him, despite our best intentions or the affection we may feel for this friend. By doing so we are only acting unethically and will drive him to inappropriate types of behavior. One has to refine and go deeper into the concept of friendship, in order to make it one of the most important transcendental moral experiences in which a man can enrich others and add value to himself through an exchange of significant experiences that will lead him to enlarge and ennoble his internal world.

If each of three virtuous friends gains two new friends to whom he can pass on higher values, and so on, it will not be long before a veritable crusade of moral perfection will spread in the service of all humanity. For this, it is only necessary to understand and create a consensus that supreme good resides in the *vertically ascendant evolution of individual consciousness,* and in the practice of the highest moral and spiritual virtue. A moral crusade of this type must transcend any petty interests in order to overcome any differences, including racial, political, philosophical, and religious interests.

Mental and Emotional Manipulation

The right to mental privacy is one of the most pressing needs at the beginning of the 21st century, for each day our minds are penetrated with greater intensity and profusion in order to become manipulated by interested parties who are foreign to the individual. Overwhelming advertising and repetitive propaganda are the most flagrant and insulting aggression to people's mental privacy, which was once the sacrosanct refuge of the "I." Now it is the agglomerated show-

room of political options, fizzy and alcoholic beverages, cigarettes, cars, designer clothes, cosmetic products, paradisiacal
beaches, objectified women, investment alternatives, pornography, entertainment, and various forms of consumerism.
Television not only disrupts our minds, but invades the peace
of our homes, aggressively bombarding us with sex, violence,
sadism, morbidity, cheap films, and vulgar sentimentalism,
with the rare exception of a few cultural programs or special
films.

In other environments, our mental faculties are affected
by high levels of acoustic and environmental pollution, all of
which dissociates and weakens our minds, thus making them
more vulnerable to external manipulation. Our minds are
continually being manipulated to oblige us to buy certain
products or to show preference for certain leaders, pop
singers, television programs, gossip magazines, or investment
options. It is an assault on free will to create artificial needs
with alienating or compulsive characteristics only with the
purpose of mere financial gain. People are unconsciously
induced to do what they do not want to do through the
hidden, subliminal penetration of their minds. It is a serious
ethical fault to manipulate people's behavior via the mass
media, and to make them tamely accept what they would
have rejected had they been in their right minds.

In democratic countries, citizens are not obliged to accept
incorrect or abusive authoritarian positions without protest,
or to passively tolerate the lack of clarity of some judicial
sentences, or to passively agree to pay abusive taxes whose
destination is unclear. However, the effects of various mental
manipulations can be felt throughout the world either directly
or indirectly, aimed at subjecting the citizen to the mandate of
obscure interests. People are subliminally persuaded to ask
for loans at usurious rates and to feel happy at having the

"privilege" of increasing the coffers of the lenders month by month. They are also subliminally persuaded to:

- Hate the rich or disqualify the poor.

- Discriminate against women.

- Imitate irrational behavioral models imposed by television and the cinema.

- Be inspired by the plot in a film to commit crimes or to adopt sadomasochistic behavior.

- Consume indiscriminately.

- Blindly imitate famous artists, musicians, and TV soap opera personalities who are notable for their vulgarity and coarseness.

- Adore false values.

- Accept the proliferation of the grotesque and the vulgar.

- Reinforce the herd behavior to thus facilitate obedient consumers.

- Indiscriminately accept any norm imposed by any relevant authority, however contradictory or unjust it may be.

- Superstitiously believe in false gods.

- Passively accept what the mass media affirms.

There are many other examples of how people are mentally controlled, and each day we have the chance to verify this for ourselves to varying degrees. The democratic principle of "government by the people" has become distorted, and confused because people's minds no longer belong to themselves, but to the mass media which directs them. Cerebral free will is destroyed at its very roots.

I alluded before to the words of Karl Popper on the dangers entailed with television, and he adds the following on the same subject:

> The consequence of the populist principle is that the public are offered ever worse programs, which are accepted only because they are peppered and laced with spices and tonics to taste, that is, with violence, sex, and sensations . . . Foodstuff is complimented with ever stronger spices because its quality gets worse and worse. With more and more salt and more and more pepper, they try to make tasty what is inedible . . . There is a considerable number of criminals who openly acknowledge that they drew inspiration for their crimes from television . . . Television has become a power that is too strong for democracy. No democracy can survive unless an end is put to the abuse of power practiced by television. This abuse is currently obvious.[1]

When that distinguished philosopher mentions "the abuse of power practiced by television," what kind of abuse does he mean? He means precisely the legal *(albeit immoral)* violation of people's mental privacy, which becomes thus conditioned to violence, vulgarity, consumerism, negative values, and the cult of the grotesque. Communication abuses by television and the press are a kind of ideological terrorism against people, which ought to be submitted to a board of ethical supervision, as was proposed by Popper himself. Just as a burglar might surprise the victim, so too does television assault with uncommon force the minds of children and adults alike, turning free will into romantic fantasy of a bygone age.

What is certain is that the mental control of people is today a flourishing business. Anybody with sufficient funds can implement an advertising campaign to influence consumer behavior that is considered highly desirable by the dominant economic systems, inasmuch as it helps to increase sales and generate wealth. Nevertheless, there is still the moral dilemma of these procedures, for we not only consume tangible goods but also ideas and values and it is in this realm that people are subjected to continual brainwashing to bend their behavior in conformity to the already created interests.

Since very remote times, ambitious people have discovered that dominion over the will of others provides an inexhaustible source of power. Unfortunately, there is still no other way to protect people from this type of invasive manipulation of their behavior. Their one possible self-defense is a strict control of their own minds. It is a contradiction that "His Majesty, the crowd," must be obeyed due to its majority of opinion while knowing that opinion is false, variable, fleeting, and does not come from an intelligent brain since that is what the crowd lacks. But rather, the crowd generally acts as an unconscious tool of certain ambitious people who, due to prestige, charisma, or oratorical skills, acquire a disproportionate influence over the crowd. It is not clear what the genuine motives of these leaders are.

Political demagogy, even though it is a bad moral example, is a good illustration of what I mean here. The dictionary gives us the following definitions of the word demagogy:

1. Tyrannical domination of the crowd with its acceptance.

2. Flattering the masses in order to make them an instrument of one's own political ambitions.

I have no doubt that cases of demagogy represent an obviously immoral form of behavior, by the mere fact that it manipulates people in order to use this power for a personal purpose, and not with the aim of serving the real interests of the people.

When does demagogy exist and when does it not? Only a higher tribunal of ethics made up of men who are virtuous, apolitical, and authorities on the subject could define it precisely. That would be highly beneficial, not only for the mental health of nations, but also for ensuring the freedom of thought of citizens, because there is no greater assault to human dignity than to abuse humble people who, because they need help, become fascinated with ambiguous or fraudulent promises. I am profoundly convinced that in the eyes of the higher order of Nature that emanates from the Creator, political demagogy is a great sin, of the type that human justice does not punish, but which natural law cannot forgive. However, it would be unjust to suppose that flattering the passions of the masses is limited to the political arena. The crowd is flattered and attracted in a thousand different ways by external sources interested in profiting in some way from their power.

There are certainly many skeptics who would doubt that it is possible to control people's behavior, even though it is by now a well-advanced science, dating back to the time of the Russian psychologist Ivan Pavlov who, at the beginning of the this century, began to experiment successfully with animal behavior. Research into the scientific modification of behavior subsequently spread to human beings with the work of the American scientists Watson and Skinner. In its repressive form, this technique deteriorated into notorious "brainwashing" which was widely employed in Russia and during the Korean and Vietnam wars.

Brainwashing is a form of psychological torture applied in dramatically modifying people's behavior, and it consists of inducing mental disorientation by keeping the victim awake indefinitely, or by subjecting him to prolonged fatigue, discomfort, malnutrition, and anxiety. Brainwashing is still employed today with renewed techniques, as a "peaceful," but not inoffensive way of modifying the individual's behavior. This happens sometimes through external chance, and other times, it happens more deliberately. Among the examples of casual or "normal" sources, the most powerful is the lifestyle that characterizes civilized existence. Our current everyday life has at least two elements of coercion with similar characteristics to those of brainwashing, namely: *disorientation* and *anxiety.* There is nothing more disorienting and stressful than the growing complexity of life in the big cities, the vertiginous growth of cultural information, the confusion of values, the informational saturation of the mass media, violence, noise, delinquency, and public corruption. The loss of control over one's own mind is provoked by continual brainwashing caused by the *disorientation* and *anxiety* that are part of our normal, albeit antinatural, lifestyles. A considerable number of mental illnesses and dysfunctions derive from the individual's mental incapacity to synthesize in his mind, in a comprehensive way, the complex realities of a civilization that does not encourage the development of individual higher consciousness, but restricts itself to merely memoristic intellectual explanations.

The parts of a total reality that should be significantly and harmoniously united in people's minds are left dissociated, isolated, contradictory, and not subordinated to the "I," which is relegated to becoming a passive spectator of stimuli that causes disorientation and anguish. The external sources of influence on the unconscious have their roots in advertising and propaganda. In the case of advertising, it has been shown that consumer behavior can be influenced by promising to satisfy the consumer's hidden needs. To this end, eight uncon-scious needs have been identified, and are used to motivate sales, and they are:

1. Emotional security.

2. An affirmation of one's own worth.

3. Finding satisfaction in one's own "I."

4. Creative outlets.

5. Love objects.

6. A sensation of power.

7. A sense of roots.

8. Immortality.

(Taken from *The Hidden Forms of Propaganda*, Vance Packard, South American Publishers.)

The foregoing are eight proven ways to manipulate the unconscious. Normal people are helpless to protect them-selves from such an invasion.

The Manipulation of the Image

On occasion one resorts to the help of marketing research to favorably change a person's or an institution's image, so that he or it will be accepted favorably by people. What are the limits to this? At what moment in the change does an image become so far removed from reality that it becomes a falsehood?

This is a particularly sensitive point in democracies where national leaders are elected on the basis of their popular charisma. We know, for example, that presidential elections of necessity entail an intense, ruthless competition in which each political party endeavors to exalt the image of its own candidate to the maximum and overshadow the adversary.

The first thing to be done when a campaign is launched is to retain an agency specialized in the marketing of the image, in order to find out what projection is more desirable for the chosen candidate and what changes have to be made in his physical appearance, manner of speech, gestures, smile, his way of standing up, and ways of moving around, etc. This man must often style his hair differently, shave off his moustache or use special glasses, wear clothes of a certain color, and have ties and shirts chosen very carefully, depending on the strata of society he wishes to reach. The topic of his speeches must be strictly adjusted to fit a plan; to project a suitable family image; to show him in charitable works, like visiting children's homes, or public schools, or being concerned with the elderly; and he must take great care to speak very prudently on taboo subjects, or even avoid them completely. His photos must exhibit his best facial angles so that his image will escape adverse connotations. If he is overweight, he must slim down rapidly; if his smile is unpleasant, he has to relearn how to smile; the same applies to his handshake.

This sort of external reengineering of a person is aimed at producing the most attractive image possible, one that is as much as possible devoid of negative perceptions.

As may be understood, this is not a simple process, for there is the risk of "inventing a person who does not exist," a fictitious being, a "hologram candidate," or an idealized person created to fascinate voters' minds. Something similar occurs in the case of movie actors, for whom the boundaries between fantasy and reality are never quite clear, for most of the episodes and experiences attributed to them are no more than advertising tricks. The need to gain popular support forces the creation of an actor–candidate, with carefully planned performances prepared by his advisors.

Presidential campaigns are remarkable in terms of their associated advertising expenses and resources, with huge mass movements, a profusion of slogans, banners, posters, party songs, stickers for cars, interviews, television debates, etc. With all this deployment one has to admit that, by and large, what is taking place is an act of concealment or substitution of the candidate's true personality—an intentional, premeditated distortion of his true nature. Thus, it may happen that the members of his party actually vote for an ideal, carefully prefabricated candidate and not for a man of flesh and blood. I refer, of course, to cases in which these excesses actually occur, it being up to the reader's discretion to judge.

What chance do voters have of knowing what the person they are going to vote for is really like? What is this individual's true behavior? Has he the necessary strength of character to withstand undue pressures? Has he the right criteria to choose what is best? What are his chief defects and weaknesses? Shall we discover them someday? Or will it be the people who will pay the consequences of certain unnoticed deficiencies at the highest level of his administration? Is he narcissistic or vain? Is he resentful or self-worshipping? Is he fair, moderate, and generous? Or, could he be a weak, cowardly, unjust, and thoughtless creature? Will he really be as charitable as he shows himself to be when performing charitable works? Or are these mere marketing tricks? What is his IQ? What does a psychological examination of him have to say? Is he a mentally healthy individual or does he possess some relevant disorder in his character? What are his real commitments to the sources that financed his campaign? Is he running to serve the people or through a desire for personal power?

Really, it is so little that we get to know about a presidential candidate of any country that it would seem that he only aspires to be a decorative figure and not the controller of a nation's destinies. It is certain that an important company has far more real information on any executive they might wish to take on. Because of the supreme importance of the position he has to fill, a presidential candidate should personify transparency itself. His defects and attributes should be known to all, beyond the veneer of publicity or marketing.

It is hard to discern people's psychological disorders or mental perturbations, even for specialists on the subject. Many people walk through the streets of our cities who look quite normal but are really not: individuals whose disorders are discontinuous and surface only during moments of great emotional tension. Is the person who aspires to be President normal? Who can guarantee this? As it concerns the maximum authority of the nation, extreme care must be taken in respect to this, and the greatest transparency in the eyes of the public should be demanded of the candidate. One cannot risk having a megalomaniac, or a borderline personality, for example, taking on such an important responsibility. These disorders are not like pimples or blackheads that can be seen on one's face, nor do they impair a person's intelligence. They only affect his perception of reality and his rational judgment, which is the most important quality a statesman requires. Unfortunately, a President is not elected technically, but emotionally. The motivations of voters are unconscious, sentimental, and with vested interest. They do not elect the man who is best prepared for the post, but instead, they elect the standard-bearer of the political party of their taste, or the "hologram-candidate" created by marketing.

A presidential candidate should undergo all manner of medical and psychological examinations, which are necessary to find out whether he is someone free of prejudice, where he is lucid, mentally sane, in touch with reality, and adequately situated in time and space. Driving a car is far less important than leading a nation, and yet the citizen who does so is obliged to undergo a psycho-technical exam to accredit his capacity to drive. What kind of psychological exam should be demanded of a country's presidential candidate? One should reflect on the huge responsibility entailed in such an important position and the pressing need to establish adequate controls. The man who delivers soft drinks with his truck needs to undergo a psychological test; the President of a country should, with even more reason, have to periodically undergo the most appropriate psychological examinations, in order to guarantee public transparency and national security.

All work ennobles and dignifies, and one kind of honest work is just as honorable as another, but if the supreme administrator of the nation makes a mistake, this may disastrously affect not only his own country but other countries as well. The excessively respectful, almost monarchic deference given to the presidents of certain countries, at times leads us to forget that they are only popularly elected representatives, so that if there were a representative with self-worshipping characteristics, he would be at risk of forgetting the true nature of his position and may even come to believe that the power he wields belongs to him. The presidency of a country should be more an example of public service, than an opportunity to impose power in order to bring about the changes desired by the majority party. It should be understood that the degree to which citizens can be led into error with regard to the true nature of a candidate to the presidency or to parliament due to an exaggerated image campaign is a very important moral fault because it represents an aggression against public good will.

Really, *the electorate will have voted for an idealized candidate who has no genuine existence in reality.* He is a marketing creation and not a man of flesh and blood. In time, this will lead to the inevitable disillusionment of the public. Once they lose their faith in this candidate, they will only be able to set their hopes on the next elections, once more exposing themselves to the indefinite repetition of the same process. Members of parliament and all those civil servants who participate in the highest spheres of a country's government are in a similar situation to that of the President if their posts require a vote by the people. All of them, without exception, are obligated to demonstrate the greatest transparency in their conduct to reassure the public that it had been right in its choice. Their lives and conduct, both public and private, should be in accordance with the image presented to the voters who elected them, for otherwise, we would have a case of ambiguous or equivocal identity. This is a very serious matter when it involves people who may be elected to their high position on the strength of the charisma which was presented by the media, while being quite different to what they show themselves to be.

I should insist that the act of moving masses through the use of an image created only for that occasion and without any coincidence with reality, in itself constitutes a very serious ethical breach which is in reality an offense of collective deceit. This is even more egregious when the potential victims are people with scant resources, or absolutely vulnerable to mental manipulation.

Dishonesty

Any moral rehabilitation, in the sense of entering and remaining on the path towards supreme good, requires the most absolute, demanding honesty of all, namely, the honesty of not lying to oneself. *Anybody who deceives his fellows first deceives himself by altering or accommodating the truth to justify his own wrong actions.* Dishonesty implies a double lie: the one committed by counterfeiting one's own inner reality and the one entailed in deceiving one's fellows.

Famous psychologists and psychoanalysts admit that self-deceit is an everyday affair, for people try to modify the reality that does not please them by accommodating or denying it. One concern among an individual's everyday concerns is how to confront the threats and dangers that produce anguish. To this end, the "I" is able to adopt a realistic type of conduct or try to relieve this anguish by using tricks that deny, simulate, or distort reality. This is achieved through the self-defense mechanisms of the "I," a subterfuge that accommodates reality to the individual's expectations, thus bringing about an artificial, transitory tranquility. As is only natural, the costs of this adulteration are incalculable, for with time, they imply a progressive distancing from reality along with the logical consequences of this. The best-known self-defense mechanisms are: repression, projection, reactive formation, fixation, and regression.

Calvin S. Hall has the following to say on the matter:

The self-defense mechanisms of the "I" are irrational ways of confronting anguish, because they deform, conceal, or deny reality and inhibit psychological development. They tie up the psychological energy that could be used in other, more effective activities of the "I." When one of these defense mechanisms acquires great influence, it dominates the "I," reducing its flexibility and adaptability. Finally, if the defenses cannot hold out, the "I" has nowhere to turn and becomes overwhelmed with anguish. The consequence of this is a nervous breakdown.

Why do these defense mechanisms exist if they are harmful in so many ways? The reason for their existence is of an evolutive kind. The childish "I" is too weak to integrate and synthesize all the demands made on it. Its defenses are adopted as protective measures. If the "I" cannot reduce anguish by rational means, it has to resort to such measures as denying the danger (repression), externalizing the danger (projection), concealing the danger (reactive formation), remaining in the same state (fixation), or going backward in emotional maturity (regression). The childish "I" needs and uses all these accessory mechanisms.

Why do they persist even after having fulfilled their function to the benefit of the childish "I"? They persist when the "I" cannot develop itself. But one of the reasons why the "I" cannot develop itself is that most of its energy is consumed in the act of defending itself. Thus, a vicious cycle is initiated. The defenses cannot be abandoned when the "I" is inadequate, and the "I" continues to be inadequate for as long as it depends on its defenses.[2]

The foregoing explains the mechanism of one of the most important causes of self-deceit. It is evident that this strategy is evolutive, inasmuch as the childish "I" is too weak to integrate and systematize all the demands made on it. One would imagine, therefore, that defense mechanisms disappear when the individual attains maturity, but unfortunately, this does not happen, for chronological age and the evolution of the "I" do not go hand in hand. The maturity of the "I" requires a prior process of individualized perfectioning and self-fulfillment, which is beyond the scope of the normal cultural tools that society offers us. It is possible to achieve this only by means of patient disciplined work and education of the consciousness, a knowledge whose basis is generally unknown, counterfeited, or rejected by the great majority of people. What has to take place in the individual's inner world, through his own will and free choice, is not a social phenomenon but a spiritual event.

When we say that the defense mechanisms are irrational ways of confronting anguish, it would seem that this implies only abnormal people, and that those who are within the normal range should not feel such anguish. However, what happens is that the "I" is afflicted whenever the individual has to face unpleasant situations typical of adults, such as "taking on responsibility"; acknowledging one's own defects; accepting one's lackings and foolish behavior; taking off one's mask of "the false adult" to fully reveal oneself in one's childishness; in saying or acknowledging the truth even when this hurts; confronting danger, risk, pain, and suffering. It means accepting and shouldering the burden of one's own lackings and failings, accepting one's own limitations, facing up to the fear and criticism of others, accepting one's own emotions, taking responsibility for oneself, etc.

Many people discover, through self-deceit, a subtle way of manipulating others who do not realize what is being done to them. By using this strategy of refusing to grow up, they remain in an indefinite state of childishness, in order to arouse compassion, affection, and protection from people through various maneuvers.

Elsewhere I discuss the childish evolutive condition of the *sapiens* despite his manifest intellectual development. A child's strongest impulse is to keep playing and not to interact with adults. Maybe adults also remain fixed in their childhood although they use the bodies, gestures, and manners of grown-ups. This childish "I" in an adult body suffers a profound anguish when faced with the requirements of existence. Such things as getting professional training, creating a family, taking one's place in society, and having success in life all represent unbearable pressures for the person who has not matured and who, driven by an obscure instinct, occasionally chooses to "exploit" his fellows by manipulating their emotions to obtain as a gift or "special treatment" what would normally require a huge, sustained effort.

Arousing pity and making people feel guilty are two of the basic tools with which people try to obtain what they want through manipulating the feelings of others, rather than facing straight up to the challenges of life. This is typical of very weak, childish people who, instead of making an effort to change, to strengthen themselves and become adults, choose the oblique path of a dishonest kind to gain benefits that do not correspond to their true merit and dedication.

It must be acknowledged that this is a malicious type of behavior, which cannot be excused only by the mere fact that one has a weak "I," since in contrast to a body exhausted by illness or mutilated in an accident, the "I" and the character can be developed at any given moment if one so decides, through one's decision and the command of the will. Dishonesty, as a mechanism of self-deceit whose ulterior aim is to cheat others, is a serious moral fault for the following reasons:

1. It is a way of avoiding one's own personal effort.

2. It is an aggression against the good will of others.

3. It is a vicious form of deception based on lies.

In order to weigh the true ethical repercussions of dishonesty, one has to understand that the dishonest person lies to himself habitually, denying or adulterating reality to take advantage of it. This mechanism is based in laziness, inertia, comfort, and a distorted interpretation of life and its events. He who behaves in this way carefully conceals his true nature by forever trying to project an attractive image, an indispensable condition for swindling the unwary. The true personal features of dishonest people are not precisely attractive. They are usually lazy and envious, lacking in discipline and will, possessed of an inner demand that everything in life should be gratis, and possessed of a profound inner rejection of individual merit and a requirement to pay for the good things they wish to have. Their parasite mentalities compel them to invent different ways of usurping goods and values from those who produce or possess them, to satisfy their personal needs by stealing from those who are laboriously successful, creative, and intelligent.

There are many levels of a lack of honesty, although the least known of these is that of the "honest picaresque"—I use this name because it refers to cases in which the person thus affected believes he is acting "in *conscience*," that is, correctly, but he is deceived by his motivations and goals, for both are really quite different than what he thinks they are. For example, he may act charitably, convinced that his motives are praiseworthy, but his true purpose may be a purely selfish one, such as that of enlarging his own public image, of raising his self-esteem, of mitigating a feeling of guilt, or producing far more murky purposes. These acts of hidden motivation are carried out through a mechanism of "unconscious intentionality" in which the individual splits his mind in two: one part is fully aware of the murky background that motivates his actions, while the other remains innocent, convinced of the nobility or rightness of his purposes. In reality, these mechanisms affect everybody to a greater or lesser extent, and in certain instances what remains concealed is really quite innocent. However, there are numerous cases of serious corruption or perversion, well concealed under an appearance of a bountiful, gentle nature. "Unconscious intentionality" occurs in all spheres of human activity.

There are politicians who believe they are serving people but who are really motivated by a voracity for personal power. There are selfish philanthropists; priests without a genuine religious calling; journalists who "misinform"; lawyers who, without consciously wishing to, act as their clients' own executioners; false friends; supposed admirers who in reality are hostile and envious people; ecologists who are only interested in wielding some sort of personal power; defenders of the poor who are not guided by any love for the needy but by envy and hate of the rich; theoretical protectors of the people, moved only by electoral interest; supposed Messiahs compelled by selfishness, vanity, and narcissism. Maybe all these people never realize that their aims are essentially corrupt and that their real motivations are murky. All over the world, in any circumstance or at any level, there are people who appear to be models of rectitude and virtue from the outside, but who are internally contaminated by base passions cunningly disguised as noble feelings so that the person thus affected may in his double game feel virtuous and worthy of being loved and respected while at the same time he pursues his sordid aims.

Just as in law, the ignorance of a law is not a mitigating circumstance if one violates it, so too in this case one cannot allege innocence through ignorance of what occurs within one's own unconscious inner world. That is because this concept is relative in the sense that, in any situation, there is a certain level of voluntary intention. At heart, each of us knows really well "where the shoe pinches," but conceals this fact very well from himself. Every day people carry out "vicious" acts: actions that, having as an apparent purpose *A* (praiseworthy aim), in reality are intended to obtain *B* (a reproachable or immoral objective).

This fluctuates from the smallest and most insignificant act to the acts of governments and well-known respectable organizations. Humanitarianism is usually a very noble enterprise but it is at times unfortunately used in a very different way, a strategy that can be either conscious or unconscious. These "vicious" acts extend from the individual who goes to a shopping mall to buy a ballpoint pen, which he needs, but he ends by buying something quite different, forgetting the ballpoint pen; or from people who deliberately get ill to unwittingly arouse others' pity; to the occasions when some government states that it is seeking transparency in a certain delicate matter appointing then an important committee of distinguished citizens to this end, all of which ends by disuniting the committee or causing the disappearance of the results of the investigation, without any more being said on the matter. One needs to recognize that the true motive for such mechanisms is always concealment or pretense, but in such a sophisticated way that it does not seem to be so, not even to the dishonest person who, without realizing it, is usually a master in the manipulation of hypocrisy and pretense.

Self-deceit always results in some form of swindling others, who in all good faith suppose that what the individual shows them is true. It is in any case an immoral act for which the transgressor will in some way attract a certain type of corrective reaction from Nature, in the form of punishment for his faults. We should remember that what is usually called "sin" represents a breach of universal order and that Nature, by seeking to reestablish equilibrium, takes from the individual something he values, of equal or greater value to the illicit benefit he had obtained. You can test this mechanism by analyzing the fluctuations between positive and negative events in an individual's life. This is because a cause and effect relationship is established between his dishonest actions and undesired or unfortunate events. It is thus possible to roughly work out the true genesis of the problems he suffers in life, which are really due to violations of the morals of Nature.

It is also painful to see that there are delinquents of all social classes who are not only knowingly dishonest but also cruel, corrupt, and vicious, albeit in such a deceitful and cunning way that they manage to keep themselves well hidden, without justice being able to unmask them or find anything wrong with them. The irony of this is that such characters, veritable "bleached sepulchres," often pass as honest, noteworthy citizens without anybody realizing their true condition. Thus, he who is not discovered continues to seem honest to the eyes of society and unreachable by human law, although not by cosmic justice. "He who sins, pays" not only is the Law of Talion, but is also the expression of that supreme law. Through the application of this supreme law, Nature seeks to recuperate its damaged equilibrium by homeostasis. If we are unaware of these sanctions, it is because the designs of the Logos are inscrutable to our eyes. It is most likely that in this case, the transgressor of cosmic law fails to establish any relationship between the present events of his life and the unlawful actions of the past, but it is absolutely certain that it is quite impossible for a crime to go unpunished according to the higher mechanics of Nature. Sooner or later, the transgressor will receive his just desserts in an equivalent form and amount of severity, independently of human law. If an innocent person is condemned by man's justice, he will be rewarded in some way by divine law, and his judges will be duly punished, particularly if there had been any dishonesty or negligence in the process.

The Abuse of Power

There are those who, on account of their profession or rank, have great power over people's lives, so that the level of their moral responsibility is very high and their ethical behavior should be strictly controlled, since if they veer off the straight and narrow path, either deliberately or unconsciously, they could cause great harm to people's honor and dignity by abusing the authority society has placed in their hands. I am going to refer especially to judges, lawyers, politicians, members of parliament, statesmen, and journalists.

A judge has the tremendous responsibility of administering justice in his hands, but *he is not justice in itself*, but merely a man with the same qualities and defects as others, susceptible to committing errors. He is also subject to the same juridical order as any other citizen, but in practice is as unreachable as an Olympian god. Behind the unintelligible tangle of jurisprudence, it becomes impossible to criticize a judge, who becomes infallible, so that it is impossible for a common person to doubt his actions. While it is true that the law has mechanisms to refute or accuse a magistrate when he has allegedly committed some illegality, it is also true that such procedures rarely succeed when the ordinary citizen sets them in motion. This may be due to the fact that the judge in question really adhered to the letter of the law or because the complaint process is deliberately bothersome or inoperable with the aim of protecting the system. Whatever the reason, it is certain that to the eyes of the profane, there is not the least transparency to this respect, and it would seem that, more

often than is desirable, the plaintiff who is right, or the innocent defendant, will lose the case or be unjustly sentenced.

Why is the common citizen not informed with perfect
clarity and in detail, using plain, simple language, as to the
legal premises that have been taken into account when meting
out justice? A magistrate has not only to answer to his hierar-
chical superior, but also to the people, and it is a moral duty
of the legal system to inform properly in a language that any
citizen can understand, lifting the veil of mystery regarding
certain sentences, to dispel the aura of "untouchability" that
surrounds the system. This way people who believe they had
been badly treated may dare to publicly announce their criticism of the system.

In which country would it be possible to carry out such a
ruthless investigation as the one carried out in Venezuela by
the journalist William Ojeda, who exposed in his book, *How
Much Does a Judge Cost?*

How many garments would he rend? How many mysterious hands would move to prevent that investigation? How
many hypocritical voices would be raised against such an
investigation? How long would the hidden inquisitorial
system of certain governments take to move so as to prevent
such an initiative or to misinform the public as to its results?
People have a right to continually test the honesty and rectitude of judicial power, not because this latter is in doubt, but
because the delicate, complex nature of its functioning at a
high level demands the most absolute public transparency.
This authority, in a democracy, has been elected by popular
will, and is therefore held accountable to it. Unfortunately,
through the lack of information in simple language, the true
grounds of the ins and outs of a trial and the true meaning of
the consequent sentence usually remains deeply in mystery

for those not initiated in the matter, who very often have the feeling, rightly or otherwise, that they have been victims of atrocious legal injustices.

This obligation for public transparency means that in a democracy the common citizen has the right to supervise the actual deeds of all public servants from the President downwards.

Let us for a moment imagine the tremendous harm an unfair judge could cause, and the magnitude of the transgression on human and divine justice represented by deliberately favoring the offender or placing the blame on an innocent person. The possibility that there could be just one single magistrate of this kind is enough reason to investigate the system in depth, not by the police or politicians, but by common citizens who are not committed to any political ideology and who are concerned merely with divulging their discoveries rather than concealing them. The manipulations of justice are a very serious moral fault when the guilty person happens to be a judge or a functionary of judicial power. The legal system also includes lawyers, since they have to participate in existing procedures. This professional individual is an intermediary between the legal system and the citizen who needs to protect his rights and as such, has great power over the circumstances of people's lives. For the same reason, the lawyer must be of irreproachable ethical training, since he is the safeguard for citizens that the law is being correctly applied and has been authorized by society to this effect.

It is obvious that, as in any human group, there will be outstanding individuals, mediocre ones, or ones that are poorly equipped for their chosen profession. I remember a lawyer friend of mine quoting a phrase attributed to a famous professor of law that said that "the touchstone of law is good faith, for if there were bad faith the system would fall apart." If a lawyer were to act in bad faith, he would not only be offending an individual, in this case his client or another colleague's client, but he would also be attacking the system, thus becoming a sort of "public enemy" of the law. Fortunately, there are many lawyers whose honesty is proof against corruption, but there could be cases of citizens who, having been tricked by bad jurists, would not dare to press a claim through fear of reprisal. This is not by any means a critique of the profession, which can be extremely noble when it is properly practiced. Rather, it is a moral denouncement of a preventive nature against certain lawyers who might attain great financial gain by, for instance, unnecessarily prolonging trials by making a deal with the other attorney.

A common man who knows he is innocent of an alleged offense resorts to a lawyer as if the latter were his savior, and if his good faith is betrayed by the very person who should advise him, this would be an atrocious transgression of justice. To repeat, transparency is the only thing that can maintain or restore the citizen's trust in his legal adviser, who because he represents him in court practically acquires a disproportionate power over his client. Who controls the ethical behavior of lawyers? They themselves, or is it some external organization? It would be too simplistic to say that any and all irregularities can be denounced in front of the law, for on account of the corporate nature of the profession, I suppose it is difficult for a lawyer to sue a colleague. Likewise, there are certain highly successful lawyers in all countries who really do not win cases by following the regular system but by means of influences that enable them to intervene and exert pressure in order to reach agreements, have cases filed, or disregarded extrajudicially. There are also examples of shysters who continually operate on the periphery of illegality, taking advantage of legal loopholes to "do what cannot be done," or to undo what has already been done. Like the rest of us, they will in due course take their rightful place within "the divine comedy," in accordance with the moral quality of their deeds.

To toy with human law brings its consequences only if one is discovered, but omniscient divine law is implacable with those who try to alter its sacred code of "egalitarian equivalence" and will always apply the appropriate punishment to those who try to provoke injustices at any level. If a good lawyer can be a blessing for a citizen in distress, a hundred of them would not be enough to wipe out the harm just one ethically devious colleague could do. As for members of parliament, they have the sacred duty of informing the people profoundly and coherently what it really means to have been elected to their high positions. As public men, their privacy becomes extremely exiguous and they have the duty to account to their voters as to how far they have fulfilled the promises made during their electoral campaigns. Members of parliament should not control themselves or dictate their own laws, and it would seem logical that there should be some committee for parliamentary ethics made up of relevant and apolitical citizens of irreproachable conduct. This review board should never be appointed because it had been suggested that there was any ethical irregularity, but because it would shed light on the system and increase people's confidence, because they often do not understand what is going on. These people would have been elected by the citizenry, be paid a salary that comes from the taxes paid by all, and be obliged to display rectitude and efficiency in their functions. They would have to be ready to give full disclosure on anything that is required of them. Otherwise, they would become an elite group divorced from any popular basis and would not in actual fact be representing the people's real interests.

One should remember that this written work is about a new morality, and that nobody should feel affected or consider themselves alluded to by the expounding of ethical norms that should form the basis of the harmonious life of a country.

If a member of parliament of any country should act demagogically, he would be committing a serious moral fault for this would indicate his attempt to manipulate people deceitfully, and this should be duly punished. The declarations by governmental representatives and politicians would also be a serious fault or immorality when they entail overt or covert pressure or intimidation of the legal system. This act could seriously interfere with the balance of justice. It would also be immoral for parliamentary committees, entrusted with investigating scandalous matters, to later refuse to inform public opinion clearly and opportunely, merely reserving such information for restricted circles. By law, an investigation carried out by committees of "virtuous men" or by members of parliament, should be quite public so that it would be a pedagogical moral lesson for all, with the sole exception of matters that might affect national security. It would also not be moral for members of parliament of the same political party to vote *en masse* on matters of national transcendence, by merely obeying the party's orders instead of following their own convictions, or by putting the party's interests before the general good.

It would also be unethical to have political negotiations in which party *A* refused to divulge compromising information about party *B* in exchange for this latter doing the same for the former. By renouncing the right to reveal embarrassing information about opposing parties in order to gain a political edge, both truth and justice are compromised, and moreover, the public is deceived. If this is the case, and if all the politicians were at the mercy of events, they would become accomplices to the concealment of facts that people should know.

Citizens have a perfect right to know how politicians behave in their private lives, and if these public men were thought to have committed any kind of inappropriate conduct, they would be under obligation to reveal the truth. It would be immoral for them to silence the accuser by using the immense power they can wield to this end. In a true democracy, the government and its agencies cannot be untouchable, and must of necessity be submitted to the enriching criticism of the citizens, unless this meant insult or calumny. If this were not the case, the idea of democracy would be a mere caricature. Furthermore, the president of a country should not treat himself like a monarch but should be normally accessible, criticizable, and available for dialogue, as corresponds to a true democracy.

With regard to journalists, they occupy a privileged place as far as the shaping of popular opinion is concerned, so that their acts must be adjusted to the strictest ethical norms. On account of the power they have, they could be the most efficient denouncers of immorality and corruption. However, they may also go too far in their comments and unwittingly besmirch a man's honor or that of his family. Personally, the type of journalist I most admire and respect is the one who knows how to inform objectively, leaving aside any political or sectarian contamination. This is the type of journalist who knows how to separate true information from mere rumor, who does not heed a malicious comment, and who knows how to accurately measure each situation. He also knows how to withstand undue pressures and justly ponder the educational and informational effect of his reports. He is the one who is committed to truth and justice and firmly refuses to divulge insufficiently proven information. He is the one who is able to persist in an investigation however many influences are mobilized to block his way.

On the other hand the one who should be repudiated is the unfair journalist who puts his pen at the service of immoral people, who seek to besmirch the honor of others by disparaging them "legally" (with legal loopholes) in order not to be taken to court. The one who investigates any scandal or fraud in which humble, defenseless people are the targets of some kind of fraud or swindle should be applauded. The one who reveals cases of public corruption at any level should be rewarded. The one who is untruthful or who was caught seriously distorting the facts with the aim of personal gain or of satisfying the appetites of third parties should be punished. Likewise, the one who intentionally with disregard, disproportionately, cynically, harmfully, or destructively offends people's honor or their dignity should be punished. High-level journalism can be a powerful moralizing force in a country, but vulgar tabloids pollute and debase the popular soul. The one who, by using the written word in a nonethical way, employing coarse or vulgar language to spread falsehoods, or attacking the honor of others, commits a serious fault—that if unpunished by social justice, will nonetheless be punished by the justice of Nature, which will also doubtlessly reward the courageous, sincere journalist who honestly fights for the truth. One must understand that the justice of Nature is of a hierarchic, discriminatory kind, that is, that one and the same fault can deserve different degrees of gravity in its punishment, depending on the characteristics of the offender and the social power he wielded when he committed the offense, which is only logical and reasonable. For example, it is almost certain that an illiterate person would receive minimal punishment, while a professional would get a much greater one.

For this reason I have focused on members of parliament, judges, journalists, and public servants, in order to stress the

fact that if those people become corrupted, their guilt is infinitely more egregious on account of its social repercussions,
than an offense committed by a common citizen. For this same
reason, there is a pressing need to duly monitor the ethical
conduct of these prominent citizens. If a tailor habitually gets
drunk, the worst that can happen is that the clothes he makes
will be badly made, but if it were a statesman who did this,
the consequences could indeed be extremely serious.

The Financial System

> Currency is a new form of slavery and is only distinguish-
> able from the older form by the fact that it is impersonal, inas-
> much as there is no human relationship between master and
> slave.
>
> *Leo Tolstoy*

> For the root of all evil is the greed for money.
>
> *Timothy 6:10*

> Thou shalt not take interest from him or usury, but thou
> shalt fear thy God and let thy brother live beside thee. Thou
> shalt not give him thy money for interest nor shalt thou give thy
> goods to usury.
>
> *Leviticus 25:36, 37*

The morality we advocate in this book is a morality in
accordance with Nature. Within the world of economics there
is probably nothing as antinatural as the financial system. The
fact that money, whose basic function is to serve as a medium
of exchange, should produce more money is not only artificial, but at heart, absurd. The reproductive function of wealth
should in common sense reside in Nature herself, from whose
womb all goods spring when she has been duly fertilized by
human effort. That a field should produce cereal or a factory
produce various objects is within the nature of things, but that

a bank should manufacture money from nothing and charge interest for it, is totally beyond logic. In the same way, it is also antinatural for banks, created without any solid backing or with scant capital, to finally become the owners of all.

Two centuries ago, Baron Von Rothschild, who financed Napoleon's campaigns, prophesied that if the money was given to him, he would not care much who governed the world. This is because money is no longer a mere convention, but has become a source of wealth and power *par excellence,* thanks to the quality of self-reproduction that bankers have discovered in it. Indeed, we have become accustomed to accepting as a normal fact that true wealth is in the banks and that these are the right institutions to guard our money and charge us interest for doing so. It would seem as if the economic system could not function without banks, and was compelled to seek its equilibrium in them, instead of having them at the axis of its natural growth in the real creation of wealth through human work. An institution such as the bank, whose original function was the custody of others' money, has spread its tentacles by appropriating everything it touches. Goods, industries, fields, and whole countries fall into its hands with hardly anyone noticing a fact as alarming as this.

The way the bank functions is apparently very simple, but at heart extremely labyrinthic, for it would seem that some sort of diabolical magic lies within it. To create wealth, power, and dominance so simply must seem shocking, at least, to the person who can only count upon his energy for work to earn the sustenance that enables him to survive. Mistrust of money—the object on which the bank operates and which it reproduces so easily, is as old as money itself. Sophocles stated that money was the worst of evils on earth, the corrupter and seducer of innate intelligence, as well as nourishment to the habit of dishonesty.

Aristotle referred to usury as a perturbation of the political economy and as a monstrosity because it attempts to make a purely conventional object like currency *engender more currency* and thus imitate the productive work of Nature, *supplanting, at the same time, human work.* That it is a monstrosity can be understood because it turns a means into an end, which leads to possession that has no limits. The great Greek philosopher had already perceived what was to become one of the greatest future disasters: the enslavement of man to usurious capital with poverty disguised as abundance.

Now, as we know, this antinatural reproduction of money was carried out in ancient times through the interest charged to the borrower, and currently through bank loans, the essential mechanism which we shall see below. When a bank grants a loan, it creates more money by the mere fact of noting it down in its accounts.[3]

A bank loan is based on a multiple of its capital and bank reserves, so *the bank lends what it does not have.* Promise of payment then becomes transferable and from then on it is abstract, paper, false money, although it is, of course, legal money. When a client pays the loan, that is, when the loan is cancelled with its corresponding interest, the bank destroys money. Frederick Soddy, winner of the Nobel Prize in 1921, pointed out that "the most sinister, anti-social feature of paper money is that it does not exist. The banks owe the public an amount of money that does not exist. By buying and selling with checks, there is only a change in the person to whom money is owed by the bank. While one client's account is debited, another's is credited, and banks can continue to owe this amount indefinitely."[4]

Promise of payment for the value of the precious metal deposited was made by the old goldsmith of a guild society to the one who deposited gold to be kept in his coffers. Goldsmiths soon realized that the people who deposited the gold only withdrew an average of about 10 percent, and due to that they began to circulate more promissory notes for the 90 percent of the gold that was not withdrawn and to charge interest for such promises. In other words, they lent money that was not theirs and profited from it, most often in a cunning way. From that moment on, the goldsmith became a banker and the metal coin was supplanted by paper money.

The generalization of a system like this that creates and destroys money with its own gain being its sole purpose and objective can lead only to a permanent distortion of the real economy. It does not matter if there are sufficient raw materials in the world, qualified manpower, technology, proper means of transport; if people have no money to buy them, poverty and shortage will inevitably appear. And if there is too much money in circulation, money loses its value and goods reach exorbitant prices that the great majority of citizens find impossible to pay. It is said that there is inflation if there is more money than goods in circulation and deflation if there are more goods than money.

All the money on the market, the basic monetary supply (called M1), is made up of the total cash in the hands of the public, plus the balances people keep in their accounts for transactions (checking accounts, financial accounts, etc.). But cash in circulation is only a small part of the supply of money, in which the private money created by bank loans increases more and more through the most sophisticated instruments of credit, such as credit cards. All transactions related to paper money expand or decrease according to the loans granted by the banks, but we should not forget that a loan is not real money. When we take out a bank loan, we tend to think that the bank is lending us other customers' money and that this is why it is logical that we should pay interest for it. Nothing is further from reality; what the bank lends us is not even banknotes, which although not convertible into gold, seem at least to have the backing of the bank making the loan. In fact this is not the case, for what the bank lends is only a promise of payment that increases the balance of our account and decreases if we sign checks (also promises of payment) on this account for other people who in turn will increase their balance with such promises when they deposit them into their respective accounts. Thus, we see that this abstract money simply grows as a notation in the accounts and has a phantasmal existence as it moves between debit and credit in the accounting books of the banks.

However, as long as the borrower guarantees the loan with his material goods, which are confiscated if he fails to keep his promise to return the total amount plus interest, this promise of payment *is not in reality being guaranteed by the bank,* because the bank can never use the deposits of their customers as a guarantee. And this is so true that if the bank is ruined, it would be the Central Bank or State Bank that would come to their aid to save such deposits. This is as much as to say that it will finally be the citizens themselves who in the ultimate analysis will keep the banks from bankruptcy with their taxes.

Of course, this accounting money gives life to the economy, but the goods and services generated by it are from the outset stigmatized by the cost of bank interest. It should be considered that all the money created by the loan with interest is created as a debt and is in itself unpayable, for if the loan creates and places money in the market, it is destroyed when it is paid back. This means simply that the bank loan cannot be paid because if everybody tried to do so at the very same moment, the amount of money in existence would not suffice.

It is not a case of enrichment through usury, but the case of a complex system of negotiating the charging of legal interest through promissory notes, which are of null consistency because the bank has no guarantees to back these promises. Of course, usury has been considered an aberration since ancient times and was forbidden both in the Christian and Muslim worlds. The usurer was ostracized and persecuted with extremely severe punishments such as the galleys or death, even from the time of Constantine.

Many Popes, such as Pius V, dictated numerous bulls and edicts against usury. Pope Benedict XIV issued an encyclical warning against the sin of usury as originated in a loan contract, pointing out that this sin cannot be condoned by the argument that the gain is neither large nor excessive but moderate or small, nor by the fact that the borrower is rich. If someone takes interest, he should pay it back in accordance with the principle of justice whose function in human contracts is to ensure equity for all. Usury is today a penal offense and the law punishes those who charge an illegal interest on a loan. But if the charging of any interest were forbidden, logically this would mean that any interest charged would be usury.

However, certain dictionaries define usury in the first place as "interest charged for money or goods in a mutual contract or loan."

With the decline of absolute monarchies and the birth of the liberal States, charging interest for money loaned became legalized; the liberals justified this measure by pointing out that an economic act cannot be judged with noneconomic criteria, that is, with criteria alien to this same act, which in the case of the prohibition of usury was certainly a moral criterion. Liberal thinking on this point, as on others, tries to map out the autonomous sphere of economy, making it independent of any other human discipline, in the same way as Machiavelli formulated his theory of the *"raison d'État"* centuries ago to establish the independence of political practice, the end of which in itself justified the use of any means, so that no ethical or theological judgment would divert a prince from his chief duty to the state, which was to strengthen and enlarge it.

One should wonder whether this methodology of disciplines, that tries to isolate the object of its investigation and the practice of "distortions" that might deform its approach (value judgments, such as moral ones) and which meant an important step forward for such sciences as physics, is also appropriate for disciplines such as politics and economics, whose ethical purpose can be no other than to be at the service of man and never the opposite. However, the fact that charging interest is authorized today in most countries does not make it blessed or desirable just because a statute permits it. Morally, and from the point of view maintained in this book, it can be neither natural nor appropriate that promised money should reproduce itself, thus systematically generating a debt for the whole of society and, as I said above, one that is also impossible to pay for the reasons given.

The most serious problem of this financial system could not in any case lie in the charging of interest, as long as it is moderate and the loan would be of money that belongs to the bank instead of a promise of payment without any guarantee whatsoever, but rather this problem lies in the possibility that the bank has to create false money, albeit legal, and charge for it. Moreover, without going into the extremely complicated mechanisms of financial engineering, the bank can use this to multiply its profits almost unlimitedly. Some experts have even calculated the real profits of a bank to be 16,200 percent[5] by using the following example of a typical transaction:

(a) With 100 monetary units belonging to a third party, a loan
     is opened for 900 units.

(b) These 900 units carry an interest of 9 percent, which means
     a net yield after one year of 81 units.

(c) The bank gives the person who deposited the money 0.5
     percent, varying according to the time, which means that
     these 100 units, which have cost the bank 0.5 units per year,
     have made it earn 81 during the same period.

(d) By carrying out the corresponding mathematical operation
     (81:0.5), the sum of 16,200 is obtained.

Personally, I do not wish to comment on the above
proportion. However, as parallel information, I would
mention as an example the case of a bank in a Latin-American
country which is today an economic model. In this country,
banks are authorized by the Central Bank to lend up to 20
times their own capital, which means that for each monetary
unit contributed by the bank's shareholders, the bank can loan
up to 20. This is of course a highly lucrative business, especially if one considers the lack of real backing of the paper
money of the loan. I would even go so far as to suppose that
the mechanics of the loan must be similar in all countries.

In any case, it is necessary to drastically reduce interest
rates in order for the credit transaction to no longer be disproportionate and antinatural, when the average profits of worldwide industry are practically ridiculous. Therefore, the real
intrinsic evil of the system lies not only in the interest rate that
is charged but in the complex mechanism of actually creating
money so as to charge the interest. This led Sir Josiah Stamp,
President of the Bank of England, to state in 1920 that
banks were conceived in iniquity and were born in sin and
that as long as it is still permitted to create money through

loans, banks will possess the earth and all men will be their slaves. Certainly, Sir Josiah Stamp knew perfectly what he was talking about. With such power in the hands of the banks, it is not difficult to calculate the influence this artificial creation of money has on the economy of our planet. Of course, banks have to be submitted to the regulations of the Central Bank of their respective countries. There is a set of obligations for commercial banks that ranges from the maintaining of reserve quotas in cash to the eventual duty of contributing the money necessary for the State to fund its needs. Yet this whole set of obligations neither reduces this fabulous business nor prevents the inflationist and deflationist distortions produced in the market by the creation and withdrawal of this artificial money.

Despite the fact that more or less orthodox economic theory tries to minimize this influence, there is another line of thought in which economists from different ideological tendencies concur, and this holds basically that all cycles are artificial, and economic crises are no more than mere financial crises produced by the loan system itself, which makes use of its mechanisms with the sole purpose of unscrupulously making profit. Pius XI in his Encyclical *Quadragesimo anno,* referring to the financial system that concentrates wealth and power more and more in fewer hands, points out that:

> Its power becomes despotic as none other, when absolute masters of money govern credit and distribute it to their own taste; it might be said that they administer the blood on which the whole economy thrives, and so to speak, hold in their hands the soul of economic life and nobody can breathe against their will.[6]

Now, when the financial system suddenly withdraws money from the market precisely when society most needs it, when this system as Pius XI says, "sucks the blood," that feeds the economic body, this produces great crises like the one that took place in 1929. This great economic crisis, which brought ruin and despair to millions of citizens, has been shown to be an example of the inevitable consequences of the practice of liberal doctrine. The postulates of *laissez-faire* required from the market a cleaning that was never going to happen, due to the existence of monopolies and other factors that would forever distort prices as a result of the game of supply and demand, deceptively being called free, but in reality, already manipulated. In fact, during those years, financial concentration in *trusts* and *holding companies* and commercial concentration in cartels, that imposed their prices on the market, already produced an absolute predominance of the bank over companies and industrial corporations—a predominance that was to facilitate the manipulation of economic life through these fictitious crises.

After the crash of 1929, all States took control of financial policy and of economic policy in matters of public expense. Such was the case in the *New Deal* undertaken in the U.S.A. which, in general terms, coincides with the postulates of the English economist John M. Keynes. These measures have not avoided fresh crises, at least not of the magnitude of that of 1929. And if such crises continue to occur with a certain rhythm affecting now some countries and then others, we should seriously wonder whether those economists who support the strictly financial origins of depressions and inflations are right.

In 1929, nothing foretold a depression in the United States of America. The country was producing, the granaries were full, industry functioned at full steam, the level of employment was acceptable, communications had considerably improved since the beginning of the century and department stores had sufficient goods to supply the population. Everything was going fine. It seemed as if there was nothing wanting, except money. Suddenly, just as the American economy was running on wheels, several million dollars were brusquely withdrawn from circulation, because bank loans that had been granted to *brokers* were cancelled. The whole thing suddenly fell apart. Without money, the blood of the economy, no one could either buy or invest. Thousands of industries went bankrupt, perishable goods rotted in the warehouses—but the crisis did not affect the bank, which had finally collected its loans by carrying out the corresponding embargoes on the goods that had guaranteed the loans, to later sell them for an infinitely higher price once the economy had recovered through the granting of new loans.

What a curious financial system that earns as much or more in both periods of crisis and prosperity! Of course, it would be natural that if the economy was going wrong it was going wrong for all. But in view of the foregoing, there is nothing strange in it, for if the bank produces the crisis, it is only logical that it will emerge reinforced from it. We are talking of phantasmagoric money and of fictitious economic crises, of a financial system in fact that, like a worldwide vampire, hypnotizes and conditions the economic body by sucking all its energy. F. Soddy, whom I mentioned above, pointed out that the bankers, who began their business with nothing of their own, have managed to make us all their direct or indirect debtors by means of the trap I have discussed here, of which society seems not to take conscious note, thus indefinitely perpetuating what J. Bochaca calls "the robbery of centuries."[7]

It is hard to believe that there is such thievery in the world and that people are unaware of it or that governments do nothing in their respective territories to remedy things. But if we take a glance at government debts and the annual interest that have to be paid on them, we shall understand that, victims as they are of the system, they can hardly be fully aware of their situation. At the end of 1995, the debt of the United States was 4.9 trillion dollars and the costs of interest on the national debt in 1992 was 292 billion dollars. In 1995, each American child was born indebted to the amount of 18,631 dollars.[8] If the most powerful country on earth owes such an amount of money, one may well ask where does its strength lie? Or to put it plainly, is it not logical to think that the one who is strong is really the creditor? If the debt of the weaker countries is quantitatively inferior, it is no less serious—quite the contrary, their situation is one of dependency on the international financial system. It is technically impossible to avoid this dependency to the extent that, as we said above, it is impossible to pay the total debt because there is not a sufficient amount of real money to pay back the paper money created out of nothing. Perhaps this is what banks desire, either to eternally maintain this situation of dependency or to appropriate the real goods that stood as guarantee for the loans. The power of the international financial system has grown to the extent that governments have lost their capacity to control money, perhaps as a consequence of the displacement of politicians from important public positions on economical matters.

There is a long standing battle between politics and practicality (in this case we would have to speak of economy), which dates back to the industrial revolution. Starting from Saint-Simon, who stated that "the government of men" would give way to "the administration of things," politics progressively lost its romantic, idealistic charge to give way to diverse forms of technocratism that have gradually substituted any political consciousness with "know-how," or to say this a different way, ideology versus technicality. Technocratism in its diverse forms has since then attempted to discredit politics, at times quite rightly. According to J. Burhan's thesis, the "media experts" (e.g., the technicians and administrators) will finally substitute the "experts in goals" (politicians and ideologists), whose usefulness is put to doubt in complex industrial societies. In the same sense, the so-called thesis of the "end of ideologies" abounded, popularized by Daniel Bell, who held that ideologies were a thing of the past, because current "intelligence" was in agreement throughout the western world on the most essential aspects.[9] Many political theorists, like Raymond Aron, insisted on the disappearance of extreme ideologies; or, as Koestler held, on the void in content of the left–right antinomy; or in the end, as the economist Galbraith states, that technical aspects prevail more and more over political ones, so that parties fighting each other had the same strategic objectives. All this technocratic "ideology" was designed to displace the politician from technical decisions, particularly in the sphere of the economy. It is obvious that these technical experts, who are no more than the agents of international finance, have gradually displaced politicians from the important positions in the economic spheres of the various governments, at the very point where important decisions are made—decisions that vary from a devaluation of the currency, to the fixing of inter-bank interest or privatization of public companies which are often undersold to the powerful, thus wasting the collective effort invested in their creation.

It may be said that the first great technocratic victory occurred on the 21st of December 1913, when the American Congress, many of whose members were absent because it was Christmas, surreptitiously passed the Federal Reserve Act, which facilitated the creation of the Federal Reserve Board, a private corporation with a state veneer that took over the monopoly for issuing currency in the country, trampling over the constitutional principle set up by the founders of the country which said, "Congress shall have the power . . . to coin money, [and] regulate the Value thereof . . ." and all this was done under the pretext that money matters should be left to the banking "experts," because politicians understood nothing about economics.

Continual economic crises, the last in 1907, cried out for the creation of a Central Bank as the sole issuer of banknotes, a solution that had been adopted since the end of the 19th century by all countries to solve the chaos of multiple issues of currency in their respective territories, and also any eventual problems of liquidity that might arise. In the United States alone there were 25,000 national banks that issued currency. Then in 1913, it was decided to abandon the idea of a State Central Bank because, apart from the technocratic pretext mentioned above, it was supposed to be incompatible with the federal system, with the individualism of the states, and because it was thought that such a vast territory as the U.S.A. would make it inefficient. Instead of a Central Bank, the Federal Reserve was, among other things, created to avoid further crises occurring through a lack of liquidity, such as the one in 1907. These good intentions however, were unable to prevent the great depression of 1929 as we said above. From that moment on, whenever the Federal Government needs money other than that which it obtains through taxes, it approaches the Federal Reserve, asking for example for 500 million dollars, which as soon as it is approved generates an authorization from Congress to the Treasury Department to print 500 million dollars in United States bonds. These latter are handed over to the Federal Reserve which then pays the expenses of issuing the money requested and gives it to the government. As a result of this transaction, the government indebts the public to the Federal Reserve Board to the tune of

500 million dollars plus the respective interest accumulated until the debt is paid off.

As a result of this system, the people of the United States were indebted to the Federal Reserve in 1976 to an amount of more than 400 billion dollars, for which they had to pay interest of approximately 2 billion dollars per month.

As the famous pilot Charles Lindbergh said, the passing of the Federal Reserve Act legalized, in fact, the invisible government of the world. The American congressmen who passed such an iniquitous law paid no heed to Thomas Jefferson's recommendation when he prophesied that if Americans one day allowed private banks to control the issuing of currency, they would in the end be deprived of everything, and their children would wake up homeless in the continent their parents had conquered. The dollar, the currency *par excellence* of the international market, is issued by twelve private banks entrusted with this function. The strings of the American monetary system are pulled from the Board of Governors of the Federal Reserve System, for those who in turn control international finances.

Little can be done in the face of this situation and in fact the governments of the different states do practically nothing, for their economies and currencies oscillate to the rhythm imposed by the interests of the great bank. Of course, a strong state whose politicians were honest and independent of the conglomerate of economic interests could beat this fateful influence, above all because the Nation-State is the ultimately important obstacle to international financial power exerting absolute dominion.[10]

Edmund Von Rothschild once stated that the structure that ought to disappear was the nation. If the fatherland, the nation, and the state are dissolved in the international order preached by the banker J. Warburg, who was associated with the Rothschilds and the Rockefellers, society would be left with scant hopes of defending itself against this worldwide power. Along more generally interventionist lines, European states have so far partially defended themselves against this influence, but could the future European Union with a more diffuse political power and a Central Bank independent of the government, following the model of the German Central Bank, guarantee this remnant of independence? Would not the Euro, the future European currency, be a more adequate instrument to more easily control finances in the Old Continent?

It would seem difficult to discipline the financial world from a just and different point of view to reach genuine independence, for the tendency seems to be just the opposite. This financial power—which lends what it does not have and charges for it; which, with a slight of hand takes money from nowhere; which has discovered spontaneous generation—what kind of difficulties could it encounter in bribing businessmen, politicians, trade unionists, and even more, all manner of institutions and corporations, when its specialty is precisely that of drawing money out of a hat? All this nonexistent money has invaded the market. We live with money that, brought from the future by long-term loans, we have to pay back with a permanent effort throughout our whole lifetime. And we have to pay back both the principal and the interest, and as if this were not enough, an extra tax assigned by the state to pay the interest on its debt. This ends up by painfully burdening the existence of future generations who will have to be able to pay the credit generated by national debt at that time. Herein lies the slavery of our time, being born indebted and working for free for more than half our lives to pay taxes and pay back the loans with their corresponding interest.

We have reached a point at which it is hard to imagine a world without credit, yet we do not realize that true credit (credibility or trust) lies in the borrower's human wealth, and not in the bank—that entity which is insolvent, because it loans what it does not have, and gets into debt in the amount of 20 times its capital in order to do so. Credit, in this case, is defined as a mere promise of payment. For instance, the company owner manufactures goods or houses with borrowed money, and we acquire these goods through an intermediary, also with a loan, which, because of successive charges for interest, generates a disproportionate difference between the original cost and the final retail sales prices. Everything that is produced bears an additional cost on account of the financial system from which no one can escape due to the schizophrenic alienation suffered by a society given up to consuming everything with unhealthy voracity.

I referred before to the compulsive quest for pleasure as one of the causes that weaken the will. In the same anguished way, the dissatisfied consumer is a social stereotype that swallows everything that the economic system produces. Any absurd, useless product, once it has hardly been introduced by the mass media, becomes immediately desired and indispensable to the consumer, to calm the permanent anxiety in which he lives. Doubtless, subliminal publicity fulfills to perfection the aim it pursues, and this in general terms means above all that the *individual will never fully satisfy his desire to consume,* so that there will always be a new desirable object and a loan available to obtain it.

Confucius said that happiness consists of desiring what one already has. Well, it would seem clear that the aim of the current financial system consists of precisely the opposite, using this consumer anxiety to enslave the individual to death, binding him for life to the cruel snare of bank loans.

Trapped in the spider's web of the financial system, current society experiences a desperate, voracious passion so that what happens is the same as with Tantalus, whose thirst was greater the more he drank. The dissatisfied consumer buys more and more objects, when behind them only the vain illusion of increasing one's self-esteem by "having" and not by "being" is to be found. Obfuscated by his passion, he persists in this process like a gambler bent on squandering his fortune at roulette without realizing that he is totally mortgaging his future and that of his family—without realizing that the magnitude of his inner void will never be satisfied either with pleasure or by consuming material goods. And as long as international finance is not really at the service of society, but the reverse, ethics will be in mourning.

Envy

Francisco de Quevedo stated that the four scourges of the world are envy, ingratitude, arrogance, and avarice. Gonzalo Fernández de la Mora,[11] the author of *The Egalitarian Envy*, says in his work:

> Envy is the malaise felt at the happiness of others, being superior, desired, unattainable, and unassimilated . . . Envy is the only capital vice that no one confesses to, in order to better maneuver against the person envied and to deceive oneself, for man has a spontaneous awareness that this is a malign sentiment . . . Envy is a feeling of all times and places . . . Although envy is anti-social, it can be manipulated as an agglutinator of the envious against the envied. Such alliances do not occur spontaneously and are promoted by demagogues, who stress the inferiorities of certain groups with respect to others, call them iniquitous and promise egalitarian Utopias . . . Envy is absolutely vile, it is negative for both the active and the passive

subject, it is pure malignity because there is no justification whatsoever for regretting the happiness of others and reveling in their misfortune; it is a perverse sentiment with not the slightest admixture of good will . . . The absolute malignity of envy is the ethical motive for the person suffering from it to keep it hidden even from himself.

This intellectual refers to the fact that envy is the only capital sin that cannot be confessed to, one eternally masked and disguised, which is due to the fact that the envious person needs to maneuver furtively and surreptitiously against the person envied, since confessing envy would make any action taken against the cause of that envy socially illegitimate.

For Plato, envy was pleasure in others' misfortune. He also attributed to it an antisocial character "for it weakens the city." For Aristotle, it was a disease of the soul that manifested itself as "grief at the good fortune of others" and "rejoicing in others' misfortune," and that envy was aroused by almost everything that brings happiness. Those who are most prone to envy would be "those who love glory."

Miguel de Unamuno classified this passion as a "psychic morbidity," "an inner gangrene," and "a terrible scourge and dreadful cancer" of the human spirit. According to Schopenhauer:

How bitter is one's own scarcity when one contemplates the well-being and property of others . . . Men cannot bear the contemplation of a supposed happy man because they feel unhappy . . . Those who envy natural gifts or personal superiorities such as beauty in women or genius in men have no consolation or hope and they have no other alternative than to bitterly and irreconcilably hate the person endowed with such qualities . . . This envy directed against personal qualities is the most insatiable and poisonous because the envious person has no hope left; but it is also the vilest because it abhors what it should love and respect . . . The envious person hides just as carefully as the secret lascivious sinner, and becomes an inexhaustible inventor of tricks, schemes, and ruses to conceal and mask himself. He is a master of dissimulation. Confronted with the brilliant qualities that corrode his soul he simulates with great refinement that these qualities are so insignificant that he has not noticed them, does not stop to contemplate them, and even forgets them accidentally. On the other hand, he is busy with intimate machinations to carefully avoid any superiority being manifested or acknowledged in any sphere. And at the same time, he projects over it darkness, hyper-criticism, sarcasm, and calumnies, like a toad that spits venom from its hole. However, he will enthusiastically praise insignificant or mediocre men and even the worst in the same type of activity . . . Envy reinforces the wall between the "you" and the "I," whereas understanding and sympathy make it fine and transparent, and when it attains full maturity the distinction between the "I" and the "non-I" disappears . . . The more brilliant one is, the more alone one is.

Other moralists have acknowledged in envy an almost incorrigible weakness and that it is "the only vice that can call itself just because it punishes those it affects with its own torment"; "It is as old as the world"; "It was the first sin on earth"; "It causes confusion between the classes and conditions of men because it is universal"; "It is anti-social and disrupts solidarity and union, separating the envious person from those who are happier."

Benito Spinoza, a Dutch philosopher of Spanish descent, stated that men are by nature inclined to envy, which is a characteristic of human nature. "Most men are envious and are unbearable to each other . . . In the measure that men are driven one against another by envy or by a feeling of hate, one opposes another." He adds that, "those most prone to envy are the proud and those who appear to be the most insignificant and humble."

Envy is the worst sin that exists because it is the most poisonous, concealed, hypocritical, and antisocial. It is a malignant force that disrupts any good, beauty, harmony, and virtue. Due to its underhanded nature, no one consciously experiences the machinations and effects of the envy of others. This envy will always make use of the most extraordinary tricks or machinations to "envy, without it seeming to be like envy in a way." The envious person will manage to combat or disqualify those whom he envies, so that at no time can anyone perceive the moral cancer that eats away at him. He will manage to discredit intelligent, valuable, straightforward, creative, and successful people, for by "chopping off" all these heads that had made him seem small, he feels that he has grown in size. He hates those who are outstanding, but so rationalizes this feeling that he manages very well to argue apparently reasonable pretexts to debase, disparage, belittle, harm, or destroy those figures who dare to break the homogeneity of the flock by standing out above it—all this on the condition that nobody realizes the horrible morbidity that invades him. Dissimulation, hypocrisy, and camouflage, allow him to disguise himself as a benefactor or defender of some public cause. The envious person is generally a "bleached sepulchre"—truly corrupt within, although outwardly he may offer an excellent appearance of social goodness.

Envy is at the same time a moral and mental disease, a vice, a mortal sin, and a malignant manifestation. It is not recognized as a disease because it is a "pathology that no one wants to see," one of those disorders that, to a greater or lesser extent, affects almost the whole species and is therefore only recognized by exceptional beings who for some reason have remained exempt from this perverse passion.

Likewise, hypocrisy, its eternal companion, makes it impossible to understand or denounce the magnitude and scope of this disorder. No one would be willing to unmask themselves to reveal the dreadful face of envy.

Lastly, it does not matter how much one talks, shows, or tests this problem; what is certain is that, just as in science fiction films in which aliens take possession of everybody's mind, only a tiny minority can calculate the terrible consequences of a sentiment that continually sets man against man, but always from the shadows of the unconscious. It is not that envy so dominates man that he should be a passive victim of it, but on the contrary, *man chooses to be envious,* in the same way as he chooses to be virtuous or vicious, except that this option obeys a mechanism of unconscious deliberation.

There are people who usually go to morbid or grotesque films without being obliged to, or who prefer to be miserable rather than happy, to be pitied rather than envied. In the same way, the mysterious catacombs of the human soul strangely make certain people sometimes prefer a painful obscurity to the light, voluntarily marginalizing themselves from the luminous brightness of virtue and happiness, choosing to be hateful and resentful rather than friendly and fraternal.

It has always had an impact on me, the nature that is so elaborate and mysterious in its passion, that it drives the individual to equalize illustrious, happy, or admired persons by "chopping off their heads." He does so with the aim of appropriating their gifts, supposed or real, or of elevating himself through contrast—debasing those who overshadow or belittle him. The final result of such machinations is sinister and unforeseeable, and consists in the automatic punishment of the envious person who through his passion dooms himself to permanent subordination, for it is really only possible to envy those we admire or those we acknowledge as our superiors. This envious obsession produces an unhealthy fixation with respect to the image of the admired person, and this mechanism inevitably means "looking up to" someone with pain and discomfort. In the envious person's mind, the admired person he wishes to harm *will always occupy a higher place, and he himself, a subordinate position.*

This is why it has been said that it is the only fair vice, for its development bears its own punishment within itself. By wishing to do harm, one harms oneself; by wanting to stand out, one becomes enslaved and subordinate; by trying to debase the admired object, one ends by exalting it; by attacking the happiness of others, one destroys one's own. One never feels envy for one's inferiors. No one envies ugly, deformed, stupid, unpleasant, or failed people. Neither does anyone attempt to attack grotesque works of art or works lacking in harmony and beauty. It is precisely these qualities that arouse rage and ill will because they are backdrops against which one's own insignificance or ugliness shows up.

According to Melanie Klein, the process of envy always starts with the initial admiration one feels for someone, a feeling that later evolves into affection and love in their positive manifestations or to envy in its negative form. Although envy is an antisocial, dissociative force that disrupts solidarity, those affected by it usually unite to go against noteworthy or outstanding people. These people may be highly intelligent, of distinguished family, or of great wealth. They may be successful, beautiful, or of outstanding moral caliber. In sum, they go against everything that stands out and possesses outstanding gifts, in whatever sphere.

Discontented people feel threatened by happy, virtuous, simple, disciplined, harmonious people. In their imagination, what these latter possess to a greater extent has been taken away from them in some mysterious way. There are political parties that exist thanks to the unifying negative power of envy, governed by the password: "to put an end to the privileges" of certain members of society—currents of thought that use envy as a binding glue to bring about revolutions. Miguel de Unamuno said that "envy is the mother of democracy" and that "peace and democracy almost forcibly engender envy . . . democracies are envious."

Envious people cannot bear others to distinguish themselves, and as a reaction, they try to even them out, for they cannot bear inferiority and difference. The background to the obsession for equality is no more than envy itself, being anxious to level people through the obtaining of some sort of political power that will enable them to punish the offense of being outstanding. In other words, to punish those who earn more money; disciplined people who master themselves; creative, intelligent, simple, happy people.

Gonzalo Fernández de la Mora holds that "it is absolutely false that nature engenders men equal; the truth is that it brings them into the world with dissimilar capacities that are obviously able to be categorized in a hierarchy. The hypothetical homogeneity announced by Rousseau runs counter to the most obvious data of genetics, physiology, and psychology. It is a fiction for the use of demagogues and the consumption of the frustrated." He adds that:

> The protagonists of the progress of Mankind are not the uniform masses, but the superior spirits, the most different people . . . the great social task of our time is not to increase the egalitarian potentialities of society and the State, but to individualize more.

The further a society falls into envious incitation, the more this will hinder its progress. Egalitarian envy is a reactionary social feeling *par excellence*. And it is an ironic semantic distortion that political currents who call themselves progressive should stimulate such a weakness in the human species.

Indeed, envy is the predominant passion that governs, and has always governed, the historical evolution of mankind. War, revolution, and social convulsions always have the unconfessable purpose of appropriating things that are envied. When the mob goes out on the streets to riot, it does not do so in protest but as a vandalistic act designed to moderate the envy that devours its guts. When the State applies discriminatory taxes by making use of its monopoly to legally use force, and ignores people's equality under law, it also does so to violently level, and thus gratify people's envy. When ultra-virtuous, successful, or original people are derided or ignored for no valid reason, it is with the sole purpose of silencing envy. The spreading of envy is the chief factor that hinders the development of nations. The cancer of a misunderstood, badly applied Marxism has poisoned the soul of the poorer countries for many years to come, by using envious passional resentment to join the masses, but in a destructive way. The collective unconscious of these nations is the bearer of the virus of hate for the rich and powerful; of the class struggle; of aversion for educated, outstanding people. They are convinced of the need to establish the dictatorship of the proletariat by demolishing established order.

Underdevelopment always means the *development and proliferation of envy,* stimulated and tactically used by political agitators in their desire to monopolize power. Economically developed countries are less affected by the scourge of envy, so that they can devote their energies to creative work, whereas other less fortunate ones are obsessed with the indefinite enlargement of the State, making use of expropriatory taxes to control the lives of the citizens and to suppress those who stand out. They do this in a desire for homogeneity that usually produces huge difficulties for economic development, so that such countries periodically experience a regression in their efforts and the thwarting of their expectations, thus generating all manner of intellectually facile explanations for the reasons behind such problems, without ever recognizing that these nations are, in fact, sick with envy, and that this disorder may turn into a terminal illness.

No one has ever tried to quantify the harm or loss suffered by a country through this practiced passion, which remains so hidden and underhanded that it forces one to invent outlandish names to conceal its true nature, for no one would dare to call it by its real name. For example, in Chile, envy is euphemistically known as "jacket-pulling" (pulling a person's jacket downwards to overthrow a successful individual). In this same country, singular strategies are used to silence, conceal, or dissimulate envious feelings. It is as if the use of an excessively affectionate or caressing language had become practiced by using diminutives that are normally applied to children. John becomes Johnny, and there are countless Paulies, Charlies, Peteys, etc. Generally, everybody speaks to each other like children to simulate a state opposed to envy.

The excess of courtesy and a desire to please becomes an excellent tool to silence or neutralize envy, which, as it is always boiling under the surface, has to continually be repressed. When this occurs, the explosions of rage usually are more profound and violent than normal, since, at that moment, an overwhelming explosion of repressed envy suddenly appears. One must visualize the huge amount of psychic energy consumed by the process of envy, and the extraordinary strategies that the envious person has to deploy in order to conceal his own vice from himself, to hide it from his fellows, and to give an outlet to the tremendous passional pulsions in a camouflaged and socially acceptable manner. All this emanates from the malicious or perverse use of one's own faculties, which if they were used positively would lead the individual to happiness and success. All those who have studied the subject have attempted somewhat unsuccessfully to discover what the real origin of this overwhelming force that enslaves the individual is. It is not sufficient to say that it comes from a "comparison with other happier or better gifted persons," or that it emanates from a desire to possess the goods that others have and that one lacks.

Personally, I believe that there are two basic types of envy, one that is located in the sex and the other in the stomach. The former is of a sadomasochistic nature, like jealousy. The envious person alternately enjoys and suffers, by knowing that he is possessed and defenseless in the face of an enslaving, overwhelming passion. This is an exciting situation that stimulates him sexually, thus leading him to perverse pleasure. The envious person both hates and desires the person envied. He watches him with the same care and passion as a person in love. He cannot forget him. He feels him ever-present and he interferes with his feelings, his mind, and his dreams. He wants to possess his belongings, to share his life and happiness, to have his respect and consideration to then spurn it—in sum, to permanently coexist with him.

It has been said of slavery that it is a symbiotic phenomenon, inasmuch as the master was usually as dependent as was the slave, for he could not live without him. There are moments when the envious person would like to dominate the person he negatively admires, not to destroy him but to share his existence, and there are other times when he would like to belong to him with the same aim in mind. The stimulus of his life is derived from the sentiment of envy by inventing all manner of strategies to harm or injure the person he negatively admires.

The envy that comes from the stomach is based on the insatiable voracity of the digestive system which reacts perversely to the abundance of others. The desire to possess material goods does not, in this case, mean food, but the goods or qualities that in some way represent survival. Just as a shark will not discriminate much when it comes to eating, so too will that voracious impulse of the stomach struggle to "swallow and devour" in some way all that supposedly makes up the happiness of others. In love, for example, the expression "I could eat you" has become common. This should not be interpreted in its erotic sense but in its gastronomic one. A pretty girl will often be defined as a "cookie," "a sweetie," "sugar," or "honey," through the envy aroused by her feminine attributes denied to men. To eat means to ensure for oneself something desired in order to thus avoid the possibility of being denied it.

Penis envy, discovered by Freud as typical of women, represents admiration for a male organ she lacks and which is the source of transmission of sperm that can impregnate her, thus enabling her to create life. It is similar to envy of the mother's breast, described by Melanie Klein, when the child discovers that milk can be denied him and that he does not control this source. The possibility that the stomach might appropriate a desirable food by the simple expedient of swallowing it leads us to accept the existence of a psychic duplication of the digestive function, whose chief appetite is to appropriate certain desirable goods or qualities. It may be that the myth of Dracula was born here. Our body is at one and the same time material and energetic. Our organs have a material ordering to them accompanied by an energetic function of a parallel nature. When this mechanism is perverted, it is not sufficient to satisfy its normal needs but, like a miser, it desires to accumulate merely to keep. Suffering because of the good fortune of others is usually somaticized by bringing on disorders of the liver and gallbladder, skin diseases and nervous disorders, and other more severe maladies. In other instances it is reflected in the face, in the pigmentation of the skin, gesture, posture, expression, and gaze. Any negative emotionality also brings about a drop in the immunological system with the consequences one might expect.

Resentment is a more subtle, underhanded form of envy, described by Nietzsche as the state of mind of those who have been refused the authentic reaction, that of action, and who make up for it with an imaginary vengeance. He states:

> The resentful person is impotent and has an insatiable instinct that he satisfies with a mental operation. The real cause of resentment, of vengeance and the like is to be found in the desire to divert an excruciating pain, one hidden and less and less bearable, by means of a stronger emotion . . . and to provoke it, the first and best pretext is to think that someone must be to blame for me not feeling well.

This enables one to transfer responsibility for one's own unhappiness onto others, thus making certain groups—one's parents, one's partner, a friend whom one envies, a race, or the whole world—the villains of the plot.

He continues:

> The resentful person lives in a world of subterranean, inexhaustible vengeance, insatiable in outbursts against those who are happy, whom he blames for his own misfortune. The supreme vengeance of the resentful person would be to convince the fortunate that it is a disgrace to feel so happy when there is so much wretchedness.

The resentful person, according to Fernández de la Mora, inverts ethics: "The villain of the morality of resentment is the hero of the other morality" (i.e., it is the world upside-down, with an inversion of values).

De la Mora further states:

> Resentment is a mental operation to discharge on others responsibility for one's own failure, to sublimate impotence and, in the ultimate analysis, to construct a scale of values that turns the villain into the happy hero, and makes the failed, embittered person good.

Resentful nations are doomed to chaos, poverty, suffering, and failure, for their lack of moral generosity makes them receive the equivalent of the seed they have sown, and this occurs with all those who base their lives on hate, ill will, corruption, and perversity. Many resentful governors who were lenient or acted weakly with envious mobs throughout the history of mankind, gave in to them in order to gain their favor. They did so out of a fear that they themselves would become the target for this dreadful passion. In his condition of impotence, the resentful individual will always seek the happy medium, not the virtuous center mentioned by Aristotle. Rather, he will seek the exact point of non-definition and ambiguity that will enable him to avoid popular envy, and apologize for all that does not succumb to envious demands.

All those who know the virulence of envy in their own flesh find it difficult to be successful, for they know that if they achieve success, they will be the inevitable targets of this passion and unconsciously prefer to fail, at times, rather than become envied on account of their success. It is a tough task to make a resentful nation progress, for in such a condition it is not even possible to keep public order, for man confronts man and the envious passion breaks out with an uncontrolled force, invariably making victims of those citizens who, for some reason or other, represent a symbol of order, merit, and discipline.

Unfortunately, the institutions or people entrusted with exalting higher values are misguided and at times end either overtly or covertly by promoting resentment and envy. Unfortunately, this type of seed is always well received by those who preach revolution for egalitarian ends. It has always been the aim of resentful, embittered, and failed individuals to level downwards, for this relieves them of the effort of emulating those who have attained higher positions. Really, it would seem easier to envy than to emulate, but the individual either ignores, or is never convinced, that the first of these possibilities is a "just vice" that entails its own punishment.

Practiced hypocrisy is the refuge of envy, for it avoids calling things by their proper name and is the chief obstacle to unmasking this capital sin. The salvation of mankind depends, at a fundamental level, on the creation of centers for researching envy, with the sole aim of studying it in depth and divulging its appalling effects, because no universal brotherhood would be possible without this. As long as people take refuge in the underworld of dissimulation and ignorance, this sin will continue to devastate the world. If its characteristics were known in detail and its mechanisms were common knowledge, it would be a compulsory subject in people's basic education so that they would learn to recognize and avoid it. If its symptoms, maneuvers, and strategies were brought to light and made transparent, it would be far more difficult to be envious, for the person who was would receive public reproval. As this does not happen today, the explosive proliferation of envy is facilitated.

If the huge destructive power of envy were revealed and laid bare, nations and political parties would have to sign a solemn pact not to promote envy with the aim of gaining the political edge. One must understand once and for all that envy kills more people in the world than hunger, AIDS, war, or the nuclear threat. By death I mean, of course, the death of possibilities and expectations for a human being who is affected by the terrible virus of envy.

No one realizes the magnitude of the harm this under-handed, destructive force can bring about: a power that kills a person from within, surreptitiously, drying up his soul and shrinking his heart, burying it in the shadows of one of the most acute sufferings man can experience. It violently sepa-rates him from the light of happiness and inner plenitude, promoting hate, rivalry, and violence, continually setting man against man, without anybody realizing the depth and dimen-sion of this phenomenon. It is a mechanism that inhibits the sentiment of brotherhood by aborting the development of both nations and individuals.

The innocent victims of this scourge are those who live in extreme poverty. Their executioners are those who, over many decades, have indefatigably devoted their efforts to sowing hate, resentment, and envy to negatively agglutinate these people, poisoning their hearts, cheating them by making them believe that what they don't have has been snatched from them by others and that it is impossible to prosper and earn money unless this be with the aid of the State and the powerful. What is true is that the established system generally prefers to spend its economic resources on paying out exorbi-tant interest on the national debt of nations. They prefer this opprobrious, unworthy human bondage to the power of money, squandering the rest in the maintaining of hypertro-phied, inefficient States, rather than deciding to train and educate the dispossessed massively and efficiently to thus enable them to choose the highest level of work opportunities and self-fulfillment. When the poor of this world turn a deaf ear to the sowers of hate and stop fighting against external enemies and devote their efforts to cultivating themselves by fighting against their own limitations—when they develop their higher faculties—they will be able to give lessons to the rest of Mankind, overcoming poverty and no longer being the tools of political power. They will also conquer the most valuable throne of human dignity, which is based on being and not on having.

Envy has to be vanquished in order for the world to effectively advance. Society must censure and punish inadequate behavior and above all, the conduct that, because it develops in the darkness of people's psychic labyrinth, is a serious threat to those who are as yet uninfected by the terrible disease. From a moral point of view, it is a capital sin and the worst of them, because it runs counter to all virtue. This is aggravated by the fact that it is a *voluntarily chosen form of conduct,* and also because of the vile, malignant, and corrupt nature of its mechanism.

When people say that the world is topsy-turvy, they mean precisely this—the false moral code of the resentful, who make heroes out of villains and villains out of heroes, who imprison the innocent and make sure that the true delinquents are never found guilty. This is the false code that encourages women who want to be men and men who want to renounce their gender; the perverse scale of values that exalts youth and rejects old age; that despises the being and glorifies having; the corrupt system that promotes easy gain and success without merit; that punishes the industrious and rewards the lazy; that worships the grotesque and disqualifies harmonious beauty; that promotes envy and frustration through the exaltation of consumerism; that continually misinforms people; that encourages war to benefit the arms industry; that cruelly persecutes certain animal species and poisons the environment; that trivializes the profound and exalts the insignificant; that mocks love and satirizes virtue; that crucifies the best and crowns the unworthy; that practices usury and promotes the financial bondage of nations and people; that brainwashes the whole of mankind through the cinema, the television, and the mass media; that in sum corrupts the entire planet. Sheer prudence advises us to flee from envy as from the plague and not to show off one's own happiness. It tells us to shun the envious, for they contaminate healthy people. One single envious person among a hundred is a rotten apple that will infect the rest. Personally, I am convinced of the truth of the ancient belief in the "evil eye," which is the magnetic irradiation of an envious person.

As far back as 1775, Doctor Franz Mesmer discovered the existence of a force which he called "animal magnetism," that emanated from the body and hands of certain people and that could be used for healing. In 1785, the French government set up a committee of doctors and scientists to investigate Mesmer's theory, but they gave an unfavorable report, which of course meant nothing. Today, science accepts the mesmeric trance and identifies it with hypnosis.

It is a well-known fact that there are people who can cure certain disorders with the laying on of hands, but it is also true that the same energy that cures can also kill and destroy when that irradiation is contaminated with the baser passions of those who irradiate hate and resentment through their gaze or by their mere presence. There are very simple means of testing whether a person's eyes are a center of radiation for their animal magnetism. In the case of the envious person, he is corrupted by the secret passion that corrodes him, and he perturbs, contaminates, or harms those who come into contact with him. If we cannot manage to visualize envy as a psychic virus that infects and destroys our minds, we shall never be able to calculate the tremendous range of this diabolic disorder, nor shall we be able to free ourselves from its appalling effects.

Egoism

Egoism is defined as "an immoderate and excessive love for oneself that makes one disproportionately attend to one's own interests without concerning oneself with others." The opposite is altruism: "concern and pleasure for the good of others, even at one's own expense," "ethical individualism opposed to egoism, which defines other people as the recipients of moral action who are not the subject of such an action." It is obvious that men are moved by their own interests, that is, *egoistically.*

An exaggeration of this attitude leads to indifference to others' suffering, to cruelty, and insensitivity to poverty or to various forms of human wretchedness.

Christianity advocates "do good without looking to whom," "turn the other cheek," and "practice charity." The mechanical exaltation of this conduct leads to servility, weakness, and self-destruction, also encouraging diverse forms of paternalism that prevent the development of those thus supposedly favored, and in the long run they are harmed through the creation of a "false virtue" (an apparent, ephemeral virtue that inadvertently ends by bringing about evil).

There are many instances in which the hard-heartedness of some powerful person mercilessly strikes the dispossessed, but there are no fewer instances in which a person is helped who does not deserve it, thus encouraging a parasitical attitude that will end by smothering or destroying the benevolent benefactor and corrupting the beneficiary. It has been said that the good of others is the supreme aim of human action, and there are political ideologies that uphold this concept. It would seem that the traditional political division between "left" and "right" concerns the matter we are discussing here, because several political tendencies advocate a more altruistic society, one based on the concept of greater social justice, and they accuse other political movements of "selfish insensitivity." In this case, the "weak" should supposedly be helped by the strong, and the latter "persuaded" to strip themselves of what they possess in favor of the former, and all this for the sake of greater equality. People talk of the "marginalized," of "extreme poverty," and "social inequality," stressing the economic gap between the respective incomes of the poor and the rich, pointing out the need for a better distribution of wealth, but the true causes of the problem remain hidden. These are: the lack of a true political will to give the dispossessed greater opportunities in education, because their votes would thus no longer be captive of economic dependency; the lack of resources, which are squandered in the payment of usurious interest on the national debt; and in the maintaining of badly administered, hypertrophied States. (No country with an economy indirectly handled by the international financial system can ever become truly rich.)

The words of Jesus Christ are often alluded to, in which he said that "it is easier for a camel to go through the eye of a needle than for a rich man to enter into the Kingdom of Heaven," in order that those who have money feel guilty and the poor may blame the rich for their own shortages. Thousands of philanthropic organizations continually remind us of our moral obligation to collaborate with the most varied types of dispossessed people throughout the entire world: fatherless children, starving children, old people abandoned, homeless citizens, invalids and sick people of all kinds, and lately such campaigns have also spread to ecological protection. Of course, charity is merely an ever insufficient palliative for poverty, whose true genesis lies in a world economy sickened by the disease of the dominant financial system, and the need will never be satisfied unless we manage to implement a healthy economic system, one free of debts and interest. Because of need, feelings of guilt are created and enlarged in those who possess in abundance what others lack. It would seem that the only ethically acceptable course would be that of self-sacrifice, for otherwise, certain individuals could come to live with a feeling of perpetual guilt by being accused of a lack of solidarity with their fellows. Of course, this is the most formidable weapon for psychological manipulation.

Likewise, no one ever analyzes the extent to which "the weak" are in fact so, or when they take advantage of a supposed weakness to manipulate others who, having worked harder and being more diligent, made better use of the opportunities life offers. It is a bizarre ethical postulate to suppose that the weak are worthier than the strong and that their mere weakness makes them better in the eyes of the Creator, whereas their real inner qualities are disregarded. I believe that a high percentage of the weak are so only in the sense of their morality and character, but not physically, and that they have never bothered to develop themselves to attain success in the art of living. I do not know what would happen in the world if all the strong people decided to become weak, in the conviction that this weak state has greater moral acceptance than strength of character, courage, order, and self-discipline. Who would take care of the weak then? Is it correct "to care for, and take pleasure in, the good of others, even at one's own expense" when it is a question of helping the underprivileged by one's own decree? I refer to the envious, the resentful, and the maladjusted, who voluntarily marginalize themselves from the opportunities life offers, for they find it is more attractive and less tiresome to envy and covet others' goods, than to work for their own development and self-fulfillment.

There is nothing in the world that can impede an individual from developing himself. It is merely a matter of perseverance and individual determination. It often happens that if citizen X is successful in life due to his own merit, personal effort, and constructive attitude, he should, in the opinion of others, give away part of his material goods to help citizen Y, who has never done anything to help himself. In the name of altruism, X is asked to "take responsibility for another person's life, to shoulder the burden that Y has so far shirked." His work and creativity are demoralized by asking him to shoulder the burden of others, effectively penalizing him for being strong. At the same time, the weak person is rewarded. At times, all this occurs by equivocally using the charitable precepts attributed to Jesus Christ. It would not be surprising if some of these precepts became distorted over time and that "do good, without considering to whom" became in fact expressed as "do good but consider carefully to whom."

In the name of Christian charity, it would be irrational to try to love perverse beings who were attempting to destroy our civilization. It is not correct to attempt "to love your neighbor more than yourself," as some do. The world of God is neither illogical nor arbitrary, and we cannot imagine that corruption is rewarded in its laws by giving the prize of love when that implies the simultaneous destruction of the one who gives it.

To maintain order in the Universe, the rules of the game have to be quite clear that good should be rewarded and evil penalized. A diligent attitude must be encouraged and sloth or indolence punished. Ambiguity and scant differentiation between good and evil lead to confusion, permissiveness, and immorality.

There is a great human mass that asks to be helped, but would never be grateful for such support because envy inhibits gratitude. An envious person will never thank you from the heart for any help he receives, even if this were the greatest imaginable. While it is true that one does not do charitable works to be thanked, an absence of gratitude in the beneficiaries is indicative of a negative or destructive attitude that could probably lead one to an irresponsible or wrong use of the resources received. We know that charity often arouses rageous, silent abhorrence in resentful people who will do anything to discredit or criticize the act of generosity. Indiscriminate charity with groups who have a high level of envy is in itself an injustice, for it means, at heart, reinforcing monstrous deformations in the soul of man, deformations voluntarily accepted because of resentment at the happiness of others. It is immoral to reward the resentful person while healthy, clean, and virtuous people are punished or go unrewarded, for there is also a great human mass that needs and deserves determined support as a passive sector of society. This is the case with the elderly, children, and invalids.

Likewise, if nations were creating an excellent standard in their productive work, and States were apolitical and impersonally efficient in the administration of their resources, charity would no longer be necessary, for normal taxes would be enough to solve the problem of poverty. One must bear in mind that these reflections are about egoism, for we need to go further in depth in the meaning of this word, which is used indiscriminately to denote those who do not display charity that conforms to the type advocated by certain people. If we are speaking of charity, the hardest heart usually belongs to those States that prefer to spend the income from taxes on their own growth rather than on helping the dispossessed. To return to the concept of "egoism," one must realize that the basis of all knowledge and all action lies in the "I" or ego, so that each act, perception, or emotion is necessarily tainted with *egoism.* The basis of knowledge and perception is to be found in the "individual I," and, from the perspective of self-interest, there will be egoism as long as there are individuals.

The lack of charity, an excessive clinging to one's personal goods, and disinterest in one's fellows, all represent a merely "external" form of egoism, a word which in this sense corresponds to the unflattering label society applies to those who act contrarily to the norms of conduct that it esteems as desirable. In its inner, more-profound form, egoism is the vital attitude of the individual who places himself, within himself, in a central point, and who is not able to distance himself from that point. According to Lersch, the following types of egoism can be distinguished: that related to the preservation of self, that is, to the preservation or protection of oneself; and that related to the affirmation of self for one's own security, and to make one's own way in the world, and by doing so, to bring about the "broadening of the 'I' " and the expansion of its sphere of action.

It is commonly thought that the overvaluing of the self, with an exaggerated desire to continually show one's worth, is a vice comparable to alcoholism and is often associated with ambition and brutality.

Egoism related to self-preservation is of a universal nature and is inherent to the diverse forms of existence. Nobody in his right mind would let his body be devoured to satisfy the hunger of others. The most civilized person can turn into a savage when confronted with a perilous, life-threatening situation.

The most common form of egoism is that which seeks affirmation of itself through ambition, greed, or vanity, in order to attain positions of personal power. In a world that is ever more complex and competitive, the need for the affirmation and expansion of the "I" has been exaggerated to pathological proportions, which makes people inevitably fall into the vicious continual desire for the esteem of others. Arrivism and the various forms of social climbing demand that the individual live permanently centered on his "self-image" with the aim of making a good impression, making himself popular, having lots of friends, and attaining success. This is the most underhanded form of egoism and egocentrism because it is the most concealed and hard to detect, since it may be accompanied by a deceitfully altruistic attitude. However, it is true that, at heart, the individual can continue to value everything relative to its usefulness to his own "I," in the sense of unhealthily strengthening the "I," converting it into the central point of existence.

Many altruists are really egocentric, and their charitable nature is not aimed at the good of others, but at the enlargement of their own image. They inadvertently endeavor to absorb the greatest possible amount of elements from society that will give them prestige or artificially enlarge their image. This is a sort of gluttony or voracity in which the individual unwittingly attempts to absorb social power in order to enlarge his ego through a sort of psychic graft that will become an "artificial," enlarged identity that will, in turn, become the central point of his narcissistic dreams. This is why, in some way, the doctor feels that "he is the power over death"; the judge, that "he is justice itself"; the policeman, that "he is authority"; and the ultimate leader of a country may even feel himself to be the true master of that territory.

All kinds of material power, whether it be economic, political, military, or unionist, emanate from society. But there are many who erroneously believe that the power they wield is part of their "I" and who in the depths of their minds say, "I am this power," an assertion which cloaks one of the forms which egoism takes. A political figure may easily attribute the power he feels in his hands to his own "I," forgetting that it emanates from the collective he represents. Material goods, particularly when they are symbols of power, also produce a false enlargement of the "I," and the individual comes to be valued for what he possesses and not for what he is, a factor that usually leads to the most-profound self-worship, a selfish individualism in which the individual disqualifies his fellows because he feels that he is worth far more than they. The different forms of egoism share an objectification of one's fellows. People come to be useful tools for one's own ends and not seen as individuals having their own thoughts, feelings, and needs.

The most altruistic individual may in reality be egoistic, a case in which his chief interest is his own image and not the material goods with which he can do charitable works. His most intense desire is to be famous, respected, and feared, and his altruism is a mere catapult to attain these ends, a preestablished cost in his career as a social climber, which in the end becomes a very profitable investment. He does not do works of charity out of compassion for the dispossessed but to increase his image and appease the feelings of guilt born from his inner conviction that all one really cares about is one's self.

One should bear in mind that doing charitable works is not necessarily a display of "unselfishness," and that it is often an act motivated by feelings of guilt, whether these be founded or unfounded. Within this latter category, there are instances of guilt deliberately provoked by external agents who are interested in manipulating the individual's feelings as a means of psychological pressure to bring about the reactions they want or to obtain a certain profit from them. It is important also to bear in mind that in this case the supposed guilt may lack any real basis, and that it may be carefully prefabricated by those who are interested in obtaining illicit political or economic advantages. It is a good moral exercise to carefully reflect on who benefits from the various types of guilt with public connotations, to ascertain whether or not the guilt is as great as it seems, or whether it has been enlarged. In the latter case, one should discover the true aims pursued by those who magnify this type of situation, as well as the immoral advantage that they usually get from it. More often than is desirable, it is surprising that those who had most vigorously reproached certain faults are the true culprits, and in other instances are also the orchestrators of misinformation designed to place those whom they wish to extort in a tight spot.

There are well-founded types of guilt and others that are merely suspect, so that one is obliged to possess the right individual criteria so as to differentiate between the two. To this end, one should make use of the old rule of observing who benefits from the faults attributed to certain people or institutions. Psychological warfare, well-known in bellicose and political confrontations, makes use of misinformation as a means of manipulating public good faith to thus obtain advantages of which only the users are aware. In the struggle for power, the destruction of public figures, groups, or institutions that hinder the plans of certain political currents is an everyday occurrence all over the world, while the blind mass never realizes what is really happening. Ethics are systematically brushed aside in such manipulations, without the relevant institutions of society ever putting in any claim with regard to this.

The blind egoism of a power struggle has as its motto that "the end justifies the means" and is one of the crudest types of immorality of our time: political candidates funded by drug-traffickers; misleading advertising campaigns; members of religious orders seduced by temporal power; corrupt judges; lawyers who are expert in the indefinite prolongation of cases; multinational corporations that control the whole world; evil company owners who exploit their workers; workers who steal and cheat their employers; drug and arms dealers; mafias that control power in various places with groups of bureaucrats at their service; politicians who live off insider dealing; pseudo-ecological campaigns with concealed aims— in short, a fauna of immorality in the everyday life of the planet.

The infinite egoism and brutality of mankind struggling for power is totally devoid of any consideration or respect for honest people. It is the realm of the man-beast, who under his veneer of civilization disguises himself as a "good man." It means the proliferation of "bleached sepulchres" at the turn of the millennium. Is this mankind's terminal crisis or is it the bondage of good, but stupid, men who are exploited by the animal cunning of other perverse individuals? All these reflections are useless if one does not possess a lucid individual consciousness, one that is free of the mental servitude of a brainwashed person. What one normally sees of egoism is not as spectacular as the case of envy, for it manifests in people's actions as a grayish ethical transgression, one that is discolored and short of humanity, generosity, and nobility. It is directly related to avarice and it represents a type of emotional tight-fistedness or meanness that prevents one from empathizing with one's fellows, unless as a maneuver aimed at some ulterior manipulation.

The egoist is usually a bad friend as far as the depth of his feelings is concerned, for his whole communication in this relationship takes place at a very superficial level. This is because he fears to open himself up to others and give them love, tenderness, or concern, insomuch as he sees this as some kind of loss or a painful shedding of something important that belongs only to him. The unfortunate man or woman who sets his or her amorous desire on an egoistic person not only will not be duly loved in return but neither will his or her feelings be valued at their true worth, or even properly accepted. He who cannot or does not know how to love is generally not in a state to receive love either. On the other hand, the egoistic feeling leads one to the use of one's partner as a tool for one's own pleasure or well-being, without the manipulator even realizing that this is the case. Unaffectionate, barely demonstrative, and stingy in giving love, he nevertheless demands continual attention from his partner.

Then there is intellectual egoism, which is the case of the individual who fanatically and blindly clings to his own ideas and shuts out any analysis of new concepts. This individual will adore his own ideas as if they were gods and he builds a sealed, obscure mental universe that cannot be penetrated by other concepts. By the way, it would also be of interest to analyze egoism in children and old people who, like extremes that touch each other, display similar characteristics. Old people, during the final part of their lives, experience an egoistic crisis which is really an instinct for self-preservation. The perception of their own weakness makes them cling voraciously to their family memories, and to their material possessions. Some of them are sure that there is a certain kind of conspiracy to strip them of their possessions and they cling tenaciously to them. Some even have to be medicated to lessen the effects of this condition. The sense of their flagging strength, the fragility of their existence, and the little time left to them all make them react strongly with a psychological voracity that drives them to fill their time with such preoccupations, dedication, or attention from others so as to raise their already depressed self-esteem. Their demands may be numerous and should be humanely understood in their true context.

Children at a certain age are the most egotistic beings in the world and demand the total preoccupation of their parents, tyrannically subjecting them to the most varied demands, demands that have to be immediately satisfied or else they will fly into tantrums of rage or tears. The proximity in time to the epoch of their fetal narcissism makes them as yet incapable of properly differentiating between the "you" and the "me" and of recognizing the existence of an external world separate from their own egos.

The basic ethical problem of egoism is in knowing how to adequately differentiate its various types, for not all egoism is bad or inappropriate. There is a destructive egoism that dries up the soul and heart, that leads to cruelty, to disproportionate ambition, to brutality, to cynicism and violence; but there is also another type that can lead to the perfect fulfillment of the highest ethical and moral norms. In order to understand this subject, when one speaks of egoism, one must ask the following question: What type of egoism are we talking about? Which ego or "I" does this passion refer to? It is obvious that we have not just one "I," but that various identities alternately take exclusive possession of our minds to make us take one or another direction. Without going too deeply into this matter, nearly everyone will accept that we are at least dual and have an animal "I" that is centered in corporeal matter, and a spiritual "I" that corresponds to the "self" or the divine spark. This bipolarity can be interpreted as the coexistence of two different identities. One is inferior and primitive, of scant evolution but with a great capacity to store information. The other is higher, immortal, and eternal, not limited by time or space, but indefinitely remains in a latent state. We could identify it with "the spirit" or "the being," man's true, higher "I." This potential seldom manages to manifest itself through the human brain on account of people's low level of consciousness. Its capacity is not of an *informational nature* but one of meaning.

The capacity for information is congenital. Not so with the capacity for meaning. This can only be activated through the development of a higher *consciousness,* which is really what makes up the highest and most-precious capacity to which a human being can aspire, a precious diamond beside which the intelligence we know is no more than a rough stone. It is an altered state of consciousness, in the sense of ascendant vertical evolution, that can be accessed only by developing the power to *comprehend significance,* of which information merely represents the epidermis. It requires many years of disciplined work on one's inner world to open up the possibility for *higher consciousness* to be born.

In this book, I do not want to discuss in detail exactly what this discipline is, for the world is full of obscure mystifiers who, in order to inflate their inferior egos, will readily counterfeit any new or different knowledge and recycle it to their own level of anti-ethics, immorality, or shortsightedness, presenting it as their own, or otherwise turning it into merchandise that can compete on the consumer market. To this end, they first have to strip it of its precious, essential content to turn it into a useless, but marketable, "piece of candy."

As the saying goes, people usually "put all their eggs in one basket" in the belief that "knowledge" is the same as *knowledge,* or "wisdom" the same as *wisdom.* This occurs particularly in cases in which there is no way to differentiate an original product from a counterfeit one, through a lack of true information. This is such a pathetic situation that there are counterfeiters who copy other counterfeiters, who had already altered what someone else had in turn already counterfeited. By this stage, the product is not even a derivative but mere waste matter, for it lacks the active ingredient that brings about the desired effects.

In ancient tales of alchemy, there are many variations of the tale of the ambitious apprentice who steals a portion of the "philosopher's stone" from his master to carry out his transmutations of lead into gold, but after trying to use it time and again, cannot achieve his purpose, which leads us to conclude that the active principle was within the alchemist and not in the stone. All these considerations are designed to speak of a "higher ego," in contrast to the "inferior I."

Inferior identity is dominated by primitive animal appetites and is susceptible to corruption from the environment, this being the reason why one can speak of an "immoral egoism" that has no respect or consideration for people and that habitually exploits them as merely replaceable pawns. One will then understand that the impulses of the "I" that normally control a person—which is the identity of the personality—may be totally immoral, as Freud quite rightly pointed out when he referred to unconscious pulsions, in this case accurately speaking of a "reprovable egoism." The case of the "spiritual I" is quite a different matter, for it is the only absolutely spotless part of what we are. Really, the individual's first duty in life is to his "spiritual I," since it is the only way to work on one's own character and will power to sublimate the passions and become a virtuous man, thus complying with the Creator's evolutive plans.

The supreme goal of human action is not doing good for others, but fulfilling the precepts of *sublime egoism* which, by prioritizing things in life, puts individual evolution in the first place. This is the only, true, and paramount contribution the individual can make to society, since to give is "to give oneself," and only a man who is correctly and perfectly self-fulfilled can give the world what it really needs and not what the economic or political interests of the moment demand. There is often talk of the need for people to participate in social works as a way of collaborating with one's fellows, but no one ever thinks that each individual, *in himself, represents a contribution to society* with regard to the excellence or corruption of his human development. Really, each man contributes himself to the world and the total sum of these contributions is what creates either social goodness or social vulgarity. Unfortunately, the contributions of many people are negative because they have never bothered to perfect themselves morally and spiritually so as to become examples of higher values. Thus, instead of contributing something valuable, they usually contaminate or corrupt the spiritual patrimony; or else they steal for themselves, and in a very dishonest way, the goods that they find around them. Society is merely an ensemble of individuals in which quantity can never substitute for quality. Progress and evolution have always come from a select spiritual or intellectual group, and not from the masses. An individual who is fulfilled from the higher point of view can contribute much good to the world, but he who has never bothered first with his own development usually has no contribution to make, except his own defects and failings. According to the laws of Nature, it is quite immoral for an individual to disdain, reject, or ignore his own spiritual fulfillment, since this is the chief purpose of life. To exist should not be a mere question of survival for man, but should instead be his faithful compliance with the laws of life, for only the person who does this is really alive. The rest are mere phantoms in search of their destiny, beings that roam erratically through life, mere seekers of apparent good or the pleasure of the moment. Only he who complies with the mandate of *sublime egoism* will have a truly important legacy to pass on to his children. As the saying goes, the greatest charity one can do is *to teach a man to fish and not to give him one.* When an individual practices *sublime egoism,* neither he nor his children will need charity, since they will be in a position to materialize their own inner wealth, no matter what their social station. This is the only course that would eliminate all social classes with one fell swoop, for it establishes equality of possibilities, not by means of a decree or an imposition, but because noble, worthy, decent, and successful existence can be within reach of anybody who takes the trouble to attain it.

As a prerequisite, one only needs to understand that this can be done, that others have done it before, and that one does not need to ask anybody for permission to get to work.

At the level of the spirit, we are all essentially the same, although we may not possess the same faculties, since it is a matter of individual work to augment them. The saddest class of the dispossessed consists of those who, having no economic emergencies, totally lack the spiritual sensitivity that enables them to desire to be more human and to become higher beings. It is the same spiritual sensitivity that will enable them to overcome their defects and passions, to conquer all vice, to temper their character and will, to be happy and virtuous through their own effort. Such people, "separated from the possibility to be spiritual," content themselves with the semi-animal existence of egoistic consumerism, self-indulgence, and the magnification of their own image. Make no mistake about it, the highest possible form of morality consists in transcending oneself to attain spiritual perfection, which will ensure genuine, lasting happiness. If we fail to pay attention to this, we are committing the sin of stupidity and pride by disdaining the most precious gift that the Creator offers us. If we continue to be concerned with the subject of charity with reference to egoism, then we must consider that only the one who has individual freedom of thought and a higher *consciousness* will have the necessary discrimination to determine what type of charity should be done, when it should be done, and who should benefit from it. He who is not in this condition can only proceed in accordance with the ineluctable mandate of his cerebral programming, thus eliminating any individual moral definition of the act, charitable or otherwise, that he is about to carry out.

Corruption

The word "corruption" means: "the action and effect of corrupting or becoming corrupt." To corrupt is: "to alter, change the shape of something; to waste, to deprave, to harm, to rot, to destroy, to adulterate, to pervert, to bribe and coerce a judge or any other person, with gifts or in other ways." If we keep to the strict sense of the word, using it to analyze internal as well as external situations, corruption to a greater or lesser degree represents something that is practiced in the great majority of people, who adulterate themselves in this way due to perturbing environmental influences.

One must accept that each individual whose nature has been alienated, altered, or adulterated through the process of subliminal training or the forced internalization of insignificant information, experiences a tremendous deterioration, frustration, "corruption," or incapacity to develop the most-precious faculties inherent to the true human condition: the higher vigilic *consciousness* that differentiates a sleepwalker from a man awake. He who is not in possession of himself belongs to forces that are alien to his own selfhood, and undergoes a debasing process of "alteration and adulteration" which leads him to the degradation of his human condition, of his inner freedom or the impossibility to obtain it. This is the essence of mankind's moral problem; the loss of his inner essence, of what makes men truly human, in contrast to animals. The corruption of his homineity leads him further and further towards behaving like a sophisticated electronic artifact that is integrally programmed, or else as an intelligent animal devoid of any self-consciousness, subordinate to the neuronal information of which he is the bearer but which slips through his control. He acts more like a subjugated nucleus of his own conduct.

What the neuronal program commands, the individual carries out unquestioningly and without hesitation. What would seem to be a complex process of thought destined to discriminating in a higher way, is usually no more than an exchange of information through chemical and electrical impulses between various neuronal groups, a mechanical or automatized association that is activated by typified stimuli that act as detonators of specific types of behavior. All this is done autonomously, without the intervention of profound comprehension or any type of elevated capacity of judgment or discrimination.

It could not be otherwise in a being possessed by a twilight consciousness living in an intermediate space between sleep and wakefulness, lacking self-consciousness and higher vigilic perception. No authentic type of higher ethical conduct is possible within this state of mental limbo or "drowsiness" in which man lives. The cerebral informational program has control over his conduct, and what we call the "emotions" are usually no more than cerebral archives of a different type, a sentimental program designed to react in an apparently spontaneous manner, but one which, at heart, had been previously conditioned.

It is not that spontaneity does not exist, but rather that it appears only exceptionally in people with a very weak program. In the rest, it is only a fair imitation. Therefore, one must agree that what we know as "human normalcy" is really a state of corruption of the faculties of authentic man, a species that is just beginning to develop. However, at the individual level, it is feasible that one can achieve an ascendant spiritual transformation by means of inner discipline.

From the point of view of the possible evolution of Mankind, the human being is so only in name, for he is really a creature that has only just begun to move away from the animal aspect, and is much closer to this aspect than to any higher entelechy. Many of the ideal things we try to attribute to the human species are in fact fantastical utopias with beings who, because they lack a similar species with which to compare themselves, believe themselves to be immensely superior to what they really are, and even feel themselves to be the lords of a creation of which they are really mere instruments.

The true dimension of the ethical and moral problem can only be appraised if one understands that "we are not what we assume we are," and that we are very far from it. The most-precious faculty is the vigilic consciousness, and not intelligence. This latter lacks higher judgment and discrimination. In practice, intelligence is an instrument manipulated automatically by cerebral information of which the individual is a bearer. Ethics is a behavioral imperative of an individual nature that must be freely borne in the depths of each individual's *self*, without pressures or threats of any kind. As long as this is not possible, Mankind must be content with the practice of brainwashing people with norms, rules, and standards that emanate from the most-important groups of power.

Subliminal messages of all kinds will penetrate the minds of common people, molding these people to the fancy of those who may derive profit from this type of conditioning. The supreme prowess of those who aspire to be truly moral is to attain psychological and mental autonomy, not in the sense of dissociating themselves from their social group, but insofar as it means attaining the power of higher vigilic discrimination. This faculty enables them to voluntarily choose and control the type, amount, and quality of the information they wish to allow into their brains; also, to revise, cleanse, and sublimate that which had entered at a stage prior to the birth of the capacity of this new power.

Only at this level can the human being become fully responsible for his own acts, for he thus attains total freedom in the sense that his mind will never be enslaved or dominated by any external influence. Neither will he be dominated by unconscious or compulsive inner mandates. On the other hand, he will be able to choose with total independence that which he wishes.

Once we understand that the nature of the whole species, with very few exceptions, is adulterated and distorted (corrupted), we shall also understand the origin of what is commonly called corruption: prevarication, bribery, vice, delinquency, terrorism, theft, swindling, deceit, and sin. All these types of conduct are no more than "normal" corruption taken to extremes. What is called "subtle corruption" is that which is practiced by the individual who, although honest, is far from being truly human and remains detached from the higher faculties traditionally attributed to the species. "Raw corruption" is everything included in the previous explanation, with the addition of all the actions that alter the judiciary and penal system.

Corruption appears in its worst form when it overpowers those who have some sort of authority granted by the State or society, for these people are precisely those who should be custodians of the purity of social order, but instead pervert the high mandate they have received, at times quite atrociously. Offenses or deceitful acts committed by civil servants in the performance of their duties deserve a more-serious moral and legal punishment than in other cases, for nobody suspects them, shielded as they are by the figure of the State. The higher their position, the greater prestige they enjoy and the more serious the offense of prevarication because this is an abusive profit of public good faith.

Not all moral faults deserve the same reprisal, because the higher an individual's public station, the greater will be the repercussion of his acts and words. This occurs with demagogy, for example. I have no doubt that in all places and at all moments of the history of Mankind there have been individuals guilty of using their political discourses to incite the masses to commit acts of violence or terrorism. In more than one case, these acts have materialized into atrocious crimes, while the intellectual authors of such deeds remain unpunished.

Really, corruption reaches unbearable limits in any place in the world where there are dishonest politicians and corrupt judges.

When can we consider that a politician has become corrupted?—when ethical laxity leads him to the practice of influence-peddling, and to demagogic discourse whose aim is to deceive the people with the sole objective of winning votes; when the desire for public service turns into a mere screen to hide money transactions and the ambition for personal power; when political parties put party power before the well-being of the people, and when their messages and actions do not have the aim of defending citizens' rights but of keeping peaks of power divorced from true community interests. Political immorality could also exist if there are attempts to intimidate or put pressure on judges or to twist the workings of justice through veiled threats against magistrates, or when high-level civil servants make public personal declarations expressing their opinion on facts that have not yet been judged.

The pressures of the press, when it carries out exhaustive campaigns against people whose supposed offenses have not been legally proven, are also a nonethical form of intervention into Courts of Justice, whose Magistrates could make prejudgments, and thus lose the necessary impartiality for justice to truly manifest itself. The independence of judicial power is an indispensable requisite for the administration of justice. However, these legal careers should remain completely protected from any political interference, which unfortunately does not occur.

The judicial system is based on the good faith of those who participate in the "social contract," and if this good faith is broken, the system collapses. Also deplorable are the scant possibilities a citizen has to successfully sue in practice for the possible abuses or errors that judges, or judicial or civil servants, can commit, in view of the power they wield over such a citizen's liberty and reputation. It would be impossible for a person affected by the illicit conduct of a judge to attempt to denounce such an error without having gathered documentary evidence of it. In any case, this would be quite improbable unless the victim were to become a spy or play the role of policeman. If, for example, in the unfortunate case of a judge being bribed, it would be hard to find evidence to verify the facts, and the perpetrators would remain indefinitely unpunished. If a lawyer acted wrongly with his own client by, for instance, taking undue advantage of privileged client–attorney information, who would the client go to for help? to another lawyer? In the field of suppositions, I imagine that it cannot be easy for one lawyer to make a claim against a colleague, or for a judge to take action against another, but if my supposition is the fruit of my ignorance of the legal system, I apologize from the outset. Nevertheless, I do believe that there are many people with similar doubts who would like to see greater transparency in the sphere of government, judicial, and political powers that are susceptible to corruption.

The most-elementary ethics demand absolute transparency in the administration of justice, and this does not exist for a person who does not understand law. I am speaking about clear transparency for what each power in the State does, and for what reasons they do it; crystalline transparency for the high authorities of the Government and the members of Congress. People need to always be well informed about what they do, how they live, and in what types of businesses or activities they are involved.

In a democracy, the people should not be left with the disturbing sensation of an inquisitorial power, both anonymous and silent, that rapidly silences all critics and attempts at unmasking the corruption in the upper echelons and that, instead of facilitating it, makes it difficult to the extreme, rendering this unmasking almost impossible.

Nor can they suspect that a blind and capricious justice imprisons honest people and never punishes, on the other hand, a certain type of delinquency, without even giving a rational explanation of the facts.

In some countries, humble people have the unpleasant experience that their judicial system forbids them to represent themselves in court, thereby obliging them to retain a lawyer. This effectively deprives the dispossessed of the right to fight personally for their own rights. Who better to defend himself from an accusation than the accused? Is it moral to deprive a person of the right to defend himself? Is it ethical to oblige an innocent person to be defended by a professional who perhaps does not believe in his innocence?

Finally, it is logical that one should be free to choose between either representing oneself or being represented by a lawyer. Otherwise, many innocent people and others whose rights have been injured or harmed run the risk of not being able to protect themselves because they lack the necessary economic resources; or these resources run out in mid-trial, and the case will then be won by the party with greater economic means. I believe that, from a moralistic point of view, a system that brings a citizen to trial and then prevents him from defending himself or taking on his own defense in that trial is highly questionable. Nor is it ethical to keep a veil of obscurity and silence over what happens within the government, and hide the real motivations that lead them to make one decision or another. Since these decisions dramatically affect the lives of all citizens, the practice of "state secrets" should be eliminated except for those which concern a country's national security.

It is deplorable that a government, for reasons of political will, should manipulate information in order to lull people's consciousness to sleep and thus keep them passive and contented, even though they are really being cheated out of an improved quality of life. Such is also the case of the government that covers up certain scandals and magnifies others, instead of making them equally transparent to all for the good of the people—governments that act on political party orders decided upon in secret meetings, while never presenting the true reasons for their acts.

It is shameful and intrinsically perverse that a state should be controlled by a circle of power that is divorced from service to the people, alien to people's real needs and interests, bent exclusively on increasing its own power and control, and thus enlarging the number of citizens who support its regime.

Each day, common man receives lessons in either integrity or corruption from the environment around him, particularly from the acts of representative bodies, among which the state occupies a prominent position. Unfortunately, it sometimes happens that the acts of high-level civil servants become suspect only because of a lack of any true, complete disclosure about their actions. The most alarming things are the covert signals that certain governments give out when there is some kind of contradictory action, for instance, not practicing what one preaches, or when the right hand ignores what the left hand is doing. Most people have a tendency to believe that if a government has been legitimately elected, all its actions will be "good," without on the whole questioning those actions. Thus it is possible for truly inappropriate types of behavior to be perceived as being normal. Through a sort of moral laxity, there are countries in which murder and corruption have come to be considered inevitable, merely a fact of normal life. In other places, everybody is accustomed to the water, food, and air being polluted. No one blinks an eye about those babies whose blood and brains are poisoned with lead or other substances every time they breathe, nor are they alarmed about the elderly who die prematurely through toxic substances in the air and in the food.

There are statutes that severely punish a person involved in a car accident, or one who could not muster the funds needed to cover a check, yet are indifferent to the offenses of air pollution, or the contamination of the seas, rivers, and our food. Perhaps millions of people throughout the world fall sick or die through polluted or adulterated foodstuffs or medicines, but there are hardly any punishments for those responsible for that.

What type of control is there on restaurants, for example? In practice, nobody knows the true sanitary state of their foodstuffs, and cosmetic appearance is given precedence over content. People's health and well-being demand that each establishment serving food should undergo a significant number of periodic surprise sanitary examinations, but this happens only in highly developed countries. If we applied the principle of transparency to the food situation, it would seem most logical that a list of sanitary inspections carried out in such establishments should be regularly published in the press. The corresponding authorities should specify in detail all the requirements, raise the level of these requirements, indicate the kitchen equipment required and appropriate methods of food storage a restaurant should have, as well as setting hygiene standards for the acquisition of foodstuffs and for people who handle them.

It is inexcusable that the result is the public becoming accustomed to poisoning from the atmosphere and through polluted foodstuffs. The authorities' permissiveness in this respect is not only a manifest immorality but also a criminal attack on the whole population and should be severely punished.

Murkiness or transparency, that is the question.

For example, there are countries where there is a national will towards transparency. Whether this is attained in actual fact or not is another matter. There are democracies in which whatever a President does is continually displayed in a very favorable light, as with his family, the sports he practices, the hours he works, the type of life he leads, as well as the lifestyle of his chief collaborators, who should also periodically undergo drug testing and offer public disclosure on any circumstance that might put their reputation or behavior in doubt.

If public action is to be at a moral optimum, it should always be clear and radiant. Citizens should have rapid access to clear and concise information of all that the government does or does not do, to thus do away with the cloud of mystery and uncertainty that invariably envelops the economy, finance, taxes, and political and juridical action.

Citizen X must be perfectly clear as to why a judge sentences him even though he believes himself to be innocent, or is in fact innocent; or why another magistrate abstains from sentencing the one who damaged his honorability or stole his personal goods. Why is murderer A sentenced to life in prison while murderer B is lightly sentenced and released? The legal system should be made comprehensible to the citizens and not shirk its responsibilities by hiding behind the cryptic web of the legal code since this reveals a lack of respect for the people. And the people should be able to understand the logic behind judicial authority when it elaborates its sentences, for if the system is closed, mysterious, authoritarian, omnipotent, and disrespectful of personal reputation and dignity, the individual finds himself in the position of a dwarf being brutally squashed by the fist of an insensitive, incomprehensible giant with the supposed aim of "rehabilitating" him for an infraction of which he was never aware, mainly because he was not given the means to find out about it.

It has always been said that one should accept the sentences of justice, and this is obvious. Nevertheless, I wonder if such acceptance should be a blind submission or enslavement to the mandate of an institution that has the monopoly on justice and the necessary muscle to enforce its mandates, or whether such acceptance should instead come from a personal conviction that justice has in fact been done; a conviction that emanates from the rational examination of a logical, clearly comprehensible process. It would be reasonable to expect the latter, for if things are not so, the individual will feel himself a victim of the police and of legal bullies. He will feel squashed by a mechanism he does not understand. Even though he may be guilty, rehabilitation would be improbable inasmuch as he would not manage to acknowledge his own deeds as criminal. In the name of ethics, justice should spare no effort in being more explicit with those affected by its sentences, so that it appears not just as a punishing, vengeful entity, since with such a reputation it would hinder its rehabilitative ability. One also takes great risk in denouncing unpleasant facts without supporting evidence, since one runs the risk of being sent to prison for slander.

However, the truth is that no single individual can take on the functions of a private investigator, so that it should be up to the police to look for the evidence that could support criminal charges. But for the reasons given above, no one dares do this, and the only ones who benefit from this situation are the delinquents. It is very likely that thousands of crimes committed in front of eye witnesses go unpunished, because of the fear of those who witnessed the crimes but did not dare to report them. Thus, there is the paradox that society never punishes certain crimes that it does not hear about, therefore, the delinquent is effectively "rewarded" by retaining the image of a law-abiding citizen. Covert corruption is the worst type of all, because no one notices it and its protagonists remain anonymous, profiting from the fruits of their crimes. From a moralistic standpoint, the most-serious outcome is for the social order to become gradually accustomed to the most-insidious types of corrupt conduct, since at a given moment they become so commonplace and habitual that people are no longer shocked by them. This implies a process of "lowering one's sights," that is, progressively lowering standards to increase general permissiveness. This usually goes hand in glove with immorality. What I am attempting to do with this book is to raise standards to their rightful position, although many may think that this is a utopian or exaggerated standard. The law of man will permit the great majority of cases of corruption to go unpunished, but in due time, natural law will summon the depraved before the court of Nature, which penalizes any arbitrary imbalance caused by those who, for example, have stolen something from their fellows or have wrongfully taken what is not theirs. What could such a punishment be like? It would simply be the return to equilibrium that had been altered by the transgressor who, having found a comfort level, had done so at the expense of, and in violation of, the law of egalitarian equivalence. The maxim, "he who sins, pays" is really a moral one which implies that justice does not come from human vengeance but from natural harmony. Eternal law says that one will be dispossessed of goods or personal possessions in the same proportion to those one has wrongfully or incorrectly appropriated.

Let us hope that Mankind's progressive corruption never leads him to have to change the name of the species, to the "Inhuman Race." The condition we now consider normal may inadvertently correspond to an advanced level of degeneration, loss, or atrophy of man's higher qualities, so that ethics, or the lack thereof, is merely a logical consequence of either a consciousness that is developed or one that is superatrophied. Corruption is unlikely to occur in the individual who, having transcended himself, sublimates his libido and forms his own character with the sword of his will power and nourishes himself on the transcendental values of life.

Depravity is normal in people of weak character who do not possess the necessary strength to withstand corrupting influences, or the necessary temperament to absorb and develop higher values. Self-indulgent people display increased permissiveness with regard to their own actions, and this inherited defect is fertile ground for the seed of depravity and vice. All corruption is based on the superatrophy of the character and will power, which leads one to seek easy gain, the contemporary hallmark in a society that has been weakened by pleasure-seeking and consumer permissiveness.

Mediocrity

To be mediocre means "to live as a gray man," to behave like a common man, to adapt to the parameters of the general norm, that is, to be normal in the statistical sense of the word. Another definition of "mediocre" is: "to be of little merit, verging on bad," or "the state of an object between large and small, between good and bad." This latter expression perhaps coincides with the most commonly attributed meaning, the one that should most concern the human being. In fact, no one is unhappier today than the one who is classified as "mediocre." It connotes an ambiguous individual who is neither good nor bad, who has neither more nor fewer defects or virtues than the rest of his fellows. Despite the fact that nobody likes being mediocre, it is true that society somehow grants privileges to, or otherwise rewards, this state by exalting its convenience. On the other hand, the social order covertly repudiates people who stand out from the average and are different, without considering whether this distance from the social order indicates a higher or lower standard of value to that of common mortals, which should be a decisive factor when one is classifying various types of behavior.

It would seem that society fears the individual as such and would wish to unify all people in an indivisibly cohesive mass, with a common identity to be easily handled. Every day there are various examples of how the individual is sacrificed for the sake of the collective, without, of course, specifying which collective or what is the caliber of the individual thus sacrificed, inasmuch as this is a matter of "persons," and it is supposed that they are all alike. There is no mention as to how clean or depraved a certain group may be or how transparently healthy and virtuous might be the possible victims of that group's wrongdoings. In the case of these victims, it would be considered merely a matter of throwing "pearls to swine," a diabolical custom that has been popular since time immemorial.

We are continually being told that "the majority rules"; we are admonished against the perils of "egoism," this expression invariably being pejoratively applied, without anybody ever acknowledging any form of higher egoism, or transcendental, ethical individualism whose aim is the spiritual evolution of the individual and not lucre or personal pillaging. We are advised to behave altruistically, to "dedicate ourselves to and take pleasure in the well-being of others," without realizing that this demands cognitive discrimination, inasmuch as the word "others" includes all manner of cunning and perverse scoundrels, whose own good is based on criminal success and who would transform us all into accomplices should we help them. This is because we would thus be favoring their perverse designs. We would be coauthors of the crimes, offenses, or the illegal acts they committed, should we lend our help.

Society tries to convince us that we must "do good without considering to whom," which from the idealistic point of view sounds great. People try to justify the goodness of this maxim by attributing it in some way to Jesus Christ, but I confess my heart feels doubt that he could have said exactly this. I think that the expression "do good but consider carefully to whom" is much fairer, although surely it will not be so pleasing to ears that have been adulterated by long demagogic speeches of various types.

"Sugar-coated" phrases usually produce addiction in people, who somehow feel purified, elevated, or absolved of their sins by the simple act of participating, albeit passively, in any humanitarian campaign. What is true is that such people do not usually distinguish the distance between the well-intentioned and those who in fact carry out whatever they have decided. It is only in the process of the materialization of good intentions that the individual manages to weigh the magnitude of the necessary effort, and it is there that the "sugar-coated" slogan becomes soured and the saying that "anything valuable costs a lot" appears in bold relief. The more valuable something is, the greater is the effort or resources needed to obtain it. Conversely, the more vulgar and devalued something is, the more easily available will it be. This is the case of garbage, which is of negative value because one has to pay for its disposal.

The mediocre person believes in easy profits, and is usually addicted to gambling in the hope of a stroke of luck.

He is a passive consumer of vulgarities, whether these be material, such as merchandise, or intangibles, such as with ideas. He lacks individuality, character, and will power; therefore, he will always go along with the majority, convinced as he is that the truth is there. He will be dreaming of somehow manipulating those who have something that he wants in order to appropriate what belongs to them, but he, himself, will be incapable of genuine effort, perseverance, and sacrifice.

Mediocrity, it has been said, may correlate with the simplicity and poverty of the spirit, and for this reason, it is pleasing to the Creator, ("blessed be the poor in spirit, for theirs shall be the Kingdom of Heaven"). Accordingly, supreme happiness would lie in contenting oneself with being just one of the masses, subsisting in anonymity and subjected to the dictates of the majority. It would mean caring for the benefit of others even at one's own expense, increasing efficiency in the role as an obedient consumer, uncomplainingly paying progressively higher taxes, obediently getting into debt with the financial system without stopping to think how much the interest amounts to, passively internalizing political and advertising slogans, and procreating a reasonable number of future citizens who will in turn become submissive consumers, thus letting the system keep up its rhythm of growth.

Of course, this will also mean "culturizing oneself" in accordance with what is fashionable, so as not to be dubbed "outmoded," and not to challenge the dominant modes of thought of the epoch. In addition, there would be the obligation to believe one is happy and that the system really works indefatigably to raise the human condition. In the philosophy of mediocrity, there is no worse sin than to stand out and rise above the shapeless masses.

To be intelligent, conscious, and virtuous is an unspeakable sin.

To dare to think differently is a lack of respect.

To repudiate hypocrisy or speak the truth cannot be tolerated.

To earn a lot of money is an insult to the poor.

To be happy is an unacceptable provocation.

To possess the higher values of the spirit is suspect.

Not to have children is suspect and not to be trusted.

To live in isolation becomes something questionable.

Indeed, the mediocre person is content to be just one more little cog in a huge machine, and he bases his security on this, rejecting any idea, attempt, or suggestion to become independent, in the sense of attaining mental and emotional autonomy in obtaining some sort of higher achievement as an individual. He is afraid to take on responsibilities and will endeavor to run away from them, preferring instead to always take orders. Although, if he is forced to occupy a position of authority, he will most likely abuse the power granted him. Servile with the powerful and arrogant with the weak, he will generally drift to envy and resentment. He always chooses the line of least effort and never wishes to commit himself to long-term projects.

Mediocrity is an assault on the eternal law that demands the gradual, progressive spiritual evolution of the individual. This evolution is a mandate that the mediocre person will stubbornly avoid, since he somehow glimpses that it is a path for great men and that it therefore entails considerable effort and sacrifice. It also requires that he take responsibility for himself and stop being an inert, shapeless, anonymous creature.

The mediocre one offends the divine spark, and is an offense to the Creator, because by ignoring this precious treasure and the responsibility it entails, he becomes interested only in coinciding with the flock. This flock is inevitably destined to repeat the same existential ritual as did its predecessors, century upon century, namely, to feed, to accumulate power, to copulate, to reproduce, to dream, to decline, and to die, leaving behind a legacy of psychological obligation to their inheritors to behave similarly.

The mediocre person is an unfulfilled reactionary, a half-man who, obsessed with ever swimming along with the current, will inevitably thwart the purpose of his own existence by never committing himself to the mandate of individual evolution laid down by the Creator. His inertia and passivity lead him always to seek a low-level consensual model with the mass in order to avoid the work of thinking for himself and taking responsibility for his own decisions.

The person who always navigates through the waters of vulgarity, coarseness, and permissiveness, instead of dignifying his own inner spiritual essence, slides down to a subhuman level of existence as far as transcendental values are concerned. He is a true egoist in the worst sense of the word, one who deprives the world of any higher contribution that would signal his own integration in society as a highly developed human individual. He prefers instead to remain like a deadweight on society.

Inertial existence has always been the main feature of the great majority of our species, and when we say "majority rules," we really refer to the undeniable fact that we will have to continue being enslaved by the inertia of the masses. This impulse does not drive us towards a higher spiritual and moral life, but rather towards materialistic barbarism whose chief slogan seems to be the permissive consumption of goods and pleasures. What prevails is a semi-human state, or even an inhuman one in which the big fish swallows up the little fish, while maintaining an image of humanism and civilization.

To be content to be merely one more among the millions of inhabitants of our planet and to tamely be subsumed into the great inertial mass, means to go against the only real form of progress there is, namely, that which eliminates all social distinction by means of individual spiritual development, thus uniting people through their higher consciousness and not on the basis of their social station. Tolerance, fraternal love, mutual respect, justice, and the general practice of the highest transcendental values can be possible only through an inner transformation of the individual, who will freely relate to other individuals, yet never through the mass movements that wipe out individuality, abuse the rights of minorities, and activate the worst characteristics of the species by creating psychological masses. As is only natural, the process of spiritual transformation can only be initiated freely, without any type of coercion whatsoever, but only through each person's own desire, sovereign will, and comprehension. In order for this to occur, however, a lot of water will have to flow under the bridges of a hypocritical society, one alienated by false values and made lethargic by the contradictory and ulteriorly motivated mandates of various power groups who view people as merely obedient consumers, useful "tools" on whose shoulders to ascend to ever higher economic or political peaks.

For the moment, mediocrity is multiplying at full speed and is an authority over common man, preventing him from finding the path of true higher ethics and morals.

Parasitical Vampirism

In defining vampirism as "the practice of exploiting others," one dictionary draws an analogy between blood-sucking bats and certain types of persons. In folklore, the vampire is a corpse who rises from his coffin at night, appearing in the shape of a bat to feed on people's blood. The belief in vampires dates back to ancient times, and was expressed in the 1897 novel, *Dracula*, by the English writer Bram Stoker. The story takes place in Transylvania and relates the tale of one Count Dracula. It is an alarming fact that the oldest fossil of a bat, the *Icaronycteris index*, dates back 60,000,000 years, just after the dinosaurs had become extinct. The largest known bat is the *Pteropus vampyrus* of Java. Its wingspan is around five feet and it is sixteen inches long. The smallest, *Pipistrella nanus* from Central Africa, measures about one-and-a-half inches and has a wingspan of four-and-a-half inches.

The bat is the only mammal that can fly, and it is an eminently nocturnal creature that rests in hiding during the day and flies by night to feed on insects, fruit, and flowers. There are also some carnivorous and even omnivorous bats that attack small amphibians, birds, rats, and other bats. There are three types of authentic vampire bats, which live in the tropics: *Desmodus*, *Diphylla*, and *Diaemus*, which live entirely on sucking the blood of cattle, horses, pigs, and occasionally human beings, therefore being a real parasite (this is said of the animal or plant that feeds on the organic substances contained in the body of another living being, with which it has either temporary or permanent contact). It is likely that this is the semantic origin given by the dictionary definition of the word "vampirism."

The English verb "to sponge" also describes the action of living off others, of being a parasite to their creative energies.

It would not be adventurous to suppose that a phenomenon found in flying mammals could not also appear analogously in the mammal *sapiens*. However, I am not referring to cases of madmen who needed to drink human blood (and plenty have been discovered in many countries) but to those people who invariably manage to maliciously avoid the honest, patient effort required for any important achievement and even to satisfy one's own needs. In other words, those who "sponge" off others resort to the manipulation of their fellows by means of dishonest tactics with the aim of subsisting not by their own effort and creative power, but by maliciously profiting from other people's simplicity or goodness.

I also refer to those who contribute nothing to Mankind, but who manage to suck the creative energies of someone or a group of people, with the aim of living through them. Such people are like the *quintral* (a parasitic plant which entwines itself around the trunk and branches of trees) in the manner in which they burrow into people, families, and various social groups to absorb their energies without contributing anything in exchange. Of course, such behavior is not the fruit of any conscious decision or planning, but is an instinctive behavior that perhaps obeys the order given by a genetic aberration with remote antecedents.

The phenomenon of slavery unequivocally corresponds to the creation of a parasitic caste, the slave-owners, who subsisted and prospered on the energies of their slaves. We can see a parallel to this today in the dependence of people and countries on international financial power. Any type of exploitation is actually a vampiric-parasitic phenomenon in which the upper crust feeds off the base.

There is also a different case in which geniuses, artists, poets, or reformers are exploited to the point of destruction by receiving breadline stipends from institutions, companies, or people who believe they can buy anything with an ounce of gold, not realizing the tremendous value of the cultural heritage such privileged beings contribute. The parasitic caste today controls most people's lives through the manipulation of usurious capital, whose interest corresponds to the energetic blood on which they feed. At the individual level, there are many who, instead of creating values that can reach a price in the free market, try to worm their way psychically and emotionally into creative persons so as to feed off them. We know that in 1772 Franz Mesmer discovered a type of energy that had an extraordinary influence on the human body, which he called *animal magnetism,* through which he carried out extraordinary cures. This aroused the enmity of doctors who then did everything possible to discredit him. Today, no one doubts that the human body possesses a sort of magnetic energy of its own, and that this can be increased, decreased, shared, or sucked.

Doctor Harold Saxton Burr, in his book *Electric Patterns of Life* or *Blueprint for Immortality,* shows how matter is organized into electric fields that are the bearers of the vital energy that organize the Universe, and which control all phenomena of existence. He successfully submitted it to rigorous scientific research for more than thirty years. If we study Saxton Burr's experiments, Mesmer's animal magnetism appears as one more expression of a universal energy that is the matrix from which physical existence springs. People's health and vitality depend upon the potency of the electromagnetic field of their bodies, which can decline or increase, and can also be absorbed by a vampire-receptor. Indeed, a considerable part of Mankind leads an overtly or covertly parasitic existence, subsisting on the benefits derived from their emotional manipulation of stronger, more creative people, who are usually the targets of envy and resentment. The phenomenon of human vampirism assumes various forms, one of which is the direct absorption of a person's animal magnetism, which often occurs in "mismatched" relationships between couples, in which one party exploits the other by feeding off his or her energies without giving anything back in exchange. Emotional frigidity usually conceals a desire to absorb energy and also a repugnance at giving up any energy, this being the typical behavior of the vampire. This type of behavior can sometimes be observed in the elderly with respect to children, and in sick people with respect to those in good health. Normally, people relate to one another in a balanced manner, there being a healthy, equivalent magnetic exchange in reference to giving and receiving.

The sharing of magnetic energy does not necessarily imply an egalitarian exchange, for this force is a medium of codified information that infiltrates with the force of a mandate. If a sick person shares with a healthy individual, this latter will give up part of his healthy magnetism to the former, who offers *sick magnetism* in exchange; that is, a means of irradiation and contact by which the disorder from which he suffers is passed on or deposited. Thus, there is a *nonegalitarian* transaction, inasmuch as one party offers *health* and receives *sickness* in exchange for it; whereas one offers illness and receives health in exchange. One has been harmed and the other benefits, and no one is any the wiser.

As may readily be understood, magnetic transactions assume the most diverse forms, but people can possess an essentially clean and healthy corporeal magnetism or an essentially filthy and sick one. Thus, magnetic contamination habitually occurs through infection.

The crowds that gather in some place for a specific activity project a strong magnetic field, which is equal to the aggregate of its members and which usually represents a dangerous source of contamination because of the lack of moral excellence of those members.

When science fully recognizes the evidence of human magnetism and its effects, then what will be appreciated is the immorality that exists in the fact of someone exploiting other people so as to steal their healthy magnetism or to use one's fellows as a garbage dump for purposes of eliminating one's own sickened magnetism. Science does not create the laws of Nature but is limited merely to discovering them. Therefore, the present unbalanced exchange of magnetism is just as immoral as it will be when science no longer ignores a phenomenon that has been demonstrated time and again, but which pride, hypocrisy, and vested interests prevent the scientific community from acknowledging.

The scientific community always starts by denying anything that surpasses its conventional limits, and will accept it only when faced with ridicule, such as when the evidence becomes overwhelming. The fact that no one notices these mechanisms, including the person responsible for them, does not excuse people before Nature, since the fact of taking something in an inequitable and unbalanced manner is an attack against natural ethics.

Parasites are these beings which produce nothing, finding it more convenient to survive at the expense of their host's creativity and labor. Human parasites usually contribute nothing to either the family, the State, or to Mankind, but they themselves manage to survive quite well. I refer to those people who, being healthy, normal, and not elderly, never bother to develop their own creativity or talent to do anything important in life, to earn a good income, or to contribute something positive to society. I also refer to those who, despite the fact that they are perfectly capable, nevertheless pass before their fellows as mediocre, handicapped, or incapable of taking advantage of their situation.

Another type of vampirism is that which concerns people who live by usurping or attacking the value produced by others, to blackmail them emotionally with the aim of obliging them to renounce or shed part of their goods to the benefit of the aggressor. Such parasites usually disguise themselves as highly honest, generous people in order to conceal their maneuvers, which are their techniques of "absorbing" their victims. To this end, they generally take advantage of public good faith by using sophisms created with much astuteness. A sophism is a syllogistic distortion or captious argument with which the speaker endeavors to make a false statement look true.

To illustrate this technique, I will briefly list certain classical techniques of covert vampirism.

1. To provoke envy and resentment in the masses with the aim of unifying them and manipulating them to better obtain their votes.

2. At the level of the couple when one of the two, with the aim of manipulating his/her companion, endeavors to inculcate feelings of guilt that make the victim feel ashamed, in order to thus keep him/her perfectly under control.

3. At the political level, the malicious use of syllogisms related to wealth versus poverty, with the aim of making those with money ashamed of it and feel wretchedly guilty on account of it, thus placing themselves at the mercy of the agitators.

4. At the level of the business enterprise, the implementation of campaigns designed to coerce, debase, or

destroy the business owner by using syllogistic arguments based on "exploitation," "excessive profits," the
lack of "social sensitivity," and others, all with the
overt or covert intention of stripping the owner of his
belongings.

There are also various overt forms of vampirism, as for
example:

1. The theft of intellectual property, exploiting legal loopholes or insufficient measures of protection.

2. The theft of scientific information, industrial processes,
   and diverse technologies.

3. The theft of lucrative confidential company information.

4. The plagiarism of words, ideas, and the works of
   others that are recycled and retouched to pass them off
   as one's own.

5. Usury, as in the case of a person who wishes to obtain
   an apartment with a 30-year mortgage from the bank
   and is obliged to pay the equivalent price of four
   apartments. This has become normal in many places.

6. Expropriatory taxes, considering under this heading
   those which in most countries are feudal in their
   proportions, and which oblige the taxpayer to work for
   free for almost six months in each year, just in order to
   pay his annual levy; this obligation is an affront to
   property rights, inasmuch as the owner of a house is
   obliged to pay a sum close to the value of rent in order
   to live in his own house; and the owner of a car to
   annually pay out 4 percent or more of the car's value
   in order to be able to drive it.

7. Hiring manual labor for miserable wages.

Within vampirism (the emotional manipulation used as a weapon of psychological persuasion against which there is no known defense), resides a knowledge as old as humanity itself. However, its true scope and techniques remain jealously hidden, and the blind masses, as always, ignore or deny that this is possible. This implies a serious intrusion into one's inner space and of people's individual liberty, but no one is bothered about this immorality.

The scant human rights which are currently in force do not protect us, even in a democracy, from the violation of our inner space. This violation refers to a sort of psychological terrorism employed by certain governments who, because they possess the legal monopoly of organized enforcement, daily transgress the rights of minorities, or exert subliminal influence over citizens' minds by sending out political messages designed to put pressure on people's consciences. And all this, for what? Invariably, it is to intimidate or coerce people with the aim of exploiting them. This is why a large sector of Mankind lives off of the rest, by manipulating their emotions and subjugating their behavior using tactics like threatening them, promising them unlimited pleasure, or making them feel guilty. This has always been so, is so, and will continue to be so unless there is an evolution in people's consciousness through individual development and perfectioning. The parasitic sector of the species does not create any kind of value; it merely profits dishonestly from the value that is created by others. In one way or another, we daily experience evidence that we are being either overtly or covertly vampirized, although we do not know how to recognize this phenomenon by name and we therefore give it clever labels to euphemize the harsh reality behind it. Really, most aspects of vampirism are totally unknown, or else they are camouflaged beneath quite legal activities. Anyone who accepts to pay excessive interest on a bank loan is vampirized on a daily basis over many years—

perhaps for his entire life—and can only helplessly watch how his initial debt grows instead of diminishing, after paying for a long time. He who fights without results against injustice, negligence, or fiscal prepotency is being legally parasitized. The victim of an inefficient or unjust legal system, of a corrupt judge, or of a ruthless lawyer, is being legally "vampirized." If a citizen of a democratic nation is subjected to the payment of disproportionately high taxes that he had never previously approved, and does not know what purposes they are destined for, or how they are administered, he is being legally "vampirized" through the "tyranny of the majority." Someone who does not receive a just salary, fee, or wages for his work, is being parasitized. Likewise, the worker who cheats or deceives his employer as far as quality or amount of work agreed upon is concerned becomes a parasite himself.

I regret not being able to develop such a fascinating subject in more depth. I trust that intelligent, unbiased individuals will reflect on the matter and draw their own conclusions. As for the rest, whatever I say in this work is all the same, because they will understand nothing, perhaps because they prefer not to do so. To act in accordance with the highest ethics is neither comfortable nor easy; it requires one to understand the genesis of sin and corruption, in order to possess the motivation that will lead one to develop the necessary internal fortitude to fight against injustice and immorality in defense of transcendental values. However, one must acknowledge that in view of the magnitude of the goals pursued, the sacrifice required becomes insignificant.

Self-Indulgence and Self-Pity

It is customary of a weak character for a person to make great demands on one's fellows, and at the same time display an extremely low level of self-demand. Such individuals have the vice of self-indulgence, a form of permissiveness that leads to moral degradation because they lack the requisite strength of character and will power to observe the golden rule: "do not do unto others as you would not have them do unto you." Quite the contrary, they use a very different yardstick to measure their fellows than the one they apply to evaluate themselves.

Any waste or annulment of one's own faculties is an important moral fault because it signifies the squandering of one's own possibilities and the act of depriving Mankind of the significant contribution that could result had there been an integration of a superior individual within the social group. It is also a way of shirking the evolutive mandate of life. It cannot be denied that a human being's first duty is to develop himself, for, as I said before, the Creator leaves us unfinished. Hence, each individual must take responsibility for himself and fulfill the great work of his transformation into a true human being, for we are only half-human as we are. We are all born equal and become differentiated through the merit of our own personal effort. The inequality we see in the world is due to the fact that some fight for their own perfectioning, whereas others are lazy or indolent and at times hateful, showing more interest in envying successful people than in growing and developing themselves.

Certain congenital faculties are created in each being, and other faculties remain in a latent state until the individual himself develops them, which is each person's primary and most sacred duty. As unfinished beings, we lack the capacity to visualize a higher ethical behavior, one that is born of a comprehension of the rights of each living entity, and of how these are harmoniously interrelated within Nature so as to maintain the cosmic plan of existence. The moral rules with which we are familiar are not consciously and voluntarily accepted by the individual, but are rather forcibly injected into him by means of an irresistible social pressure. Only very few individuals in the world act correctly through an internal mandate that is born of their own reflective *consciousness.* There are very few who individually choose the path of righteousness absolutely freely and voluntarily, without any coercive pressure. However, these are the only ones who will continue to act correctly if, in the event of a social catastrophe, punishment for immoral, criminal, or illicit deeds were to be waived. The rest, in the pursuit of mere lucre or personal gratification, sure of not being punished, would transgress the limits of ethics and virtue. In order for any individual to act in an authentically moral way, his actions must be conscious, free, and voluntary, and not the result of cerebral programming carried out by an external authority. We would have nothing to gain from a world of "ethical automatons," just the opposite—we would regress considerably in terms of our hominal quality.

The fact is that on this planet there is an abundance of "immoral automatons," who are a predatory humanoid species that can exterminate life on the planet.

However, the remedy does not consist of reprogramming them in the reverse. Rather, it consists in promoting the creation of a new society through the implementation of an educational system which will permit the development of the superior individual consciousness, through the process of a non-memoristic learning, to be carried out in a state of higher awakening—a process by which comprehension and judgment are given predominance over mere information. To this end, however, it would be necessary to somehow eradicate the disproportionate influence of those multinational corporations which view man merely as a potentially obedient consumer, a necessary artifact or tool with which to cement the basis of power groups. When individual vigilic consciousness is developed, they would lose their influence to manipulate people's minds. It is therefore, logical to expect that they would tenaciously oppose this type of liberty.

The educational process should be defended against any type of pressure or interference from economic or political interests, with the aim that children may develop absolutely freely and have a real chance to choose what they individually desire. One should remember that while it is true that the mind may be enchained, the spirit, which is the being, grants access only to the individual himself, and it is the sacred precinct of free will and individual judgment. Man will be truly free, virtuous, and morally adequate when he manages to attain his development and spiritual perfectioning. This is the great challenge of the 21st century.

Self-indulgence, a vice or a disease of the character, also implies a malicious profiting from this disorder. It generally leads to self-pity, which is a psychological attitude whereby the individual visualizes himself as a victim, and dramatizes this role in his interpersonal relationships, ending up, deliberately or not, taking undue profit from other people by manipulating their emotions.

In this book I often refer to "weak" people. I should point out that I do not indicate those who suffer from some organic or mental disorder, but those who, because of their negative mental, emotional, passive, and parasitical condition, weaken their character through nonaction, their passions, their vices, and their destructive inner disposition. The origins of this condition can often be traced to a childish fixation caused by a great amount of rage against their parents that they have not managed to overcome. This leads those thus affected to the madness of unconsciously seeking "to be handicapped" as persons, to then blame their parents for wrongly fulfilling their duties. They may also develop a blind rebellion, the result of arrogance, which drives them to gradual self-destruction. It also happens that they act like this as a simple reaction to the horror of organized, patient, painstaking effort.

In any case, the self-indulgent person is incapable of voluntarily disciplining himself in order to become a higher being, and blows through life like a leaf in the wind, which is moved, in this case, at the impulse of the stimuli that originate in the masses. He usually has poor relationships with people because of his intolerance, inasmuch as he demands of others all that he avoids demanding of himself. He is critical and aggressive, prone to envy and resentment. Although he may possess excellent personal qualities, he refuses to develop them or use them, but prefers to subsist in mediocrity, taking advantage of the kindness of others.

He is a recalcitrant, "unfinished" being, and the exaggerated inertia of his lifestyle leads him to a destiny that is incongruent with a being who is the bearer of the divine spark. His permissiveness leads him easily to immoral types of behavior, to which he is either unaware of its immorality, or he does not consider it so. One should flee from self-indulgence because it is the fatal enemy of apprentice man, whose challenge in life is to take the tools of his intelligence, decision, and will power, to fulfill himself as a true human being. Permissiveness with oneself is also the mother of frustration, suffering, and failure, for it goes along with a lack of foresight and a lack of executive power.

It is important to consider that the self-indulgent person, like many others, is not generally a limited individual who has been prevented from obtaining the best opportunity, but that, like everyone else, he is the faithful result of his own actions, and the frustration that usually pursues him is no more than the logical result of his prior behavior.

Living for One's Image

As I said above, the individual's first duty is "to live for himself" as concerns his spiritual self, the divine spark, the being, or the spirit, for only in this way will he be able to attain human excellence. Far from being a selfish attitude, in accordance with the usual connotation of this word, "living for oneself" is a path of renunciation of the passional "I." It is also a path on which the individual has to go through a long process of sublimating his inferior passions and appetites until he manages to live in terms of his being and not of his personality.

Only the person who achieves this can be classified as a genuine human being. Through a painstaking work of perfectioning, he complies with the great work of completing himself as a being who is in possession of higher consciousness, the supreme attribute to which a man can aspire. He also identifies himself with capacities that the species would have when reaching the ascendant level of its possible evolution.

Although it might seem contradictory, there are only very few individuals who manage to "live for themselves" as far as the selfness of their being is concerned, for this must of necessity originate in a conscious personal inspiration, an in-depth "realizing" of one's own position and the need to change it, which occurs only during great crises.

Most men live for their image, through their image, and in terms of their image, that is, the motivation for their existence is to obtain the approval of others. All they do is to try to please or impress the masses, so that they irreversibly have to cover themselves up in the trappings of triviality and coarseness, or else echoing the audience of the moment.

The individual affected by this problem has no life of his own and only exists in terms of the acceptance or rejection of others. Thus he transforms himself into a mere projection of the common mass, continually struggling to obtain its approval and affection, a mechanism that ultimately divorces him from his "individual I" to destroy it and replace it with a "grafted I," a mere appendix of the collective psyche of society. Carl Gustav Jung defines a person as "a more or less arbitrary slice of the collective psyche."

It is of great interest to our study to understand certain concepts of Jung's regarding the individual and collectivity. We shall, therefore, begin by addressing his expression: "psychic inflation." In his work, *The I and the Unconscious*[12] Jung says:

> This definition [psychic inflation] seems accurate to me for the state in question means an extension of the personality beyond its individual limits. In a state of inflation, the psyche occupies a space which could not normally be filled. And this is only possible if one is owner of contents and properties that, through their independent existence, have to be located outside of our limits. What is located outside of ourselves belongs to another, or to all, or to no one.
>
> As psychic inflation is in no way a phenomenon produced exclusively by analysis but is recorded just as frequently in ordinary life, we could also examine it in other cases.
>
> A very common case is that of the identity, and this is not a joke, between many men and their occupation or title. It is true that my position is the activity that corresponds to me; but it is at the same time a collective factor historically shaped by the joint labor of many, and I owe its dignity solely to collective assent. Therefore, if I identify with my position or with my title, I will behave as if I myself were equivalent to the whole complex social factor that is a position, as if I were not merely

the one who holds the position but at the same time also represented the assent of society. Like this, I would have become abnormally inflated, usurping qualities that are in no way to be found within my person but that lie outside it. "I am the State." This is the motto of such people.

Jung considers that many men are no more than the dignity granted them by society, and that behind a grandiose image there hides a tiny man, the reason why such a person is so seduced by the position or by the outer mask used to this end.

Jung also holds that society usually accentuates collective qualities and rewards the mediocre, thus disfavoring people's individualism, a situation moreover made worse by the fact that if there is no liberty there can be no morality. "To live for one's image" means to give up one's own "I" to become part of the reflection shown to us by the mirror of society; to build ones' identity within this echo of the mass in the erroneous belief that "we are just that," consequently thinking, feeling, and acting in this way, totally alienated in the intrinsic essence that belongs to each of us; the sublime flower that, smothered by the weeds of mediocrity, immorality, vulgarity, coarseness, and insensitive materialism, ends by being extinguished, leaving behind only a sad, insignificant screen, doomed to roam throughout life by feeding on the recognition and approval of others and of social dignitaries.

Only the Prince of Darkness could imagine such a contradictory situation: the individual working with all his might to inflate and protect his image, which is nothingness itself, while he neglects, denies, and abandons his true being, or immortal spirit, which is everything. Disloyal to himself and being the unworthy bearer of the divine spark, he is the worst possible moral example, who like all transgressors of supreme law, will receive, at the proper time, the punishment that corresponds to his sin.

I should point out that I use the word "sin" in the sense of aggression against universal harmony, a violation of the energetic ecology of the Universe, rebellion against the Creator's designs, and noncompliance with egalitarian equivalence, which is the supreme pillar of justice.

It is not an old man sitting on the supreme throne of heaven who will take particular care to punish transgressors; it is the law of eternal harmony that directs the ordering of the Cosmos by controlling everything from the atom to man as well as the different realms of Nature.

The kingdom of the masses has turned the world into the cemetery of souls, into a huge dump for those who wander through life on this small planet in pursuit of good and happiness and who fall victim to the social monster that they themselves feed, which ruthlessly strips them of their own essence, giving them in exchange mirages, visions, fantasies, and illusions, in order to keep them seduced and subjugated so that they do not notice the death of their true egos. In accordance with this Dantesque display, the teachings and knowledge that could save man are counterfeited, ignored, hidden, or adulterated. This happens for example with Christian wisdom, which when quoted at some point in history was misinterpreted.

Let us recall certain sayings:

"Allow the little children come unto me, for theirs is the Kingdom of Heaven."

This phrase is interpreted to mean that children are imbued with a sacred aura, and some believe that the world indeed belongs to them. It is true that Jesus, who probably belonged to the Essene sect, as the *Encyclopaedia Britannica* suggests, did no more than refer to the ancient Greek mysteries of initiation in which it was held that "to be re-born, you must first die." This statement that had a psychological and spiritual meaning referred to a process of sublimation of the libido during which the undesirable "I" had to gradually die, that is, the vulgar identity of a passional, personalistic, and egotistic nature, to be replaced by the "luminous I," the individual's true spiritual essence. In this way, "children" were the "twice-born": once of a mother of flesh and blood and then of their own spiritual work. It is certain that Jesus meant these people when he said "theirs is the Kingdom of Heaven."

In the case of the Christian recommendation to "turn the other cheek" if one is struck, this has been interpreted literally in the supposition that the greatest virtue lies in tamely accepting being thrown to the lions. What is certain is that this saying concerns man's need to overcome his instinctive, passional reactions, to be able to act in a truly ethical and moral way. If the first impulse is to give back blow for blow, then proper discipline of self-control will enable one to behave more intelligently and suitably.

Again, when we read statements in the Bible such as "go ye forth and multiply," in all good reason, one cannot think that this was not a command designed to make the family grow indiscriminately, but rather to increase the number of the "twice-born," individuals who had really followed the path of evolution desired by the Creator.

The exaggerated exaltation of the virtues of childhood and youth is no more than an expression of the bitterness felt by those adults who, feeling failed and observing the vain attempts of civilization to create a society of greater moral and spiritual weight, renounce the world and hand it over in their imagination to children, in the hope that future generations will do better, without realizing that the same absurd ritual has been performed for centuries and that no new generation has to date attained a more perfect and durable existence in the spiritual and moral sense.

As long as adults continue to avoid responsibility for their lives, they will be anxiously and compulsively handing over a symbolic staff of authority of civilization to the children who paradoxically, as is only logical, are just as incomplete as the adults. That an "uncompleted" being should attempt to leave his position to one who is fundamentally a smaller copy of himself would truly seem a mockery or a tragedy. Mankind is no more conscious today than at the time of the crucifixion and has not the intelligence to recognize and follow the true great men, but is seduced by the splendor of flickering images of individuals who are mere bearers or containers of information they do not understand. These containers of information lead Mankind to the perpetuation of the deficient model of consciousness we saw above, with its great miseries and scant greatness. The others, the few who manage to be "twice-born," are ignored, disqualified, stigmatized, or persecuted. Their work is adulterated or ridiculed, while the "screen-men" copy their creations and profit from them, for after they have emptied these creations of their essential content, they recycle them in accordance with general mediocrity, baptizing them with a new name and launching them as if they were their own inventions.

The important figures of the epoch, with few exceptions, suffer from "psychic inflation," thus becoming "empty shells," imitated by those who, dazzled by the deceitful reflections of such screens, wish to become the type of person they suppose their admired personages to be.

It is easy to understand that a world of phantoms, with few higher examples to emulate, will irremediably drift towards a materialistic, cynical, insensitive, empty, cruel, and immoral society, albeit one well presented as "humanistic," "progressive," and "civilized."

I believe that all those who have suffered in their own flesh from the harshness of this supposed era of progress, humanism, and reason will agree to this description. The rest will merely defend their own life-script, wasted on pursuing fantasies and mirages of all that "glitters and twinkles," the easy, downward path that imperceptibly leads to the existential void, tedium, and death. The absurd thing about this image is that it only exists in people's minds, for it only refers to the way one perceives oneself and the way one is perceived, or to the way in which companies, institutions, or persons are visualized. As may be understood, this representation is totally subjective and probably dramatically different from reality.

Advertising and marketing companies study the way to manipulate people's minds to thus promote consumer behavior with the aim of making people blindly buy or accept everything they are subliminally ordered to buy, from a television set to a president, and they are quite successful in this. However, the secondary effects are disastrous and chiefly concern an increase in suggestibility, weakening of character and will, and extreme difficulty in appreciating reality. The abuse of this practice weakens the real world, and leads the individual to make choices based on appearances and not on content, to have sentiments based on the external, and to value everything that glitters.

We buy what we do not need and vote for imaginary people who do not exist as such in the real world. We fall in love with the attractive image projected by a person of the opposite sex and after several years we realize that this person has none of the qualities we had attributed to him or her. On the contrary, we are incapable of discovering the extraordinary capacities of others to whom we are indifferent, so that we may even reject them and fall in love with ourselves, that is, with what we believe ourselves to be—our own image. From childhood we are taught to value appearances and ignore depth, to emphasize the frivolous and despise serious matters, for seriousness is identified with boredom.

A huge battery of systems of entertainment is carefully planned so that children and adults alike do not get bored, a procedure that discourages or prevents any attempt at introspection, profound reflection, or spiritual growth. Emptiness, superficiality, and frivolity are idealized and all that lies outside the person is exalted, thus diminishing their inner world.

One of the most destructive modes of living for one's image is the case of narcissism, commonly defined as falling in love with oneself, which is really a fixation on one's image. The individual does not really fall in love with his authentic self, but with his image, which brings a marked impoverishment and paralysis of his emotional life. At various levels of intensity, this disorder affects a significant sector of Mankind. It is an exclusive perturbation because it isolates the individual in a world of uninterrupted contemplation and adoration of his own image, something that does not exist in the real world. The narcissist only has eyes for himself or for whatever reinforces his own image and is incapable of perceiving at a profound level anything that does not coincide with this image.

Contemplation of his own image gives him intense pleasure and he will seek all those situations which offer him the amount of enjoyment he expects. However, he is doomed to never be satisfied, so that this contemplation and search continue hopelessly until the hour of his death, at each moment of the day or night seeking situations that might stimulate him. Narcissistic enjoyment cannot be cumulative and can never be satisfied, and this is the great tragedy of this disorder.

Notoriously egoistic, the narcissist objectifies people, using them as mirrors that reflect back his own glittering image, feeding on this false brightness. He cares not for those who refuse to act as mirrors since they can be of no use to him. His sole interest lies in the exaltation of himself through the applause and continual attention and admiration of others. It might be said that his true being has died and that he feels obliged to devote all his efforts to the survival of his image. Cold and calculating, he seems quite lacking in feelings, but it is true that he suffers deeply on account of his immense solitude and incapacity to love.

It has been said that on account of her natural coquetterie, woman is more prone to narcissism than man, but it is possible that hers is only a different way of expressing this problem, which in the male sex provokes a struggle for power, and among women, competition for men. This latter is what leads a woman to a climax of narcissistic pleasure when she is "preferred" among many others, or when her clothes are the most beautiful at a party and she becomes the center of attention. With other people in her everyday life, she will continually go over in her mind her clothes, figure, and make-up, which gives her great pleasure. A large slice of her life lies in the mirror of her imagination and she will consult it time and again as to what is acceptable or criticizable in her appearance and the ways in which it can be improved upon.

It is true that there are countless human beings incapable of genuine contact with reality and the outer world, because they cannot manage to detach their "I" from their image, but on the contrary, struggle desperately to remain just where they are. Such people are in a certain sense blind, deaf, and dumb. They cannot see, hear, or speak from a territory that is beyond their image. To put it more crudely, *they have no territory other than their own image.*

It should be understood that I refer here to pathological narcissism, since it is normal for all of us to have a certain dose of it. However, this should not surpass certain limits. When this happens, it becomes the most immoral form of psychic incest: "the erotic relationship of the 'I' with the ''I,' " in which any external partner will become a mere trophy, or passing and disposable ornament, and at the same time food for the ego.

The individual who is in love with himself is forever immersed in this forbidden romance, like a sort of Onan, enchained to his own perverse concupiscence with no other hope of freedom other than death or an inner revolution.

Lack of Individual Merit

At some point, the perverse idea that our lives should be intrinsically pleasurable and prosperous was conceived of, and that if it did not turn out like this it was due to bad luck or some sort of social injustice or imbalance. Existence is visualized as a strong, powerful, agreeable, maternal bosom that is obliged to suckle us, even when we lack any merit because we have not made any significant individual effort to earn a right to it.

In accordance with the irrational logic of this belief, the abundance and happiness of others arouse rage, envy, and resentment, through the belief that someone is stealing the food that is ours and that for some reason has not reached our mouths. And all this is because of the harm caused by pseudo-humanitarian slogans that repeat the same messages time and again, reaffirming that everybody has a right to life and that everybody has a right to a home, that everybody has a right to good health, welfare, education, food, justice, and prosperity. As is only natural, these slogans refer to ideal situations that ought to be reached, but they cause great harm on account of the superficiality of their statements, since they fail to explain that a "right" must be based on individual merit and not on the plunder of others, so that they are of a plainly demagogic nature and do not have the welfare of the people as their real aim but the agitation of the masses.

This is how the role played by merit and personal effort in the satisfaction of our most important needs is so cunningly concealed. In this way, true statements are voiced, albeit captiously or incompletely formulated, in the manner of the best sophisms of antiquity. People have come to think that the aim of life is to attain a happiness along the lines of uterine nirvana, to live without effort or work, without trouble or contradiction. In order to sustain this absurd concept, gibberish such as "equality among people" has been developed without ever revealing what this really means, while this premise is stated in the style of a demagogic sophism.

Disregarding bad faith, I suppose there is excessive naivete or ineptitude in those who were responsible for the creation, considering the harmful side-effects of the celebrated trilogy minted during the French Revolution by the ideologues of the Constitutive Assembly: Liberty, Equality, and Fraternity. What is all this in practice but a high-sounding slogan?

There can be no liberty without self-control and without breaking through the shackles of usurian debts; there is no equality because we all possess different capacities and different motivations; fraternity only exists at the level of good intentions and when all goes well.

The problem with these slogans is that each individual interprets them in accordance with the personal hunger he is mastered by, that is, in accordance with the dictates of his passional appetites, as happened from the outset during the reign of terror of the French Revolution, in which all alike took advantage to carry out their private revenges, protected by the principles of Liberty, Equality, and Fraternity.

A slogan is usually a phrase with a high emotional content and extensive subliminal resonance, but one quite devoid of meaning, not because it has no meaning but because the meaning is concealed or ignored. Once it is stripped of its semantics, a slogan is empty and can be used as a mask, standard, or battle flag for almost anything. Moreover, it could quite well occur that two warring bands had exactly the same slogan or banner, each with opposite interpretations.

It is true that in a matter of such transcendence as morality, values cannot be handed over to the passional, limited interpretation of people who are not trained for it, and in this case, chaos would ensue.

The eternal truths are the basic pillars of the Universe; they have always been, are now, and will always remain so, independently of man. Nor can they be submitted to intellectual speculation or passional manipulation without their intrinsic content becoming adulterated or distorted. They cannot be apprehended by the exclusive use of reason and the senses, for it is only possible to have access to them in states of higher spiritual consciousness, since they are part of God, and if they are to be apprehended, require a process of personal illumination, which is part of spiritual discipline.

The true prophets or messengers of truth have always been and will always be those who at some point in their lives have successfully undertaken the great work of "completing the rough work" of the Creator, the portion given by him in the form of human corporeal life, as we know it in its sense of "statistic normality."

This process culminated in some in the form of inner illumination. In order to attain this, all without exception had to go through the ordeal of overcoming themselves and renouncing the different selfish manifestations of their "I," of dying through their personalities and being reborn in a more perfect form, thus becoming the "twice-born," those whom Jesus invited to come unto him.

The true prophets do not invent such truths, nor do they devote their efforts to predicting the future; they merely pass on the significant realities that are as valid in the past as in the present or future, since they are projections of Nature which transcend both time and space. They are those who, as in Plato's allegory of the cave, manage to come out into the exterior, no longer contemplating shadows, to confront the splendid Universe of light and genuine reality.

The prophets, who have always been ahead of their time, are those who maintain the light of Humanity, just the opposite of those who manipulate the truth to attain selfish, despicable purposes.

As is only natural, every coin has two sides to it, so that false prophets are the curse of the world, and the great limitation of common man is his incapacity to discriminate between truth and falsehood, because he lacks a state of higher consciousness since his normal condition is like a sleepwalking trance caused by the myriad stimuli that overwhelm his mind.

In this way, mediocre man is generally doomed to follow false prophets, since the messages these latter pass on flatter the "I" by promising to satisfy his most common passions.

Many of the human being's most frequent statements do not emanate from his own brain but are mental grafts provoked by the most fashionable false prophets. These grafts feed on the fantasies, hopes, and illusions of the people who bear them, so that they are strong enough to provoke disastrous conflagrations and wars.

Millions of sleepwalkers wander obediently through the world, driven by the subliminal messages that nest in their brains, that drive them to unknown goals, making them advance towards a chimerical goal that only exists in their fantasies and that they can never reach since it is a mere subterfuge to use them in the service of obscure, concealed purposes. I have no doubt that there is a worldwide conspiracy that aims to revive the obscure epoch of slavery, although now in a more sophisticated form, without discrimination of race or color and without shackles or fetters to imprison people's limbs. It is even simpler and quite legal to enslave people's minds by means of audiovisual technology and subliminal messages with the aim of directing their conduct and thus creating the perfect slave: an obedient consumer, a submissive voter, and a forced worker. In any case, nothing is to be gained by revealing this reality; the subliminal graft of such mental serfs makes sure that any attempt to show the truth will be discouraged.

I believe that only the stupid, the gullible, and the sleepwalkers think that life is "open" and without mysteries, and that science has the last word. It is true that this world is intrinsically mysterious and that everything fundamentally occurs through unknown causes. Science is only beginning to take its first steps in the study of the mind and totally ignores the phenomenon of states of higher consciousness, which it mistakenly associates with visions produced by drug-taking, calling them "altered states of consciousness." The narcissism of scientists prevents them from accepting the possibility that Mankind's normal condition is really that of daily living in a pathological state of altered consciousness, and that the suppression of this disorder could represent the antechamber of the higher state of consciousness.

A pathological condition is no longer regarded as such and becomes normal when it becomes generalized. In contrast, spontaneous healings that occurred in an exceptional way would be considered as madness by the mere fact that they represent a different statistic pattern.

As a well-known expression says "not all who are here, are, and not all who are, are here." Neither are madmen as mad or the sane as sane as they seem to be. However, what is true is that people's covert mental disorders are the cause of all society's problems, since they cause serious limitations of inner judgment.

From the French Revolution to the present day, liberty and equality have acted as a pretext to justify a huge subculture of people's inner demands, in the sense that the State or the powerful would be obliged to supply them with the welfare they themselves have been unable to make for themselves, because instead of developing their best faculties, they prefer to take the line of paralyzing their own self-fulfillment, since they are more concerned with remaining immobile and devote their time and energy to the unconstructive "art" of envy and resentment. Instead of imitating those who make their own way, they take the passive stance of beggars, waiting for political or state alms that will mean greater welfare. They do not realize that they are really aiming like this at equality in mediocrity rather than in development.

The only cure for this malignant disease is that those affected manage to overcome the immense fear reality provokes in them, in order to stop manipulating it and instead of living in the ideal world of their own facile fantastical accommodations, dare to face reality as it is, stripped of dreams and ornaments. This type of person would be ready for anything except for contemplating himself in the regal mirror of truth to find out exactly what he is like beyond his own speculations.

The true confrontation with reality is the supreme test for the individual, and there are only very few throughout history who have dared to experience this ordeal, because people prefer to always maintain an idealized image of themselves, in order to justify their inner demands, the source of all their misfortune.

The weak demand the satisfaction of their needs by the rest of the world; they ask people, the powerful, the State, the Church, and also cry out to God, rationalizing their requests so that it would seem an atrocity not to satisfy them. They never even try to ask themselves if they have sufficient merit to be rewarded in this way, nor do they question that their painful situation may be the natural punishment for their own indolence and lack of responsibility. In some way, they perhaps guess that they might discover something that would not appeal to them, such as confronting the concrete fact that their own indolence often leads them to paralyze their development as human beings, and that they merely subsist like vegetables, rooted and immobile in an energetic environment from which they draw their nutrients, passively depending on some sort of sun that gives them light and warmth. The lack of practice of the human faculties makes them atrophy progressively, and they run the risk of even living a semi-animal existence, one chiefly motivated by instinct. Character and will power become rusty and atrophied, remaining only as latent capacities. The cure for this malignant disease begins with the acceptance of the simple realities that obscure interests try to conceal; to accept that life is really a continual succession of problems and that these problems never end but merely take other forms or give way to other different ones, is equivalent to the fact of being alive.

If we are alive, we shall always have problems, imbalances, alterations, crises, adjustments, and breakdowns. It is not a matter of having or not having problems, since this is not debatable as there is no alternative. I repeatedly say that to be born means to immediately inherit a huge problem with a myriad of variables, and that one has to devote one's whole life to solving them, in the same way as students have to acquire progressive knowledge of certain subjects until they manage to become properly trained with time. Some, in a very healthy way, approach this difficulty by choosing the alternative of facing existential problems as an unavoidable, immutable fact, one that is an integral part of life itself. Others, on the other hand, endeavor to rationalize existence and attempt to accommodate it imaginatively to their own position, defects, and failings, systematically eluding the responsibility of accepting reality as it is. These dreaming idlers do not realize that they are transgressors of the divine mandate that says "thou shalt earn thy bread with the sweat of thy brow." This maxim does not only mean the need to work and make an effort to earn one's keep, but also entails the fundamental importance that the individual "pay" or give back to Nature the equivalent of what he has already received from her. Among her gifts there is the one which is called the "gift of life," but it is not really so in practice, for each individual is obliged to give back a hundredfold the life he has received.

So what should one live for? To subsist as a parasite on the effort of others, or bitterly and unvaliantly complain about the things one lacks without ever making any great effort to obtain them? To earn one's bread with the sweat of one's brow symbolizes far more than just this. It means facing reality in a truly responsible way, doing one's utmost to justify the "gift" of life, developing oneself to a maximum as a human being, which in the first place means to break through the hypnotic trance that enslaves the mind, to later cleanse it of all the destructive rationalizations accumulated in the past, tempering one's character and will until one achieves proper self-control to progressively increase the superior qualities of mankind through the development and practice of the supreme virtues in order to attain ascendant vertical evolution.

It means to accept inequality as a logical event in life and not as a disaster. We should not look for equality beneath us, since we would be unwittingly guided by the poison of envy. To descend, to regress, to involute, are not concepts inspired by divine luminosity but by the obscurity of the great tempter.

God demands an individual effort of evolution from us. If we shirk this effort, we shall be straying off the path set by the Creator, and as the world of the Creator is "the whole," we shall be in nothingness. One must not believe in the word "gratis," since this expression is an invention that warms man's heart but actually does not exist in Nature where nothing is free, and in which the law prevails of a cosmic mercantilism in the highest sense. This law states that "the same as I take, I pay back to you," "the same as you give me, I must pay back to you."

There is a popular expression that says "there are no free meals, for somebody always pays for them," which in some way implies a negation of the concept of "gratis."

Ordinary people are not willing to pay what something material or immaterial is really worth, since they expect to receive what they want in some miraculous way without any cost. To try to take without giving anything in return is closest to the concept of theft, but here it represents the fantasy or anxiety of stingy hearts and idlers, despite the obvious immorality of this desire.

Once more, the parasitic impulse can be stronger than the honest desire to earn things through great effort and personal sacrifice, and the "Draculian" instinct may lead many people to either unconsciously or deliberately invent or create dramatic situations in their lives with which to manipulate people's feelings by arousing pity or guilt in them, situations in which the manipulated individual is ready to give away what he has legitimately earned, in order to benefit somebody who may not only be lacking in any merit, but who may even be in debt to Nature through his reprovable actions.

No one thinks of the possibility that if a divine authority of an infallible, omniscient type wished to do immediate justice to all people, it would be perfectly possible for many of them to have the little they own taken away from them on account of their extreme lack of merit, so that an egalitarian equivalence would be established with regard to what they really deserve.

Those who demand justice always think in terms of some privilege being restored or granted, or else they believe they deserve it. As no one has eyes to see himself when it comes to establishing egalitarian equivalence between what one deserves and what one wants to obtain, it may be that what one has at that moment is already excessive, and that it may be taken from one in proportion to one's tiny merit. This is similar to what occurs with convicts who when they ask for a reduction of their sentence find it increased by the court.

The word "liberty" has been interpreted by the mass in a licentious sense, as an excuse to give free rein to one's own passions, to not subject oneself to any higher authority or to respect any type of hierarchy, or else in the sense of the freedom of the people to govern themselves, as occurs in theory in democracies.

To this respect, I would like to quote the words of André Frossard of the French Academy, taken from his book *Man in Questions* (Dolmen Edition, Colombia, 1995, p. 96). This distinguished thinker says on democracy:

> According to the Americans, it is the government of the people by the people and for the people. According to Jean Jaques Rousseau, the spiritual father of the modern world, it is the realm of the general will.
>
> These are the most deeply rooted definitions of democracy, but both are politically illusory and sterile. In fact, we have never seen a people that governs itself, except in tiny regions of Switzerland where it is possible to gather together the whole population in the main square and consult them on any matter. With regard to the general will, which should not be confused with the expression of a majority of citizens, it means the annulment of all individual wills, a type of abnegation that is only to be found in contemplative monasteries. Democracy then, has never existed anywhere, unless we take into account the two small exceptions mentioned above, the second of which is also unconvincing because monasteries are closer to a monarchic régime. However, democracy is the most widely accepted system of government at present and one should believe that it exists, for so many nations boast of calling themselves democratic.
>
> The American formula is a romantic way of remembering that in an ordinary democracy, the people have the first and the last word; the first through the designation of those elected; the

last, by their eventual revocation, but in the interim, the people have no word . . . all bourgeois democracies have a bad conscience to the extent that they cannot, without destroying themselves, ensure to each individual the integral liberty that should arise from its sovereignty of principles.

It is astonishing to visualize the possibility that true democracy does not really exist but is for the moment a mere romantic adaptation of an infeasible utopia, conceived in Greece as a form of government for the most highly evolved of men. In fact, individuals with the category of citizens were only a small percentage of the total population; women, children under a certain age, and those submitted to the tutelage of others were excluded. Really, it was a sort of artistocracy; representation did not exist; government posts were by rote among the citizens and the sovereignty of the assembly was absolute.

Aristotle defined three classical forms of government: monarchy, aristocracy, and democracy, which is considered as the form in which the majority governs for the good of general interest, whereas its degenerate or impure form was demagogy, in which government was for the private interest of a class which, for Aristotle, was the poorer class.

To return to the concept of *liberty*, it must be understood that true, ultimate liberty bears no relation to any external phenomenon, since it is a person's inner situation. A person cannot be free as long as he is enslaved to his passions and acts on the orders of the mental grafts implanted by the manipulators of behavior. There is no worse prison than a limited, shortsighted mind, or a heart invaded by hate, envy, and resentment. Nor can a person be free if he depends on an inequitable and inegalitarian economic system which acts as a parasite on people through the antinatural reproduction of money, which as it should increase solely in virtue of work and personal effort, does so perversely through bank loans and their interest. The supposed freedom of the consumer is also a fiction, for much of what is bought is quite unnecessary and superfluous, and is acquired because people have been brainwashed by continual advertising, television programs, and the never ending bombardment of news from the mass media. All this creates a colossal, subliminal informational inertia due to the meaningless reception of messages, which makes the individual become a sort of slave to information, a mechanized executor of the information that has not been subordinated to the "I" that has taken possession of his brain.

The different advertising campaigns war over the individual's brain and the only option he has is to "mentally belong" to this or that product, or this or that ideology or political party, but never to himself. The information he carries in his brain defends itself against any knowledge that does not coincide with its own structure, and blindly rejects any attempt to confront true reality. Mental blindness is typical of brains inundated by "insignificant" subliminal messages (lacking in meaning), which from a level of "half-sleep" usually descend to that of "sleepwalking with one's eyes open," the terminal phase of freedom and consciousness.

As will be understood, no moral system can function correctly in psychically deteriorated people with scant perception of reality. The problem of immorality and a lack of values is no more than a matter of man's subdevelopment as far as his hominal qualities are concerned. Unless the dilemma is tackled from this angle, no genuine solution will be possible.

Unfortunately, too many financial, company, and political interests would be affected in the whole world at the very moment that man attained his full liberty and individual consciousness, for he would no longer be a submissive consumer as he would be immune to the hypnotic trance and would be able to think with total independence and without any undue pressures to reach through to his true human dimension.

In this way, there would be an end to modern slavery, a thousand times worse than that which shackled only the body leaving an inner space of rebellion or free will. But, this inner terrain is the one that is invaded now, and as a result, the present-day slaves enjoy being obedient automatons and never tire of thanking their masters for having granted them the honor of serving them.

Who are these masters?

Like the State, they are anonymous, but do in fact exist and continually offer proof of their power by controlling the world in diverse ways.

Ignorance of Good and Evil

In order for a person to behave correctly, he needs to perfectly distinguish between good and evil and know precisely what each of these concepts means. It may be argued that this is not possible and that it depends on each person's point of view, a reflection which is in fact immoral in itself. In fact, values as important as love, duty, fraternity, friendship, justice, and good, cannot be given over to the "individual point of view," for either through gravity, inertia, or entropy, individual opinion is polarized exactly in the center of what the individual's animal appetites and impulses are.

To put it in other words, each individual's opinion is usually no more than the manifestation of his superstitious beliefs, an expression of a narrow segment of reality that corresponds to the justification of his own hereditary defects, vices, failings, and sins, and to the defense of the territory that has been colonized in his brain by the information that has penetrated it.

Therefore, we cannot expect individual opinion to be very important or significant, since it is generally almost a reflex action of colonized neurons, or a mechanism of visceral reaction before the fear that certain realities inspire. Therefore good and evil must be defined from the absolute point of view, that is, beyond circumscribed individual experience or carnal or emotional appetites and beyond the informational guest we bear in our brain, the fruit of the ruthless programming of man by man.

Without a doubt, good that resides beyond any point of view, epoch, or territory *is what enables the individual to awaken from the environmental hypnotic trance that alienates him so that he will not have the space, lucidity, and force to carry out his own process of evolution, making ascendant vertical progress through the development of his higher consciousness, his aim being the spiritual perfection that will lead him to encounter his roots and union with the divine spark.*

Evil, on the other hand, beyond any personal consideration, *is all that is produced by the hypnotic trance that is of a cosmic and environmental origin, and that impedes one to awaken, paralyzing any attempt at individual evolution. It is that which programs and empties the individual, putting him to sleep, hypnotizing him, destroying his "I" and leading him towards involution and loss of his soul and spirit. It is that which alienates and disintegrates the intrinsic essence of what we really are. It is the dark force of the Universe that is trying to destroy all that is genuinely good and to devour the divine spark.*

It is each person's ineluctible moral duty to reflect profoundly on what good and evil really are so that one can properly identify their agents on Earth. In this way, people will be able to avoid situations that, while promising some apparent good, really deviate them from the supreme good. There is nothing more deceptive than the apparent good of the moment, based on the material pleasure that makes us believe we have found happiness and that if it gives us such pleasure it has to be good. Likewise, there is nothing easier than to classify a situation of suffering and pain as "evil," which might really mean a healing process that is highly beneficial to the soul.

Material pleasure usually hypnotizes us and puts us to sleep, whereas suffering moves us so dramatically that we are temporarily removed from the hypnotic trance that dominates us.

However, one cannot be so simplistic in this matter and one must also know intermediate situations that are not at one extreme or the other. It is true that we have to learn to look beneath appearances and not identify the pleasurable with good and pain with evil. There is pain that can be sterile and pain that can be healing; pleasure that empties and pleasure that fills. Unfortunately, this second fact is very little known, so that most enjoyable situations leave us exhausted and inert.

Really, people have no idea how to enjoy themselves without sinning or degrading themselves, in order not to empty themselves or extinguish their energy. It is of supreme importance to bear in mind that evil does not always present itself in its true appearance, but that it often does so disguised as something beneficial or elevated. It would mean ignorance of Satan's cunning to suppose that his manifestations have to be enveloped in sulphurous vapors, hooves, horns, and an animal's tail. On the contrary, he may envelop himself in an aura of innocence, respectability, and goodness, a useful mask under which to hunt the unwary.

It is obvious that without a higher criterion as to good and evil, one cannot penetrate through the appearance of the senses, above all when what we see or hear is pleasing to our ego and physically enjoyable. Dreadful atrocities and massacres have been committed throughout the course of history in the name of higher causes or some apparent, supposed, or feigned good.

On the contrary, acts of patriotism, good, and justice have been manipulated and stigmatized by attributing to them devious purposes or intentions. Jesus was accused of committing serious offenses, Gandhi was considered to be a dangerous delinquent, and many times the founding fathers of different countries were once considered to be mere criminals.

Great benefactors of Mankind have been derided or murdered while delinquents and murderers have been applauded and glorified. The problem is that it is becoming progressively more difficult to know who the good ones are and who the bad ones are, and more often than one would wish, their roles are totally inverted, the honest man passing for a thief, and the delinquent, for a respectable person. The worst criminals can go scot-free while worthy, honest men are imprisoned.

"Bleached sepulchres" have always abounded but very few citizens have been able to identify the overwhelming rottenness that underlies their bounteous, honorable appearance. One cannot tell who is who, and social respectability is no guarantee of cleanliness, nor is the reproval or sentence of some individual or specific situation any guarantee either.

The only thing that is certain is the persistent reality that can only be glimpsed when it is no longer the present but has become part of the past. We are more or less sure when we pass an opinion on the past we have directly experienced, but are incapable of properly evaluating our present existence and the sequence of its events. As far as knowing truth and reality is concerned, it would seem that the sun shines backwards in time, and that today were forever shrouded in mist and obscurity, from which doubt, ignorance, disorientation, and vacillation are born.

The truth generally lies in the past. With the passing of time, it is far easier to perceive it, not merely because we can take an emotional distance from it, but also because the events that take place as the days go by tend to shed more light on what had hitherto remained in the shadow.

It might be thought that it is not of great use to know the past when what we need is clarity in the present. However, by scrutinizing the past, we may come to understand the causes of our present failure and thus implement the ideal means to achieve success.

The true analysis of the past is far more useful to those who blame their frustration or misfortune on fate, the environment, or certain groups or people, for they will thus be able to establish a relation of cause and effect between what they reap today and what they sowed in the past.

This could be extraordinarily useful from the pedagogical point of view if we really perceive that the positive or negative events of the present are no more than the direct result of our past actions. Not only must we learn to distinguish between external and inner manifestations of good and evil, but also view more clearly which are the positive or good actions we have to carry out at this moment and from which ones we must abstain.

The past reveals that we normally make the same type of mistakes throughout our lives and to this end, a clear, descriptive list of such mechanisms could help us put an end to them in the different spheres of our life. Likewise, processes that lead us to success should also be studied in depth, since nothing could be more profitable, both materially and spiritually, than discovering the way to achieve success, thus avoiding frustration and failure. However, it is essential that we are not impressed in this analysis by expectations of attaining a good that we think is valuable and lasting but which is maybe a mere mirage of apparent good, which in the long run will only bring us pain and frustration.

We shall never make mistakes if we aim our best efforts and energy to cultivating and developing the highest moral and spiritual virtues, for this path will not only lead us to lasting happiness but also to the spiritual perfection that comes from completing our human faculties, thus culminating the rough work received from God. Within this context, the individual urgently needs to be able to clearly differentiate between good and evil, which also includes being able to differentiate between what looks good and what is apparently evil.

As I said above, such knowledge cannot be the result of sentiment, the impulse of the moment, or the deceptive gratification of the pleasure of the senses. On the contrary, it is a lifelong task to perfect such wisdom in depth. Only by such means can one find peace in life, which on the whole comes from the certainty that one is acting correctly, and this is only possible if one is certain as to what is good and what is evil. Once this is understood, the individual will have effectively developed the compass for his *moral consciousness.* This is usually the mere fruit of social customs and mandates, but only very rarely is a reflection of some higher ethical system that is consciously and voluntarily introjected. The individual usually finds what the majority does acceptable or advisable, or in some cases imitates the models he admires—however all this without any process of reflective introspection.

It is very common to hear of the need to "decide in conscience," and there are people who boast of repeatedly doing just this. Nevertheless, one might ask what type of conscience they mean when man's normal mental state is that of "unconsciousness" or what I call "hypnotic trance" or the sleepwalking state. When a phenomenon is unknown because it has not been directly experienced, it is very easy to suppose that one has some capacity that one really does not possess, as in fact occurs in the sphere of consciousness, will power, and free choice, that are only faculties in a latent state, however much some may boast of fully mastering them.

When we speak of "consciousness" we fall into quick-sands or marshlands, for this word is used in practice as if it were elastic by adapting it to any situation whatsoever. If we speak of "psychic consciousness," it is obvious that we all have this, and it is certain that animals do too. If we speak of consciousness in the sense of *being conscious in a superior way*, it is also obvious that very few of us are. It is also possible to see that this *superior consciousness* only occurs when one escapes from the hypnotic trance that controls our minds, and that it therefore has myriad levels, from the most rudimentary to the most elevated. The most primitive level is that of the individual who had freed himself from the hypnotic trance but has still done nothing to cultivate and develop this new faculty. The most elevated is typical of the individual who has culminated the process of development of his consciousness, and has in fact attained a level as high as that of certain myth-ical wise men of antiquity.

This wisdom has nothing to do with formal knowledge, for it concerns the spiritual experience which is only possible within the interior of one's own soul. One must think that if an individual understands and accepts that absolute evil is the force that prevents man from awakening from the hypnotic trance he is afflicted by, and that the terrestrial manifestation of this evil incarnates in all the instruments that in one way or another keep people in the sleepwalking state, it will totally change the individual's perspective of existence, for it will take on purpose and meaning and will no longer be merely accidental or purely material.

There are occasions when the television, the press, the mass media, and certain publicity campaigns or political propaganda inadvertently become useful instruments for the designs of the Prince of Darkness. More often than one might wish, people are misinformed instead of informed, and are barbarized rather than cultured. People's thought is obscured and muddled instead of their minds being illuminated. Their brain is scourged by all manner of contradictory subliminal messages, thus reinforcing the hypnotic trance which they are afflicted by, instead of sending them warning messages that would help them to awaken to a more elevated state of awareness. Quite openly and legally, without any type of precaution or secrecy, an authentic conspiracy is waged against the human species, the despicable purpose of which is to progressively reduce the level of awakening in their mind with the aim of making them prone to manipulation by the dark force and its involuntary terrestrial allies.

These forces benefit from their unconscious collaboration with a progressive increase of obedient consumers who will contribute more and more resources to their coffers. As all of us without exception are affected by the environmental hypnotic force through its infinite and continuous suggesting stimuli, the only hope for man to improve his inner condition, which has not changed since remote antiquity, lies in taking control of his own mind, making it refractory to the influence of environmental hypnosis, a prior requisite for any true spiritual progress.

Authentic morality is "the knowledge of one sole person" and this means the fact that it is consustantial with a state of higher consciousness. This can only be attained through freely and voluntarily accepted individual work. This is the reason why such knowledge does not belong to the masses, neither can it be vulgarized, for it is the undeniable fruit of merit and personal effort. The mass as such will never be able to raise its conceptual level in the sense of "higher consciousness," for it can only increase the information that penetrates its brains.

From the point of view of these concepts, the computer could be a veritable "thief of consciousness," a destroyer of the higher human capacities, by reinforcing the hypnotic trance. I have not the slightest doubt that anyone who uses a computer loses his "I" while he is using it, or is manipulated by the machine. The loss of the "I" is a fundamental mechanism of the hypnotic process and, in the present case, the computer devours it through identification with the images on the screen and returns it battered, exhausted, and empty once the machine is switched off.

Any type of progress and technology may offer undeniable advantages, but like medicines, there are little-known side effects, or effects that are totally ignored. At the outset, it was never thought that a car engine could become a polluting nightmare, or that insecticides could be so dangerously poisonous. Computer technology is very recent and we do not know its side effects. All that has been studied in this respect are the harmful rays from the screen, and only in a very basic way. It will be far harder to test its negative effects on a field as little known as that of hypnosis, in which the surface of its true significance has barely been scratched. It might even be that everything has been coldly calculated and that the true purpose of the computer's existence is to create huge masses of mental slaves, susceptible to being manipulated in the desired direction by those who handle the whole system. Who really knows the true structure of the software on the market? Who can ensure that it is free of subliminal messages? Is it really harmless for the brain and mind, or does it cause addiction, dissociation, or other harmful side effects?

This is a problem that no one has studied in depth and that corresponds to the appropriate authorities. However, the results of such possible research would be just as dubious as research carried out to determine the harm caused by marijuana or other harmful drugs, in which there are always people who will minimize or deny their negative effects and consider their consumption unimportant, or will even add that it would be more convenient to legalize them.

The interests of the computer industry are so vast that it is very unlikely that there could be serious research as to the possible mental deterioration caused by such equipment. Therefore, to this end, there would have to be great progress in the research of the mind in order to accurately ascertain the essence and magnitude of the higher qualities it possesses which could thus be inadvertently damaged. However, once the present situation belongs to the past and sufficient time has gone by, we may perhaps come to know the exact dimension of the problem I am discussing here. It is also possible that this situation could get notably worse.

It is no easy matter to accurately specify if something is or is not progress, for the computer that helps the individual in the mechanics of his work could also as a side effect deform his mind and impoverish his inner potentialities. This, however, will never be known in all certainty without scientifically establishing which of the mind's most precious faculties is thus damaged, that is, consciousness. At that very moment, it will be understood that there are technologies and situations in everyday life that might increase people's IQ, but that at the same time destroy the level of their higher consciousness. That will be the day when there will be a reinforcement of the certainty that the only viable path to rescue transcendental values, to practice truly ethical behavior and find happiness, lies in the spiritual perfectioning of the individual, to which the environmental hypnotic trance of our time is tenaciously opposed.

Swindling

Swindling consists of acquiring money or valuables by means of tricks and deceit, and with no intention of paying for them. The definition also includes any of the offenses that are typified by lucre as an end, using deceit or an abuse of trust as a means. When a swindle is uncovered, the full weight of the law usually falls on the perpetrator, but there are certain areas in which dishonest manipulation remains ambiguous or concealed, so that it goes unnoticed or unreported, since it is not even considered a swindle in the strict sense of that word.

What is a transgression? Is it only what is contained within the penal code? Or are there uncoded transgressions?

In order to understand this problem, one should consider that almost any swindling that manages to deceive people in general would never be discovered. Furthermore, the basic requisite for a swindle to be discovered is that it deceives only a portion of the population, in order for the rest to be able to realize this fraud. For someone to fool the whole population, it would have to be a new type of swindle, some dishonest manipulation of such scope and style that most people would never suspect that there was any deception at all. I think, for example, that there may have been many historical swindles, whether deliberate or inadvertent, since the evidence of such deceit is so old, which were either very cunningly manipulated or the corresponding evidence was made to disappear.

Certain heroes may not have been quite so heroic as they have been held up to be. On the other hand, illustrious forerunners of science and philosophy have been vilified or obscured because they dared to think differently or because their theories shook the foundations of powerful economic, political, or religious interests. It is most likely that the overwhelming majority of such dishonest manipulations that use, as their only purpose, cheating and an abuse of trust for profit remain totally ignored, with those responsible for them looking perfectly innocent in the eyes of human justice. In accordance with these patterns, irregular deeds that remain undiscovered or which are not codified carry no penalty for their perpetrators. Nevertheless, they are fatefully punished by Nature.

It may be presumed that delinquency, evil, and corruption are as fertile as the ravings of an unhinged mind and that there are millions of offenses that we know nothing about or which have been neither invented nor discovered. The struggle between legality and delinquency never ends, since as soon as some offense is successful, other people think up new and better ways of either preventing or circumventing it either to safeguard or break the law. It should be acknowledged that there are many dishonest manipulations, that are essentially a form of swindling that go unpunished due to the fact that they are so difficult to prove, as well as on account of the indifference of most people to accept the realization of such things.

Profit does not necessarily imply economic gain. Rather, it includes any type of income or utility derived from something. Now, as it happens, there are illicit as well as legal means of taking profit. Honest work is legitimate and swindling is one of the illicit methods.

If we agree that any dishonest manipulation whose end is gain *may in fact be a swindle,* then we shall also agree that the scope of this concept is considerably broader. If a wrong action goes unpunished by human law, this does not mean that it is not an offense before Nature. Supreme law is based on the transaction of *equivalently egalitarian values,* and swindling consists of a maliciously fraudulent process intended to alter the equality of the exchange. In order to illustrate this point, I will give a series of examples which, although imaginary, could quite well occur in reality.

First example: publishing in the press

Newspaper "X" publishes a series of articles about certain scandals and in a wealth of detail describes the alleged offenses committed by such and such a person, who stands accused of having stolen a large sum of money, whereas the case against him has hardly begun. After some time, the accused is declared innocent of all charges.

Consequence: *the public has been deceived and somebody has taken profit from this defamation of the accused and his family. It will be hard for them to recover their reputations because the press will never deny its unsupported allegations as profusely as it had first promoted them.*

Of course, it may be argued that the newspaper had acted in good faith, and believed that the original information they reported about the case was true. However, one might well wonder why accusations are so profusely divulged before being adjudicated when a judge's initial conjecture may, at best, have been wrong, as is only logical and human. To conject means merely to suspect—to judge or to guess something because there are traces or signs of it. However, nobody can avoid projecting themselves psychologically when they presume, and therefore proceed in accordance with their own emotional sympathies or suspicions, or based on personal shortcomings (which we all have), rather than with strict higher rationality.

The fact of ignoring the innocence of the accused is not reason enough for justifying the previously mentioned news story, because, by spreading such information that was ultimately exposed as false, people were cheated with the sole purpose of benefiting from selling more newspapers. Despite the fact that the information had never been proven, it was exposed publicly as the truth and not as the mere presumption it had been up until that moment.

The accused's reputation was destroyed and his image may forever be besmirched. No one would dare suppose that there had been a swindle, but public good faith was indeed cheated with the motive of profit, from a slur having been cast on the security, tranquility, and honor of a citizen and his family. While it may be true that there was no intention of deceiving, it might have been presumable that the information could turn out to be false. Similarly, the newspaper in question would only be interested in satisfying the sick morbidity of the masses, who are always avid for bloody or sensational facts. Please remember that I am using an imaginary example, and that if this should bear any resemblance to reality, it would not be my responsibility.

Second example: demagogic political speech

Gratification of people's passions to make them the instrument of one's own political ambition is one of the cruelest and most barefaced of swindles by which people can be victimized. Millions of people become enthused by believing in utopian promises that will never be fulfilled, for they are only used as electoral bait. Power is the gain thus obtained—power at the service of top party circles and not of the people. These people, who never understand, usually react violently when they discover the fraud, mistakenly blaming the wrong people and never those who had deliberately lied in order to seize power. As L. Dumur said in *Petit Aphorismes 6:* "Politics is the art of making use of men by making them believe one is serving them." Meanwhile, D'Alambert sustains in *Mélanges de Littérature,* Chapter V, that "the art of war is the art of destroying men, just as politics is the art of deceiving them." Collective hypocrisy impedes the acknowledgment of certain truths when those truths are exposed. The pre-established concepts are the source of emotional security for all those who, being accustomed to a system, fear to recognize any defect and vice that such a system could have. This is the danger of "democratitis," a sort of malignant disease that leads one to emotionally believe in the democratic system of government and to indiscriminately reject any criticism aimed at perfecting it. Democracy does not exist merely as a matter of agreement or decree but rather represents a state of consciousness that requires a long, laborious process of perfecting in which each citizen is obliged to renounce government paternalism and take responsibility for himself—an understanding that individual merit is the only source of wealth, peace, and prosperity, these attributes being the fundamental condition to become immune to electoral sirens' songs.

It should be understood that covert swindles practiced on a large scale, that is, that affect the great majority of the population, are usually successful because they are caused and developed by an overwhelming deployment of advertising, in which the mass media are generally innocent accomplices. As we live in the age of ambiguity, it is very common to see something "as a swindle when it is not."

Indeed, for those affected it is a swindle, but not so when the moment comes to acknowledge it or to punish the perpetrator.

When certain promises are made before a candidate enters the government or assumes political power, and these commitments are not fulfilled after he has won the elections, there is a common swindling of public good faith. That figure is an immoral figure whose aim is premeditated deceit and profit, and this will certainly be punished correspondingly when the moment comes for nations to duly weigh the magnitude and effects of such manipulations.

Third example: commercial messages

The constant repetition of certain messages makes people convinced that certain commercial promises are effective or real, whereas they may later turn out to be exaggerated or totally false. This happens, for example, with most of the "miracle" systems for slimming down or with some wonderful cosmetics and creams that promise rapid rejuvenation of women's skin by removing or reducing their wrinkles. No advertising agency puts the products it promotes to the test, leaving that responsibility to the company that commissions the advertisements. However, it is true that the elaboration of advertising messages is what deceives the public more often than one would wish, by offering them something they will never be able to have, and that they would perhaps not acquire if they were not under the hypnotic influence of advertising. There are areas, for example, in which there is an overwhelming mathematical improbability that people's expectations will be satisfied, as occurs with lotteries, raffles, and gambling, which of course are no more than a market of illusions. Is it licit to sell illusions? The person who buys them should decide this, but it is a fact that we once more verge on ambiguity because we are presented with the hope of travel, houses, luxuries, and the solution to economic problems by the mere fact of buying raffle tickets. Of course, this cannot be fulfilled—people know this beforehand. There is a sort of deceit because it is not clearly stated that what is being sold is only *the supposition that the buyer of a ticket may win a prize, a supposition that looks like a childish promise when confronted with the calculation of probabilities entailed.* That people like being cheated is another matter, but it is not an extenuating circumstance.

It should be the duty of lottery and gambling commissions to warn players about the overwhelming mathematical improbability they have of winning, perhaps showing them a calculation of probabilities to this end.

Let's analyze the possibilities of picking the shortest matchstick out of a packet of 50 ordinary ones that had been specially prepared in this way, awarding a prize to the person who blindly picks it. Let us now multiply the number of matches by ten thousand or forty thousand and we will have a rough idea of the dimension of the illusions we are buying when we take part in lotteries. Here again, we are confronted with an ambiguous situation that verges on swindling and that is possible only if consumers' minds are fascinated by images that suggest a variety of pleasurable situations.

The sale of illusions is quite legal but in practice it really means cheating the buyer, at the same time as it means an alliance with the dark forces, represented by *anything that prevents the individual from awakening from environmental hypnosis. This latter is the most difficult obstacle to attaining higher states of consciousness and higher evolution, man's transcendental goal.*

Likewise, one must acknowledge that anything that promotes fantastical illusory expectations in people weakens or disrupts their contact with reality and progressively annuls their individual capacity to materialize their projects, the chief instrument for the prosperity of nations.

He who dreams of a stroke of luck does not usually bother much to struggle to make his way in life, and when this condition spreads in a country it negatively influences people's economic and mental health, so that they end by living in a virtual reality of abundance and pleasure whereas, really, they barely subsist.

Fourth example: consumer loans

Consumer loans are not free of ambiguity either, although consumers either ignore or do not accept the real cost of the money loaned to them. An economist in the Chilean press maintains that interest in commercial establishments is between three and seven percent a month, whereas a bank offers an annual loan of between one and four million pesos with 1.99 percent monthly interest, which, once insurance is added, is equivalent to 26.8 percent per year.

According to this expert, this means that the consumer pays a debt equivalent to a certain amount of units ("units of economic development," used in Chile, with a value that increases progressively) plus 18.5 percent per year. Dazzled by the object he wants to acquire, the obedient consumer does not bother to get proper information as to the true cost of the loan transaction. Even if he does, he remains in a state of unconsciousness that makes him refuse to accept an unpleasant reality, being quite blinded by his chosen expectations.

In this case we have an example that to a certain extent resembles the clauses in fine print on insurance policies, which as I believe, have lately been restricted, in the sense that they must appear in the same size type as the rest of the contract. There is no clear warning to the consumer about the real amount of money he has to pay back to comply with the obligations he undertakes. When he is not in a position to pay, he is excessively reproached for having irresponsibly undertaken a debt without any clear idea of the sum of interest and expenses.

As a corollary to this unpleasant adventure, an insidious "prejudicial" persecution is begun to obtain reimbursement, this being the moment when the debtor finally realizes the full amount of the charges on his loan.

In other circumstances, it usually happens that when someone wishes to buy a house with a mortgage, he pays very dearly for his dream, for after paying for several years, he realizes that his current debt is higher than at the outset and that his monthly payments rise to such an extent that it is in many cases impossible to continue paying them. In many cases, this means selling the house and certainly having to face a large debt, since it is very likely that the settlement price is not enough to pay off the original debt.

The immorality of such situations lies in the premeditated directing of people's behavior, with money-making aims, adulterating unsuitable or unattractive realities for them to such a degree as to make them appear in the consumer's mind as desirable options.

It is quite probable that in the 21st century such maneuvers will be viewed by man's law quite simply as a *vulgar attack or violation of the human mind*. Persuasion tactics must be limited because in many cases they may oblige people to make decisions that are very harmful for their pockets, health, and peace of mind.

Fifth example: the relationship within a couple

The decline in values has led people to try to conquer a partner of the opposite sex by profusely resorting to swindling, through the carefully systematic concealment of their own defects and the forcedly artificial heightening of invented qualities that really do not exist. Both men and women endeavor for years to *adulterate their own psychological profile by hiding behind a false image that bears no resemblance to their real being, feigning virtues they do not possess, thus managing to cheat the other party who, deceived in this way, will take this fiction as reality without realizing the true nature of the person he finds attractive.* Should this relationship end in marriage or cohabitation, the passing of time will implacably bring these true characteristics, hitherto concealed, to light, with the counterpart wrongly thinking that his partner *"has changed for the worse,"* and usually blaming this change on third parties. What has really happened is that the setup of a swindle has crumbled through the incapacity or lack of interest to continue hiding one's own true condition, which becomes obvious when reality is confronted. In this example, only one person is swindled, but there are cases in which a whole nation is taken in by its leaders or administrators, when the people discover with the passing of time that the image such leaders had projected in no way corresponds to concrete reality.

One has to consider that in manipulations of the image there is a clear desire to cheat, and that there is a malicious usurping of attributes and positions with the intention of obtaining profit. The greater the number of people affected by these swindles, the greater the offense committed, and the punishment for it should be proportional. Advertising endows products with false images that arouse fantasies and unconscious appetites in the consumer, who in most cases is not overly interested in the product he buys. The real attraction emanates from the *fantasy that is added to it*. This is the true reason why certain goods quickly lose interest for the consumer once they have been acquired, *since the consumer is looking for a fantasy in them that he can never find* and thus has to brusquely confront the objective reality of his purchase.

Faced with this dilemma, the consumer thinks that maybe he made a mistake to buy the goods and that he should have bought other products which now seem more attractive to him, since as is only logical, they are still endowed with the fantasy with which they are marketed, as they still do not have to pass the test of confrontation with reality.

I do not wish to belabor this point, and I am sure that readers will easily be able to find many more examples of this covert or ambiguous type of swindling. *In other words, it is something that at one and the same time is and is not a swindle, being not legally typified as such, but which in the material reality of the person thus affected is a genuine swindle.*

Abortion

According to the Catholic Church,

The respect for human life is not something imposed only on Christians; reason is enough to demand it, based on the analysis of what a person is and should be . . .

A human being's first right is his life. He has other possessions and some of them are more precious; but the right to life is fundamental, a condition before all the rest. This is why it should be protected as no other. It is not up to society or public authorities, of whatever type, to recognize this right for some and not for others; any discrimination is wicked, whether it be based on race, sex, color, or religion . . .

A bias based on the diverse periods of the life cycle is not more justifiable than any other discrimination. The right to life remains intact in an old person however much he may be handicapped; a person with an incurable illness does not lose this right. It is no less legitimate for a new-born human being than for a mature person. Really, respect for human life must begin when the process of gestation begins. From the moment the ovule is fertilized, a new life begins that is not that of the father or the mother but of a new human being who will develop by himself. He will never become human if he is not then. *(Official Declaration of the Holy See, 18th November, 1974).*

Both the Church and many scientists state that the fetus is a person from the very moment of conception, that every one has a right to life and that therefore an abortion cannot be carried out, as it is a crime.

I do not intend to start any kind of debate on this sticky subject, but merely to add a few different reflections on the matter.

The ardor with which life is defended is praiseworthy, but the candor with which people defend the idea that the fetus is a person right from the first moments of gestation is amazing. Great emphasis is given to the fact that it begins to have human characteristics at a very early stage, for example, pointing out that by the tenth week it already has a face, arms, legs, and fingers; it has internal organs and a certain activity of the brain can be detected.

Although I understand the laudable purpose of such statements, I believe that the concept is extremely naïve, when one can only with difficulty state that an organism is a person because it has human form similar to that of other bodies also considered to be persons in the highest sense of this word. According to the dictionary definition, a person is "an individual of human species."

In accordance with Friedrich Dorsch's *Dictionary of Psychology*, "the word 'person' does not come from the verb *personare*, contrary to what was thought before, but appears to come from the Etruscan *fersuna* meaning 'mask,' and more precisely the mask that characterized Fersu, the god of the Earth." In modern times, one understands by "person" not only a human being, the individual belonging to the human species, but a man and his specific character—*the being who has a conscious and unified "I."*

If we understand the definition of *persona* as the man in his specific way of being, not having any individual merit, there is no doubt that all human beings are persons, and as such there must be an unlimited respect for their lives, except in the case of the death penalty that is contemplated in some legislations. If we accept the condition of having "a conscious unified 'I'," we must also accept, after mature reflection, that only few specimens of Homo sapiens fulfill this requisite and that only these few should indeed use the title of "persons" in the sense of adult, conscious human beings. Nevertheless, respect for life must of course be extended to all, whatever their class, race, or condition, or to the interpretation given to this word.

Do you believe you have a conscious, unified "I"? Do you know anyone who has one?

To be conscious means to be free from the hypnotic trance, which is the very low level of awareness displayed by common man; to be immune to the influence of advertising; to have access to higher states of consciousness (generally unknown); to be the master of your own mind, the master of your own thoughts (to think voluntarily and not "to be thought"); to perceive reality as it is, without distortions or accommodations (overcoming the defense mechanisms of the "I"); to be above the passions and baser emotions; to be strong and virtuous, to mention only a few of the capacities of the conscicus being.

As far as the unified "I" is concerned, it is obvious that the people we know do not have it, for they have multiple fragmentations of their identities and have thousands of more or less important "I's" that successively fight for control of the psyche and the body. And this explains the continual changes in a person's behavior.

As for their more continual, stable types of behavior, these are so mechanical and automatic that the notion of a higher human "I" in the sense of a level of *higher consciousness* is naïve.

The great obstacle most scholars have when they analyze a person is their insistence that all people are equal, and therefore have the same rights (albeit not apparently subject to similar obligations). For hundreds of years, we have been brainwashed to believe in the imperative fiction of equality.

It is true that in the strict sense of what a person should be, one can say that a person is truly human only if he possesses a higher consciousness, a quality that man presumes to be one of his inherent attributes, but which in reality can only be attained at the individual level after laborious, patient spiritual discipline.

Although not with regard to the same subject I am discussing here, André Malraux approaches this concept in his novel *The Human Condition*, in which the following dialogue appears in one of the final parts:

"You know the saying," said Gisors, "It takes nine months to make a man, and only one day to kill him. We have always known it to be like this . . . May, listen to me; it doesn't take nine months, it takes fifty years of sacrifice, of will, of so many things. And when this man is made, when nothing of his infancy or his adolescence is left in him, when he is truly a man, he is of no more use than to die" . . . She looked at him in terror; he was watching the clouds.

The above quotation offers a glimpse of what man's true situation is: the fact that most die in the attempt of trying to become a true human being, and the few who succeed usually remain ignored by Mankind.

The normal person is *only a rough draft of what a human being should really be,* and he barely surpasses this initial level. As is only natural, some reach higher levels while others can only be identified with a humanoid condition and well deserve to be called such. In the middle of the spectrum, the great majority remain in "a latent state," like beings that could, in theory, reach a genuinely human status but in accordance with the law of probabilities are far more likely to never get any further than a common mediocrity.

Therefore, to speak of *a person* is like saying a "person at level one, at level ten, or level eighty," (on a scale of one to a hundred), using arbitrary numbers that express a deficiency of or an excellence, although this division cannot constitute a reason for discrimination against the modest ones in reference to the right to existence and the quality of life. The different degrees I have mentioned have no more social connotations than those to be observed in the different courses in which school children study until they perhaps attain a university degree, after which, a small percentage will in time attain human and academic excellence. Although nobody says this, society notably discriminates against those who have not reached the level of higher education, without mentioning equality between people in this case. Is there perhaps equality in the salaries of the literate and the illiterate?

In the same way, Nature recognizes qualitative differences between human beings, which concern their different levels of individual evolution. The problem is that between the humblest degree and the highest, there are light years of difference with respect to the level of hominality possessed, so that in all fairness, when we refer to one person or another, we are speaking of quite different things. There are also huge differences between the intermediate degrees.

From a cultural perspective, the word "person" always denotes the same thing, except in cultures with a caste system where there are first-class or third-class persons, for example. However, this separation does not in this case express real differences in *individual human quality* but only obeys religious, political, or economic reasons. The semantic imprecisions of language which form the normal material of our minds give rise to all manner of misunderstandings that, with time, come to form an immutable part of culture, and when clearer heads appear that attempt to go deeper into concepts for the sake of truth, they are generally persecuted or ostracized for the offense of thinking more profoundly and differently.

As far as a person is concerned, it is true that there are thousands of beings all of very different condition who are indiscriminately and arbitrarily grouped under the same label. Therefore, it could hardly be said with accuracy whether a fetus is or is not a person in the profound sense that this word has, if this cannot even be said with certainty about adults.

If there are those who insist on saying that a *person* is anyone who displays the outward signs of the human body, the fetus could probably be considered as a person. But if we speak of a person in its complete, higher sense, the fetus is certainly not a person, nor can the viability of it attaining this condition be assured. We know that, in clinical terms, abortion is the spontaneous or provoked interruption of pregnancy before the fetus can develop, that is, before it begins to show signs of more-advanced vital activity. Within different legal frameworks, a variable duration is given to the period of viability, which is the chief cause of controversy on this matter, so that it is a duty of the scientific community to give their last word on this subject. It is obvious that there is a point at which the fetus is like a "seed" of a human being, and we cannot confuse a seed with a tree.

Another of the most commonly used arguments on the subject is that "everybody has a right to life" and that therefore the fetus also has this same right. It is obvious, even more truly, that the millions of children and adults who starve throughout the world also have a right to survival. I think it would be rash to speak of a "right to life" in any congenital sense, as if it were free, and as if one did not have to earn it in any way, so that it represents a mere gift aside from any individual merit or effort. This notion clashes with the reality of Nature in which the concept "gratis" does not exist inasmuch as everything is the result of a mercantile transaction, if you will allow me to use this expression, in the sense of barter or egalitarian exchange. Only the naïve think that "there is free food"; what is true is that, without exception, someone or something always pays for it.

There is not a single cell in the human body that is maintained "gratis" by the organism, for each of them has to earn its keep by carrying out the tasks within the whole that correspond to it. Unfortunately, the social body is a sick body, since it requires arbitrarily that everybody will feed it without properly distributing the right nutrients to each of the human cells that make up this social body. It is also true that a great number of these cells want to feed for free and not do any productive work, intending the State to keep them, even though they are in a perfect state of bodily health.

Among the superstitions that poison our lives, filling us with rage and frustration, there is the belief that the mere fact of being alive, gives us the right to demand from the world, when it is the society that is in the position to demand an appropriate type of behavior from its citizens. In the same way, it is the parents who should demand correct behavior from their children, since they have created and sheltered them, since they are flesh of their flesh and blood of their own blood. In accordance with the laws of Nature, we have no right to anything congenitally and we have to earn everything through our personal effort. As the fetus can earn nothing for itself, due to its parasitic condition and its state of underdevelopment, its rights, in practice, come from its parents, the fetus itself being a extension of them. Unfortunately, it usually happens that, as the Bible says, "the sins of the fathers shall be visited upon the children," which is further proof of the defenselessness and precarious condition of the fetus.

Although parents are responsible for the birth and later care of a child, they should think beforehand of their guilt in causing conception of the fetus through negligence in coitus, which is usually carried out in a purely animalistic way, devoid of any loving sublimation, and with no intention to procreate children, so that these children more often than one might wish, are born more as the result of a libidinous instinct than of love.

I have no doubt that this fact has a profoundly negative influence on the child's development, since the magnetic impact of the state of animal consciousness in the parents is inherited by the child, so that he will experience an exaggerated attraction to primitive impulses. We not only inherit the influence of the genes, but also the magnetic fields that predominated in our parents during coitus, which take possession of the fetus' structure. Added to this, there is the transmission of their magnetism during the whole period of pregnancy. To a great extent, this entire process conditions the future life of the fetus which, parallel to the positive qualities it inherits, will come to life "burdened with the sins of its fathers," that is, with a handicap that comes from the negative vibratory energy of its parents.

For quite some time, and unfortunately, coitus has become an act for "pleasure consumption," totally detached from love or any other romantic connotation. It is contemplated in the same direct manner as someone does when wanting to eat a hamburger, simply doing so, without considering the possibility and consequences of conceiving a child without the inclusion of any higher feelings, but driven solely by an irresistible libidinous explosion. In this way, couples suddenly discover that the woman is pregnant, without them having the slightest intention to this respect. This means a rude awakening from an act that was for them a mere "consumption of pleasure," so that they resort to abortion as a means of solving the problem. I am convinced that the thoughts, impulses, and emotions of the parents during the period of pregnancy decisively influence the psychic and physical formation of the fetus. I very much doubt that an unwanted fetus can develop as it should, and I believe that it could rather display malformations of the brain or behavioral problems through projection of the magnetic energy of the baser emotions and instinctive impulses of its parents which, because they are deposited in the womb, come to form a part of the child's structure, thereby perhaps becoming destructive energetic pulsions; or they lack in vitality because of the rejection or lack of love for the new life form.

In order for a child to develop normally, he must be the fruit of love and not of an animal impulse. He must be consciously and deliberately engendered, spend a pleasant period in the womb, and be educated by a couple who are united by genuine love and who possess higher moral values. Therefore, to condemn abortion should not be a pretext to indiscriminately promote demographic growth, since we would thus be attacking the quality of life of all Mankind. It is society that commits the sin of hypocrisy by condemning abortion when it has not even bothered to create a "School for future parents" beforehand, in which people are taught to educate their sexuality so as not to be slaves to their animal impulses and hence procreate only when they have consciously made the decision to have a child.

Why do groups who condemn abortion not show the same zeal in preventing or regulating pregnancy through the education of people's sexuality? What educational campaigns are oriented to sublimating sexuality so that it becomes controlled by higher consciousness?

Really, society chastises with the left hand what the right hand will not prevent, turning a blind eye, as well, to realities that are just as shocking or more so than abortion.

With respect to life in the womb, for example, the shocking, aberrational, and incestuous attack on the fetus when the couple continue to indulge in the sexual act during pregnancy has never been mentioned, due to hypocrisy. No one denounces or condemns this openly immoral phenomenon, despite the fact that the fetus is indirectly submitted to the barbarous experience of prenatal sex, since it is still one with its mother.

No one stops to think that the fetus experiences everything the mother feels, and that its weak, unstable nervous system is time and again submitted to the exacerbation of orgasm, the couple being totally indifferent to what this really represents. In reality, the tiny creature is a single unit with its mother and participates fully in her emotional, mental, and instinctive states. Coitus during pregnancy is a clearly incestuous act, one that is harmful, violent, and senseless, since it obliges the fetus to participate in an erotic rapture. It seems that this act is not condemned because the fetus is not considered a *person* in this case.

Therefore, I would ask why is it that a fetus is considered a person for purposes of the abortion issue and not when it comes to incest?

These remarks are not intended to conceal or reduce responsibility in abortion, but to point out the hypocrisy and inconsistency there is with regard to this subject. People preach about the need to protect the life of the fetus, and when its life is ensured, the fetus is attacked in diverse ways, having everything possible done to it, although in a covert way, in order to provoke the underdevelopment of his human capabilities.

The truth is that we are not rabbits and cannot procreate like them. If there is anything that separates man from other animals, it is the self-control of his own sexuality. However, for some strange reason, it is supposed that the biological animal capacity to procreate and conceive offspring is condition enough for someone to be able to function properly as a good parent, when it is quite possible, that through ignorance of technical child rearing, many parents become the worst destroyers of their own children, despite the love they might feel for them. Thus, the moral poverty of mankind is not surprising under these conditions. Parents who were procreated and brought up to be incomplete beings repeat the cycle and ensure that their own offspring cannot attain total development either. And all this with a strange kind of pseudo-love and good intentions.

Because of the strangely twisted ordering (or disordering) of certain social customs, relatively few people consider it immoral to have children without the parents being duly trained to raise them. On the contrary, the idea of proper training to this end, that is, to procreate consciously, and do one's utmost to improve the quality of human life from before conception, definitely annoys people. It seems contradictory to me that man has improved the animal species from which he profits and the fruits and plants that he uses, without having managed to improve his own human condition to date, as far as inner quality is concerned, acting in many instances in a far inferior way to beasts. Among beasts, there is no corruption, cruelty, lasciviousness, or sadism, nor is there unnecessary violence.

Man has not managed to attain the level of consciousness that would enable him to respect and protect his natural and human environment. He is a predator of natural resources and is not able to respect the rights of his fellow beings. In the case of the fetus, for example, man begins by stating that it has a right to life, so that making himself its representative, man brings it to life, obliges it to live, submits it to intrauterine participation in its parents' sexual relationships, and condemns it to be one more future servant of the world conglomerate of obedient consumers. As if this were not enough, that fetus will grow up to be deceived by demagogic political discourse, and will be used for the creation of bodies of power that are totally divorced from the real interests of the people. It is handed over in a defenseless condition to an educational system that uses subliminal and alienating pedagogical techniques, and its mind will be left inert before the massive and formidable penetration of information from the mass media. It will grow in ignorance of its own lackings, ignoring that it is an incomplete being, doomed to exist as "half-man," unless it experiences the miracle of a genuine spiritual revelation.

Obviously, in the opinion of *sapiens*, the fetuses of other animal species have no right whatever to life, being at the disposal of man's whims. Fully developed animals are slaughtered, exterminated, devoured, or cooked alive, tortured in laboratory experiments or dissected for the sake of science.

Why then does the human fetus have more right to life than the offspring of other animal species?

It is easy to argue that this is because one is human and the other an animal. However, there are times when the human condition is debatable, and man, in fact, descends to the level of the beast. We also know that if we are stripped of our hypocritical cultural veneer, we are still "naked apes," who exert the right of the survival of the fittest, in this way to sacrifice the weaker species.

On speaking of abortion, one has to analyze not only what the death of the fetus implies, but also what its survival entails within the context of the reality of this epoch and this planet, and the quality of life that awaits it, beyond the fantasies of future success that are so common nowadays. It should be clearly understood what is to be gained and what is lost by the fact of being alive or of not existing.

To return to the condition of the fetus, I believe that it can be considered a person in the strict sense of the word, only when it attains its true human condition as an adult, which may or may not occur. Of course, this cannot be a justification for abortion. Before reaching this maturity, *it is only the draft of a person,* or perhaps to put it in other words, *a half-person.* If we agree with the definition of *person* in the sense of *a body with human form,* it is most likely that we would have to accept that the fetus is a person from the moment there is an appreciable physical development for it to look like a human body.

As regards the conception of the fetus, I would stress that most often the sexual act that gives rise to the fetus is an episode of erotic madness in which the participants are no longer masters of their own acts, so that they display a temporary loss of consciousness and a reduced or annulled responsibility. Coitus is experienced by the great majority of people as the sudden eruption of a force beyond their will, which drives them to genital coupling and to momentary obliviousness to the possibility of conception. This is the true cause for the birth of most children, and abortion is consequently used as a violent means of avoiding unwanted offspring.

One should also reflect on whether it is licit to be obliged to have unwanted children in a society in which no one is educated in such a way as to possess an adequate control of his genital impulses, which consequently results in an orgiastic type of coitus as a general practice, that is, one that gives free reign to the passions. I consider it immoral that society should punish what it does not bother to prevent, and in all environments we encounter numerous examples of this. For instance, why is the sale of alcoholic beverages to drivers permitted if it is forbidden for them to drive under its influence? Why is it legal to manufacture and sell a car that can run at 140 miles an hour if the speed limit is 55 or 65? If 800 million people suffer famine in the world, why is stricter birth control not established? Why should we be scandalized by underdevelopment and poverty if not enough is invested in public education, and the necessary level of efficiency is not attained either? How will the poor manage to earn enough money and get on in life if they are not acculturated to this end from birth?

A society that punishes what it has not bothered to prevent beforehand and that repudiates and punishes the absence of certain abilities for success in people's lives when this can be attributed to its own lack of educational policies is a totalitarian, lying, unjust, and hypocritical society. It is one that is unjustified in sending a poor woman to prison for having had an abortion in deplorable sanitary conditions, when her behavior is no more than the reflection of the social imperfection and inconsistency that has previously conditioned her conduct.

We find a great deal of evidence as to the existence of a psychic heritage passed on from parents to children in the form of a cellular magnetic archive, which makes the descendants mere bearers of adequate or inadequate mandates that have their origin in their parents' instinctive, emotional, and mental states. I do not believe it is possible to expect a great deal from an unwanted or unloved child, one born from a mere genital outburst, since its parents' rejection could be a negative branding on their descendants' psyche, these children being the bearers of flaws and deficiencies that cannot be attributed to genes or health or environmental conditioning.

A loveless sexual relationship, originating solely from libidinous desire, will produce a child in whom the highest qualities of the species will hardly be able to manifest themselves.

Just the opposite happens in higher procreation, which is originated by a sublime attraction between two conscious beings who, because they love and respect each other, fervently desire to have children. The wanted child, who is really the fruit of love and not of animal passion, will have the best chances of developing the higher qualities of the species. In the same vein, I believe that there are different levels of guilt in abortion. It is probable that, for example, by aborting an unwanted fetus, one prevents conception of a creature which might be less viable as an integral human being due to the psychological impediments it inherits from its parents. Conversely, if one would provoke the abortion of a wanted child, which nevertheless is unsuited to the couple's circumstances, it would probably mean preventing the life of a fetus that was far more viable as a human person.

I must insist that having a child should not be the result of chance or genital outbursts, but rather of mature reflection and the parents' responsible decision. They must analyze very clearly the type of life they could offer their children, with respect to the quality of the environment in which they will live and the type of education to which they would have access. As long as people have intercourse in the same superficial and intranscendental way as animals, they cannot be seriously asked to take mature responsibility for the consequences of this genital contact with the associated temporary loss of consciousness that it entails. This is because to demand this would be to commit the sin of stupid hypocrisy. We should not forget that abortion does not only occur because the woman is pregnant, but is the unhappy final stage of a chain of circumstances whose primal cause is coitus, that is, she is pregnant because there was a relationship that was consummated in her fertile period perhaps through a sudden and irresistible sexual excitement. The true sin or offense of abortion lies in a society that is incapable of supplying the

individual with the moral and spiritual tools for him to sublimate his sexuality so that he is no longer a slave of his animal
impulses. At the same time, this society contradictorily
expects him to raise, in a superior manner, the child he has
procreated in an animalistic way, this behavior being only too
often the normal sexual behavior of both believers and atheists regarding this subject. Abortion cannot be analyzed as
individual guilt but as a social flaw, and society has no moral
authority to condemn it lightly, for the incapacity to control
oneself sexually also derives to a great extent from collective
artificial exaltation of the libidinous impulse which is
provoked by the exciting, ardent erotic publicity of diverse,
well-known advertising campaigns. These campaigns sell
covert sex, and society tacitly condones and even applauds it
by the fact of promoting consumerism. This means that the
pressure of the individual's erotic boiler is raised to a
maximum, and when his reason has been totally obliterated
by desire, he ends by giving free rein to his instincts, in an act
of momentary madness that often generates a child, so that he
is obliged to accept through his reason what was only the
product of madness.

Likewise, there are those who forbid or discourage contra-
ceptives, thus forcibly increasing a human mass that is
unwanted by its parents, its members being limited in their
chances of development for this reason, even from before
birth. Furthermore, it is acceptable for the parents to be
untrained in their parental functions, therefore becoming "bad
parents" in the technical sense of the word. They are totally
ignorant of how their offspring should really be raised to
ensure them a prosperous life and good possibilities in
attaining the status of a real human being. Otherwise, they
may drift towards the state of "humanoids" or forever remain
incomplete. Harsh reality shows that the great majority of
parents, whatever their social or cultural condition, have never

attained the condition of true human persons in the strict sense of the word. This is why it is so difficult for them to teach their children what they themselves do not even know, nor were able to experience in themselves. In a sense, therefore, there is a sort of fatal outcome by the fact that incomplete parents will always educate children to be the same as themselves, thereby depriving them of the chance for any type of human and spiritual development surpassing the limits of common habit and custom. This higher development will lead an individual to fulfill himself as a real, authentic human being.

It is not culture that humanizes people, it is spiritual growth in the technical sense—that is, the fact of having the possibility to experience life at higher levels of consciousness which, as I have repeatedly said here, is possible only through an absolutely free and individual decision that will lead the seeker in the right direction.

All these remarks are intended to draw attention to the different levels of responsibility incurred by those who provoke an abortion. The following could be circumstances that counteract the feasibility of the fetus being able to become a real person in the higher sense of the word:

(a) Parents may have had intercourse in an animalistic way, so that this act can hardly be attributed to God.

(b) They subject the fetus to the immoral abuse of having to share their sexual relationships while it is still in the womb.

(c) The parents do not want a child, nor are they in a position to feed it properly or give it the necessary love and care.

(d) The parents are themselves *incomplete,* so that their children can hardly be viable as *persons,* in the higher sense of this word.

(e) They are bad parents in the technical sense of the word.

I would like to ask the readers what would have happened if, before they had come into this world, they could have chosen their parents in some way. Would they have chosen to be procreated by parents who were not united by love but by instinctive passion; who would leap into intercourse in a purely animalistic way, without wishing to have offspring of any kind; knowing that when faced with the obligation to have them, they would be unable to feed them properly or to give them the necessary love and care; besides the fact that they themselves are *half-men and bad parents?* Would they have really chosen brutal, selfish parents, or parents incapable of giving them love and tenderness?

The first and greatest violation against the fetus is to procreate it unconsciously, thereby transmitting to it the inferior qualities of its parents and forcing it without its consent (how could they ask it for that?) to come into this world imposing on it the heavy weight of all their flaws. It is forced to have parents it did not choose, who subject it to the trauma of a prenatal sexual relationship through their coitus. Furthermore, they give it over to an inadequate educational system, and force it to a kind of life for which they never asked its consent.

One could argue that a fetus did not exist before it was procreated, but this is as much as to say that life comes out of nothing, or that it begins only at the moment of procreation. I believe that the child, as an archetypal form, exists in a latent state within each person, and that before making the decision to procreate, one must make contact with this part of oneself to know whether this part of what we are would really like to become a child once more, and if so, would it like to have parents like oneself and one's partner?

It is indeed unfair to bring a being into the world without its consent. I have deliberately chosen this specific phrase "to bring a being into the world," to denote that before it is brought into the world it must be somewhere else, both in the biological and metaphysical sense. There is no doubt that in an ideal world, where possible, everyone would want to be consulted before coming to life, and to "approve" of their parents. This concept will be understood by those who believe in life after death, which logically assumes that there must necessarily be *life before birth.*

The second type of violation then, is the possibility of an induced abortion. The third violation is when the fetus is doomed to lead a life that it does not want or a kind of life with which it disagrees. The fourth type of violation against the fetus is the enslaving of the mind through advertising and audiovisual communication. In Manhattan, there is an advertisement which is posted on the side of bus stops that I have kept a photo of. On it, there is a couple embracing, with the following slogan:

Every 27 seconds the average man thinks about sex.

The rest of the time he's all ours.

Worldwide Networks. On line. Radio integrated events.

Targeted opportunities. ESPN. Now much more than cable TV.

No comment!

Of course, no one questions the fact that a child will be converted, almost irremediably, into a being who does not possess himself, and that is the type of life that its parents can offer, because they do not possess themselves either. For the aforementioned reasons, those people who do not want to have a child at the present moment should restrict conception by voluntary birth control through the most suitable method, making the decision to procreate only after a profound analysis of their consciousness, fully grasping the huge responsibility entailed in the process. We should not be puppets of the passions, but rather conscious architects of our own destiny. If we make the decision to bring a child into the world, we must take full responsibility for this and understand what is really entailed in our action. However, this indubitably demands a self-discipline that only few people possess.

The fifth type of violation occurs when our bodies are effectively snatched from us and given over to the State by the mere fact of being denied the option of euthanasia in the case of terminal illnesses.

In practice, a woman is not the owner of her own body either, for she has no choice in whether or not to foster a little parasite, which is the fetus, even if the fertilization may have taken place against her will, or in the absence of it, such as when she is raped or took part in intercourse in a state of passional madness that entailed a temporary loss of reason. This latter situation would constitute an extenuating circumstance in the case of a passional crime.

What exceeds the limits of what is permissible is that pregnancy frequently occurs without the woman being ready for maternity, because of careless irresponsibility. As regards the limitation of liberties, the person who does not wish to live on account of ill health cannot dispose of his own body either, for however painful his life may be, he is not in control of leaving it when he wants to. What kind of liberty is this when the State takes control over citizens' bodies? It seems quite logical to me that the person who, with good reason, wishes to end his life should be free to do so, being thus allowed to choose the moment and manner in which he abandons his body in a dignified way. All this, of course, should be done with style and high aim, in accordance with an adequate legislation. In some cases, this is one of the most terrible forms of discrimination, in which a court of bureaucrats denies a citizen a dignified death when he is suffering from a terminal illness or some other disease that is unbearably painful or denigrating. Of course, the bureaucrat who forbids voluntary death does not do so out of compassion, but out of insensitivity, for he cannot feel the atrocious pain or discomfort the person who wishes to end his existence can experience and therefore, as he is not affected by this, he can easily decide that a self-provoked death by one's own decision is illicit.

Medical science is totally incapable, for the moment, of guaranteeing a dignified death to certain people. Therefore, society should not impose, as an atrocious punishment, the maintaining of a life whose quality has dropped below the bearable limit, becoming undignified or denigrated. Certainly, none of those who are opposed to euthanasia have suffered in their own flesh the dreadful pains of certain extremely severe illnesses and therefore cannot calculate the need to put a voluntary end to such suffering.

Once more, we come across similar arguments to those related to the condemning of abortion: the right to life. It will then be said that "everybody has a right to life" (where is real life, "here" or "there?"). This means that the State, by obliging someone to live, assumes the role of torturer of all those who are suffering in the grasp of incurable illnesses or irreparable accidents, condemning them to put up with a miserable, undignified, and painful life. Of course, if it were a case of the torments of their own bodies, the same inquisitors, as in antiquity, would doubtless issue some license for one to be able to stop living in a dignified way at the chosen moment. If our right to life is recognized, why not do so with the right to die as well? In many cases, it is an act of savagery, and not a civilized act, to coldly make a decision about the suffering of others through the mere fact that one cannot feel it in one's own flesh, thus denying the sufferer the possibility to decide voluntarily on the matter of his own death.

Just as the fetus was obliged to come to life, the sufferer of an incurable disease is now obliged to tolerate the torture of the pain and bodily misery, as if it made him more pleasing in the eyes of God. As far as the fetus and the indiscriminate increase of procreation is concerned, they are really saying: "It does not matter whether this fetus is interested in living or not; it must be obligated to; it does not matter whether its parents are sick, inadequate, degenerate, or incomplete, it must be obligated to bear them; it does not matter if it is born in the middle of a war or in the middle of a catastrophe, it must be obliged to, even though it may have hereditary diseases or be handicapped, a down's-syndrome baby, mentally retarded, insane, or deformed. Let it put up with the torture of its own misery or let it die of hunger or violence, but never by abortion. It must be obliged to live in an alienated, sick world and be violated so that it is forced to accept the patterns of pseudo-normality, which in reality, is a pathological condition. It must be enslaved psychologically, given over defenseless to the mass media that controls its mind. It must be registered in the world conglomerate of obedient consumers in order to survive the prevailing economic system; it must be enframed, twisted around, entangled, blinded, deafened, polluted, pawed, and whatever else is needed to adapt it, by reason or by force, to the norms that a sick society considers desirable."

I would ask how many of them would "regret their lives," how many people at this very moment who, if they could turn back the hands of time to the moment of conception, would choose the option of not being born to terrestrial life. It is evident that there are many who in that moment, for different circumstances in their lives, would be thankful to their parents for having abstained from conceiving them. It is certain that, for the mentally retarded, for those suffering from Down's syndrome, for the paraplegic or the deformed, life becomes a great torture. If we could consult the forty million people brutally killed in World War II, including both civilians and soldiers, it is most likely that the great majority would have preferred not to have been conceived instead of going through the horrendous suffering they must have experienced.

Paradoxically, there is license to die during a war, to die of hunger, to be poisoned by environmental pollution, to collapse through stress, or be slowly killed off by the toxicity of certain food products. For the law of man, it is also licit to nullify people's minds and souls with excessive advertising, information, and educational "messages." In sum, people die both physically and psychologically in many different ways: of drug overdoses, through dangerous ingredients in food-stuffs sold in supermarkets, through the venom of political demagogy, and through informational saturation.

Every day the hopes and illusions of countless people in the world are killed, the world welcomes thousands of children who will die of starvation, and old people are left to die totally abandoned.

On account of its ethical connotations, the subject of abortion, as is only logical, shocks people's consciousness. Therefore, it is not licit that certain "Pharisees" should take advantage of this circumstance as a smoke screen for closing people's eyes to other indirect ways of depriving life, these other ways being more underhanded, slower, and more cunning—being practiced against both children and adults or even against entire countries. Why, for example, do they not defend with equal vigor large families of humble origin, who literally slowly die due to extremely poor nutrition, by lack of proper medical attention, and by indirect enslavement to certain taxes and financial debts? Why do they not firmly denounce the sad neglect of the elderly and the pollution of the air and food? Or the irreparable brain damage caused by drugs? Why do they not also advocate reducing the size of the State in order to implement a massive educational program that would favor the most needy, thereby helping to prevent abortion, delinquency, and drug addiction? Really, we would not have enough space to list the diverse, sophisticated ways in which, legally or indirectly, human life is assaulted. Therefore, each can draw his own conclusions in this respect. We have inadvertently reached a sanctification of the fetus to the detriment of adults, to the point that it is even considered to have more rights than its mother, and that she ought to sacrifice everything for it, thus dodging the biological evidence that "there is only one mother," but children, many.

We are convinced that this protection of babies and children is merely a question of a mother's natural love for her offspring, but what is certain is that this originates in a "moral indoctrination" that goes back hundreds of years and is not motivated by love but by reasons of State. Before the year 1760, the child meant nothing different than what it does today, being basically considered "a nuisance," while for St. Augustine, the child, as soon as it is born, becomes a symbol of the forces of evil, an imperfect being, one burdened with original sin, and of such a corrupt nature that the task of correcting it must of necessity be very exhausting. This line of thought dominated pedagogy until the end of the 18th century. Elizabeth Badinter writes in her work *Does Maternal Love Exist?*:[13]

Currently, we are profoundly convinced that the death of a child leaves an indelible scar on its mother's heart. Even the mother who loses an incipient embryo, if she wanted it, will keep the memory of its death. Even though she may not sink into pathological manifestations of grief, every woman will remember that day as the day of an irreplaceable loss. The fact that she can give birth to another child nine months later does not cancel out the death of the former. No quantity can substitute the quality we attribute to each human being, including the viable fetus. Formerly, the opposite approach had been predominant. F. Lebrun writes in his thesis: "at the human level, the death of a small child is experienced as a banal accident that has to be remedied by another birth."

Elizabeth Badinter continues:

Perhaps the greatest proof of indifference is the parents' absence at their child's funeral. In some parishes, as for example in Anjou, neither the mother nor the father attend the funeral of a child under five years. The ultimate proof of this indifference is offered by the opposite phenomenon: to display grief for the death of a child is a type of behavior that the environment always considers as curious.

Professor Badinter shows that at that time there was a general rejection of motherhood, because maternal duties were not given any attention and were not valued at all by society. Women earned no glory for themselves as mothers and yet that was their main function. Children were generally handed over to nurses a few hours after birth, and it was not rare for their parents to first meet them only once they had grown into adults, if they ever reached adulthood.

Badinter continues:

As from 1760, there are many publications that advise mothers to personally take care of their children and tell them to breastfeed them. They create an obligation for women to be mothers above all and engender a myth that would be more alive than ever two hundred years later: the myth of the maternal instinct, of every mother's spontaneous love for her child.

Moralists, administrators, and doctors set to work and deployed their subtlest arguments to convince women to return to better sentiments and once more breastfeed their children . . . It was the discourse of happiness and equality, a discourse that concerned them to the highest degree. Over almost two centuries, all ideologues promised them wonders in the event that they undertook their maternal duties: "Be good mothers and you will be happy and respected. Make yourselves indispensable to the family and you will obtain the right to citizenship."

One should understand that the current evaluation of motherhood is the result of a two-hundred-year-old advertising campaign, and that the original reasons for such discourse had nothing to do with love, but were chiefly based on the fact that at the end of the 18th century, the child acquired the value of merchandise, for it was perceived as potential economic wealth. The distinguished demographer Moheau said, "If there are princes whose hearts are deaf to the cry of nature, if vain tributes have made them forget that their subjects are their fellows, they should at least stop to think that man is simultaneously the ultimate end and instrument of all types of products; if this is the case, it is sufficient to consider him as a being who has a price, in order for him to be considered the most precious treasure of a sovereign." Also consider that the defense of population explosion has only one origin—that each human being is an essential economic unit as a producer-consumer, and is therefore useful to the system. This is the real reason why certain sectors are so reactionary to any form of birth control, for if the birth rate drops, the expansion of capitalism is thus restricted.

I believe that the practice of indiscriminate abortion must come to a stop now altogether, but the blame of those who practice it cannot be the same in all cases, since there may be extenuating and aggravating circumstances.

Indeed, as with all ethical and moral dilemmas, the problem would not exist if the human being could evolve spiritually. Ethical dilemmas affect only "half-men," inasmuch as the "complete" ones invariably act on the strength of the highest form of ethics, simply because their minds could not conceive of any other option.

Really, abortion is not a judicial or moral problem but rather a jigsaw puzzle for those who are incomplete; it is merely a matter of paucity of consciousness in the common man, with all the shortcomings that this kind of underdevelopment entails. This underdevelopment is the most grave, cruel, and pernicious of all. Highly developed people usually make love consciously, choosing fertile or infertile cycles in accordance with their intentions, but if an unwanted pregnancy should occur through carelessness or error, they would take full responsibility for this before God and Nature.

The rights of the fetus emanate from its parents. They procreate it, breast-feed it, care for it, and educate it, or prevent it from developing. It is obvious that while its parasite life lasts, the fetus is only a guest of the mother who harbors it, and it attains individual status only once the umbilical cord is cut. Obviously, as the pregnancy advances, the fetus becomes more and more viable, so that as it progresses, an abortion would also be a more serious violation.

I believe that proper family planning and birth control are important if we are to overcome the human being's quantitative mania as regards the continual growth of the flock. This approach entails a preference for increasing quantity instead of quality, which has doomed the species to the moral and spiritual decadence that is the logical consequence of a proliferation of vulgarity and coarseness, of a mass that increases at lightning speed, displaying the very worst characteristics of the species.

The People's Republic of China has provoked controversy by approving a law declaring that couples who wish to marry must have their genes examined to detect genetic errors and mental disorders that, although they might not be apparent in the couple themselves, could in fact affect their children. Permission to marry is refused to the bearers of such deficient genes, or they are allowed to marry only if they agree to sterilization beforehand. Despite the fact that many find this to be an inhuman act that offends human dignity, one could quite rightly ask: "which is worse, to procreate sick or mentally disturbed children or to prevent them being born? Is it a barbaric act or an act of perfect humanism?" Each must decide for himself in his own inner world, setting aside hypocrisy and blind obedience to the slogans of the majority.

However, it is a concrete reality that, with the passing of the years, there has been an increase in the number of deficient genes in the human gene pool. Deficient mutations occur by chance, but the probability that they might occur increases through exposure to certain mutagenic agents such as chemical substances or products of nuclear irradiation. Moreover, coupling between blood-relations brings about a higher proportion of deficient genes. Likewise, medical advances also influence this matter by prolonging the life of patients such as diabetics and hemophiliacs, who used to die at an early age, which once meant the elimination of part of that gene pool.

There are rules for shaping good citizens, obedient consumers, efficient professionals, intelligent people, but not for individuals with a high level of consciousness and ethical and spiritual values of a transcendental kind. It appears that in our culture, there exists only the concept of "quantity" in the physical sense, but not of "quality" of people as far as spiritual development is concerned. There is great concern in certain sectors to ensure the continual population growth, but total disinterest in improving people's inner quality. This means ensuring the progressive increase of bodies and sensations that are more and more intense, forgetting the need to promote the development of the spirit and the higher feelings. There is nothing more exhausting than to await the duplication or triplication of a massive population devoid of any spiritual content, with subhuman inner qualities, capacities limited to the survival of the body or reproduction, consumerism, and animal pleasure. This means to indiscriminately increase the number of *incomplete or half-men,* instead of making an effort to complete those who already exist.

The sanctification of the fetus may make us believe that the only important thing in life is the survival of the body, and that the phrase "grow and multiply" means merely to increase the density of the human flock. It is oblivious to the true purpose of life which is the shaping and proliferation of higher human beings who will comply with the Creator's evolutive mandate—complete men who can guide their fellows along the path of spiritual perfection.

There are as many different motivations for bringing on an abortion as there are diverse life situations in a couple, but it is obvious that abortion provoked through the inconvenience of having a child is the most common. This could be avoided with birth control that utilizes infertile cycles, but people unfortunately are not being educated in these techniques.

I have repeatedly insisted that the moral question is a matter of the *individual level of evolution,* and that one can act with authentic rectitude only when one attains this level.

A person's acts are the expression of his spiritual measure, and if this latter is at the lowest level, one can expect from him ethically acceptable behavior only if he submits to the moral rules imposed by society, since between two evils, it is always better to choose the less evil. Of course, an enforced code of ethics is preferable to deliberate immorality.

However, in the strict sense of what morality really is, it needs to be pointed out that it is only genuine when its rules are carried out freely and voluntarily by an individual who, because of his own level of comprehension of what is good and what is evil, is convinced of the ineluctible need to act correctly. The rest, those who neither understand nor who are interested in doing so, are for the moment the majority.

To act morally means to decide in conscience, but not the "conscience" of facile speech. Rather, it is "conscience" in the highest sense of the word, that concerns the individual spiritual evolution that gives birth to the total consciousness of those who find their transcendental selfhood through knowledge of themselves, thus becoming the most suitable vehicle for the manifestation of the divine spark, the individual's luminous identity—the individual who will later attain the capacity to recognize this same spark in all human beings.

Every conscious person must, as much as possible, prevent unwanted pregnancies by using adequate birth control, using the system of the cycles of physiological infertility in order to avoid the problem of an unwanted birth. Also, the fetus should be demythified in the sense that people need to become aware of the huge hypocrisy there is concerning this subject, when abortion is indiscriminately condemned and, at the same time, the problem of the 850 million people who suffer famine in the world is ignored, (according to a United Nations report), and of other forms of violence and slavery that are exerted against both children and adults.

Neither should one forget that abortion is an unhappy choice but one that corresponds to real situations in people's lives, and that penalization means making it clandestine which raises the risk of complications such as traumatic hemorrhages, infections, and chronic inflammation of the fallopian tubes, apart from the psychological trauma derived from social reproval of provoked abortion.

Once again, it is necessary to insist on the fact that sexuality has to be taught in such a way that it becomes a conscious act of human beings and not of animals, thus birth control should be used in order not to be faced with the temptation of abortion.

Masturbation

Like many other vices, onanism has in modern times been stripped of the immoral aura it had in former times, and many professionals openly recommend it as an advisable form of therapy to release nervous tension. It is no longer a practice that is merely excusable in adolescence, but rather, has become a habit that needs no justification among adults.

In various countries, there are "masturbation workshops" which teach how to perform this under the pretext of its supposed or imaginary benefits, which are really a mere justification for a type of permissive self-indulgence that destroys one's character and will power.

It is a sign of our times that there is a repeated intent to suppress the concept of "sexual aberrations" so that any type of sexual behavior, however perverse it may be, is justified as a matter of "individual preference." This is a process that goes in parallel with the loss or deterioration of moral values, as if there were a power in the shadows that for some reason wished to pervert all of humanity.

Nobody today is shocked if an adult habitually masturbates, and this is supposedly not only natural but also healthy. Men usually do it to relieve anguish of various types, and women to unconsciously try to overcome "penis envy" or envy of the male role by obtaining sexual stimulation without the agency of a man, something that many women either overtly or covertly desire. These women usually dream of dispensing with the male sex to thus be able to satisfy their own desires and needs by themselves. This yearning desire is unconsciously mixed with disqualification and contempt for men.

The high level of nonspecific anguish in some women makes them resort to the solitary pleasures as an escape valve, a manipulation to which they have to return constantly since their anxiety resurfaces time and again with increasing intensity. Thus, masturbation has become as common as having a cup of coffee, eating a candy, or tasting an exotic dish.

The scientific community supposes that this habit does not harm people, but to the contrary, views it as recommendable or healthy. I do not know how the "solitary vice" lost its reputation as a reprovable habit to become a desirable manipulation. What is true is that those who habitually masturbate become morose, sad, unsociable, and forgetful and experience a deterioration in both character and will power. In antiquity, it was thought that the solitary vice caused various psychic disorders, but it is now thought that such solitary practices are only one of the elements in a clinical case that can bring physical exhaustion and obsessions.

Antoine Porot, in the *Dictionary of Clinical Psychiatry and Therapy*,[14] states:

> Masturbation is a symptom of many mental disorders, psychoses, or neuroses, either isolated or associated with other practices of morbid eroticism. In the biographies of sexual perverts, it appears as a manifestation of emotional childishness, and is often connected with bestiality, fetishism, and exhibitionism. It is also to be found in acute states such as drunkenness and infectious deliriums.
>
> It is also significant at the beginning of schizophrenic states and is associated with the odd attitudes of moodiness, shyness, autism, and inherited retardation. It is commonly to be observed in idiots, in which it can take on a frenzied aspect, and in other forms of mental retardation such as imbecility. It occurs also in psychastenia and neurotic states with depression of the will, manic psychosis, and dementia.

Personally, I believe that masturbation brings psychic disorders, a functional perturbation of the brain, altered emotional states, a deterioration of the character and will, and a narcissistic introversion, thus representing an immoral perversion of the sacred nature of sex. This was alluded to in the Bible with respect to the original sin when God commanded Adam and Eve not to eat of the fruit of a certain tree in Paradise. It is said that they were expelled from the Garden of Eden for not obeying this prohibition. I believe this story conceals a profound meaning that transcends appearances, and the true sin of Adam and Eve was to lose respect for sex as a divine gift or a sacred manifestation of the Creator, in the supposition that sexuality was a mere instrument to satisfy their concupiscence and not the divine source of all creativity.

On the subject of masturbation, the remarks of Sandor Ferenczi are of particular interest, in his work *Sex and*

Psychoanalysis,[15] as to the difference between onanism and normal coitus. Ferenczi says:

> In a series of cases in which analysis brought awareness of the terror of castration and thoughts of incest, and therefore put an end to the psychoneurotic symptoms, but in which there was not total abstinence from onanism, even during treatment or after same, on the day after masturbation, patients displayed a typical psychic and somatic perturbation, which I shall call day-neurasthenia. These patients' main complaint was: marked fatigue and a leaden heaviness in their legs, especially when they got up in the morning, insomnia or disturbed sleep, great sensitivity to light and auditive stimuli (sometimes clearly defined sensations of pain in the eyes or ears), gastric disorders, paresthesia in the lumbar region, and sensitivity to pressure in all nerves. In the psychic sphere, [they experienced] great emotional irritability, bad temper and a tendency to find fault, an incapacity or reduction in the capacity to concentrate (aprosexia). These perturbations lasted right through the middle of the day and gradually diminished in the early hours of the evening. Towards night, there was total restoration of the state of the body, calm in the sphere of the emotions and total recovery of the intellectual capacity.
>
> I should like to expressly point out that these symptoms did not coincide with any relapse of the psychoneurotic symptoms and that in no case could I reach these symptoms or influence them through psychoanalysis. Therefore, honesty demands that we leave aside here psychological speculations and that the symptoms be recognized as the physiological results of onanism.

Ferenczi states that the activity of masturbation can bring on physiological effects that do not occur in normal coitus. He points out that when a man had sexual relations with a woman who gave him complete satisfaction, he felt invigorated after the act, often enjoying a short nap on the same day, and the next day behaved in an unusually competent and efficient manner. After onanism, on the other hand, there came day-neurasthenia, with all the symptoms mentioned above, namely, pain in the eyes at the stimulus of light, heaviness in the legs, psychic irritability, hyperaesthesia of the skin, and a special sensitivity to tickling.

He adds that "the real masturbatory neurosis can be conceived of as chronic, as the sum of the symptoms of the onanistic neurasthenias of one day . . . It is obvious that the nervous processes of coitus and masturbation are not physiologically identical."

The differences pointed out by Ferenczi between normal and onanistic coitus show that one of them, the normal type, is a source of satisfaction and energy, whereas the other brings vasomotor, sensorial, sensitive, and psychic over-stimulation, that persist after onanism. Add to this the sensations of sadness, oppression, solitude, and exhaustion.

There is a profound reason Nature has in condemning masturbation, and this is the fact that unipolarity does not engender anything. Only bipolarity is fecund. Everything in Nature, from the atom to the most complex structures has two poles, and this bipolarity is the origin of creative power. Neither the solitary male nor the abandoned female is fecund, and this should be understood beyond the concept of materializing offspring and be taken to the sphere of personal creativity.

The masturbator deliberately withdraws from his polar partner (a partner of the opposite sex), so that he is isolated from Nature and experiences a considerable restriction of his creative capacities. This results in a loss of virility, difficulty in materializing his personal projects, diverse psychic disorders, a lack of mental concentration, solitude and unhappiness, abnormality in his relations with the opposite sex, and a deterioration of character and will power.

The normal sexual relationship between men and women is an interaction of two magnets, which by uniting, increase their potential, from which a good deal of erotic pleasure is derived.

The woman, as the negative pole, and the man, as the positive one, are united during coitus in an energetic feedback that means giving and receiving, exchanging the magnetism of their bodies, a process that renews both the cells and vitality. That onanism is an aberration, comes from the fact that everything in Nature is dual and has two poles, and unipolarity does not exist within the normal schema of life.

Sexual attraction is a phenomenon equivalent to two magnets sticking together, but the fundamental impulse of sexual activity is the survival instinct that leads to procreation. The power to create new life lies in sex, and represents a sacred faculty that emanates from God.

Coitus is intended to be creative only when it engenders a child, but one might ask what happens in those cases in which there has been a normal relationship without the ovule being fertilized. The obvious reply seems to be that nothing occurs; the seed simply drops onto infertile ground and conception is not carried out. This idea has a basic flaw, and this is the fact that life is polar; it has two sides to it, and mass and energy cannot be separated when examining either one or the other in isolation, for they are indissolubly united. This means that all bodily functions have an energetic counterpart of similar importance, a fact well known to acupuncture since time immemorial. The fact that the physical seed is lost does not mean that the same occurs in its energetic counterpart.

The process of the sexual act, from beginning to end, is equivalent to the organic one in the field of energy. This means accepting that there is an energetic sexuality, the counterpart of the organic one, which is the true source of sexual attraction between the two sexes.

The fact that the scientific establishment does not know and has not proven its existence does not mean that it does not exist. It often happens that the pride of scientists causes us to be taken further away from the original sources of truth through the argument that "that was what was believed in olden times." This is quite true at times with respect to ancient concepts such as the one that says the earth is flat or that the planets revolve around it, but it is quite likely that there are other areas in which ancient wisdom could offer us lessons, and one of them is that of animal magnetism, or merely magnetism.

In 1760, Franz Mesmer, a German physician, attempted to cure illnesses with the use of magnets, for he had discovered that by applying them, certain sick persons could be cured. He then discovered that the human body was also a magnetic accumulator, and that cures could be effected by "the laying on of hands," from which the theory of animal magnetism was born. A royal committee disqualified the bases of his doctrine, so that after being highly successful in Paris, he returned to Germany where he died in oblivion. Today, whether the scientific establishment likes it or not, alternative medicine can successfully cure many illnesses with the use of magnets and machines that project magnetic impulses. It is, moreover, quite likely that the future of curative medicine lies in irradiating the organs with magnetic energy to reestablish the order that had been altered in the body's fields of energy.

Harold Saxton Burr provided a great deal of evidence supporting the fact that matter is structured through the irradiation of electric fields and that these influence man, plants, trees, and animals alike. In his work *Blueprint for Immortality*,[16] he shows how it is possible, with the aid of a voltmeter, to detect illnesses at the potential or incubatory stage. Saxton Burr believes that the whole Cosmos is full of these intelligent electric fields that are the "pattern" or template around which atoms and any material structure are organized, and that illness is a disorder of the potentiality of these fields, which he calls *L-fields* (life-fields).

Saxton Burr says:

The electrodynamic fields are invisible and intangible, and it is hard to visualize them. Most people who have been in contact with higher education will remember that if iron shavings are scattered over a metal plate with the aid of a magnet, they will order themselves into the form of the lines of force of the magnetic field. Something similar, although infinitely more complicated, occurs with the human body. Its molecules and cells are constantly being discarded and reconstructed with new material from the food we eat. Modern research has shown that the materials of our body and brain are renewed far more often than one might think. All the proteins in the body, for example, are changed every six months, and in some organs such as the liver, they are renewed more frequently. When we encounter a friend we have not seen for six months, there is not a single molecule in his face that was there six months before, but thanks to a controlled *L-field*, the new molecules have slipped into the older familiar form and we can recognize his face. Until modern instruments revealed the existence of controlled *L-fields*, biologists got lost explaining how our bodies were kept in form by the metabolism and the endless changes of material. Now the mystery has been solved. The electrodynamic fields of the body serve as a mold or matrix that preserves the form or ordering of any material that is emptied out of it, even when this occurs frequently . . . the inspection of the *L-fields* is carried out with voltmeters and special electrodes that reveal different forms or degrees of voltage in different parts of the *L-field*.

The *L-fields* can be detected by measuring the differences in voltage between two points on or near the surface of the life-form. In man and woman they can be measured by locating an electrode on the forehead and another on the chest or hand. Alternatively, the index finger of each hand is submerged in containers filled with a saline solution, which are connected to the voltmeter, which must be a special model with an empty tube, for an ordinary voltmeter needs so much electric current to make the needle swing that it would consume the potential of the *L-field*, thus making any reading useless.

Saxton Burr recommends Hewlett-Packard model 412A, that has been discontinued but has been replaced by other models. In the preface to his book, Saxton Burr writes:

> The Universe in which we live and from which we cannot be separated, is a place of Law and Order. This is neither accident nor chaos. It is organized and maintained by an electrodynamic field that is able to determine the position and movement of all charged particles. For about half a century, the consequences of this theory have been submitted to rigorously controlled experimental conditions and no contradictions have been found.

In accordance with Burr's experiments, there is no doubt at all that the electronic field characteristic of a living system is a basic property of life. Likewise, it should be remembered what the basis of electromagnetism is: the fact that any magnetic phenomenon is produced by electric currents, and that when two electric charges are in movement, there is manifested a magnetic force between them. This could be a point of contact between the concept of the *L-fields* and so-called "animal magnetism." I believe that the electromagnetic fields of man and woman complement each other in a harmonious interrelation, mutually revitalizing each other through erotic attraction between both sexes, and during coitus and orgasm. In the same way, I think that the *L-fields* of the masturbator will be altered and disordered by solitary stimulation, for in this case there is no complementation with his counterpart of the opposite sex.

Dissociation, disorder, and decline of the *L-fields* may decisively cause the body to weaken, as anybody can certainly prove for himself if he has time and interest enough for it.

Normal coitus is carried out between man and woman, one of positive polarity, the other of negative, the sperm and the egg, and it usually ends in orgasm, the moment when the semen penetrates the woman who, if she is in her fertile period, will likely conceive a child.

In this way, only a small proportion of sexual acts result in offspring, so that those that do not could be classified as "infertile coitus." Nevertheless, I believe that we are eminently creative, and that there is no infertile orgasm, because there is an energetic counterpart of the male seed and the female uterus. Every sexual act is creative, even though we may not be able to visualize the fruit of it when there is no physical offspring. However, I have no doubt that the magnetic-sexual irradiations of man and woman always create a certain type of child when they have intercourse and that this probably corresponds to some type of coagulation of magnetic energy that has a certain level of consciousness in accordance with that of its parents, and that it continues to live through them. Those who believe only in what they can see and touch should recall that visible matter is only a thousand millionth part of the Universe, since the relationship between amounts of energy (photons) and particles of mass (nucleons) is roughly a thousand million to one. Thus, the great majority of life in the Universe consists of invisible energy.

This is why it is absurd to suppose that the only creative possibility of coitus is a material offspring. It is more logical to suppose that any sexual act gives rise to energetic offspring, forms of energy which, having already existed in the father and mother, are projected outside them in orgasm to become independent and start a form of life not known to science: the human being's *magnetic residue,* an energy that, once it separates from its creators, continues to exist as a sort of fetus made up of pure energy that remains attached to its parents by an energetic umbilical cord, and feeds on them in order to subsist. When the sexual act gives rise to conception, these energies are reabsorbed in the physical fetus.

Masturbation will always be sterile and represents an aberration of Nature, by trying to make the coitus unilateral, by using the energies of life granted by the Creator, in a vicious self-stimulation of sensorial lust, devoid of love, romanticism, and any relationship within a couple. The sublime nature of the creative act of life, becomes denegrated to the manual or mechanical stimulation of the organs.

The word "masturbation" is derived from the Latin *man(u)stuprare. Mano* or *manus* means "hand." *Stuprum* means "dishonor, profanation, and disgrace." He who masturbates profanes his own body, and what is an almost necessary evil in adolescence becomes vicious behavior in adulthood.

In sum, masturbation does not represent normal sexual activity, and has always been, is, and always will be a vice, and one should remember what this expression means. The dictionary says that the word "to vitiate" means: "to damage or corrupt physically or morally." Likewise "to corrupt" means "to waste, to deprave, to harm, to rot," and also "to ruin," "to vitiate," "to pervert." The masturbator is addicted to the lasciviousness of stimulating his own sex, which debases, wastes, and perverts him, because it is an aberration of normal coitus. The arguments of those who defend this vice come under the heading of rationalizations, which are mental thought processes to justify an act or opinion that is really founded on other motives or causes than those expressed, although this need not necessarily be evident to the person who rationalizes.

There are addicts of masturbation who, in order to justify their vice, rationalize it, embroidering it in such a way that instead of accepting it for what it really is, make it appear as a healthy, recommendable custom, and sometimes even endowing it with mystical connotations. Thus, what should be the product of love is debased and defiled to become an act of giving free rein to the animal we all bear within us. Any moral and spiritual perfectioning needs a sublimation of the libido. Masturbation seems to be the opposite of sublimation, and represents a moral and spiritual degradation that has become characteristic of Mankind in our time. Besides, one should also consider the selfish, antisocial nature the masturbator develops, for he withdraws into himself, avoiding normal contact with the opposite sex and also at times with everybody else.

The normal love relationship between a man and a woman is something that requires effort and work, for each will unwittingly attempt to assimilate the other party to his own needs, which sooner or later provokes friction and confrontation. Friction and confrontation are a vehicle for working on one's own defects such as egoism and narcissism, to one day merge in harmonious, happy, and balanced union. For this, one needs character, sensitivity, will power, tolerance, and generosity.

The onanist shirks all this work and effort to get quick, immediate genital satisfaction, thus depriving himself of the beauty, harmony, internal satisfaction, and depth that a relationship within a couple can bring. Really, the proof of a human being is his partner, for it is in this relationship that all demands and defects that have not been worked on will surface. He who continues to compulsively masturbate after adolescence and cannot stop it, is fixed at a childish stage that prevents him from maturing, very often depriving him of the happiness and plenitude one can achieve in a good relationship of a couple. The solitary onanist who has no partner merely squanders his creative power uselessly, discharging the magnetism of his body and thus making it impossible to accumulate it properly. This has negative consequences for his health and personal fulfillment. The semen spilt by the masturbator cannot become similar, biologically and energetically speaking, to that which is issued in normal coitus, and in some way, it is marked or contaminated by the dark side of the universal force. The masturbator in himself is not usually a luminous person but a surly and taciturn one. If we accept that the human body is a magnetic accumulator, the sexual act cannot be any other than an exchange of magnetism in which both parties give and receive. I believe that animal magnetism is essential to life and bodily health and that all vitality is at heart vitality of the cell. When Ferenczi points out that man feels invigorated after sexual relations with a woman that gives him total satisfaction, he means a revitalization of the man's own magnetic potential through the exchange of magnetism, for the same thing happens to the woman.

The masturbator on the other hand only gives, and receives nothing in exchange, resulting in an orgasm in which there is a veritable discharge to the earth of his electromagnetic potential, which explains the extreme weakness he feels afterwards.

I believe that a sustained drop in the levels of the body's electric potential makes it vulnerable to diverse physiological disorders, among which one could mention the loss of a capacity to concentrate and a drop in the activity of the immunological system. It is quite likely that the brain is also affected because the cerebrospinal axis is a magnet with one pole in the brain and the other in the genitalia. Like all cells, the neurons need to feed on magnetism, which in this case circulates through the cerebrospinal channel, being renewed or replenished through bipolar sexual contact with the opposite sex. This type of coitus, when one does not overdo it, nourishes and stimulates the brain, but this does not occur in masturbation in which one is continually being depleted of cerebrospinal magnetism through one's sex, with a resulting perturbation of neuronal nutrition and vitality.

Dr. Paul Le Moal, in his definition of the normal sexual act, says that if it is to be effectively valid, it must have attained a triple maturity: genital, psycho-sexual, and emotional.

Le Moal points out that:

Sexual maturity is usually attained at the end of puberty, when the genital organs have acquired the same characteristics as in adults. This maturity is what makes a complete sexual relationship possible, and with it, procreation. Psycho-sexual maturity is the heterosexual eroticism to be especially found in a youth who has attained the elective stage. Emotional maturity, particularly characterized by the offering of one's self (offering and a spirit of sacrifice) is attained when the possibility to give oneself can be materialized without restrictions and definitively. In other words, when there is full recognition of the "other" as a person in the full meaning of the word, then it is possible. Therefore, a sexual act, of any type, that does not correspond to this triple requirement is sexually abnormal and at the same time morally abnormal.

> Let us point out that what gives the human sexual act its specific values is not sexual maturity or heterosexual attraction (these two conditions occur and exist among animals), but emotional maturity which implies electivity. In men and women who have attained maturity, it is the sentimental impulse, that is self-offering love, that must condition the carnal act; the mere genital link in evolved beings cannot be sufficient unto itself because, in isolation, it brings no more than mere "pleasure," which is not even the shadow of the joyful happiness (in which pleasure is included) reserved for those who fully love each other.[17]

As Doctor Le Moal points out, it is emotional maturity that enables the sexual act to be considered normal, and that when this component is missing, coitus between persons is no different than that practiced by other animals. I echoed this point of view in a former chapter when I said that most offspring are not the fruit of genuine love but of the instincts. I have no doubt whatsoever that the child engendered without real, complete affection cannot be qualitatively the same as the one who is in fact the product of love. Unfortunately, our era is not characterized by an abundance of people who possess a mature and evolved "I." Rather, what abounds are neurotic, weak, childish, and evolutively frustrated parents.

Love is probably what brings the *L-fields* of a couple into harmony thereby bringing about the "joyful happiness" that Doctor Le Moal attributes to those who fully love each other. It is the sublime happiness that the onanist will never attain, unless he manages to gain maturity in the field of the emotions and overcomes this vice.

The great obstacle that men of science have in grasping certain simple truths that concern people's condition of normalcy is the fact that there is an accelerated decline in moral values, a decline that sweeps along all Mankind in a veritable involution of ethics, so that something that was considered a perversion 50 years ago is now regarded as normal. When man wishes to justify his own vices, faults, or offenses, he resorts to a manipulation of the concept of normality, arguing that "this is normal," however aberrant or perverse it may really be. As is only logical, all those who feel attracted to perverse types of behavior will coincide in calling them absolutely normal.

Even though a bad habit can be widespread and accepted by everyone, this will not mean that this habit is normal in the higher meaning of the word. Unfortunately, if the whole species follows the most aberrant habit imaginable, it will by this very fact take on the condition of "normality." However, it is easy to understand that this normality has nothing to do with real normality.

Suppose for a moment that the entire species decided in fact to practice masturbation as the ideal form of coitus, collecting the semen for test-tube fertilization. Without a doubt, the moment would come when those who carried out the normal sexual act would be persecuted or punished, and one day, people would altogether forget how to really make love.

The perversion I describe here has fortunately not occurred, but it has certainly occurred in the past in an equivalent manner in other spheres of human life, and it is possible that a considerable portion of what we call "normal" is really abnormal, perverse, or depraved. I have pointed out that common man is far from being normal, if we discard the statistical concept of normality and focus on the "optimum normality" of Nature. In fact, the common man is indeed "incomplete," and what is incomplete is often abnormal.

The most prized capacities the human race can aspire to are contained within it only in a latent state, and can only be activated by genuine individual evolution. From the point of view of the emotions, masturbation is a withdrawal into oneself in a selfish complacency that is situated at the opposite pole to empathy and interest for one's fellows, and it is a serious obstacle to the correct development of the "I." Spiritual development is incompatible with masturbation or other vices, because it demands an adequate tempering of character and will, which is not possible when one remains enslaved to the passions.

As for love, I cannot see how the onanist can attain it in its true meaning, unless it be through real spiritual and emotional maturity, for love is a mixture of renunciation, virtue, and higher consciousness.

The vice of masturbation can be easily overcome by educating the will and by entering into normal love relationships with a partner of the opposite sex. However, it requires overcoming one's own selfish tendencies to learn to give of oneself and acquire the right emotional compromise in the couple's relationship.

NOTE: (Cf. the Appendix for scientific experimentation as to the harm caused by masturbation.)

Relations Against Nature

There are those who so distort the course of their sexual activity that they fall into relationships against Nature. Among such aberrations is anal coitus which has proliferated to the extent that it has become considered "only a sexual variant," as normal as any other. It would seem that a certain type of "brain fever" had spread that leads some to carry out the sexual act with inappropriate parts of the body, thus contravening both God and Nature, who have provided the organically correct channels for genital contact. Only a very sick or perturbed individual could desire penetration by the same channel through which excrement is normally eliminated, and he who lends himself passively to it must be equally unhinged. One could ask what type of mad desire leads a human being to reject the body and organs God gave him according to his sexual gender, which for example occurs with males who seek to turn into women through surgery, or women who wish to have male genitals, thus repudiating their own sexuality.

The one who seeks anal contact reduces sexuality to a purely genital and mechanical affair, like the complement between a nut and a bolt, in the supposition that coitus is merely a material stimulation of his organs. Thus love, romanticism, and respect for both oneself and the opposite sex are erased with one act. Similarly, the union of the virile member and excrement is a sordid mixture, but we know that there are many individuals who feel attracted by this vice or anything else that degrades and distorts the natural channels, and it is up to the psychiatrist to explain the causes for this perturbation. Because we live in a society that is profoundly hypocritical, this subject is usually never mentioned. However, it is not possible when discussing morality to omit this type of conduct, for we run the risk that in the course of time we may come to think that violating Nature is just as normal as respecting it, and we may perhaps also forget what normal sex is, as opposed to aberrant sexuality.

Under the pretext of respect for individual freedom there is perhaps too much permissiveness as regards this subject, and children may grow up in the midst of total ambiguity or absolute ignorance as to sexual normality. It is obvious that the individual who wishes to be perverse, through his own tastes, will in any case be so. However, I believe that it is important for people to know the cost of such deviation, for only by knowing about it will it be possible to assess its real consequences.

As is logical, in the minds of men of plainly instinctive behavior, female sexuality represents a mere "cavity" that offers pleasure, an orifice that as such need be no different than any other cleft. With this approach, they not only lack respect for and debase women or humanity, but also lower themselves to the condition of mere animals. In any case, I do not believe that any of these or other even stronger considerations could serve to make those who have slipped into antinatural vices abandon such practices. Something similar occurs here to what happens with tobacco addiction. The smoker knows that smoking may cause cancer or other diseases, but is still addicted to it because he does not have the necessary will power or because he deceives himself into believing that he does not have it. At heart, he manipulates himself in order to continue smoking, fully aware of the harm it causes him, due to the fact that his inner world has neither really understood nor accepted the destructive effects of tobacco.

One human peculiarity that has always astonished me is the fact that a man may "know" something and yet not incorporate it, because he does not deeply understand the information he possesses. It is a bit like simultaneously knowing and ignoring, and this is why people are not consequential with what they do and what they know, there being no cause–effect relationship between both things. This is also the reason why people are not interested in knowing the genuine truth regarding the fundamental questions of life, for the truth demands that one commit oneself to it to act consequentially, which perhaps may mean a total change of conduct and habits that may deprive the individual of the abnormal or deviant pleasure he derives from "incorrect," immoral, or anti-ethical situations.

The one who practices anal sex sees nothing unseemly in it, apart from a moral prohibition or social rejection, and does not distinguish it as different from natural coitus. What is certain, however, is that the creative nature of any sexual act ensures that the result of anal penetration will be a "magnetic child," born from the mixture of the magnetic energy of the penis and the anus.

There is no need to give much thought to the matter in order to discern what the qualitative condition of this freak could be, one of whose creative poles consists of the magnetic irradiation of the penis, which is the natural channel used for coitus, and the other, the magnetism of the anus, which is the sewer of the body, used in this case as a perverse substitute for the vagina. What type of vibratory creature could be produced by using the channel through which excrement is eliminated as one of the creative polar extremes? The duality of all that exists shows that any living matter has an energetic counterpart, of an equivalent vibratory condition, as is the case of the *L-fields*, which are in keeping with the specific function of the bodily organ or system they accompany.

In the present case, an act of energetic creation is carried out by using the magnetic projection of the male organ and the anus, which is the channel for eliminating organic waste. In this way, the one who carries out this manipulation will *generate an energetic offspring, the fruit of the magnetic projection of the male organ and of the magnetism irradiated by the sewage function.*

Although this creation is only real in the world of energy, the same happens to it as to any child of flesh and blood, that is, it lives in close symbiosis with its parents.

The price paid by the addict for the practice we are discussing is that he must always be accompanied by a being who springs from his own energetic seed, a freak of perverse nature in this case dominated by the dark side of the universal force. This creation will certainly provoke unsuspected trouble in its progenitors' lives.

There is a popular Spanish expression that says that "the devil put his tail in" to refer to such excessive complications or sudden obstacles that appear, opposing people's designs. It is quite likely that in these cases it is not precisely a question of "the devil's tail" but of "the hoof of a magnetic offspring" engendered *contranatura*.

The development of research on magnetism and techniques similar to Kirlian photography, which will be intensified in the 21st century, will enable us to prove that the creative nature of the magnetic projection of the human being, whose basic vibratory tonality, which could be either love or hate for example, can influence living beings either constructively or destructively. I should point out that there is nothing in modern physics to contradict this statement. On the contrary, there is outright certainty of everything I state in this work on magnetism, the proof of which is unfortunately silenced, discriminated against, and ignored, as always happens with new and different discoveries that are usually manipulated so that they remain ignored.

One has to lay aside "scientific superstition" and pride for a moment, to accept the possibility of a mystical view of reality that surpasses the separation between matter and spirit. This possibility has already been accepted by certain scientists such as Heisenberg, Schrodinger, Planck, Einstein, Pauli, Eddington, Koestler, and others. As has been said, "a little science makes the individual proud, but a more profound, complete science makes him humble." I suppose that any scientist with sufficient inner humility would be prepared to open up to the study of new truths in an unprejudiced way, but superstitious scientific prejudice that leads one to believe in immutable, definitive scientific knowledge, as someone said, may make one forget that "science is today's truth and tomorrow's lie."

As will be understood, in a book on morality one cannot evade a subject as controversial as this, and one has to pay the price that many feelings could be hurt. In any case, caring for others' feelings can never be important enough to hide the truth, and it is the duty of every authentic philosopher to proclaim this fact.

The only objective that guides me in this chapter is the denunciation of the consequences of anal coitus, and it is not my intention to offend or disqualify anyone. There are times in the life of certain people, when certain nefarious events occur and are only attributed to chance, whereas their true genesis may lie in certain cases, in mechanisms of the unconscious self-creation of destructive forces that perturb, disintegrate, or decompose people's *L-fields* and their environment. The laws of affinity and magnetic induction make it possible for a person to unwittingly influence the arrangement of his natural environment, at times perturbing the schema of forces that in some way maintain order, condition, or influence the material plane and its events.

I am amazed at the way in which so many cultured, intelligent people dissociate matter and energy, supposing that they are to be found in separate compartments when the truth is that they continually and extensively interpenetrate. The disintegration I mentioned leads them to invariably deny that the cause of facts of unknown origin, which could be attributed to chance, might lie in complex transactions that take place at a certain level of Nature, this level being "physical" (in the sense of physics) but invisible.

The above-mentioned people are those who could also think that repudiating these "bad habits"—to say the least—might respond to an old-fashioned or over-traditional approach, one perhaps far removed from progress and modernity. If this is my case, I feel greatly satisfied by it and happy to be able to adhere to traditional and transcendental values. I would like to be repetitive in affirming that anal coitus is an aberration of Nature, and it is a shameful rejection of the female vagina and womb, which is practiced by unhinged minds. A woman's sacred chalice can be sullied by individuals who practice anal coitus occasionally or habitually and are incapable of differentiating between both orifices. I could go on at length on this very sensitive subject, but I prefer to be brief and mention another type of antinatural relationship, which is menstrual coitus. With the exception of certain Eastern religions, I have never heard of doctors, priests, or moralists condemning this type of relationship. The general objections I have heard go no further than recommending proper hygiene in the process, and I know men who prefer to have sexual relations during this time. I want to mention the ancient belief, quoted in Hindu texts and others, that the woman takes on a marked attraction for men when she has her period, which is not hard to see by careful observation. In past epochs, it was said that a woman is controlled or dominated by strange forces during her period, forces which are precisely those that give that power of attraction to her. However, one can also tell in an ambiguous, blurred way that "one should not give in to such charms," for they obey some kind of dark force whose intentions are unsuspected. Chilean peasants believe that a woman who has her period should not gaze upon any sowed crops, for if she does, these crops might dry up or die. This belief is so extensive that in order to protect certain plantations from the woman's gaze, they put up curtains of large plants such as maize to protect more susceptible crops.

In many other places, it is also the custom that when a woman has her period she must refrain from working the land or from the task of sowing grain. Although those who superstitiously worship formal science as if it were an untouchable goddess may mock, it is nevertheless true that these customs have a completely scientific basis. Great discoveries do not begin when science takes them up; they have always existed in Nature, hidden from the knowledge of man. In reality, science neither discovers nor invents anything; it finds only what previously existed in the memory of Nature. Electricity did not begin with man; it has always existed. At this very moment, everything that could come into existence has its own reality within Nature, even though it remains invisible to our eyes.

The period of female menstruation corresponds to a process of eliminating old, worn-out, bodily magnetism, which is the bearer of negative energetic pulses of cellular waste; it is a cycle of sexual repose that should be respected, in as much as it corresponds to a phase of elimination and renewal. Women are renewed each month by expelling energetic waste through menstrual blood, which is not the same as normal blood, for it is saturated with negative magnetism, as has been proven in the research that appears in the Appendix to this work. If normal blood is under the vital influence of Eros and could be considered pure, menstrual blood is impure, being the bearer of a vibration of death, exhaustion, and waste. The former corresponds to the luminous side of the force, and the latter to the dark side.

We can, therefore, understand that a woman is influenced during her period by the dark side of the cosmic force, and that her blood is impure as she eliminates the negative part of her organic waste through it. Some Hindu religious precepts forbid any sexual relationships on days when a woman has her period, considering that she is then impure and that she has a contaminating power at that time.

Really, coitus during menstruation produces a situation which notably harms the couple, for apart from being morally impure, it results in a process of vice-ridden creation. Even though the normal channel is used, it is in a phase of elimination of residual waste, being saturated therefore by negative, dirty, impure, and worn-out magnetism. The fact that this phase corresponds to the manifestation of the dark side of the force makes for a coitus that puts us into contact with the universal destructive energy. The energetic offspring engendered by this process will be marked by the sign of the shadows, and will negatively influence the life of its creators. It is an inappropriate act from the moral and physiological point of view, and a harmful practice for the couple's *L-fields* which are the shared or common vital fields. If offspring were to be manually created by the parents from a diversity of materials, just as a sculptor molds a body, I would ask myself: Who would be so lacking in common sense as to create from waste material? This, nevertheless, is the case of the sexual act during menstruation—there is no visible offspring, but there is indeed an energetic offspring engendered from the waste energy, a magnetic field that will negatively influence its parents' destiny, who are also sinning against the purity and harmony of Nature.

NOTE: (Cf. the Appendix for scientific experimentation on the harm caused by anal coitus and sexual relations during menstruation.)

Adultery

According to certain religious precepts "marriage is indissoluble and the couple must remain united until death." This is a heavy burden indeed, that presupposes extraordinary clear-sightedness in the choice of the right partner, and great impeccability and patience in order to harmonize different characters and overcome the ups and downs of everyday life. In practice, the breach of conjugal fidelity is habitual in a high percentage of normal married couples from different social strata. When this occurs, there is immediate talk of the moral decline of certain people, but the true causes for this conduct are never really researched. Neither are different types of adultery classified in accordance with their seriousness.

I believe that one cannot generalize on this matter and that one can only speak of the case of a certain person whose motivations must surely be due to very diverse causes. It generally happens that the concept of conjugal fidelity is limited to exclusivity in the sexual contact of bodies. Each undertakes to grant the sexual exclusivity of his/her body to his/her counterpart. As regards what might happen in their thoughts and feelings, no one says anything. What would happen, for example, with an individual who was faithful in body but adulterous in thought and feeling? Could not the type of infidelity that entails the heart, soul, and thought be far more serious than that which merely affects the physical body? For example, no one would call the indiscriminate sexual intercourse practiced by animals "adultery," since they lack the consciousness that human beings have. The term "adulterer" can therefore be applied only to a human being, for he is supposed to have free will.

Is the man faithful or adulterous who respects bodily exclusivity at the same time as he desires so many women, and desires them every day, and even evokes their images during marital coitus? Is sex limited to mere genital contact? Are not erotic pulsions also sex? What about the faithful wife, who nevertheless continues to dream of her Prince Charming or who habitually meets men she feels attracted to, but does not share her erotic fantasy with her husband—this fantasy usually being more intense than the real act—rather, she shares this fantasy with the images of the ones in the fantasy.

It might be argued that it is one thing to desire something and not put it into practice and quite another to effectively execute it. This is very true, but in a different sense to what might be thought, for when something is put into practice, it might disappoint exaggerated expectations that are thus deflated and come to an end at that very moment. On the other hand, unsatisfied fantastical desire can remain active a whole lifetime, in this case becoming a person's "hidden lovers." The longer such fantasies last, the greater power they acquire in the mind of the person thus affected, and the stronger the tendency to overestimate the happiness or pleasure given by such images, the greater the tendency will be to criticize or disqualify the relationship that is in fact maintained.

Of course, the foregoing cannot be an excuse for adultery. There are many people who begin to love their partner once they have lost him/her, since prior to this they were subjugated to their own erotic dreams, veritable mental lovers who with their sirens' song had impaired an appreciation of their counterpart's qualities. There are those who consider that infidelity is something that almost exclusively concerns men, but statistics belie this for the proportion is not noticeably different.

Thus, the myth is done away with that a woman's sexual needs are weaker than a man's. What happens is that they have different types of sexuality that are satisfied in different ways. One of the strongest motivations for male adultery is usually genital dissatisfaction, whereas the predominant motive in women is a lack of affection. However, the true origin of adultery without a shadow of a doubt, lies in the fact that neither men nor women are prepared for marriage and are, respectively, bad spouses from a technical point of view. Neither of them has the level of consciousness needed for the practice of genuine love, which far from being a wild flower, is the fruit of an art that has to be carefully and perseveringly cultivated.

There will never be adultery if the couple has in fact learned how to practice the art of loving, and this expression has nothing to do with those books on pseudo-sexology that merely recommend the best positions for coitus. True love is far beyond the purely genital, although it is complemented by the carnal aspect.

What is commonly called "love" is usually no more than the erotic attraction of two bodies, unleashed by chemical factors (pheromones) and not by the harmonious vibration of two souls that, when they meet, are enraptured in mutual contemplation. The art of loving needs a long training process and centers on the person's spiritual development, the only valid means to develop higher consciousness, which is the source of genuine love.

I believe there is a proportion between genuine love and a person's spiritual development, and that unless one attains this stage of evolution, any attempt at love will be reduced to a mere imitation of something that is only glimpsed at the imaginative level. A true, profound love relationship requires that both the man and the woman have highly developed consciousnesses. The art of loving is no more than the faculty of exercising one's own spirituality in the sphere of coupling or human relationships.

Conjugal infidelity should be analyzed from the perspective of immaturity and a lack of expansion of consciousness. More than anything else, adultery is a means of betraying the trust the couple have placed in each other. It is not a mere transgression of bodily exclusivity, but the breach of a pact of honor established between the two parties. As in all moral matters, I believe that this problem is fundamentally due to the fact that ethical systems are generalized for everybody's use, and as people are not the same, what is of use for one may not help another, except of course those minimal norms that are designed to avoid dishonest habits, protect the stability of the family nucleus, ensure the individual's rights, or improve cohabitation and people's personal security. I am referring to the fact that the individual generally lacks any capacity to discriminate between good and evil, between what is right and what is wrong, and usually only imitates the habits of the majority, which by the way are not outstanding for their rationality and perfection, but rather for their lack of higher consciousness.

Neither does the individual put himself empathically in the shoes of others to respect their rights and to do justice to their basic aspirations. Honor, in the higher sense, means to nurture the trust given by others as if it were a precious treasure, paying continual attention that interpersonal relationships adjust to the concept of egalitarian equivalence. Now, only individuals with a fully developed higher *consciousness* can apply this wise principle, for they are conscious of their own rights and can wisely harmonize these rights with those of their fellows.

As may be understood, there would be no problems of any kind in the world if most of its population acted in this way. Not only would there be no adultery, in the profound sense of the word, but neither would there be famine, war, delinquency, or violence. Adultery is only one of the many facets of human imperfection, and to combat it by using religious or moral anathemas is only a makeshift solution to what is *Homo sapiens'* supreme wretchedness—his total lack of spiritual development, for a man's inner content (his spiritual content or spiritual quality) has not varied noticeably from his origins to the present day. In fact, when we speak of "spiritual development" it would seem that some dark machination had filched the meaning of this expression at some point in history, for when it is used, darkness penetrates people's minds, people who do not know what it is and who merely project their individual fantasies to define or pigeon-hole it along with the labels normally used by different cultures.

Some will link it to religion, others with a renunciation of material goods, metaphysics, esotericism, parapsychology, fortune-telling, and even swindling, but very few will have a good idea of what it really means, that is, the genuine evolution of individual consciousness, with everything that this entails in a technical and non-superstitious or mystical, dreamlike sense.

Wherever there is a truly evolved individual, he will take good care to keep to the principle of egalitarian equivalence in his relationship with his partner, since he will possess sufficient spiritual quality to assess his own acts and those of others in depth and with fairness, without overdoing it or falling short of what corresponds to himself or his spouse as far as obligations and rights are concerned, beyond any selfish interpretation.

He will never betray his companion, but if she should fall for some reason into the temptation of adultery, he will know how to keep calm and transcend the problem together, without harming the family or children. "Egalitarian equivalence," nevertheless, implies a higher equilibrium in the couple in the sense of individual consciousness, for in marriage, as in the whole of society, each brings his own contribution, more or less significant, and if this contribution is under the limit of what is acceptable, it means that only one of the spouses bears the burden of the whole relationship whereas the other remains as a dead weight to it.

The immaturity of one of the parties may cause his/her most important contribution to the marriage to be merely his/her own body, or just keeping house, in which case it is hard to maintain equality. As may be appreciated, should the one who contributes less to the marriage, in the integral sense, commit adultery, this is a more serious form of betrayal, just as if he who owes someone a certain sum of money also stole part of this person's belongings; or if a person who received only favors and kindness paid back the person who had been kind to him, by betraying him.

When understood as betrayal, adultery can never be justifiable, but if it is committed when one is "taken out of oneself" through unbearable psychological pressures, then this is a considerably important extenuating circumstance. For instance, there are cases in which a man harasses and maltreats his wife, who because she feels bullied, will easily slip into infidelity.

When the woman extorts the man, depriving him of sex with the aim of obtaining exaggerated concessions from him, she also risks making him seek a substitute, and perhaps no one could reproach him for this.

Whenever there is a lack of affection and care by one of the parties, there is a danger that the abandoned party will commit adultery, and this is a very real possibility in such cases.

Common (unevolved) people need a repressive code of ethics to dissuade them from committing orgiastic adultery, since they do not have the right self-control to properly withstand temptation, nor do they have the necessary force and frankness to take responsibility for their actions.

However, one must understand that sexual deprival is the antechamber to infidelity in the man and emotional deprival, the beginning of adultery in the woman. This does not mean that the sexual aspect is not important in the woman or the emotional aspect in the man; they are merely critical factors that precipitate adultery. The mere fact that there are moral rules condemning infidelity as reprovable makes one wonder whether this commandment, like any other moral requisite, should be observed to comply with the ethical code or to satisfy an inner need to do what is just and right.

This is where the crux of genuine human morality lies; the fact that an individual, or a group of individuals, has the necessary discernment of *conscience* to always act in accordance with what is just and right, not because there is any set of rules that demands it, but rather out of an inner certainty that this is the only feasible path to attain supreme good and happiness. Correct action is not easy within a corrupt context for it usually demands that one possess the necessary strength of character to go against the current or to denounce injustice, immorality, or arbitrariness that others either do not notice or ignore.

To oppose corruption when this type of conduct has become prevalent is an act of heroism for the person who keeps a clear head, and this may cause him to be considered as a dangerous rebel by the established system, which rewards massification and disapproves of those heroes of the spirit and the arts who make huge efforts to keep their own mental freedom and independence. The culture of the masses blindly worships hypocrisy and applauds those who, unclean, rend their garments when criticized or take the mote out of another's eye.

In any case, it would seem that the human being cannot bear a life free from hypocrisy, since this acts like a soft wadding around the "I" of those who can hardly bear to come into contact with reality.

Today there is a widespread desire to do what is immoral and forbidden, at the same time as all manner of strategic machinations are carried out at both the internal and external levels to whitewash one's image before society.

I should point out that on account of the paternalism of our culture, male infidelity is permissively regarded and is even considered a demonstration of virility, whereas the adulteress usually is unfairly insulted, not that it is just to be unfaithful, but there is no need to atrociously increase female guiltiness when male infidelity is brushed off lightly. Besides, it is obvious that the woman has a far higher level of tolerance towards male infidelity than that to be observed in men in the same situation. The woman usually forgives, but the man never forgets, and can hardly recover from an experience so injurious to his male chauvinism.

Practiced hypocrisy makes it accepted as normal that a man should feel attracted by any woman who is not his wife, but on the other hand, the woman is expected not to take her eyes off her husband for any reason. It has even been supposed that infidelity has a genetic origin, but really motivations for it are quite diverse. The commonest of these could quite well be the boredom caused by an over-routine relationship, which drives people to seek new sensations. The main culprit for this routine is usually consumerism, which obliges people to work much harder within a very strict timetable in order to save up the necessary funds to satisfy their desires. Nevertheless, one should consider that there is a necessary and well-founded type of consumerism, which is that destined to satisfy basic needs, and another that could be called superfluous or exaggerated. The problem lies in that the normal levels of material well-being required by the family are continually being raised by the multiplication of consumer offers. It then occurs that after exhausting days at work, there is not much space left for variation or creativity in one's conjugal relations, and people very often feel that they have had their bellyful of repetitive patterns. Together with this, tiredness and stress come into play too, becoming the antechamber for the search for some escape valve which in many cases is infidelity, this usually being devoid of routine on account of its very characteristics.

Another cause for adultery is the sexual dissatisfaction of the woman because of the man's premature orgasm, or noncoincidence between the man's and the woman's genital appetites.

Men who are rough in bed; women who remain indifferent to their husband's requests; over-passive individuals married to hot-blooded women; a lack of love and care by one's counterpart; a desire for change and adventure are all some of the most frequent causes for adultery.

There are other, well-founded motives such as cases in which one of the parties suffers serious disorders of the personality, as for instance occurs in borderline, schizoid, and cyclothymic personalities, which manage to make life impossible for those around them, incurable cases that, without a shadow of a doubt, justify putting an end to the relationship. With regard to this problem, I should point out that the symptoms that accompany these disorders are usually quite insidious and hard to recognize for the nonprofessional in this field and can be confused with nervous disorders, which explains why a relationship of this kind can last for a long time. Really, among common people, there are only few who can "throw the first stone" to condemn a case of adultery, for this should only be done when one knows the real reasons that drove a person to fall into the situation under discussion here.

It is quite understandable that only certain men arouse a woman's hormones, and the same goes vice versa, but the usual question posed in these cases is why the unfaithful party did not notice that his partner did not satisfy him from the beginning. If adultery is "a sin of the flesh," I should point out that one cannot favor the flesh to the detriment of the spirit, but one must also accept that the body has needs that must be satisfied to maintain health and psychological equilibrium. There is nothing worse than rigid sexual repression while the boiler of the libido is at full steam, for it could collapse in the form of diverse types of depravation, like imaginary, morbid, pornographic, or sadomasochistic games that are perverse substitutes for normal sex. Repression is usually the source of the most common psychological disorders, although licentiousness only leads to the animalization of man. The most suitable choice is normal sex and the sublimation of the libido, to gain access also to higher spheres of creativity and spiritual perfection. Hypocritical prudishness could be as close to sin as a licentious attitude. A good example of this is the case of puritanism when it represents an unconscious defense against the sinful morbidity or sinful temptation that invades the mind and heart.

Both man and woman have a full right to seek sexual satisfaction within the correct limitations, but not through incorrect or aberrant procedures. The golden rule in this situation is still the one that says: "Do unto others, as you would have others do unto you." There are legitimate and illegitimate ways to have access to sexual satisfaction. The ideal situation should also invariably include love as a prior requisite and ideal motivation.

The consumerism of orgiastic sexual pleasure, devoid of love, delicacy, and romanticism, makes adultery worse in the moral sense, although at the level of human feelings, it may be more painful to be betrayed in love than if one is deceived because of a temporary unhinged state provoked by passion. It does not matter how much or how deeply we analyze conjugal infidelity; we shall always reach the forcible conclusion that it is a phenomenon inherent to human imperfection and carnal weakness, and that the most adequate way to avoid it is by means of a true love relationship. However, the development of one's own individual consciousness is a prior requisite to this end, if one is to master the science of love.

Divorce

Divorce, just like any other moral problem, has to be seen within a double context:

(a)   The divorce of common (unevolved) persons.

(b)   The divorce of spiritually developed persons.

I believe the moral question will never be satisfactorily resolved unless one accepts that there are persons of very different categories, more or less human according to the variability of their inner content, within a broad spectrum that goes from the subhuman to the higher human condition, without these differences having anything to do with the social stratum such people belong to. A truly evolved individual does not need laws or rules to oblige him to behave in a certain way, for he will always act through his own will in accordance with the highest good and untarnished respect for his fellows and Nature. However, the great majority of Mankind—which is certainly not in the former case—needs very strict rules and repressive laws to comply with the prevailing legal system in order to act more or less morally. If this legal system were to be suspended for only three days, with an anticipated amnesty for all infringements of the law that might be committed, there would be absolute chaos. Such people only act correctly because the law punishes wrong-doing, and in the case that the law does not discover specific offenses or is itself corrupt, then immorality and delinquency proliferate.

This huge mass of human beings, which I call the "common beings" to denote those who are still at an early stage of significant evolution, are in no way a sample of human normality, for the overwhelming majority of them are really "incomplete" beings, individuals of a species that barely 15,000 or 20,000 years ago began to show signs of a relatively conscious behavior in circumstances when man first existed as a human being from the time of Cro-Magnon, for there is evidence that he already existed in the era when the last glaciers disappeared. Therefore, we should not be surprised at man's imperfection, who is ideally described in a well-known encyclopaedia as "occupying a supreme place on the scale of living beings, and through his intelligence and thirst for the infinite is the worthy lord of the world he inhabits."

Like many others, this description violently clashes with the everyday reality of a being who does not belong to himself, a slave to his passions and to the autonomous infor-mation he carries in his brain, a predator of Nature, the lord of exploitation and war, a defender of violence and injustice, a servant to the golden calf incapable of controlling his own thought, impulses, and emotions, an inhabitant of the mental shadows of the state of drowsiness; a tiny little man dominated by his dreams of grandeur, which he uses as analgesics to calm the anguish he feels before his inner certainty as to his own defenselessness and smallness. It can be just as great a mistake to idealize man as to disqualify him. To expose the weaknesses of the species does not mean to debase it, but to place it where it should really be, to end the myth of the "king of Nature." Besides, in the cultural and psychic aspects, this exposition is the necessary source for all those who, in their search for self-fulfillment first have to discern the error and falsehood of certain beliefs before they attain the highest peaks of spiritual or artistic perfection.

One should recall that terrestrial man, so proud of his human condition, has still not had the chance to compare himself to an alien counterpart of greater evolutive caliber than himself and that perhaps, after such a confrontation, his dreams of grandeur would vanish as regards the great human quality he attributes to himself.

We know that man is capable of very noble deeds, but also of very base ones, due to his dual condition—that of an animal that bears the divine spark—one who lacks real consciousness in the higher sense. This is the reality of our existence, for when one observes his environment one has to accept that one's quality of life does not correspond to that which the world would have if those who rule it were in fact possessors of a high human condition. With this, the total failure of science, economics, and politics—in their desire to ensure human well-being and happiness—is made quite clear, unless we measure this by people's standards of comfort.

The air we breathe in the big cities, noise and food pollution, delinquency, terrorism, the exploitation of man by man, political demagogy that swindles the people, the scant efficacy of justice when one has no money, the struggle against the "big fish," the attempt to defend oneself against the diverse abuses of the State, war, famine, the institutionalization of usury in certain financial systems, are all undesirable characteristics of the world of this man so brashly idealized as the king of Nature and of living beings.

I apologize for going on at such length on a subject that might seem far removed from divorce, but what I want to show here is that divorce, like abortion, delinquency, immorality, corruption, or so many other human flaws, is no more than the very imperfection of man's scant level of evolution. The huge mass of humans, in which lies the kind of imperfection only to be expected from beings of a corrupt childish condition, must supposedly evolve toward higher strata of *consciousness*.

However, spiritual evolution is not a matter for the masses but rather a strictly individual concern, because the development of consciousness is only possible at the level of "an individual," whose experience can of course be repeated in many others, but hardly be projected as a phenomenon of the masses for it first requires a free, personal decision motivated by some inner awakening and not by a process of external persuasion.

As I have already pointed out in this work, it is unfortunate that man's inner content has not increased much with the passing of the centuries or millennia, and this is why a serious study of moral problems must forcibly begin with the recognition of man's scant evolutive stature, so that he may, by dropping his aspirations to become king, take on the role of a humble apprentice. It is a fact that, however proud he may become of his science and technology, it is the logical result of the multiplication of inherited experiences through the cultural transfer between successive generations.

One has to acknowledge that however stupid an individual may be, if he were able to live for 500 years, he would eventually be able to learn how things work and perhaps would become a great inventor. However, a very different case is when one attempts to attain the type of wisdom that includes higher spiritual consciousness, for this is a process that first demands that one overcome one's susceptibility to environmental hypnosis. I am not by any means putting man's intelligence in doubt. I am only saying that this capacity has been overestimated, for one can be intelligent and at the same time incapable of measuring the consequences of one's own acts and controlling oneself so that one attains a truly civilized type of behavior. I also believe in the existence of the "half-wise," blockheads who, like library mice inflated by their own knowledge, lack any inner judgment, vision, modesty, and the high aims that true wisdom demands, veritable living computers directed by unknown programmers whom they submissively obey in the conviction that all these external mandates are in fact their own.

Without a doubt, higher *consciousness* is the maximum capacity man can aspire to, for without it, intelligence is like a ship without a compass or a helm—its behavior is absolutely unpredictable—and at times terribly destructive—as occurs in cases in which diverse scientific advances end up by being used for war or extermination. The learned man without a higher consciousness is no more than any other intelligent animal, his brain being saturated with information that enslaves his behavior, turning any attempt at genuine freedom into an illusion. I am convinced in my inner world that we live in a "prehuman" era, if we take what a true human condition really means, and that the inconsistencies of Mankind are the logical result of this fact, and not an anomaly. However, I am certain of the existence of beings who are more evolved than usual, and history tells us of such supermen of spirituality who are now converted into mythical figures.

Jesus, Buddha, and Mohammed correspond to spiritual archetypes of diverse cultures, and should be a permanent reminder of the need to attain higher states of spiritual perfection. Nevertheless, as in other cases, "hidden hands" have sequestered the truth by the expedient of making people believe that it is impossible to emulate the development of these outstanding beings by alleging that "they were gods" or "sent by God." Hence, common man can do nothing to imitate them, for he is not sent by God, so therefore he can only adore these divine beings and beg for their blessing while he remains in spiritual poverty.

Indeed, anyone who so decides can start out on the path towards higher spiritual evolution. Of course, this is not an easy, frivolous, or light-hearted undertaking, but requires character, will, and determination, so that it is usually more convenient to limit oneself to praying to a deity. If one accepts that despite the foregoing there is a certain number of conscious and more highly evolved people than is common, one must understand that if one of them gets divorced, this will not have a negative impact on his family, or on his children, nor will his separation be the cause of hate or discord between the spouses, but rather a matter of mutual agreement. All the negative effects anticipated by society as the result of divorce will simply not occur in this case.

However, society is right to make laws for the majority, for they are incapable of accepting and emulating spiritually developed beings, nor are they in a position to visualize or accept this elevated behavior.

Really, people cannot conceive that there are people who, by withstanding the animal impulse, can "turn the other cheek" or abstain from doing to others what they would not want to suffer themselves. Nevertheless, such people do exist, even though their number is small, although they remain unknown, not through any wish of their own, but through the stubborn blindness of the human collective. If they were well-known, they would be ridiculed by the mass, which could not, however hard it tried, imagine the reasons for such "outlandish behavior," and would certainly have serious suspicions with respect to the rectitude of such people. Epictetus[18] in his time, warned that all those who seek wisdom would be ridiculed. In *The Art of Living,* he says:

> Those who pursue a higher, wiser life, those who seek to live in accordance with spiritual principles, must be prepared to be the object of mockery and reproval.
>
> Many people who have gradually abandoned their personal norms in an effort to obtain social approval and the commodities of life, bitterly resent those of a more philosophical inclination who avoid negotiating their spiritual ideals and seek to better themselves. Let us never live reacting against these poor souls. Let us be compassionate with them and at the same time, let us cling to all that we know is good.
>
> When we begin our program of spiritual progress, it is most likely that those around us will mock us or accuse us of arrogance. It is our job to behave humbly and pursue our moral ideals in a disciplined way. Let us cling to what we know in our hearts is the best. Then, if we are strong, the same people who had ridiculed us will come to admire us.
>
> But if we allow the mean opinions of others to make us hesitate in our purpose, we will incur a double shame.

It is necessary to analyze divorce from the angle of the spouses' level of consciousness, hence the reason why I have given so much space to this subject.

From the point of view of common sense, and on the margin of any religious or legal considerations, it would seem totally out of place to oblige two people who do not love each other, or who perhaps hate each other, to remain united forever. I believe that this is a monstrosity supported by a superstitious or fanatical view of the true meaning of religious precepts. In order to briefly summarize the kind of abuse that we can observe in so many places, as far as individual liberties are concerned, let us consider the following:

1. **Forbidding Divorce:** the individual is not the master of his own body. This belongs to the State, which forces him to share his life with a person with whom he does not wish. Of course, the body includes the mind, the heart, and the soul.

2. **Abortion:** the woman is not the owner of her own body, for in most countries she has no freedom to have an abortion except in certain cases.

3. **Advertising:** man is no longer the master of his own behavior, which is motivated by advertising agencies.

4. **Political Propaganda:** the citizen is deprived of his own brain through psychological brainwashing techniques.

5. **Television:** the individual no longer belongs to himself and loses the inviolability of his own mind and home.

6. **Agglomeration:** the mass absorbs and directs the individual, depriving him of what is his own, forcing him to behave dubiously like the collective, the state

of the psychological mass in which the best qualities of the species cannot blossom.

7. **Euthanasia:** the State is the master of the citizen's body, and implacably tortures it in the case of incurable illnesses, forcing it to a shameful, undignified agony, preventing it from voluntarily leaving this life.

8. **Money:** the financial and banking system is the master of the soul and efforts of labor of all those who resort to loans, either directly or indirectly, whereas the State subjects us to taxes similar in amount to those which the serfs had to pay to their feudal lords.

9. **Consumerism:** the individual's whole effort is directed towards a dehumanized consumerism through the penetration of advertising.

10. **The Power of the Majority:** the enslavement of minority groups to the tyranny of majorities.

I am aware that the prudish approach of the general majority will make many readers annoyed at this crude analysis. Nevertheless, I believe that it is necessary to remind people of things that we always forget or refuse to see in our endeavors to please the majority.

There are many people who acknowledge truths in their inner world that they would never dare accept in public. The fact of getting divorced or not is insignificant, when compared to the magnitude of the moral deterioration of Mankind, which compromises and injures Humanity in all aspects. This gives rise to a pressing need to begin the great crusade of the 21st Century—the recovery of traditional and consensual spiritual values to be massively, clearly, and profoundly incorporated into human culture. In this way, the irrefutable fact that the noblest aim a person can pursue is that of spiritually perfecting himself, will no longer be concealed from the individual, so that he can offer himself as the most valuable contribution he can make to society—that of a truly evolved human being, one who will be the best example and inspiration for those who seek self-fulfillment.

To forcibly impede an individual from getting a divorce may lead to an authentic "devil's cauldron" in the family, in which for perhaps many years, the children have to witness in amazement the exchange of insults between their parents.

It is far more constructive in a psychologically adult marriage to nip the situation in the bud and obtain a mutual agreement divorce, explaining to the children what is happening in an objective, mature way. The children's problems always derive from their parents' immaturity, for they pass onto them their own sentimental burden, which will manifest itself both within and outside marriage. The truth is that, as this is a case of individuals of scant moral stature, neither the marriage contract nor the option for divorce or mere cohabitation will be favorable, for in all these cases the family will be likewise harmed or diminished in their possibilities.

Nor should one forget that marriage cannot be a goal in order to acquire identity and social recognition, and that the only valid reason for marrying is love. If the spouses no longer love each other, they cannot be forced to remain together, and the only solution is to negotiate special measures to protect the children.

This leads us to another problem, which is the fact that love is generally falsified because people ignore its true essence and cannot therefore truly love. However, I believe that this impediment can be remedied, and that people can learn to love. To this end, however, they have to begin by breaking their own egotism in the profound sense of what this means, and not only with regard to human charity as we know it. Unfortunately, experience shows that it is very hard for the individual to *decenter* his own "egotistic I."

Sadomasochism

Friedrich Dorsch's *Dictionary of Psychology*[19] defines "sadism" as: "a concept introduced by Krafft-Ebing, that takes its name from the French writer Marquis de Sade (1740–1814), a behavioral deviation in sexual matters in which satisfaction is obtained to the point of orgasm by inflicting pain, maltreatment, and humiliation. In extreme cases, it can even cause injuries and death. Sadism is the opposite of masochism. In some cases, sadism means the obtaining of pleasure from exerting physical force without the accompaniment of sexual activity (aggressive behavior)."

In the same text, sadomasochism is described as "the combination of sadism and masochism with the aim of sexual satisfaction in one and the same individual. Only clearly defined forms can be classified in this way, because, to some degree, both tendencies are present in the human being."

The Dictionary of Psychoanalysis[20] by Jean Laplanche and Jean Bertrand Pontalis defines sadism as: "a sexual perversion in which satisfaction is linked to suffering or humiliation inflicted on others." When one speaks of these perverse impulses, everybody steers clear, as if it were something totally alien to common experience, and pertaining only to mentally sick or disturbed persons. In the first place, we know that no one is absolutely exempt from a certain level of mental perturbation, and it is true that sadomasochism is a far more commonly perverse conduct than one might think and explains many behavioral aberrations. It should be dealt with in a work on morality because it is a devious conduct of the archetypal patterns of universal harmony, and is therefore a moral dislocation.

Freud thought that there was a connection between sadistic and masochistic perversions, considering both as two aspects of one and the same type of corruption, whose active and passive forms are to be found in variable proportions in one and the same individual.

Freud says: "a sadist is always a masochist at the same time, which does not prevent either the active or passive aspect of the perversion from predominating and giving special character to the prevailing sexual activity." In the long run, two basic ideas of Freud can be defined:

1. The correlation between the two terms of the pair is so close that they cannot be studied separately in either their genesis or in any of their manifestations.

2. The importance of this pair goes far beyond the plane of perversions: "sadism and masochism occupy a special position among the perversions. The activity and passivity that make up its fundamentally opposite characteristics are a constituent of sexual life in general."

It should be pointed out that what for Freud and other psychoanalysts was a sexual perversion, is "modernly" usually classified, not innocently, under the heading of "variations of sexual experience." Something similar occurs with most depravations, whose pathological meaning has been obscured in order to give the deceptive appearance of normal behavior. Thus, the broadest possible showcase of aberrations, suitably decked out to give them an appearance of normality, is what is being offered to young people. This is only one example of how the "moral toboggan" of humanity functions today, in its accelerated plunge, through the patient work of these anonymous entities who, for some reason, devote their efforts to stamping with the seal of legality or normalcy types of conduct that really represent a progressive deviation of man's fundamental transcendental values.

If it were not an overbold supposition, one could imagine a conspiracy designed to destroy the integrity, the character, the will, the mental health, and the cleanliness of Mankind by twisting, besmirching, discrediting, or mocking traditional values, thus bringing about the decline of the species, or perhaps only of a previously specified faction of it.

Yet who could be capable of such a conspiracy? I myself, would not dare to suggest it, but it is true that Mankind is on an accelerated moral decline and that there are very few who dare to recognize the true extent of this decline. There is no room here to give further information on a type of behavior whose characteristics can be studied in any specialized text. What I intend here is to refer to two little-known aspects of sadomasochism—that it is a sexual vice and that it relates to moral masochism.

Common vices are characterized by the fact that the person affected knows about his problem, and can perhaps perceive it in others. In the case of sadomasochism this does not happen, for except in extreme cases, it is usually a sexual vice so cunningly hidden or dissimulated that nobody can recognize it by examining the behavior of the person affected. When I say vice, I mean the fact of being dominated by an imperfect, licentious type of behavior that in this case alters the very essence and reason of sexuality, a procedure in which the disorder in question in many cases remains quite invisible, and is therefore a disguised vice.

Freud held that *every sensation is sexual* and that even sucking a candy or chewing food at heart entails a libidinous stimulation. The infant's first erotic pleasure is to suck its mother's breast and later its baby and other foods. Therefore, it must be made quite clear that any sensation indirectly provokes a sexual stimulus. Food, for example, is not only a means of raising one's self-esteem, but also of experiencing erotic stimulation, which is obvious when we taste certain delicacies that elicit in gourmets a type of orgasm that is located in their stomach.

There are other cases in which the imagination becomes a source of sexual stimulus and the same occurs with certain emotional experiences. Sometimes, this is an integral part of the normal process of sexual excitement, but at others it represents deviant, dissimulated forms of sexual pleasure, as for example what happens with people who enjoy roulette, cards, horseracing, and gambling in general. It is during the excitement of gambling and betting that the individual experiences an intensified pendular oscillation in his sensations that comes from the hope of winning and the fear of losing. This leads him to an abrupt alternation between pleasure and pain, and sparking off sadomasochistic enjoyment. There is pain because of losing or of expecting to lose, and pleasure for winning either in reality or in hopes of same. At moments, an individual is on the point of losing huge sums of money that perhaps entail a large part of his possessions, and the next instant he could be winning significant amounts, a process which when repeated in diverse ways, *triggers off successive psychological orgasms in a deviant type of pleasure.*

When an individual becomes an incurable gambler, he is at heart subjugated to a vicious, aberrant sexual dependency. We could also think then, since most gamblers lose, what predominates in them is the masochistic impulse that leads them to derive pleasure from the pain caused by losing. No gambler would really gamble without betting, since this would mean preventing or thwarting the pleasure mechanism. The greater the risk and the higher the bets, the more intense will be the succession of aroused psychic orgasms.

In order to understand the real mechanism of sado-masochism, it is useful to resort to the simile of a pendulum and compare it to the oscillations of the sensations and human sentiments, which because of their dual nature (pleasure/pain, sadness/joy, euphoria/depression) usually lead the individual from one polar extreme to the other. This oscillation, however, usually occurs slowly and gradually, almost imperceptibly, so that it can be compared to the sensation of driving in a car at low speed.

Generally, entertainment and pleasure are based on an intensification of the sensations, and this could be compared to what one feels when one accelerates the car to high speeds. The human being's sensations have both movement and speed, and are determined by this pendular oscillation. When the pendulum is immobile in the center, or its movement is too slow, the individual gets bored and is in an almost lethargic state. For common man, enjoyment means to *accelerate*, and this is the aim of most forms of entertainment.

As long as the pendulum moves at its natural slow speed, the polar extremes remain clearly defined, but when the speed is increased they tend to become blurred, and it is at this moment that the individual can begin to enjoy himself with pain, or suffer with pleasure. There thus comes a moment when the oscillation is fast and sharp, like in roulette, bringing about a sudden, violent contrast of polar extremes (pleasure/pain), that sets off a chain reaction of deviant psychic orgasmic enjoyment.

An addiction to high-risk sports is also based on this same principle, since after risking one's own life, there comes a moment, as for instance in parachute jumping, when one is safe on the ground and there suddenly comes the pleasurable relief of being alive and safe. In the brief lapse of a jump from a plane, the individual abruptly alternates between the fact that he is risking his life with the later security of being on the ground.

This is how an individual can become accustomed to such experiences, even though, in a certain way, they are sado-masochistic. However, except for certain cases, this never reaches the limit of the pathological, unless it becomes an addiction. On the contrary, it may be the reason why the individual feels humbler and more satisfied, grateful for life and the achievements he has attained. Unlike the case of gambling, high-risk sports are a challenge to self-discipline and can notably help to shape both character and will, that is if one is prudent.

The pendulum mechanism of the sensations explains why the common human being finds it so hard to find happiness, and why he so often ends addicted to painful situations which are repeated time and again in his life. These painful situations are usually attributed to destiny or external factors of an adverse nature but never to his own unconsciously made choice driven by a masochistic addiction to suffering.

There are many who, apparently not wanting to do so fail in love, in business, or in life in general, for at the peak moments of their own projects, they somehow manage to cunningly sabotage the projects in such a covert way that they would be the last to admit the existence of any such manipulation. In this case, it is sadism applied by the individual against himself with the deliberate aim of provoking a masochistic experience.

It should be understood that this pernicious habit, because it causes addiction, seals the destiny of the person thus affected with the bitter fate of defeat and suffering, while the other part of his mind is still conspiring from its airtight compartment to bring about failure.

We cannot help pointing out that immorality implies a huge waste of the individual's inner resources, which instead of being used creatively to help both himself and Mankind, are squandered in an inebriation of perverse libidinous stimulation that leads to destruction and pain.

Really, there are countless situations in everyday life that come under the mechanism of sadomasochism. A very clear example is jealousy in a couple of such destructive intensity that only he who has at some time suffered it can assess the inferno it brings about. The pendulum principle is rigorously fulfilled in jealousy, and this is why it is addictive. The man or woman thus affected suffers on account of the supposed or real betrayal he or she is victim to, with the inseparable result of violence and vengeance against his or her companion or against the hated rival. However, at peak moments of doubt and suspicion, all manner of erotic pictures flood his or her mind as to the type of sexual contacts that both (his or her companion and the other party) may be having at that very moment, which brings intense erotic pleasure that when mixed and alternated with the pain he or she is suffering, gives rise to an intense, deviant type of pleasure that is typical of sadomasochistic situations; pleasure at the gallery of erotic pictures he or she imagines, and profound pain at simultaneously feeling betrayed, humiliated, and mocked.

Once more, the pendulum has swung violently and rapidly with the consequences mentioned above. It is known that the repertoire of situations that could cause jealousy is infinite, as far as its plots are concerned, but it does not matter whether jealousy is founded or not, the same principle of intensified pendular oscillation always occurs.

There are also totally unfounded, pathological types of jealousy, the product of the individual's imagination. In this case, it is of interest to understand why he imagines such situations, and by carefully analyzing many different cases, we come to the conclusion that they are not engendered by well-founded suspicion that the individual is being betrayed, for such mistrust is independent of concrete facts, and is a mere pretext or justification to give free rein to his sadomasochistic inclinations. This means that most jealousy is based on insignificant facts, but that there are self-provoked overreactions with the sole aim of reaching a perverse psychological climax, at times based on the excuse of an insignificant suspicion as to a totally transparent action on the part of the spouse, albeit one which is interpreted deviously, and this can give rise to the craziest, most outrageous conclusions.

In other instances, jealousy is well-founded, but there is a huge disproportion between the magnitude of the offense caused and the other party's explosive reaction, for he or she undoubtedly exaggerates with the clear intention of obtaining erotic pleasure of a sadomasochistic type.

The woman at times is far more prone to fall into sadomasochistic habits through her fondness for romance novels, and for erotic and romantic films which make her head work in an accelerated way. Only in this way can one explain the success of films which are a mere excuse for spectators to be able to identify with the protagonist and openly enjoy being in the hero's arms. Being more intuitive and imaginative than men, she carries out in her imagination many things that society and its customs forbid her. This intensified imagination is what also leads her to silently enjoy the pictures that form in her mind with regard to erotic situations of a forbidden nature.

The woman does not like romanticism merely for the sake of experiencing pleasant emotions, but because it is a suitable cover for her to find an outlet for her repressed sexuality. Famous psychoanalysts maintain that the woman is intrinsically masochistic, and that her life is marked by suffering which she accepts and learns to enjoy.

From the menstrual cycle to the delivery, obligations of motherhood, her submission to men (which is getting less and less), the drudgery of household duties—all these show a patient and often painful sacrifice for the children's and the family's sake.

The success of soap operas with their invariable dose of melodrama, pain, and passion is mainly due to the woman's masochistic attitude. The part she most enjoys albeit unwittingly, is when the protagonist is humiliated, derided, raped, or imprisoned, or when she takes revenge by destroying the person who has offended her. I can remember the huge box-office success of a film that ran for many weeks and was a classic case of sadomasochism. Women patiently lined up for it and left the cinemas enthralled by it, without realizing that they had been given "a brief course in sadomasochism," this in fact being noticed by very few spectators. Slavery was, in its day, a very crude manifestation of sadomasochism, some people having total power over the lives of others who were thus enslaved, as are the diverse forms of oppression still in existence today, such as:

1. The despotism of large majorities over small minorities.

2. The tyranny of drugs.

3. The monopoly of legal violence exercised by the State.

4. The financial exploitation of people through usurious interest rates.

5. The growth of organized crime.

6. War.

7. Terrorism.

8. The brainwashing carried out by advertising and political indoctrination.

9. Dependency on hypocrisy, for he who does not use it is repudiated.

10. Racial discrimination.

11. Environmental pollution.

12. The despoiling of Nature.

13. Consumerism.

14. Corruption.

15. Political demagogy.

The moral offense of sadomasochism does not only derive from the fact that it is a sexual perversion, but also because it is a corruption of people's motivations. This is because they idealize their own motivations in order to classify themselves as virtuous or noble, without suspecting that these motivations are corrupt at their very core and obey aberrant or twisted impulses. Man is supposedly a hedonistic creature who continually seeks pleasure, but not only is masochism not a flight from pain and malaise, but is in fact an attraction to them.

Theodor Reik believes that it is possible that man could have become a "masochistic animal" after thousands of years of transformations in the environment and in his psychic structure. Daily experience confirms the truth of this statement, which can be understood by Reik's definition of moral masochism, which is: "a peculiar attitude to life, which is to enjoy one's own sufferings or misfortune, unconsciously seeking physical and psychic pain, voluntarily submitting oneself to deprival, accepting sacrifices, shame, humiliations, and insults deliberately." Moral masochism is a disease of the individual, of groups, and of whole countries. There are collectives of citizens who make a show of such submission and tameness at the diverse abuses committed by the State or private individuals, that their conduct cannot be otherwise explained except as moral masochism; cities in which the long-suffering inhabitants tamely breathe in the polluted air that threatens their lives and those of their children without really protesting, and put up with deafening noise pollution, which destroys their hearing, and habitually consume polluted foodstuffs that are not controlled by the authorities, or remain passive before corruption, crime, and delinquency; cities in which those whose job it is to fight against such situations endeavor to ingratiate themselves with the offenders due to fear; cities in which citizens, intimidated by the power of the State, which has the monopoly on legal violence, docilely accept to pay disproportionate taxes without having any clear, detailed information as to how these taxes are really used—taxes that grow higher and higher without the taxpayer being able to ever find out where this money goes; cities in which property is repossessed from its legitimate owners by the usurers' loans that could not be paid on time, in which such a high tax is charged for living in one's own home that it is in many cases almost like paying rent, or the high annual percentage charged on the taxable value of one's car which is simply for permitting one to ride on the streets. In his work *Masochism in Modern Man*,[21] Theodor Reik says:

Moral masochism should deserve the attention of every educated person, because it sets its particular seal on an important part of our inner life. It is not restricted to isolated individuals, but is a significant factor in the life of social, national, and religious organisms. Masochism is an important component of many neuroses and peculiarities of character. Furthermore, research shows that in the tendencies and behavior of each of us there can be found traces of moral masochism. The common feature of all these psychic phenomena is the unconscious inclination to seek pain and to derive pleasure from suffering. Psychoanalysis first discovered the existence of such masochistic tendencies when it studied neurotic and anti-social characters, although some time passed before it was shown that there is a proportion of moral masochism in every human being. The case of neurosis and deformity reflect what is in all of us in an exaggerated and pathological way. These cases have not exceeded the bounds of what is considered normal.

Those persons whose psychoanalysis enables us to study the phenomenon, behave in a characteristic way which according to Freud is the effect of a desire for punishment. This desire need not manifest itself consciously. People who fall victim to it neither know about it nor will confess to it. However, its effects manifest themselves quite clearly both in their acts and in their thoughts. It is as if such people were their own worst enemies. In everything they do, or do not do, they manage to spoil their pleasure and their work, denying themselves a well-deserved happiness and even in extreme cases putting their own life at risk. In almost all cases, the casual observer may think that the misfortune or bad luck that governs such people's lives comes from external circumstances, and that they have to constantly struggle against unlucky events and afflictions that ceaselessly crop up in their fate. One might get the impression that a hostile fate had cursed them, or that they are victims to everybody else's trickery and everything with which they come into contact. However, psychoanalytical observation justifies the statement that it is these same people who, albeit quite unconsciously, are responsible for most of the disas-

ters and misfortunes they suffer. Nevertheless, they make it look
as if fate or some evil god had assigned to them the losing
numbers of the lottery of life.

Analysis of the sensations of ourselves and of others can
considerably help us to understand the phenomenon of
masochism. It often happens that by overstimulating their
senses, people lose the ability to find anything that fulfills
them, and thus remain in a state of apathy and passivity. The
death or thwarting of cherished illusions also creates a sensation of inner void that the individual will try to fill in any
way. Suffering may be painful but it certainly fills people's
inner worlds so that they can, albeit negatively, attain or
recover a sense of inner plenitude. This happens for example
in the case of the elderly who encounter in their aches and
pains a stimulus to fill their lives with, and although painful,
it can make them feel important.

There are people who, having undergone surgery, tell
their friends in a wealth of detail all the ins and outs of the
operation and exhibit those parts of their anatomy that have
been removed like trophies, all of which makes them feel
important. They might also unwittingly accept an illness as a
gratifying experience with regard to their sensations.

One problem with sadomasochism is that it is an underhanded motivation that is concealed behind many of man's
negative patterns of behavior. Violence and destructiveness,
for example, are no more than a sadistic impulse aimed at
deriving erotic pleasure by making other people suffer.

There are also many who fail in love, business, and lucrative activities through some inner decree of their own, and
they never imagine that *their own unconscious makes them deliberately bring about the failure of their projects, although they do not
perceive this at the conscious level. This will bring the painful expe-*

*riences that give them masochistic suffering through which they can
obtain the deviant pleasure they so desire.*

It is at the same time a moral fault to become addicted to
such maneuvers, a defiling and deterioration of mental and
emotional life that leads the individual to know himself less
and less, thus gradually distancing himself from the possibility of guiding or controlling his own person in the sense of
being able to act in the higher manner that corresponds to a
true human being. As occurs with all vices, these are alienating factors that imprison the individual's "I," for he will
waste all his energies in a continual endeavor to justify
himself and at the same time multiply and intensify the sensations that possess him, whereas his creativity and inner
freedom are nullified.

To become conscious of the way in which the sadomasochistic mechanism works may be a great help to the
person thus affected but unfortunately there are very few who
are willing to acknowledge their own deviations. On the
contrary, they try their utmost to hide, dissimulate, or deny
them, with the covert intention of not missing the perverse
pleasure that they provoke in them.

The Weakening of the Family

The family is the basic unit of human society and the
formative center of the individual's affective and moral life. It
is essential to human civilization because it is the medium for
developing personalities that are to be socially useful, but at
times, unfortunately, it misses its mark. The family and the
home become the first structural model of the world that the
child knows and his psychological, moral, and spiritual development emanates from this formative environment. Man's
ethical and spiritual defeat is really the failure of parents, who

because they are usually not sufficiently developed themselves, and are therefore *incomplete,* cannot pass on to their children the necessary spiritual values, for they themselves lack them.

This is the true genesis of the spiritual misery of the world: the great majority of us are children of *bad parents,* in the technical sense. Morally undefined parents, ambiguous with little knowledge of how to raise their children properly, since to date they themselves have been unable to educate themselves in what is supreme human knowledge; that is, how to master one's own person to attain a higher level of human behavior in the spiritual, ethical, and moral sense; to master oneself in order not to be controlled by animal passions. It is obvious that people's behavior is more instinctive than rational, otherwise wars and other scourges could not be explained. Human intelligence does not obey the spirit, or a superior reason, but rather is at the service of the passions.

This is why it seems so odd to improve the world by increasing people's level of intelligence, since unless intelligence goes hand in hand with a parallel development of higher consciousness, it would ineluctibly lead to an unbearable sophistication of criminality, precisely because delinquents would become more cunning and intelligent. The worst misfortune that can befall man is to attain the IQ of a genius without having first attained the spiritual consciousness that becomes the compass and helm of his faculties, without which he would not take very long to destroy the entire planet.

The greater man's intelligence, the more exploitation, the more sophisticated immorality; the greater the number of the morally blind through pride and narcissism; the more destructive and cruel wars, the harder it is to enforce law and order; the greater the moral deviation or dislocation of science, the more intellectual tools to deceive oneself and to behave dishonestly with one's fellows; the greater control over consumers' minds, the greater the efficiency of brainwashing through political discourse—in sum, the less individual freedom through the reduction in opportunities for spiritual regeneration.

This spiritual regeneration is not a blessing that falls from heaven like rain or sunlight, but depends on personal spiritual work of a painful, sustained nature for which the individual must, as a prior requisite, become conscious of his own smallness, which he can hardly do in the triumphalistic intoxication derived from inflated personal importance. I dare suppose that the average IQ of today's parents is considerably higher than that of former generations, just as happens with the vertiginous advance of science in our time, which is a reflection of man's greater intellectual development, although this capacity does not make them better parents.

If we keep to what spirituality really means, science has brought no spiritual progress to man, and its contribution to facilitating the development of higher consciousness is null.

However great the man of science may be, his knowledge cannot help him to have greater self-control or to consciously carry out actions with a higher moral effect. Neither can he manage to master his passions or place his intelligence at the service of his own spirit. In other words, his inner content is not noticeably any different or greater than that of any man in the street. Many people think that science will save Mankind. I believe that it is more likely that it will bring about the spiritual atrophy of man or that it will lead him to the verge of destruction, since as science in itself is absolutely amoral, it is incapable of guaranteeing correct use of the technology it develops.

In an attempt to protect the family and to help society, certain religions have decreed that marriage is indissoluble. Unfortunately, this praiseworthy intent to keep the family united contradicts its own aims when it comes up against common reality, which cannot be changed by decree. This is why the marriage of an incomplete man to a similar woman entails the duplication of their respective incapacities, since instead of uniting through genuine love and plenitude, they do so on account of their respective failings, this being the reason why such a family can hardly be an adequate nucleus for the proper development of their offspring. Save exceptions, it will on the contrary mean dooming the offspring to the most vulgar type of mediocrity, making it very hard, if not impossible, for them to develop higher human faculties.

The personality of the child from a marriage that is neither conceptually nor spiritually developed can hardly surpass the limits of its parents' psychic and cultural mold. Despite the fact that the child is biologically normal, *it will be limited or impeded with regard to its level of consciousness,* and *correspondingly thwarted with regard to its higher homineity.*

It is true that there are exceptions to the rule, and that great men have been born in homes that are very restricted in this sense. The truth is that culture does not manufacture human content but only too often diminishes it because of its alienating style, thus creating a sort of learned barbarism, as occurs in the case of intelligent people without criterion or sensitivity, and in cynical, dishonest, or wicked persons. In the same way there are also beings who are poor in cultural or encyclopaedic knowledge but who are veritable magnates of the soul and the spirit. The Apostles, for example, were not characterized by their culture, education, or good manners, but by the grandeur of their souls.

There are great souls in bodies that are socially rejected or restricted, but unfortunately there are also many people of great social relevance whose spiritual substance is in fact unbearably insignificant.

From the reality of the world, it is more than obvious that the typical family does not have the capacity to train its offspring in adopting transcendental spiritual values, and that there must be a veritable process of human reengineering in it in order to develop its correct shaping power. It is a fact that common parents cannot manage to control their children or pass on transcendental values to them. This is a great pity because the pre-teen years are usually fertile ground for the seed of contamination or perversion.

Of course, I do not mean that parents must handle their children repressively, or oblige them to adopt their own habits, but that they should exert true moral authority over them, so that they are figures worthy of imitation and not a motive for disqualification and disdain, which only too often happens. On the contrary, it very often occurs that it is the parents who blindly admire their children and become their psychological lackeys. When children find themselves idealized in this way, they think they are in possession of the truth and absolute freedom of choice, so that they will easily fall into moral depravity and underdevelopment of character and will.

Just as descendants at times inherit the capacities of their forefathers, they also take on their worst defects, which results in a total incapacity of the parents to guide them properly. Of course, if a parent is a slave to his own defects, and they are inherited by his child, his enslavement and lack of control of the child will be only greater since the child is the incarnation of his own deficiencies. It often occurs in the case of a large family that the child who has inherited its parents' worst defects is the favorite and nobody can explain why the naughtiest, most perverse child can be the family pet, while the brothers and sisters who are better in every respect, are only treated indifferently. This phenomenon can be explained because such a parent never managed to control the imperfections and deficiencies of his own inner world, now encountering them outside of himself and as a result, they are almost totally uncontrollable. The lack of a proper patriarchal figure, in the sense of a person who exerts moral authority in the family on account of his age and wisdom, may bring a climate of chronic ambiguity in which the child imitates bad examples or cannot find a significant figure to emulate and respect. The strongly materialistic environment makes him unduly disqualify adults or elderly, who are viewed as *invalids* by the young, who in their emotional insensitivity call their mothers "crazy" and their fathers "poor old men."

This cynical, materialistic approach leads certain young people to look upon the elderly as dusty or primitive junk, and to consider themselves as perfect modern artifices. This is why they normally use pejorative nicknames like *archaic, outdated, old crocks, mummies,* and so on.

However, one cannot only blame the young for this, since in order for a parent to be respected, he must have the necessary "guts" to deserve this dignity and to not be a mere ambiguous, timorous, masochistic, undefined, or contradictory figure. When I speak of "guts," I mean possessing an integral character and strong will, that will enable an individual to carry out his actions within the turmoil of everyday life by maturely facing the struggle against corruption, vice, and temptation; by having the inner force to be honest and virtuous; by persisting in such behavior despite disqualification from others; by having the power to reject any instinctive behavior or animal violence; by being able to "turn the other cheek" in the spiritual and technical sense of what this means, as a supreme effort of will to withstand the temptation of the facile or violent response; by being able to act as a truly human, civilized being; by being so strong, honest, and virtuous, that he is the best, most clearly defined example for his children.

These are parents who do not intend their children to do what they have not been able to do and who are satisfied with a measure of success equivalent to the demands they make on themselves; paternal figures who, because of the magnitude of their inner achievements as human beings, can arouse respect and admiration in their children to make them want to imitate the extent of their parents' spiritual fulfillment; moral patriarchs, *complete* individuals, who unite the family around them, thus becoming the optimal formative nucleus for its members.

Unfortunately, cases abound in which the patriarchy is exercised in the lowest, most violent way by brutal, selfish, covetous, and materialistic individuals who become the corrupting force for their offspring and whole family.

Just as nations depend on their leaders, the family group is subordinate to a leader who is the one who maintains family cohesion. The ideal situation is when this leadership is shared in a balanced way by both father and mother, each in their respective spheres, for in this way the child relates properly from an early age to male and female figures. In this way, the woman will develop a harmonious relationship with the opposite sex, as will the man.

It is obvious that a couple must be united by true love, for otherwise married life becomes a complete fraud that threatens the integrity of the entire family. One should ask what the object of marriage really is. To have children? To obtain a social identity? To legalize a sexual relationship?

What we have to agree on is that marriage cannot be considered as a goal but as a means to perfection for two people who are united by love, in order to work on their respective imperfections and mutually complement each other. To understand the true meaning of marriage and therefore of the family, one has to go deeper into its true significance. Usually, it represents the legalizing of cohabitation between a man and a woman, on the strength of an imitation of love. For Nature, it is the union of a man and woman through a genuine, true love, with or without a legal contract. If their love is true, then it is a real marriage; if their union is legalized but there is no true love, then there is only concubinage. It is either very simple or impossible to understand this, depending on the degree of unprejudiced lucidity of the person who analyzes it.

People are like musical instruments that can be well-tuned or out of tune, harmonious or discordant, and by joining in an orchestra can play either the most sublime melodies or the most dreadful discords. Each person sends out vibrations that come from their mental, instinctive, and emotional states and these tonalities take on a similar harmony or discord to what there is in the individual's inner world. Only genuine love enables a couple to complement both the man's and the woman's vibratory tones harmoniously, so that they will in turn harmonize with the music of the spheres mentioned by Pythagoras. The family in turn is a more important "musical ensemble," and the quality of its harmony is what ensures its happiness, stability, moral quality, and spiritual life.

The proper ordering of the family's *L-fields* is the best guarantee for the child's correct development and proper moral training, which in turn are the foundation for the couple's emotional stability. It is easy to understand that the "musical vibratory quality" of an individual dominated by his baser passions can never resemble the higher harmony of a virtuous man whose vital motivation lies in the transcendental values of the spirit.

External regulations with regard to marriage, divorce, abortion, infidelity, or ethics are no more than poor substitutes for what the fulfillment of an integral or *complete* man is; this means the handling of his own behavior in accordance with the supreme principle of *egalitarian equivalence.* It means the self-adjustment designed to respect and love whatever is just and correct in itself, and not in accordance with personal interests or subjective social opinions. It is the individual's moral coming of age, the level at which he is fully conscious and responsible for his acts, taking from the world only what he deserves and giving to those who deserve to receive. It is the state of impersonal consciousness in which the individual relates to himself and other people in accordance with justice and supreme good.

This type of development is what permits the shaping of a family that can withstand the polluting or disintegrating influences that come from the environment, being a refuge of peace, harmony, and love.

The universal habit of "living for the outside" makes the individual extremely vulnerable to outside influences and to falling into the vice of adjusting his conduct to anything that pleases the environment around him. If most people approve of something, then it will suffice for it to be classified as good, without any further analysis.

This habit of indiscriminately accepting the opinions or ideas of relevant figures because of their social prestige and not through any comprehensive agreement impoverishes and weakens the individual's inner world, preventing or thwarting the growth and maturing of his "I."

A real family must be a "workshop of life," a place in which truths are accepted only through comprehension and rational consent, and not through the unbearable weight of majority opinion or the social or political charisma of whoever might be presenting them.

The true family must be resistant to subliminal penetration in order not to become easy prey to the messages of advertising, for any subliminal training creates a sort of "second man" alien to the individual himself, a phantom born of social, cultural, political, or advertising grafts. In a very short time, this "second man" alienates and totally thwarts the real being, who is left buried under a tangle of external messages or mandates that condition his behavior; patterns that are incorporated into the cerebral neurons as "autonomous information," thus creating an independent thinking entity and turning the individual into a mere bearer of the alien creation that dominates him, in turn serving the external sources from which it had emanated.

Our world is no more than a planet full of deluded wanderers who devote their lives to seeking the mirages that the alienating phantom has caused, whereas the real being is left paralyzed and distressed in the most profound solitude, sadness, and impotence.

As life would be unbearable in such conditions, man has had to create a gigantic supermarket of consumerism, entertainment, and illusions, so that the individual can at least transitorily relieve the inner misery of being divorced from his own essence and, therefore, far removed from God and Nature.

The nonspecific anguish that afflicts man corresponds to his inner intuition of feeling uprooted from the place from which his real existence emanates, a prisoner of the collective soul of the mass, a tiny insignificant cog in the huge social machinery that smothers his individual identity. Only the conscious shaping power of a family made up of a couple of *complete* beings with a highly evolved consciousness can guide its members towards a higher quality of life: that quality which, by respecting others' rights and the integrity of Nature, also defends individual identity, and gives priority to spiritual development with the values this entails, beyond the cynical, ruthless materialism of those who, although well disguised, only wish to use the human being as an obedient consumer who will buy this or that, who serves as cannon fodder for economic or political experiments and who votes for a certain candidate.

It is a quality of life that allows for the individual's only authentic freedom, which is the one based on overcoming one's own passions and taking control of one's own mind, that permits the individual to be in possession of himself in order to be able to exist as truly corresponds to a real man in his quality of being the channel for the manifestation of the *being*, wherein his genuine, intrinsic identity originates.

It is the level at which the individual becomes aware of the true meaning and purpose of life, which is not merely to subsist, or grow and multiply, nor is it to promote the geometrical progression of the quantity and diversity of consumer goods.

A hundred conscious families, directed by *complete* patriarchs, would change the life of a nation, and a thousand families will change the destiny of the world.

However, there are reactionary forces that oppose the implantation of a higher morality, forces that lie in ambush in the informational mandates that come from subliminal persuasion and remain active in the depths of people's unconscious, ready to set them against anything that might mean that the obedient, compulsive consumer became a *conscious consumer* immune to subliminal penetration, capable of choosing what he wants with total inner freedom.

These messages, which are continually and massively sent out by those who in some way profit from man's mental enslavement, have brainwashed almost the entire planet so that people accept as normal and desirable the antinatural lifestyle which such exploiters wish to impose.

The Declaration of Human Rights, which we all know, should be changed and completed in this new century if one wants individual liberties to survive. *Among others, the right to one's own mental privacy should be added, to not be tyrannized by the majority, and to be able to avoid excessive advertising. The right should also be guaranteed to be able to vote for a candidate of flesh and blood and not for a phantom created by marketing, or the right to have truly impartial justice, to be protected against state violence and all forms of discrimination, monopoly, violence, and exploitation.*

The current situation of the average family is negatively affected in all cultures by an excessive consumer offer, which fills people's heads with a myriad of fantasies. Once they fall into this trap, they have to devote all their time and effort at work to earning enough money to satisfy their desires, which prevents or thwarts any chance of a minimum self-analysis and possibility to question either life or oneself. Instead of doing that, the individual, without thinking at all, prefers to accept ideas and customs coming from the majority or from leaders who are the most attractive just because they coincide with his own needs.

When a person has no time or interest for introspective analysis or for the world around him, he merely blindly obeys the dictates of the autonomous information that lies in his brain. For a man to be truly free he must not be mentally manipulated or content himself with what is familiar to him, but must seek access to transcendental truths that by their very nature are kept pure throughout time.

An individual who is a "bad man" in the technical sense of the word, by the mere fact that he does not have an appreciable dose of inner quality, will also be a bad father, for he will not be able to pass on to his children the qualities he himself lacks.

It very often happens that, instead of educating, he himself is badly educated by his children who, perceiving their parents' weakness, resort to emotional manipulation to get their own way. Only parents who have a high level of consciousness themselves will be capable of guiding their offspring properly without attempting to turn them into a copy of themselves or allowing themselves to be absorbed and dominated by the whims typical of childhood. It is the parents who must think up and implant adequate norms of coexistence within the home so that this will truly be a fitting model of higher values. One should never resort to authoritarianism to make children do what one wants, but one has to explain the reasons or motives why they have to do this or that coherently and without contradictions. Children usually understand considerably more than one might think when one uses the right type of language with them. A father who is caught lying loses his moral authority to teach his child to tell the truth, for the child will immediately disqualify him.

One of the greatest weaknesses in parents is to give in to the hero-worship his children give him, for this is a continual narcissistic pleasure; to allow oneself to be adored as a distant god who manifests his authority without offering explanations, for it is the least pedagogical attitude of all. One cannot expect a child to come up to its parents' level to understand them. It is the parents who should come down to their children's level and begin there to communicate with the child in its own language and make it realize with time that its father is human and fallible, subject to fear, pain, anxiety, and suffering, just like his offspring, but that his character and will allow him to overcome conflictive situations.

When a father makes himself a god to his children, he will eventually become the clay-footed idol, who at the slightest slip will display his lack of infallibility, thus undermining the respect and love of his offspring. In marital squabbles, it usually happens that the children, disconcerted, ask what is happening, and the parents in order not to tell them the truth, invent any excuse or justification, which in the end will turn out to be false or contradictory, generating situations that will negatively affect the child's mental health.

There are times when both father and mother try to blame each other to ensure the love of their children, which has a devastating effect on the children's minds, because for them their parents make up an inseparable unit. Sincere, opportune communication among the members of a family is a vital necessity, for otherwise the unity of the group would be broken, making it more vulnerable to external and internal dissociating agents.

Among the external factors is television, which although it physically joins the group together, also mentally and emotionally isolates its members, for silent evenings become a habit in which there is practically no conversation so as not to miss a single detail of their favorite programs. Television entertainment is usually the worst rival to any pedagogical endeavor on the part of the parents, for they do not know how to explain the fact that the screen, despite the fact that it is based on things that could be real, generally shows a false reality, absolutely divorced from true life. It is important that the family keep a certain time exclusively for communication, and that all its members understand the need to comply with this rule, this being the chance to manifest their diverse preoccupations. Dialogues should deal with each member's problems and emotional condition, what makes them outraged, what annoys them, and what they do not understand, and all members should give their opinion to this respect.

These meetings could be held weekly and should be surrounded by certain formalities so that they are given the importance they deserve as the opportunity chosen to communicate emotionally and mentally in the understanding that this practice could be vital to the happiness, prosperity, and spiritual development of its members. It is also advisable to choose subjects of conversation on moral dilemmas or problems in life, so that all learn to communicate by manifesting what they think about them.

The parents, who should direct these encounters, can choose subjects that correspond to a knowledge of higher moral values, stressing the importance of honesty, value, friendship, patriotism, work, respect for the rights of others, tolerance, discipline, controlling the passions, and so on. This will make the children reflect on how important it is in life to behave correctly as good citizens and good people.

When a member of the group has behaved incorrectly, he should be spoken to in the presence of all, not to reprimand him in an authoritarian manner but to make him understand the magnitude of his lack of respect and the harm it might cause to both himself and the family nucleus.

There is nothing better than a family based on humanistic intentions and higher spiritual goals, for it can become a reservoir of moral wealth passed on to the descendants of such a family like a torch that goes from hand to hand becoming considerably multiplied through time.

The moral misery of certain half-men cannot reach those who are protected by a family united by love and true moral and spiritual knowledge.

It is the surest hope for a more human, more beautiful and better world, for it ensures a spiritually superior quality of life in people's inner worlds, which is where everyday experience can be wisely elaborated to nourish the spirit.

To allow the weakening of the family is a manifest type of immorality on account of the immensely positive or negative projection it has in the training of youth, the hope for the future. This permissiveness can be passive or active, by omission or disrespect, and in both cases the quality of life of the whole of Mankind is being threatened.

It should be pointed out that it is a profound mistake to try to measure family unity by the time its members share physically. It is not the hours in time that count but the depth of communication, the love and loyalty that remain ever latent, even though everyday life may restrict the physical time that can be shared.

It is also obvious that a father or mother exhausted by work, worry, and stress cannot offer a very positive emotional and psychological contribution to the family, however long they may have lived together. Therefore, it is a fact that both have to give priority to their own spiritual development so that their best human capacities can surface. This means that the more elevated their inner condition, the more valuable their contribution to the family will be, beyond limitations of available time so common in our era. If the parents do not have their own space for healthy, periodical reflective introspection, they will not have the inner equilibrium necessary to guide their children effectively. As for everyday relations, intense, profound, warm, and opportune communication is really needed. In this way, one half-hour of being together in which one says and does what is appropriate can be far more beneficial than entire days of noncommunication or behavioral, emotional, and psychological wrongdoings. Children should know that they can *count on their parents*, but not in the narcissistic sense of using them as objects, but as sources of true affection, union, and preoccupation.

Within another context, one has to stop and think that when the union of the family is mentioned, this concept is usually circumscribed to its social meaning, whereas an analysis of its moral condition is excluded in the supposition that just because it has kept together, it is blessed. This is why we can observe the contradiction in the case of families that are strongly united although not by virtue, but by immorality and bad habits, or even by crime, hate, violence, envy, and resentment, thus becoming a disturbing social and moral influence and the worst training ground for the development of the children.

In this way, the undeniable fact is avoided that from the "technical" point of view there are good and bad families, despite the union of its members, so that moral and psychological ideal models of family coexistence should urgently be created with the aim of incorporating these concepts right from schooling, which is the best chance to develop the authentic wealth of a country. The moral concept of *family*, then, should be reserved for family groups united by higher spiritual and ethical values, their principles spreading not only to religious people but also to the profane, so that they may also have access to spirituality through a rational, technical message that does not demand unrestricted belief if one is to agree with its content.

Comfort

People have a common habit of comforming their psyche to the level of lowest demand, with the aim of attaining as soon as possible in life, a rigid, unmovable mental and emotional posture in order to feel secure and avoid the fear and anguish provoked by change, ignoring that life is continual change and that psychological petrification constitutes death in life. From his youth onwards, the individual will seek to neutralize insecurity by somehow attaining a certain type of inner equilibrium that will enable him to withstand the infinite variations of his existence.

The young person will copy the habits and manners of people he admires for the social impact that these figures inspire in him, or their popularity among the groups he moves in, and not for what they are really worth in themselves. This will unwittingly lead him to the imitative acquisition of presumptuous patterns of behavior that give him a sensation of security before the mass. The anguish that gnawed at him before is gradually replaced by a sensation of superiority, which at some point will lead him to feel relatively safe in a world that had previously seemed hostile. There is a moment when his stabilizing effort lessens or ceases because he feels that people regard him with respect, fear, or admiration, so that he believes he has reached the high level of individual security that a socially successful personality usually gives out. When the individual feels that he has attained proper social status, he ends his individualizing efforts and becomes mentally and psychologically petrified with the aim of protecting and perpetuating the identity he has obtained, for he feels that this not only safeguards it efficiently against aggression from others but that it also offers him a position of social privilege. This process can take on a pacific form of self-protection, yet there is another in which the individual decides that the best defense against the supposed or real aggression of others is to attack, so that he turns into a psychological bully who uses disqualification and verbal and psychological provocation on people as a way to feel secure. Undoubtedly, there are other cases in which the aggressive personality is deliberately adopted with a clear intent of intimidating people to obtain illegal advantages.

It is obvious that this same mechanism can also turn an individual into a shy person, for this corresponds to a very convenient defensive approach. There are other instances in which an individual who occupies a declining socioeconomic position manages to justify his poverty by means of complex rationalizations, turning it into a sort of proud indigence in which pride allows him to overvalue his own lackings and disqualify "those above." From another point of view, the same usually happens with many truly undesirable individuals who, by manipulating their own minds, see themselves as the best representatives of the human race, when truly they are the dregs of Mankind.

Indeed, the individual at a given point discovers that his typical way of behaving can bring advantages in his relations with people, so that everything he does from that moment is aimed at seeking the necessary elements to reinforce his own patterns of behavior. It is from that moment on that his personality becomes petrified and will never be modified in its essential structure, merely growing in the sense of the increasing or reinforcement of its own mechanisms. This situation gives rise to a sort of comfort that goes beyond mere laziness, in fact becoming an impulse of inertia or death to be psychoanalytically identified with Thanatos, the opposite of Eros—which is the irradiation of life. Possessed by an inertia that emanates from an identity molded by mechanical patterns, lacking consciousness, the individual refuses to come out of his habitual way of being or thinking in order to try to understand different realities. This is the general attitude of the whole of Mankind, and a source of incommunicability and violence among people.

The changes adults seem to undergo generally take place on the surface and not in their primary structure, so that there is usually no evolutive transformation between the moment the personality becomes petrified and that of physical death. This means that there is only a change in social habits, like a person who changes his clothes in accordance with fashion or acquires toys that he has not played with yet. The *having* part is modified, but there is no real change in the *being*, which constitutes a deviation of the evolutive mandate of Nature. Once the individual acquires the psychic immobility typical of petrified personalities, he merely blindly defends his own patterns of behavior, applauding those that coincide with his and repudiating those that diverge from them, without any further analysis.

Whatever their social or cultural level, such men come to constitute the inert class, beings incapable of opening up to new or different ideas, and like a chicken in its nest, spend their lives crouching in the depths of their own beliefs, fearful of approaching the light of more profound realities.

It is not at all satisfying to have to recognize that this is the measure that is being used in order to define what is wrongly called "normality," that impulse of being a good "social automaton"—mechanically speaking—an individual with a brain integrally programmed by fashionable messages, whether these be cultural, political, or religious. Comfort, in the sense we are analyzing it, is a moral transgression because it is opposed to the Creator's evolutive mandate, which is the significant purpose of existence.

Through convenience, many elderly people are indifferently allowed to languish; millions of children are allowed to starve; people remain indifferent to such suffering while their own spirit lies in the limbo of being unable to manifest itself through its corporeal vehicle. Likewise, people become accomplices of perverse ideologies or devious leaders; scandal and public corruption are tolerated; the manipulation of justice is allowed; and in some countries unnoticed and underhanded, it comes to be a political instrument of the State. One dies slowly in the daily conformism of the moral cowardice of those who, through their atrophied character and will, are incapable of overcoming their own animal nature, remaining like passive instruments of their own passions, with their intelligence placed at the service of covetousness, resentment, hate, violence, indolence, or destructiveness.

Every day, honor and dignity die—of those incapable of committing themselves to truth and justice; of those who hypocritically complain of darkness in the midst of light; of those who prostitute their minds to defend immoral causes; of those who in the name of humanism and peace sell their country to foreign interests; of those who through convenience or fear keep passively silent before infamy and corruption.

Comfort or convenience, with their lethal poison, destroy man's best intentions. He loses all his strength and bolsters himself in daily inertia, like the sick person who falls on his bed resigned to give himself up to death. It represents an inner impulse to continue to do what one has always done, to not move away from one's typical emotional repertoire, and to continue thinking as one has done to date. Through inertia, one continues to fail, to decline, to passively assent, to thwart one's inner desires; to deny the truths that do not fit one's own beliefs, however obvious they may be; to manipulate ethics in order to act wrongly and to continue thinking that one has acted rightly; to cling to old ideas as if they were idols; to resist opening up to new or different paradigms; to take refuge in hypocritical self-indulgence so as not to disturb one's own comfort; to let oneself be manipulated and intimidated by the opinion of the majority, however insane it may be.

Once more, one should remember that to act correctly one has to develop both character and willpower, which is impossible as long as we are dominated by such facile, idle conduct that leads us to yield and break down when something requires a strong, sustained effort.

Comfort produces addiction to habitual patterns of behavior and this automatized permanence in our physical, mental, and emotional habits both damages and thwarts any possibility of positive change. There are many people who feel unhappy and whose greatest desire is to attain the happiness they seek. However, they cannot understand that persistent misfortune is also a form of comfort. This is why happiness can be at one and the same time both desired and feared, for it implies work, effort, and responsibility, so that the individual unconsciously opts to continue being unhappy.

Of course, no one would admit to being unhappy through their own decision, and even less to have been driven to such misfortune by the vice of comfort. Usually one blames one's unhappiness on external factors, and rarely on unconscious mechanisms of a destructive nature. The easygoing individual usually complains about everything that happens in his social or personal environment, attributing his failings to specific people or situations, excluding himself from this analysis. It is a popular custom to take on the role of victim, for there are cultural and religious messages that covertly state that all victims, whether apparent or real, are good people who are suffering at the hands of some perverse persecutor. This place is often occupied by a ruler who is not popular among the people, or by a certain institution or certain ideologies, but as long as this mental adjustment works in the brains of the inert class, they feel themselves as "good."

One of the problems of the world today is the difficulty to distinguish between real and feigned victims. Things which seem clear are usually the most turbid, as philosophers have been telling us for thousands of years. For example, it is not rare for innocent people to be victimized by a blind justice that issues its verdict of guilt without having gone into the facts in depth, because it does not have the necessary independence to withstand certain pressures. Those affected remain indefinitely under a false stigma of wickedness or corruption.

In fact, the "easygoing" sometimes find that it is far less tiring and easier to somehow align themselves as the victims of something, whether it be true or supposed, as a means of acquiring respectability and avoiding the sustained, painful effort required to voluntarily become winners through their own decision, happy and free from aggressiveness and resentment. It is much easier to complain than to work hard, and to demand that the State, or somebody, solve problems which in truth are a matter of one's own individual effort. The more easygoing a person is, the greater will be his unjustified complaints and the more disproportionate or arbitrary demands he will make. It would seem as if the lazy person is conscious, in his inner world, of his behavior, so that in order to polish his image to himself, he goes to the other extreme, convincing himself that he deserves everything (which is the opposite of not deserving anything as a logical effect of his own laziness or indolence). As he probably does not have much, he convinces himself that he is the victim of the most ferocious type of injustice and becomes bitterly resentful. In this way, the blame is put onto society, onto a certain person, a system, or a certain social class, anything to avoid the inevitable result of feeling his aversion to making an adequate effort and acting efficiently in a disciplined way.

Do not think that an individual stops being an idler by the mere fact of working regularly. As we all know, inertia is the incapacity of bodies to modify, by themselves, the state of repose or movement in which they find themselves. The one who rests all the time is just as inert as the one who moves mechanically in frenzied activity, which because it is unconscious or disorderly can be quite unproductive. One has to learn that it is not enough to work; one has to do so efficiently, and only in this way can one attain one's personal goals. One must think that it may take years to acquire efficiency in a certain area and that it cannot be improvised, so that one has to discard the concept of "easy gain." Anything that is really worthwhile has a high price, and in this case, the price has to be paid in the same measure as our effort and perseverance. As for moral behavior, one generally needs a previous stage of sacrifice and self-discipline to become a truly virtuous being, a stage in which the individual must crystallize his character and will, withstand vice and corruption, and overcome many temptations before he attains an incorruptible condition.

All those who are averse to sustained effort over time will think the foregoing a sterile or futile process, one incompatible with facile effort and the pleasure of the moment. They are incapable of renouncing the immediate for the sake of distant goals, however valuable or transcendental these might be, ever pursuing the immediate satisfaction of their own impulses, like children. The merits of organized effort have even been questioned, arguing that it is a concept that corresponds to a certain political tendency, as if there were an honest system in life for success that excluded laborious work and personal merit.

Comfort is the cause and consequence of premature aging and decline. He who gives in to it ignores that his motivation resides more in death than in life. The usual image we have of comfort is that of an inactive individual who spends most of his time resting on a couch, who does not bother to try to attain what he wants, or who lives in a sybaritic orgy of material comfort. This type of behavior is easily recognizable and can hardly be denied by the individual himself.

However, this does not happen with psychological inertia that affects the mind and emotions, and that consists of a visceral, mechanical resistance to moving away from the habitual channels of thought, behavior, and feeling. This is a very subtle mechanism that is interpreted by the individual as his own desire or will, as the free choice of one who wishes to persist in forms of behavior chosen by some higher rationality. At no time would this person then think that the origin of his behavior could lie in the idleness roused by inertia, which by affecting the movement of all bodies also influences his own psyche, driving it to similar behavior.

This is one of the reasons why there is such a strong tendency for people to continue doing what they have always done and thought or felt, in accordance with their usual habit, a situation that can only be changed by means of the development of a state of consciousness of a power higher than inertia. Nobody can deny that it is far more laborious and difficult to open up new paths than to travel along well-known roads. When it is a case of the brain, it becomes a superhuman task, reserved only for heroes or those who aspire to be so, for the information we bear in our brain in the form of knowledge or conditioning, *opens up paths or channels of communication between neurons,* which like electronic circuits, become obligatory sidetracks for the circulation of energy, in this case, the information exchanged between the brain cells. In other words, our brain also has *circuits of comfort,* paths of neuronal communication through which the nervous impulses pass in an extremely fluid manner and which are available for habitual cerebral activity.

Normal thought means, therefore, the inevitable circulation along well-known paths, the falling into the continued repetition of one's own schemas, and this can only be avoided by higher mental activity, which is not a congenital capacity nor is it learned through education or culture. This quality can only be obtained after a long apprenticeship in states of intensified awakening, a process through which one can one day attain what I call *neuronal spontaneity,* which corresponds to forms of neural association not previously registered, nor automatic, as if the complete neuronal structure were to forget every day the habitual form of communicating, so that each day a new method would have to be improvised. This phenomenon corresponds to true vigilic consciousness. In this way, comfort entirely rules our lives, making us *accommodate* our view of the world to what corresponds to our own mechanisms, flaws, defects, vices, or failings and not to any authentic image of reality. This is why one blindly obeys the implicit authority of the majority, however little morals its habits may bear, adhering passively to inappropriate forms of behavior, particularly when they are disguised with beautiful words such as *liberty, justice, equality,* or *tolerance.*

In the name of humanitarian ideals and Christian charity, but also in that of easy, lukewarm conformism, the suppression of the death penalty is advocated, even in highly justified cases, with the argument that it is a barbarian sentence because it goes against the most precious possession of all, which is human life, and that society has no right to take revenge for itself. The very act of meting out justice has been called "taking vengeance." However, the permissive attitude is taken to enable other criminals to feel free to put an end to others' lives because they are not afraid of the punishment. In this way, in order to save only a few, we risk not only the lives, but also the tranquility of peaceful people. To die slowly, second by second, could perhaps be far more cruel than being executed, as in the legendary oriental torture in which a drop of water falls on a condemned man's head until it drives him mad.

Despite what is said to the contrary, millions of innocent children, adults, and old people are killed every day because of the polluted air they breathe, through insufficient control of polluted food mixed with additives, the effects of which cannot be foreseen, their brains battered with acoustic contamination and their minds invaded and poisoned with a myriad of subliminal messages that are contradictory and induce neuroses.

People remain indifferent while the dispossessed have no real access to justice, for this usually only goes as far as the money available for it. The elderly are attacked by being prematurely criticized as heavy burdens for society or the family. Drug consumption grows more each day and many of those affected are dead in life due to their atrocious dependence on them. Why is human life not defended in these cases with the same vehemence as that used to suppress the death penalty? It is obvious that in the midst of refined, underhanded mechanisms of death and destruction, the only form of eliminating a person which is neither hypocritical nor dissimulated, but which corresponds to a transparent act of social justice, is attacked.

One should ponder whether murder is merely to destroy a person in an instant or whether the crime does not also spread to diverse forms of slow death. If an individual poisoned a person with a slow-working poison that took 20 years to kill him, would this be considered less of a crime than eliminating him with one single blow over the head? On the contrary, the premeditation and ill will needed to regularly supply a poisonous substance for some time would make the crime considerably worse.

Traditional medicine does not hesitate to surgically amputate cancerous tumors, in the knowledge that if this is not done, the whole body may die. Through hypocrisy and false charity, society refuses to accept that certain forms of delinquency are a veritable social cancer, to which the only solution consists in the definitive elimination of the perturbing factor, before there is greater damage to the social body—and if we do not do this, we become the allies and accomplices of such destructive elements. In the end, it could perhaps be more merciful to physically eliminate an atrocious delinquent than to imprison him for life. It is argued that, "God gives life and therefore, only He has the right to take it away." In reality, by the fact of killing a fellow man, the murderer deserves a punishment which has been previously established by society. Therefore, he becomes his own murderer in the event that he is condemned to death. This is not vengeance, but the reestablishment of justice and the security of society.

The contradiction of suppressing the death penalty lies in the fact that we implicitly punish at one and the same time both the victim and his family, because we allow his death, and secondly, because we prevent the egalitarian equivalence that would mean the physical elimination of the murderer, giving both different rights under the law.

Likewise, the person responsible is doubly rewarded, first because he is allowed to satisfy his perverse criminal impulses, after which he is rewarded because his board and lodging and health are perpetually taken care of, thus preventing the biblical anathema which in virtue of original sin condemned man to "earn his bread with the sweat of his brow." If the death penalty is rejected through compassion, one must understand that a life sentence is not the right substitute, because for many people, in particular those who live in extreme poverty, the deprival of liberty could mean a reward as far as it puts an end to having to struggle for one's daily bread.

It would seem that at the beginning of the 21st century society is getting into the habit of changing the names of many things to thus satisfy practiced hypocrisy and avoid the envy of the resentful. Society is beginning to call the maximum penalty of traditional justice, "vengeance"; depraved conduct, "variations of sexual experience"; sexual consumerism, "love"; ambiguity, "the center"; consumerism, "well-being"; licentiousness, "freedom"; and denouncements of corruption, "attacks on people's honor."

The type of verbal deals in which two honest, integral men shake hands to seal an agreement, seems to be a thing of the past or a reason for laughter or mockery.

Accumulated inertia gives us a surprising mental agility to *accommodate* our moral judgments, tastes, and preferences to the tonic of our instinctive impulses and thus justify the immoral excesses of the unconscious.

There is no doubt that immoral conduct represents a decline in human faculties, being a *descending* process, one of an easy, facile downward drop, whereas it is an arduous, laborious task to become virtuous for it requires ascending to a level of higher behavior that, as I have repeatedly pointed out, demands proper development of character and will.

To be virtuous means the antithesis of comfort; it is a continual act of power that requires all the individual's inner strength. Vice, on the other hand, does not even have to be desired, for to acquire it, it is enough for the individual to passively assent and he will unwittingly go further and further down the scale until in some cases he will reach the defiling of his own human condition in the blind conviction that he is acting correctly.

In the midst of its great contradictions, Mankind says that it adheres to a virtuous way of life, but at the same time disqualifies and attacks elitism, as if it were a sin as serious as any form of corruption, ignoring the fact that virtue has never been a privilege of the mass but the quality of certain individuals who because of their own effort and free choice, are able to integrate into the select minority of those who manage to free themselves of their own passions.

Masses are by nature uncontrolled and fickle, lacking a responsible head that would guarantee their proper moral behavior. When we are asked to practice *equality* indiscriminately, there is an underhanded attempt to press us to adopt types of behavior similar to the blind masses in order for us to fall into the same moral ambiguity as them. It would seem that it is an attempt to stop us from abandoning our passive role as obedient consumers for any reason whatsoever.

The obvious path of comfort is naturally to give oneself up to the mass and to lose one's own identity there so that one cannot be either criticized or attacked due to one's lack of differentiation from that mass.

People's mental commodity makes them seek *canned culture* in books, pre-digested, beautifully bound concepts that make one agree with them blindly and not take the trouble to really think, but to merely pay attention to the publicity or prestige of the publishing house.

Reading preferences fall as is only logical into the category of "candy-coated" literature especially designed to flatter people's vanity or to satisfy the idle fantasies of the lazy and the self-indulgent.

People also join the most powerful or prestigious political parties through inertia, and applaud those artists who cultivate a grotesque style of art merely because "prestigious" critics praise the "beauty" or the "depth" of their work. On the other hand, they disqualify those who could become geniuses similar to those of the Renaissance. Comfort is without a doubt the enemy of ethics and morality and from the darkest abyss of the soul conspires to prevent man from ascending.

Hate

St. Augustine said that "wrath engenders hate and from hate, pain and fear are born." According to Goethe "hate is a deadweight that sinks the heart deep into the breast and, like a tombstone, weighs heavily on all joys." Hate, antipathy, and aversion to a person or thing whom we wish harm is a moral disease that affects a large part of Mankind. As occurs with other negative feelings of concentrated intensity, such as envy and jealousy, hate is highly contagious, as it manifests itself so virulently that it ends up by sweeping away the will of the weak. As in the cases I described above, the feeling of intense hate, like any other intensified exaltation of the senses, represents a perverse exacerbation of sexuality that in this case takes on a destructive mode. The same ardor, in its positive creative manifestation, was what drove Michelangelo to paint the Sistine Chapel or to give form to any of his works.

Sexual energy can have three different outlets: the most common is its reproductive function; it can also be sublimated as a driving force for spirituality and the arts; or in its lowest form, become depraved and will, in the guise of hate, trigger off people's sadistic impulses. Most hateful people are sadistic and through the overflowing of their perverse erotic sensations attain a *psychological orgasm* that is prolonged throughout time. This explains the recurrent intensity of passions such as wrath, jealousy, and violence, and the difficulties encountered in controlling them. Very intense sensations cause a projection of the individual's animal magnetism. In the present case, hate elevates the individual's destructive feelings to an extraordinary potency and will issue his own magnetism saturated with mortal intent.

The ancient Samurai were able to perceive beforehand, and at a certain physical distance, what they called "the murderer's air," equivalent to the murderous intentions of those who wanted to attack them, so that it was very difficult, if not almost impossible, to take them by surprise. Naturally, this perception was the result of a long period of training, and thus common men lack this sensitivity. However, the "murderer's air" was the projection of magnetism impregnated by the destructive intentions of the one who wanted to kill the warrior. People's intentions, feelings, and impulses impregnate and saturate their biomagnetism either positively or negatively, and this is not a metaphysical manifestation, but a phenomenon just as normal and common as saving information on a diskette or hard disk of a computer. He who hates *archives* a destructive vibration in his personal magnetism and in his *L-fields,* projecting this energy on the person or thing he so detests. The first to be harmed by filing away hate is the hateful individual himself, for as this is a passion of a destructive and ill-willed nature, it *disorders, dissociates, stains, perturbs, and contaminates his L-fields,* with the consequent damage to his health.

There are many people who catch serious illnesses because of the hate they are affected by. Resentment, hate, envy, and destructiveness are all discordant and destructive musical tones issued by our psyche that act as messengers of death to the cells of the body.

The destructive influence of negative emotions is fully accepted in medicine, and certain scientists agree that "there is no illness that is exempt from a psychosomatic factor." For example, it has been observed that postoperative recovery is far quicker and more profound in happy, harmonious individuals, with a family who loves them, than in cases of hateful, solitary, embittered individuals.

The "evil eye," rather than a superstition, is a natural phenomenon of biomagnetism projected through the eyes, which can cause a negative or destructive influence in living beings brought on by the envy or hate the individual feels, in this case, by the individual who glares in fury. It is known that there are glances that pacify and calm us down, because this is the nature of the individual who gazes, and others that paralyze, alter, annoy, or disturb the soul. Very little is known about what might exist "beyond" or "behind" a person's eyes, except for the saying that "the eyes are the mirror of the soul." What is true is that when we look at them, we feel that they put us in touch with something very intimate that either pleases or displeases us, and this is either the harmonious or the discordant condition of what is filed away in the individual's bodily magnetism, a message that we manage to decode at moments of greater receptiveness.

Lovers never tire of looking each other in the eyes, since the delight they experience comes from the fact that they share their respective magnetic fluids. Cupid's arrow is an intuitive symbol of a person's magnetic irradiation that reaches another of the opposite sex, who, fascinated by the pleasure to be derived from it, succumbs to the attraction.

In Mesmer's time, hypnosis was known as "magnetization," since it was supposed that this was the way in which the hypnotic phenomena was brought on.

Probably, the custom of shaking hands was born at a time when man's intuition was more highly developed, as a means of "touching" or "feeling" the other person's magnetism to see whether he was a friend or an enemy, whether he was good or bad. The individual who hates is without a shadow of a doubt a sender of magnetism that bears the mandates of death and destruction, that comes from the archive of his vibrations of hate. This archive becomes a source of vibratory projection, which, when caught by other people, penetrates in the magnetic current of their bodies, destructively influencing their vital, intellectual, and emotional centers.

The person hated will feel depressed, crestfallen, and dispirited, and will in turn begin to detest things that had never bothered him before. Hate, and most vices, are extremely contagious, and this is why certain forms of corruption can spread so dramatically.

To hate is a very serious moral fault, for it represents an attempt on other people's lives, who can be negatively affected in their psychic or biological integrity when the destructive magnetic projection reaches them, and will experience problems for which they will never discover the origin. The individual who hates punishes his own sin very efficiently, for the negative passion that consumes him will gradually become a destructive part of the cells of his body, and will also deform his facial and bodily expressions and give rise to a variety of mental and biological alterations.

There are people who deteriorate their conduct instead of perfecting it by becoming more cynical and aggressive with the passing of the years. The dishonest interpretation of their own life circumstances pollutes and dirties their feelings due to the fact that they blame external sources, whether these be people, groups, or institutions, for the misfortune or unhappiness they suffer, whereas it is really their own responsibility. Once sullied, polluted, and embittered, this person will get into the habit of unconsciously shaping in his mind a sort of "chameleon operation" in which he manages to blame or hate others through a series of complex rationalizations, with the true intent of concealing and denying his own faults and weaknesses. Once he has convinced himself of his own innocence and of the guilt of others, he will give free rein to his hate, the sadistic impulse which makes him indefinitely experience an emotional orgasm of depraved pleasure over and over again. As will be understood, the magnitude of this sensation makes him addicted to it, so that he will habitually resort to the same mechanism to satisfy his perverse needs.

Hate, just like envy, is a sin against any form of life and is severely punished because its appalling nature will naturally rebound back onto the one who hates. Like any other vicious conduct, one may ask if it is freely chosen or if it is an irresistible force that takes possession of the individual's will. I personally believe that what the individual chooses is in all truth his own weakness or strength. In the former case, just like a sponge, he will absorb and appropriate the vicious types of conduct that most attract him, thus reinforcing his position as victim by being left impotent before the force of the bad habit by which he is dominated. Thus he also has the chance to satisfy his masochistic fantasy of falling down in a faint, or lying inert, unable to escape, before a strange force that overcomes him. He who prefers to choose to be strong and to possess a well-tempered character can well withstand the temptation of acting incorrectly and the attraction aroused by vices.

When we are in danger, we have two options: either to flee or to attack. To flee may be physical or mental, in order to evade or deny the dangerous situation. Aggression has to be viewed in its lower aspect as a physical confrontation and, in its highest form, as the capacity to confront stressful, problematic, or threatening situations of everyday reality.

Both options are symbolized by Eros as the force of life and by Thanatos as the force of death. Eros was the name the Greeks gave to love and the god Love, and it was used by Freud in his theory of pulsions to denote the ensemble of life pulsions, opposing them to death pulsions, or Thanatos, a Greek word which means death. There are those who choose to commit themselves to Thanatos and become specialists in fleeing from the truth, from responsibility, virtue, good, and love, hiding their heads in the basement of their mind. They invariably justify their errors, vices, and failings, blaming others to cleanse their offensive image through the subterfuge of turning into victims.

I believe that the human being chooses either the role of victim or that of an adult, mature, responsible person. Of course, I have no intention of denying the fact that there are many real martyrs; I am only saying that a very high percentage of Mankind chooses, rightly or wrongly, the role of victim. This choice, of a sadomasochistic kind, psychoanalytically represents a regression to the womb, as a self-destructive impulse that leads the individual to seek and to encounter situations of pain and suffering.

Those who choose the luminous impulse of life refuse to consider themselves victims, for they are perfectly capable of confronting dangerous situations with a controlled aggressiveness that is expressed in the form of a force at the service of the "I." Really, our existence is a continual succession of problems, and one must understand that this is a situation that is inherent to being alive, and not something "abnormal." He who feels a victim may believe he is the object of a great injustice, and easily fall into a sort of resentment that will in time lead to hate.

I am convinced that the individual deliberately chooses the role of a weak or strong person, his choice depending on whether he wants to fully face life or to evade the painful effort implied in adapting himself to an uncontrollable and ever more problematic and complex external reality.

I believe that most of those who seem weak are really inveterate idlers who have chosen this type of behavior because it enables them to subsist with the minimum effort by surreptitiously manipulating their own emotions and those of others. These idlers do so by camouflaging themselves as a member of the inert class in order to arouse compassion or to avoid responsibilities.

When I speak of a strong individual, I chiefly mean strength of character and will that can be fortified by means of proper self-discipline and a real confrontation with everyday conflicts. This individual takes life with love and joy, as something that has to be lived positively and creatively, and far from avoiding his problems, will face up to them with a harmonious, balanced inner disposition, an attitude that signals a good beginning to finding happiness.

There is an even greater sin than hate, and that is to sow hate in the masses, who are always susceptible to this type of manipulation. This operation is analogous to someone deliberately "infecting" a crowd with the virus of his own illness, multiplying and magnifying its destructive effects, since the entire family is infected in the end and then a whole country, in many instances causing an escalation of death and destruction.

Fernández de la Mora referred to certain political agitators as "engineers of envy," beings whose daily activity consists of infecting the people's minds with the venom of hate and envy. Whole towns are contaminated with this venom, which, once inside a person's mind, becomes *autonomous information*, that is, it is *not subordinate to the "I."* This totally alienates an individual's behavior, turning him into a socially resentful being, not because he has any powerful reasons for this, but because of his dependence on the mental toxin he bears within himself. Once this resentment becomes that of the majority, the country is lost, for the force that drives it is no longer constructive and controlled but becomes destructive and blind. This happened with the bloodbath of the French Revolution, in which the heads of several of its leaders rolled in turn under the guillotine.

A country infected by envy and resentment can remain indefinitely in economic underdevelopment, because to envy *means to unconsciously choose a subordinate position in life, for one can only envy "those above" so that to do so, one has to place oneself "beneath" in a subordinate position.* One can only envy those who are above one in some way, permanently looking upwards. Wallowing in envious malaise obliges one "to be beneath" and to remain there.

It is said that "he who sows winds will reap tempests," and this is very true, for in due time, the effects created by people's incorrect actions will inevitably fall back upon themselves. It is true that Nature possesses its own morality and, in accordance with its laws, at some point, "he who does so will always pay" without there being any chance of him escaping from it. Normally, we do not notice this because the time of Nature passes far slower than that of man, so that perhaps the punishment of certain people will only come after death, as some religions hold when they say that a person who has sinned too much will go to Hell when he dies. There is no need to go very far into modern physics to understand that the existence of Hell is not even remotely a physical impossibility, since there are many planes of parallel realities.

One must understand that true sin is not a violation of the codes whimsically invented by man but rather it is an infraction of laws with which Nature maintains life and universal equilibrium. To sin is to violate this supreme ordinance and it does not matter whether the offender is a believer or not, he will receive his punishment nonetheless. For example, there is no need *to believe in the law of gravity* for an apple that has been thrown into the air to return to the ground.

Authentic morality should be a compendium of the laws of Nature, applied wisely to human existence, and not a compendium of prohibitions and recommendations born of the good intentions of people who desire good, but ignore the patterns of natural law. One should understand that we as human beings live within Nature, and that we are not its master, as is presumed by certain arrogant people.

On our dear planet Earth, we are no more than tiny cells in a huge macrocosm. Imagine what would happen to a cell of our body that believed that it was the lord of the whole organism, and proceeded to transgress its biological rules, for instance by attempting to attack and destroy other cells, to steal their nutrients, or turn them against the central government of the brain. Something similar to this is what happens with immoral people. They are individuals who do not respect the holographic structure of life as a single body in which all living forms are linked by constant biofeedback through a subtle connection. They cannot understand that by damaging others, they also destroy themselves.

"Do unto others as you would have them do unto you" is not only a nice sentence but one that obviously also expresses the universal holographic principle, which could be summed up as follows: "all are within oneself and one is within all others." Each cell of our body possesses the complete memory of the whole organism. Each particle of the Universe is also a reflection of its total structure. As long as people believe that moral rules represent no more than the behavioral preferences of certain moralists, and that each can choose his own actions in accordance with his personal desires, there will be no hope for man for any type of higher behavior.

To return to the subject of hate, it stems from a desire to suppress something that irritates or perturbs us in some way, and not necessarily because the object of our hate is bad or perverse. This helps to explain the true origin of certain revolutions, the driving force of which resides in hate, envy, and destruction. The aversion we feel towards a certain person often derives from the fact that he is a "noncompliant mirror," for when we confront him, his superiority becomes evident, as well as our own smallness. This is the reason why we unwittingly try "at all costs" to discredit or tarnish the image that perturbs us so.

This is the reason for the wrath and rejection exuded by the masses against certain people who seem to be "too clean" or "too perfect," becoming thus moral mirrors that reflect the magnitude of others' meanness. I believe that people who are mediocre, weak, sickly, or otherwise physically unappealing, have a better chance of being preferred by the masses than those who are too harmonious, both internally and externally. The most popular leaders or candidates are usually elected by virtue of the inner parameter of their voters, and are seldom of greater stature than the inner reference of each voter, being thus the expression of the level of spiritual perfection or imperfection of each. In its true expression, an individual's cognitive standing never surpasses his quotient of spiritual consciousness, and this is why the mass, the concrete manifestation of mediocrity, has no power of discrimination with which to recognize great men, so that more often than one might wish, it accepts the orders of dummies.

It is impossible for an ignorant person to evaluate a wise man, but the wise man has the capacity to detect a fool. In any case, the worst form of ignorance is not that which concerns the lack of cultural or scientific information, but that which concerns the individual's lack of knowledge of his own being, his inner world, and the transcendental states of consciousness. This subject is like a blind spot in the minds of those who are considered the most cultured and intellectual, or else it is a topic for indifference, mockery, or disqualification for most people. The gravest ineptitude lies not in illiteracy nor in the possession of a modest IQ, but in the lack of *significant consciousness,* a capacity which is not innate, which we possess only in a latent state. Without it, man is no more than a *container of information,* a mere archive for autonomous information that is not subordinated to his "I."

One either ignores or fails to understand the words of Sir Arthur Eddington when he said that "the only thing that can be studied is the contents of one's own consciousness." This is a major declaration for those who, because they lack any knowledge of how to handle their own consciousness, are not in a position to carry out any profound, accurate study of internal and external reality; and this is the concrete situation of people who are wrongly considered to be normal. Those who are asleep cannot see those who are awake, but the awake ones can invariably recognize the sleepwalkers.

Drug Abuse

The vice of drug abuse represents the most violent, destructive way to avoid confronting reality. It entails taking refuge in a world of dreams, hallucinations, and altered perceptions, in which the individual slowly destroys himself at the same time as he denies the harmful effect of his addiction. Apart from being a vice, it is also a serious moral fault, because it assaults one's own physical and psychological integrity, so that one rejects the opportunity to fulfill oneself as an authentic human being.

The drug addict is a sick person, but he is also a vicious person and the former condition is no justification for the latter. Drug dependency is a psychological, and at times physical, condition characterized by the compulsion to consume a narcotic so as to experience its enervating effects. Addiction is a severe form of dependency, characterized by a physical submission. This condition occurs when the narcotic has caused physical changes in the body, there being a development of tolerance and the need to increase the dosage so as to experience its effects, and resulting in a syndrome of disorders such as nausea, diarrhea, or pain, which appear once the effects of the drug have worn off.

The most popular drugs are: the opiates, such as morphine and heroin; sedative-hypnotics, such as barbiturates and tranquilizers; stimulants, among which one could include cocaine and amphetamines; hallucinatory drugs (LSD, mescaline, and peyote); *cannabis* (marijuana); and inhalants such as neoprene, gasoline, and diverse aerosols. Because of its great impact on young people, I will mention the injuries caused by marijuana, so that both young people and adults know the price they have to pay for the smoke they inhale. An ancient, polemical aphorism that says "spare the rod and spoil the child," most certainly refers to the severity needed in order to teach something that people refuse to learn.

Perhaps moral rules are easier to comply with when they are no longer simple, well-intended recommendations, so that people can concretely visualize the magnitude of the harm and self-destruction generated by not complying with them. As far as marijuana consumption is concerned, this is quite clear, however much smokers may argue that "it is more inoffensive than tobacco." The *Cannabis sativa* plant is the source of marijuana and hash. The leaves, flower, and branches are ground to produce marijuana, while hash is its concentrated resin. Marijuana elicits a state of relaxation, an acceleration of the heart rate, a slowing down of the perception of time, and an intensification of hearing, smell, touch, and taste. Its negative perceptual effects include confusion, panic reactions, attacks of anxiety, fear, a feeling of defenselessness, and a loss of self-control. Its active substance is tetrahydrocannabinol, known as THC. A Swiss scientist who injected THC into rats and rabbits analyzed their excrement to discover that both their urine and feces remained radioactive for a minimum period of three days. He also discovered a similar duration of the concentration of radioactivity in dissected portions of the liver, spleen, kidneys, and suprarenal glands, both in rats and in rabbits. The importance of the spleen is that it is closely involved in the immunological system of our body.

There have also been experiments to inject THC into the veins of several volunteers. Some of them had never smoked marijuana, while others had smoked it daily for over 10 years. In both cases, the radioactivity in urine and feces was detected for over a week, for THC is stored in the fatty tissues such as the liver, brain, bone marrow, and the suprarenal glands and is slowly excreted in feces and urine. As THC dissolves in fat, it remains in the organism to produce effects that will last for days or weeks and even months. Certain clinical observations show an increase in the speed of the heartbeat, redness in the eyes, a lack of coordination, weakness in the muscles, an increase in passivity, transitory changes in the brain waves, and a short-term loss of memory. There is also a deterioration of one's motor skills and slowness of the subjective moment.

In 1977, it was estimated that a total of 43,000,000 people had tried it in the United States, and that over 10 percent of them were between the ages of 12 and 17. More than 12,000,000 people use this drug more or less regularly. In 1971, the radioactivity labelled as Delta-9-THC showed that the active metabolites from marijuana are stored in the tissues, including the brain, for at least eight days after the initial entry of the drug into the organism. This means that so-called "moderate smokers" will never be free from the effects of marijuana. There are studies that have established that three out of every four smokers of marijuana have certain lymphocytes with a diminishment of the speed of cell division. When the lymphocytes were studied for three days, they showed high abnormality in the number of ruptures of the chromosomes. These are the threads of the DNA that bear the hereditary characteristics of our cells. Doctor Akira Morishima observed that 30 percent of marijuana smokers had fewer chromosomes in their lymphocytes than the normal amount required. A research committee informed the U.S. Senate that "THC, the most important psychoactive substance of hemp, tends to accumulate in the brain, sexual glands, and other fatty tissues of the organism in a way very similar to that in which DDT is stored."

Five scientists declared before a senatorial subcommittee that "the products of marijuana prevent the normal multiplication of lymphocytes in cells, as happens with other cells under study." Each of these researchers expressed his fears that "such cell damage could lead to cancer, to an increase in various diseases, and possibly, to an increase of genetically damaged offspring."

Really, there is evidence that marijuana can cause irreversible damage to the brain when it is used regularly for several years. Doctor William Paton, a professor of pharmacology at Oxford University, discovered in a group of young smokers that the atrophy of their brains was equivalent to what one would normally find in people between 70 and 90 years of age.

There is evidence that the male hormonal level was reduced to 44 percent in young men who had used marijuana at least four times a week for a minimum period of six months. The sperm count in this same group had dropped in proportion to the amount of marijuana smoked, causing sterility in those who smoked large quantities. There is also evidence that the cells of the sperm of certain animals exposed to marijuana bore reduced amounts of DNA and that its regular use ended with three times as many wasted chromosomes as the chromosomes that are normally found in nonsmokers.

The committee also informed that habitual use ends in a deterioration of the working of the mind, pathological states similar to paranoia, progressive habitual passivity, and a lack of motivation. Nine of the scientists who testified before the Senate's subcommittee, some of them professors of psychiatry, gave a wealth of evidence and observations of aberrant and dangerous behavior among marijuana smokers, even among the moderate smokers. Doctor Tennant said that "the principle manifestations in users' personalities were apathy, insensitivity, and lethargy, with severe deterioration of judgment, concentration, and memory. Their physical appearance was stereotyped and all the patients seemed stupid, with a lack of personal hygiene and they displayed a slowness in their speech." There is well-founded evidence that concentration and the number of cells accumulated in smokers' sperm is notably reduced, on average by 50 percent. The reduction in the production of sperm is usually associated with abnormal sperm, that is, with low-quality reproductive cells. THC dramatically affects the white globules (lymphocytes), causing a remarkable drop in people's immunological systems.

In the Helsinki conference of 1975, three thousand pharmacologists met for a week and hundreds of studies were presented at dozens of sessions. In the symposium on marijuana, an impressive film was shown in which a white globule appeared that had been separated from the lung lining. The cell and all its parts continually moved in a natural way, but after adding a small amount of THC, the same cell became completely paralyzed as if it had lost its life. The psychiatrist Professor Costas Stefani and Professor of Cell Biology Marietta Issidorides reported that they had discovered fundamental chemical changes in the white globules and in the sperm cells of those who regularly smoked hash, which indicates an abnormality in the cell nucleus. By using various slides, Stefani was able to show the fundamental cellular changes that had taken place in the white globules and sperm cells due to the use of marijuana, which could explain its interference with the formation of the fundamental chemical materials of the cell. Professor Robert Heath, of Tulane University, showed in his experiments with Rhesus monkeys that primates exposed to marijuana smoke displayed permanent alterations in the patterns of the brain waves of the limbic system, which is the part of the brain that controls emotional behavior. Doctor Gabriel Nahas[22] sustained that one of the fastest effects of marijuana is the progressive loss of will that can be clearly observed after six weeks of moderate use, and that the ability to enjoy a real pleasure disappeared, to be replaced by a noisy pretense of happiness. While healthy young people will diligently participate in different types of sports and other activities, those who use marijuana will display a growing tendency to talk endlessly of their high aims without doing anything to attain them. And instead of feeling profound affection for others, the marijuana smoker is prone to wallowing in superfluous sentimental emotions.

The investigations of the NIDA (National Institute on Drug Abuse) of the Department of Public Health of the United States showed that marijuana depresses man's reproductive hormones, causing important changes in the sexual organs, such as a drop in the weight of the testicles, seminal bladder, and prostate gland. All this is accompanied by oligospermia and sperm abnormalities.[23] The NIDA also sustains that the chronic use of marijuana causes a drop in the function of the endocrine organs, such as the pituitary gland, the testicles, the thyroid, and the adrenal cortex.[24] The hypothalamus is the area most affected by THC, and it is believed that there is an alteration in neuronal input to this area. There is also well-documented evidence that the cannabinoids alter cellular functioning, causing changes in the sequence and form in which genetic information is processed and transcribed. Naturally, the effects of these transformations are unforeseeable.

Professor Jerome Jaffe, Professor of Psychiatry at the College of Physicians and Surgeons of Columbia University, Robert Petersen, Joint Director of the Research Division of the NIDA, and the psychologist Ray Hodgson of the London Institute of Psychiatry sustain that: "one of the most important aspects of daily tasks affected by marijuana is driving vehicles, for the most careful research carried out recently indicates that if the driver of a vehicle smokes marijuana, he is exposed to adverse effects exactly the same as if he had taken alcohol and driven a car in that state." They add that a particularly important fact is that some of the visual problems caused by marijuana may persist for hours after subjective stimulation has ceased. For example, peripheral vision is not immediately recovered. They state:

> The person who drives a vehicle under the effects of *cannabis* is irremediably exposed to diverse risks. The combination of alcohol and *cannabis* is quite common and could be more dangerous than the consumption of either of the two toxic substances taken separately.
>
> The American scientists who study the effects of marijuana in angina pectoris, that is, retrosternal pain in patients with heart problems, have observed that its use caused pain quicker and after less effort than those who smoked cigarettes. Others who maybe should not try marijuana are those who suffer from serious emotional problems: the study of a small group of individuals who had suffered from schizophrenia and recovered showed that the disease reappeared after consuming this drug. Among university students, it has been discovered that those who are most concerned about their health and have the least capacity for self-control or to govern their lives, are those who most often suffer the fearful, unpleasant effects of marijuana.

Other causes for preoccupation about marijuana abuse are centered on the possibility of bronchitis. They continue:

> The Leuchtenberger's, Swiss researchers, have shown that the tissue of the human lung exposed to *cannabis* smoke in a test tube, displayed cellular alterations far more serious than those observed in similar tissue samples that had been exposed to

common tobacco smoke. The changes observed were similar to those of cancerous cells. When extracts of *cannabis* smoke were inserted into the skins of study animals, tumors evolved similar to those produced by the tar from cigarette tobacco.[25]

As for my own observations, I have been able to discover diverse alterations produced in frequent marijuana smokers. All of them, without exception, develop a sort of emotional narcissism that makes it very difficult for them to feel empathy for their fellows, tending rather to manipulate the feelings of those around them. Despite the fact that their emotional manifestations seem to be of great intensity, they are really mechanical, superficial, and stereotyped, leading to "emotional frigidity" disguised under an apparently highly sensitive temperament. In many of them, it is also obvious that with the passing of time, the drug profoundly affects the higher cerebral functions to the detriment of higher discrimination, criterion, and inner judgment. The capacity to open oneself up to new paradigms of thought or higher forms of conduct is also dramatically reduced, even when the person affected is convinced of just the opposite. It is, therefore, not surprising that men should display reduced sexual potency and secondary feminine characteristics such as the exaggerated development of the breasts or a tendency toward homosexuality. In the October 27, 1986, edition of *Newsweek* there appeared an article entitled: "One of Reagan's Assistants Declares: *Marijuana could turn you into a homosexual.*" This comment referred to the White House antidrug adviser, Carlton E. Turner, who was convinced that the vice of marijuana could lead its addicts to homosexuality. He also stated that homosexuals, by the mere fact of consuming marijuana, dangerously increase the vulnerability of their immunological system with respect to AIDS. Each time he visited an antidrug treatment center for patients under 18, he was able to see that more than 40 percent of these underage drug addicts had had homosexual relationships. Turner, who is a doctor in organic chemistry, was convinced that the drug is the first step and that homosexuality comes immediately after as a second step. He firmly defended his opinion that marijuana makes its dependents far more susceptible to AIDS, because of the way in which it affects and damages people's immunological systems.

The abuse of marijuana, from the moral point of view, damages the individual—as will any vice that produces dependency—by annulling his character and will. Furthermore, as we have seen, the use of cannabis is also an aggression against one's own body, which, as it is the bearer of the being, possesses the spark of divinity and is thus the temple of the spirit. It is this sanctuary that we attack when we poison our organism with marijuana, cocaine, or other poisonous products, and our moral fault is equivalently serious. It seems that what occurs with cannabis is within the context of those things which hinder our virtuous behavior, stimulating only the passional, since the cerebral center which is most impacted is the limbic system, and that is where the greatest amount of the drug accumulates.

The paleoencephalus or "old brain," was the most important part of primitive man's brain, and also that of animals, while millions of years of evolution developed what has come to be called the neocortex or "new brain," also known as the cerebral cortex, or "roof of the brain," a name given to it by Charles Sherrington.

Our intellectual faculties such as language, symbolic expressions, an analytical capacity, and self-knowledge, all derive from the new brain, while our emotions and instincts are stored in the ancient one, along with the subconscious.

Human conduct results from the interaction between both brains and when this interaction is altered, behavior is also modified. Doctors Pennfield and Jaspers discovered that the electric stimulation of the limbic area in patients who were awake caused a loss of identity, fear, paranoia, distortions of perception, and alterations in the sensation of time. Olds and Milner, of McGill University, carried out an experiment that consisted of inserting tiny electrodes into the limbic area in rats, which the animals could activate by pressing a small lever to stimulate this region. Once the rats associated the stimulation with a pleasurable sensation, they set up a pattern of stimulus that lasted until the animals were quite worn out, pressing the lever up to three thousand times per hour.

The researchers reached the conclusion that there is a specific area in the old brain which, when stimulated, provokes a type of behavior associated with reward and pleasure.

Professor Robert Heath, of Tulane University, came to the conclusion that electric stimulation of the part of the hypothalamus in the old brain produces sensations of well-being and euphoria in primates and in man. After inserting electrodes deep into the limbic area of rhesus monkeys, he made them inhale marijuana and observed "bursts" of irregular electric activity, or "punctures" caused by the marijuana in the septal area of the brain, which is the focal point for reward and pleasure. After a time, he killed several specimens to examine the old brain and discovered damage to the synapses of the limbic tissues.

Smoking marijuana stimulates the limbic system, and it is not far-fetched to suppose that it unleashes the passions, preventing self-control, making higher rationality difficult and altering emotional behavior.

As with any solitary vice, the use of *cannabis* means an easy reward through the stimulation of the pleasure centers, thus eluding the natural process in which the pleasurable is usually the final prize for a long, arduous process to earn this reward. This is one of the reasons why it harms the character and erodes the will, for the concept of an easy reward becomes a habit that prevents true personal effort, which is essential for tempering the will and attaining proper self-control.

The addict expects to get everything without doing anything, through some kind of miracle or fortunate chance and develops a terror of making a painful effort. This becomes obvious not only in the sphere of work, but also in interpersonal relationships, for this requires continual care in order to put oneself in the place of other people and to be able to understand them better. The marijuana smoker will habitually complain that "they don't understand me," "they don't support me," or "they don't love me," and will refuse to acknowledge that what he perceives is really his own reflection.

I believe that the drug develops a sort of pathological narcissism that is more serious than that provoked by other causes, because it isolates the individual in a world of fantasy to which his fellows have no access and places him on the verge of antisocial behavior. The *cannabis* addict objectifies people in his mind, so that they come to exist merely as useful objects for him and not as individuals who have their own needs and feelings. Thus, his friendships are limited to companions in the same vice and people who are useful to his own ends.

For a high percentage of addicts, the concept of friendship or love does not represent an equivalent exchange but merely a "receiving." The emotional alteration resulting from their vice makes it very hard for them to maintain an interpersonal relationship that means true love and care for others.

Fear of the opposite sex means that once the higher cortical barriers have been broken down, the individual will seek a homosexual relationship as the easiest and least demanding as far as giving is concerned. For a man, relating to a woman implies learning to give in many varied ways, and also entails being left exposed with regard to his true condition by renouncing the image he usually projects. It also means taking the trouble to understand his female companion, which demands properly decoding a type of behavior that for the man is translated into complex, incomprehensible messages. Faced with these options, certain characters that have been softened by the drug prefer a sexual-narcissistic relationship with an individual of the same sex, for both in this case speak the same language. In this way, many men remain isolated in their own egotism, depriving themselves of knowing "the other face of truth," that is, the feminine version of reality which is necessary if one is to know both sides of existence.

For the woman, relating to a man means giving herself emotionally and accepting to be penetrated, which represents a confrontation of her femininity with the man's virility. She feels that her own feminine nature is being put to the test in this act, which causes great fear and often drives her to choose weak, unintelligent companions who will not represent a challenge for her. In such circumstances, it is not surprising that women marijuana consumers take up some sort of relationship with a person of the same sex. In order to justify their habit, habitual marijuana smokers maintain that, unlike alcohol, the drug reduces aggressiveness, and this seems to be a unanimous opinion among them. However, it seems to me that its effects in this area are quite different and that instead of reducing aggressiveness it brings on over-passivity, which, of course, appeases aggression. It is obvious that an individual asleep or in a state of forced immobility will not attack anyone, but this is not a display of self-control.

I believe that one of the most relevant aspects of the conduct of habitual marijuana smokers concerns their difficulty in properly assessing the moments in their life in which they are not under the recent or direct stimulus of the drug. The hyperevaluation of their experiences under the effects of THC leads them to devalue normal sensations, and to feel that when they are not drugged life becomes flat, monotonous, and boring. Of course, this leads them to an obsessive concern with once more experiencing that so-desired stimulus. Depression, anguish, and self-devaluation continually stalk the person thus affected, for an inner tendency arises to consider that the true world, the one that is really worthwhile, is the one of the fantasy-based experiences caused by the drug; and that the other, that of normal everyday existence, in which common people fight for survival, make efforts, suffer, enjoy themselves, succeed, or fail, appears false and alien to them. It is therefore not surprising that many marijuana smokers become cynical, materialistic, and skeptical, for they consider that life is not worth living because it is devoid of meaning and purpose.

Rehabilitation of addicts lies in the recovery or encounter of true joy of living, and the comprehension and internal acceptance that all valuable things have an equivalent price. They must come to realize that one of the maximum laws of human life consists in the reward of one's own merits, and that we can attain very valuable goals if we make sufficient effort in this respect. Those who depend on drugs are not able to conceive the fact that they do not need such toxic substances to feel stimulated, and that sports and concern for others can give them new, greater incentives to free themselves of their bad habit.

Likewise, to discover the meaning of existence by developing and cultivating spiritual values can totally transform a person's life. The true work of spiritual perfection, which is at the same time technical and mystical, enables one to experience higher states of consciousness that no drug can emulate. There is no kind of drug that can *create consciousness;* they only produce a sort of passing euphoria through the stimulation of the individual's fantasies. It is only possible to access transcendental consciousness by means of long, persevering, and disciplined cultivation of one's own latent faculties, a process that should be exempt from any vain expectations. Undoubtedly, the words "long," "persevering," and "disciplined" will strike terror or disdain in those brains that have been washed by the advertising messages that make people believe that easy gain exists or that, for a price, one can obtain everything that is important here and now at this very moment. However, what is true is that authentic, lasting happiness cannot be anything else but the reward that awaits us at the end of a long, painful journey. Let us not commit the error of following deceptively easy paths that in the end can lead us to unforeseen precipices. Legitimate personal effort applied to *non-illusory* things is preferable, for it leads to gradual success and happiness with time, because it interacts correctly with reality. One of the most fashionable hereditary defects of late, a product of indiscriminate advertising, is the fact of feeling that problems, duty, effort, and merit all represent *lackings that steal something from us,* while the pleasurable or good is unconsciously considered to be a *gratuitous wild fruit,* a product of luck or chance, for which one does not need to pay any price at all. The most successful people are those *favored by luck,* while those who have many problems are the *victims* of something. This is why the *fantasy of gratuity* dominates the minds of a high percentage of those who live in underdeveloped countries, and this latter is no more than the natural consequence of the former. The first requisite for the success both of people and nations is based on the genuine acceptance and internal conviction that everything has a price, that this is equivalent to the value of what is desired, and that one has to pay happily and in advance, for this payment will allow one to possess what one yearns for, that is, to attain what one desires. The use of marijuana and other drugs that promise *easy reward and immediate pleasure* leads to laziness, passivity, and the disqualification of personal effort as a necessary element to attain well-being, success, and happiness.

Not Keeping One's Word

We are so used to not keeping our word that we cannot even glimpse the harm that this bad habit causes. The cells of the body are sensitive to our emotions, words, and thoughts, for to a certain extent they tend to follow the mandates of the "I." Because the "I" as an entity is made up of a conscious area and another subconscious one, it usually sends out its mandates mechanically, just like an electronic device that sends out a certain signal because it is ordered to do so by its program. There are many who have accidents or fall sick because of the manipulations of the unconscious, which attempts to avoid responsibility, elude reality, or satisfy a feeling of guilt. Negative emotions, such as depression, anguish, or sadness, are powerful detonators or elements that are generally present in diseases as serious as cancer.

There are cases of spontaneous remission in malignant tumors and the individual's positive psychological behavior is probably decisive in his healing. I think that laughter, joy, optimism, and good humor all boost people's immunological systems, while depressive states weaken them. It is very common for moments when people catch an illness to coincide with painful thoughts and feelings, as if this type of state annulled or weakened the lymphocytes, activating viruses, microbes, and bacteria.

The human being will often unwittingly act against himself by means of self-destructive psychic maneuvers. One of these is not keeping one's word. It is habitual for people to commit themselves verbally to do something and to end by doing something quite different. Such people give no importance to this behavior without understanding that it is a self-destructive mechanism. As is only logical, it does not refer to cases in which an individual says that he is going to go north and ends by going south, because a more detailed analysis of the facts shows him that his first decision was wrong.

The harmful mechanism is that which, when one has committed oneself verbally to do something right and correct, one ends by not keeping one's promise, out of laziness at the prospect of the effort entailed or the illusory prospect of an easier way to do it.

There are two ways of not keeping one's word, and both are equally harmful. One of them is to break the word that one has given to a certain person or institution, and the other is to damage the word that one gives to oneself by stating something aloud in full conviction of what one is doing, to later break this promise to himself. To break the given word is typical of men without honor who neither respect nor believe in themselves.

It is necessary to analyze what there is within an individual for him to not give the slightest value to his own word. It means just this: *to not be trustworthy even to himself*; to not believe in what he himself *affirms*.

In reality, there are people who lie so much that they lose their own credibility, that is, the *subconscious does not believe what the conscious says*, so that there is dispersion of these two areas, in the sense of perturbation and damage to the normal interaction between the two. The individual who does not respect his own word, but who uses his word to lie and to cheat others, or who uses his promise to persuade his fellows, and violates an agreement without batting an eyelid, *thus acquires a hidden enemy within himself that will react against what he intended to do.* This entity is the subconscious, which, because it has been submitted to deceit so often, no longer believes what the conscious says and has no desire to collaborate or take part in its machinations. On the contrary, it is very likely that it will systematically oppose the individual's projects.

There is a form of covert immorality, even for the individual himself, in which he behaves as a swindler, a liar, and a dishonest person, upsetting his mind and making it neurotic, for he will usually say one thing and do another, so that certain matters appear to be correct and straightforward which at bottom are really murky. This habit leads him to the acquisition of a mental duplicity, a sort of dual personality in which one of them (the conscious) only knows a tiny portion of his motivations and an infinitesimal portion of the information from the brain, while the subconscious, the major area, knows everything, except the most subterranean area of the unconscious.

The "I" acts in accordance with its good or bad reasons and based on the restricted information it possesses. It reasons, but only based on a meager amount of the elements of the whole mind. It believes that its motives are clean, whereas they could really be corrupt, or mistaken, despite the fact that the individual is convinced he is right.

Freud classifies psychic processes into *conscious, preconscious,* and *unconscious.* Within this analysis, it is of interest to consider what the *unconscious* represents in human consciousness, a level more profound than the subconscious. The subconscious correlates to the *preconscious* psychic process pointed out by Freud. The truth is that the individual's unconscious is a mere projection of the *collective unconscious* of Mankind, a sort of primitive soul made up of an inheritance that ranges from the simian to present-day *Homo sapiens.* The collective unconscious is the psychic archive of the memory of the species, from its remote origins to the present.

The most distinguished Egyptian and Greek wise men believed that unlike man, who has an individual, immortal soul, animals are moved by a primitive collective soul, a sort of energetic nucleus that directs all the functions of a species, such as migrations, mating seasons, etc.

The unconscious is thus the inheritance of the collective soul of the simian, which never died in the course of its cerebral and biological evolution, but remained intact, manifesting itself from some corner of the old brain, the paleocortex, activating itself and interacting under certain circumstances with the new brain or neocortex.

The ape lurks in ambush in our inner abyss, as likewise the Neanderthal, Cro-Magnon, Australopithecus, and the Pithecanthropus. On nights when there is a full moon, they awaken within the depths of our unconscious, obeying the call of the jungle. Their common soul is part of our collective psyche and is incorporated into the unconscious of each individual of the species, irremediably interwoven with his feelings and behavior.

This explains the abysmal contradictions of a species such as *Homo sapiens,* who speaks of peace but lives in a constant state of war; who preaches love but usually acts out of hatred; who possesses great scientific and technological advances, but displays an insignificant or nonexistent spiritual advance. This can be understood if we abide by what spirituality really means: a change of a techno-functional character in the mind that enables the being (the spirit) to manifest itself in the reality of the present moment. This type of concrete spirituality is what goes beyond superstitious words, pseudo-esoteric entanglements, or theoretical or unreal philosophical speculations. Now, what has all this to do with keeping one's word?

The fact is that language has a very profound neurophysiological basis, and *what we say and how we say it* profoundly affects our brain. At the very moment we speak, our cells and neurons prepare themselves for an action equivalent to that stated in words. If what we say is lacking in consistency and seriousness, it will negatively feed back to our brain. If we often break our word, our cells will be thwarted by receiving contradictory messages. A cell in this condition cannot be any different from a frustrated, cheated person and will develop similar symptoms: stress, tension, disagreeableness, and neurosis.

The internal and external effect caused by a person's word who, without knowing what he is saying, will merely repeat another's concepts, cannot be the same as what is said by an individual who understands in depth the meaning of what he is talking about. In the former case, his words will be absolutely empty: mere sounds articulating words that make up phrases and concepts devoid of any meaning in the speaker's mind, with a negative cerebral feedback.

It does not matter how well a preacher may repeat the words of Christ, or how true they may be; if the level of meaning they had in the Messiah's mind is not in the speaker, his words will be like empty ears of wheat, mere pods without any real content. The fact of habitually not keeping our word causes us to contradict our own purposes, thus slowing down their capacity to materialize, making the subconscious lose respect for us and to finally turn against us. The fact of strictly keeping the word we have given to others or to ourselves makes us true men of honor, integral persons with the maturity and discipline necessary to carry out our own purposes, even at the expense of postponing an immediate good for the sake of a future good of greater significance or transcendence. Likewise, the respect and collaboration offered by our subconscious will impede us from falling into the unfortunate mechanism of sabotaging our own projects without ever being aware of it. I am not exaggerating by thinking that this fact could be a touchstone for our success and happiness—each time we manage to keep our word clean of lying, calumny, injurious statements, or bad language. It would not be too far off to state that the School of Pythagoras had pursued far more profound purposes than is immediately suspected when it recommended a vow of silence to those who yearned for spiritual perfection. In fact, the purifying of the word through a stage of voluntary silence can lead to a sort of introspection that will enable the individual to know himself in a very profound way, filling him with new life and energy, for people usually waste too much energy through speech.

One must consider that common forms of speech are so machine-like that words are rarely elaborated cerebrally in a conscious way, this being the reason why this mechanized modality of expression feeds back into the brain in a single direction: without any possibility of choice, it merely reinforces the cerebral circuits already in existence. This means that it increases the individual's mechanicalness, proportionally reducing his consciousness and level of alertness. Banal, repetitive chat hypnotizes people more profoundly than usual, sinking them into a comfortable, passive, and indolent self-indulgence that progressively distances them from reality. The lack of significant depth of thought generates a stereo-typed, mechanical, monotonous, and repetitive form of expression. The wisest or most profound words placed in the mouth of the person who has learned them by heart and only has access to the informational portion of knowledge do not constitute wisdom, but, like a computer, a mere "accessing" of a certain file.

It is said that the words uttered by Christ caused an extraordinary influence on those who understood them, his message becoming a source of eternal life. The same phrases in a preacher's sermon would only have the effect of inspira-tion, by giving examples that comfort the soul and the sense of morality, but that never become the "water that quenches one's thirst for all eternity." This is so, since the word in some mysterious way is the bearer of the significant content of the thought of the person who utters it, and as is only logical, the preacher's mind (despite the fact that he may be a simple, good man) does not possess the level of meaningfulness which the Divine Master possessed.

The Gospel according to St. John begins by saying that before the world was created, *the word,* or the verb, already existed and was with God and was part of Him. By means of *the word,* God created life and all things in life. In this way, *the word* seems to be endowed with a certain status and sacred power.

Man, as bearer of the divine spark that emanates from the Creator, possesses a tiny fraction of this power in an inactive state. In order to activate it, he first and foremost has to purify his speech, refrain from using bad language, refuse to hurt or insult his fellows in words, avoid speaking too much, renounce speaking ill of others, jealously keep the secrets with which he has been entrusted, and take care to fulfill a promise once made, to thus purify and cleanse himself so that his language is the expression of his own transparency and not of his hate or resentment. He should keep periodical lapses of silence in order to become conscious of what he is talking about and how he expresses it. He must avoid *meaninglessly* repeating messages or information learned by heart (that are devoid of meaning), just like a sound-reproducing machine, in order to not feed back to the brain nonconscious recordings that have a mechanizing effect on it. He must become aware that the word is sacred, and must be respected and used for good, honorable works, and never to bemire people's honor or dignity.

A particularly grave sin is that of those who prostitute their word by putting it at the service of lies elaborated with underhanded aims. For example, those who spread false accounts of the actions of a person or of a group of persons merely to discredit them, harm them, or for political convenience destroy the public image that they may have; those who bear false witness in courts of justice; those who, through the improper usage of the power of influential groups, intimidate or pressure those who know about cases of public or private corruption to not reveal what they know; those who by using their word and influence in some way try to threaten, pressure, or intimidate judicial power to tip the scales of justice; those who lie indiscriminately to satisfy their personal ambitions or silence their moral conscience.

Undoubtedly, it is a noble moral battle to rescue the word from the clutches of lies, frivolity, mechanicalness, emptiness, or aggression toward one's fellows, thus placing it beyond the reach of our passions and making it the expression of inner virtue and not the dark side of the human being. On only too many occasions the simian we bear within us takes over our mouth to grunt and threaten, and only very seldom does the soul manifest itself through it.

Words can move the world, but the Tower of Babel of language separates and antagonizes men. Speaking the same language is no guarantee of understanding each other, for in people's minds, similar words have different meanings. How often does it happen that two individuals argue heatedly for hours, without realizing that they are saying exactly the same thing, although their minds are registering different concepts? It is necessary to understand why the abuse of the word is a serious moral violation that is equivalently punished by Nature, since everything that comes from man returns to him at some moment.

Deceiving the Eye and the Ear

This consists of silencing, falsifying, or denying what we hear or see, because it perturbs our moral consciousness, is detrimental to our self-esteem, does not coincide with our ideas, or causes us anguish. It is a moral fault because it is the unconscious mechanism we make use of to act dishonestly, in an underhanded way, to avoid confronting reality when it is inconvenient for us.

When it suits us, we deny that we have heard something which we surely have heard, or we magnify those words that could even remotely imply flattery or approval of our own acts, using this message to balance some lacking that could be left pending within us.

Hearing is one of the great snares of our mind, since in practice it is no more than one of so many threads that manipulate the puppet we have become.

The fact is that we regularly and even daily deceive ourselves. We only listen to what suits our image and reject the rest. We allow access to our brain everything that flatters us or that coincides with our own ideas or represents a type of paradigm that enables us to justify our own defects, hereditary defects and deficiencies.

Our hearing becomes particularly sensitive and sharp when we are spoken well of, and suddenly becomes deaf when we are criticized or when we hear ideas that contradict or diverge from our own. Our sight is particularly sharp to discern the "mote in the other's eye" yet has singular difficulty in perceiving the plank in our own.

We only see what we expect and wish to see, and close our eyes to the rest. Our conversations or discussions on certain subjects are so sterile that we really listen to nothing which we do not want to and only pay attention to words that could mean we are right in our statements. Political or religious debates are usually dialogues for the deaf, for nobody is interested in listening but merely in imposing their own ideas. Quarrels between a couple are generally only a process of impatiently and deafly waiting for the other party to finish speaking without caring what he or she is saying, unless it coincides with one's own version, in which case the faculty of listening is immediately recovered.

We only listen when we are flattered and remain deaf to any criticism. This enables us to develop all kinds of exotic mental and emotional maneuvers to convince ourselves that red is really blue, because this is our favorite color, and that green is yellow, because we do not like green. Dialogue is rare even if there are two or more people involved. It is common for there to be a monologue in which each merely gives out the messages generated in his cerebral program, without any inner disposition to listen to divergent opinions.

It is quite common when people hear something for it to clash with their own mechanisms so that there comes an episode of psychological deafness, characterized by perceiving a sort of "music" or "noise" of words or concepts, the meaning of which is misunderstood or ignored. Something similar occurs with children when their parents scold them, for they experience great emotional turmoil that leaves their minds blank and prevents them from perceiving the truth of their parents' message. I should point out that psychological deafness is not an accepted pathology, since by it being a universal pandemic, the rare exception of it consists of the few who truly listen. Obviously, we do not listen with our ears but with the brain and although our hearing may be quite normal, the brain is the one that has to process and record what is being heard.

Everything that reaches our minds is perceived unconsciously and filtered, and only the fragments accepted by the ascendant reticular system penetrate to the *conscious level*. The ascendant reticular system is the section of the medulla oblongata that instructs the cerebral cortex as to when it must pay attention to something. The rest of the stimuli end up in the basement of the unconscious, without the individual ever being aware of it.

This situation can be experimentally proven by means of hypnosis, a process in which the individual accesses a large amount of information that he does not know about in his normal state of awareness.

One has to accept that we are beings with a diminished, atrophied consciousness, because intensified attention and awareness are not voluntary faculties, except on rare occasions. We rarely pay sustained attention to what we should really concern ourselves with; we cannot stop thinking at will;

nor have we the capacity to enter into states of higher awareness through our own volition.

Our attention is captured by all that is a pressing duty or arouses our desire and attraction, whereas it is almost impossible for us to focus it on what is not shocking, impressive, flashy, or anything that does not offer an immediate reward.

It would seem that the object of the cerebral filters is to act as a shock absorber between the "I" and reality, perhaps being the physiological counterpart to the self-defense mechanisms of the "I" such as denial, repression, projection, regression, fixation, and reactive formation which are studied in psychoanalysis.

On this topic, Calvin S. Hall states:

One of the most important tasks of the "I" is to confront the threats and dangers that lie in waiting for the individual and cause anguish. The "I" may try to control the danger by adopting realistic methods to solve the problem, or it may try to relieve anguish by using methods that deny, falsify, or distort reality. These methods are called self-defense mechanisms of the "I." They are irrational ways of facing up to anguish because they deform, conceal, or deny reality and create obstacles against psychological development.

Why are there such defenses if they are so harmful in so many ways?

The childish "I" is too weak to integrate and synthesize all the demands made on it. The defenses of the "I" are adopted as protective measures. If the "I" cannot reduce anguish by rational means it has to use such measures to deny the danger, to externalize it, to hide it, to remain in the same state or retrogress.

Why do they persist once they have fulfilled their purpose in the childish "I?" They persist when the "I" cannot develop by itself. Yet one of the reasons why the "I" cannot develop is that a great deal of its energy is consumed in its defenses. Thus, in this situation, a vicious circle occurs. The defenses cannot be abandoned because the "I" is insufficient, and the "I" continues to be insufficient whenever it depends on the defenses. How can the "I" break through this circle? One important factor is the maturing process. Under the influence of the maturing process the "I" feels obliged to evolve.[26]

At the moment of birth, we are faced with the anguish of having to breathe and feel stimuli and other needs which we formerly did not have. We miss the well-being of the womb, but in exchange we receive the reward of our mother's breast. Therefore, at the same time that we experience this, we also experience the threatening anguish that the deprivation of that food could represent for us. When the time comes for us to acknowledge ourselves as beings separate from the mother, we begin to experience the agonizing need to receive care and company. As we grow, we become aware of adults as menacing giants who draw back the curtain on a world that is distressingly wide and alien. To silence the anxiety that dangerous or threatening situations cause us, we unwittingly begin to evade a reality which forcibly disrupts our lives by denying or counterfeiting what we see. This evasion usually acts like an emotional placebo that momentarily calms us. Unfortunately, this habit causes addiction and marks a tendency to escapism and evasion, which, to the extent that it is repeated, defines a person as a being who usually lives outside reality. Taking refuge in his own dreams and mental juggling tricks, his perception is tainted and altered by this fact; he is centered on his own schema and dramatically far away from the good things which the true world offers.

The sin of manipulating reality to adapt it to one's own fears and desires represents a moral dislocation, as it deprives us of the pedagogical lessons of life, for we shall never understand what the true cause of our frustrations, pains, lackings, or sufferings really is. This is the same as saying that the teacher gave us a bad grade at school because he does not like us instead of recognizing our own ignorance or lack of diligence in our studies. It is a way to artfully avoid what the Creator and Nature expect of the human individual—*apprehending the reality of life in order to evolve from it.* God only knows how many religions, beliefs, ideologies, and systems have been born in the history of Mankind as emotional placebos, sugar-coated schemes whose only aim is to facilitate the evasion of an unpleasant reality. As long as Mankind suckles on the colossal placebo of consumerism of all kinds, he weakens himself by swallowing his own blood, as in the fable of the snake who happily licked a file and then constantly drank its own blood.

Nor can we ever know the magnitude of the historical deceits that man has been victim of, with the aim of concealing dishonest doings or obscure political or financial schemes.

As long as the explanations given about a certain scandal satisfy general hypocrisy, then all will accept this version as the truth, "wash their hands," and remain tranquil. If the most obvious truth reveals people's faults, dishonesty, and common psychological mechanisms, then it will be rejected by the majority, whereas the crudest lie will be unanimously and readily accepted if it calms their anguish or the collective envy.

Truth is a food reserved only for those who in some way manage to escape from the clutches of the defense mechanisms of the "I," and who manage to develop a mature, adult, conscious "I."

Psychological games that deform, deny, or alter reality are partly responsible for the lack of understanding between people, since each one disqualifies ideas or concepts that do not coincide with their own. The mass media cleverly handles the "candy" and the "bombs." The former is all the information that focuses or magnifies scientific, medical, or technological advances, or shows the huge range of entertainment and pleasure at people's disposal: various types of "candy" are food, sex, the raising of one's self-esteem, trophies, trips to escape from oneself, clothing to disguise oneself adequately and lose sight of one's own identity, and narcissistic gratification of all kinds. The "bombs" are the negative, dramatic, bloody, or morbid events that make one yearn for the "candy" to calm one's anguish.

The manipulation of one's own mind may make the individual perceive a saint as a con-man, a boor as an important man, the truth as a lie, and falsehood as authenticity. It makes him visualize himself as a model of honesty and nobility even while he is committing the greatest infamy. It may make him disqualify a wise man and flatter an ignorant one. All this is in accordance with the fluctuation of his desires, faults, and fears, and not with reality.

The act of counterfeiting himself is the individual's greatest machination. This counterfeited self possesses three different identities:

1. How he sees himself.

2. The way people see him.

3. The way he really is.

Each person "dreams himself up," models himself in his imagination in accordance with his own fantasies, which usually correspond to delusions of grandeur and power. In this way, an ideal "I" is established which the individual assumes as his true being, believing deep down that it corresponds to his genuine identity. His personality thus splits between the image he has of himself, which he takes to be his true "I," and what he is in reality. Thus there may appear the existence of two personalities that do not know of the existence of one another. In reality, the splitting of the "I" was only approached by Freud at the descriptive level and not at the explanatory one; the following paragraph gives us a broader explanation of this:

> In 1911 E. Bleuler created the term *schizophrenia* to denote a group of psychoses, the unity of which Kraepelin had already pointed out classifying them under the heading of prococious dementia and differentiating them into three forms that have become classical: hebephrenic, catatonic, and paranoid. Clinically, schizophrenia diversifies into forms that are apparently very different to each other in which the following characteristics are usually noted: incoherence of thought, action, and affection, separation of reality with withdrawal into oneself and predominance of an inner life given up to the productions of fantasy (autism), a more or less accentuated delirious activity which is invariably wrongly systematized; lastly, the chronic nature of the disease that evolves with very diverse rhythms towards an intellectual and affective deterioration and often leads to states resembling dementia.
>
> **—Jean Laplanche and Jean Bertrand Pontalis**[27]

It would be no exaggeration to sustain that most perturbations of the character, mind, emotions, and conduct originate in disorders of the attention—in an inability to attend to what one has to, in the way that one has to, in order to perceive reality as it is.

Invariably, a distorted perception of reality will lead the individual to a false existence that takes place in his own arbitrary, personal universe in which the laws that govern such a world correspond to his inner delirium. This inner delirium can be understood as the state of having illusory experiences analogous to those of one's dreams or hallucinations, an alteration of the consciousness of reality that manifests itself in the forming of wrong judgments that are far removed from reality. If we understand the world as a place in which each generally lives immersed in his own delirium, we can see how difficult it is for people to communicate honestly, since they really do this "from image to image." *This means that "A" communicates from the image he accepts as his true identity, while "B" listens in the same condition from a false identity, at the same time supposing that what "A" perceives corresponds to genuine reality, whereas in all truth it is only virtual reality.*

In this way, communication between virtual identities becomes the habitual means of contact between people, without their legitimate beings ever able to glimpse each other.

To speak, think, feel, or behave on the strength of what one believes one is and not what one really is, is no different to the performances of Batman or Superman: pure fantasy. It is possible that the ancient saying *nosce te ipsum (know thyself)* was designed with the fundamental purpose of attaining honest, truthful communication between people, thus avoiding interminable and useless chatter in which the part of an individual's mind that is governed by fantasy dialogues with its counterpart in another person.

To a certain extent, people perceive the spurious, irrelevant nature of these contacts, for after conversing, people will often feel dissatisfied, annoyed, or doubtful, just as if they had expressed something in an improper way or still had not said what they really wanted, seeking it always in their minds without ever finding it. What happens is that at that moment they glimpse their true identity, smothered beneath the foliage of the image, and this emotional perception also shows them by contrast, the falsehood of their daily behavior, in which the being is continually relegated and attacked in order to defend its own idealized image. As a result of all this, there appears a vague discontent or frustration, like a feeling of having lost or forgotten something, or of not having managed to do what one really wanted to do. One must consider that when one takes on a false or fantastical identity, as in the case of the idealized image, the "I," as the central point of this formation, attracts around it all the elements of new daily experiences, which, instead of augmenting the being, pass over into the image, as if a computer operator had made a mistake in filing information and put it where it does not belong. The image feeds on all the individual's experiences; this is the reason why such experiences lose their evolutive usefulness and merely come to augment the effigy, whereas the being, which is the transcendental "I," remains deprived and underdeveloped.

This, and no other, is the reason for the foolishness of Mankind: we are giants at the level of the intellect and pygmies as far as the being is concerned, and this amazing smallness is reflected in an equivalent ethical and moral wretchedness. We achieve nothing by increasing material comforts and over-feeding people's stomachs or intellects if their spirits remain in a state of abject poverty. This is the general misery that attacks people regardless of their social class, creed, race, or color. However rich, famous, important, charitable, magnanimous, or intelligent an individual may be, his respective being will most likely be in a state of profound impoverishment, whereas his false identity will suffer from chronic obesity. In this way, each does no more than defend what he sees in the image created by his own dreams, on which he has imprudently and wrongly hung his own identity. The authentic being, meanwhile, languishes in oblivion and abandonment.

However, there are many who in a hollow, mechanical way make theoretical apologies for humanism, morality, and ethics without really understanding what they are saying and limit themselves to imitating what charismatic celebrities sustain without having bothered to polish their own rough stone beforehand in order to recover their inner essence from the clutches of their image. This is a prerequisite for authentic spiritual development that may confer higher cognitive content to their words.

It often occurs that certain people, with the covert aim of washing their images, will, throughout their lifetime, wave the banner of fine concepts or ideals that they do not really feel, understand, or practice, and they certainly do this sincerely with no conscious intention of cheating anyone. As you will understand, it is very pleasant to boast of frankness and humanitarianism even though this bears no relation to the individual's true inner reality.

To confront inner and external truth as it really is, is both an honor and a privilege, and he who does not do this commits a moral offense against God and his own divine spark, thus dooming himself to spiritual exile.

Alcoholism

Alcohol is the most consumed drug in the world, since it is socially accepted and is openly sold. By technical definition, "a drug is any natural or artificial substance that on entering the organism causes alterations, that are more or less persistent, in its structure or normal functioning."

Alcohol is not a product that harms all those who consume it, but harms those who by drinking too much, end up addicted to it.

Alcohol has been defined as a *psychoactive* drug that acts on the central nervous system, affecting the brain and modifying the way a person sees himself and the world. When one drinks too much, one's perception of reality is altered and one's ideas become undefined and confused. It is a depressive substance and not a stimulant, since a person's fictitious happiness is due to the fact that alcohol numbs nervous centers that act as censors or inhibit certain types of behavior or feelings, thus making the person in question act in a loose way.

As alcohol is a depressive substance, it is very risky to consume it in combination with barbiturates, since, as the depressing effect is potentiated, the organism functions so slowly that it can cause a heart attack, or arrest the person's breathing. The following progressive changes have been defined in a drunk person:

First stage: Feelings of well-being and uninhibitedness. He becomes talkative, sociable, relaxed, and unconcerned.

Second stage: Euphoria and excitement, loquaciousness, hyperactivity; he becomes insistent and repetitive, irritable. His mental acuteness diminishes; his judgment gets worse; his behavior becomes erratic and his movements uncoordinated.

Third stage: Confusion and disorientation. He is not able to coordinate his movements. He is not able to keep his balance and coordinate his speech. Feelings of sadness, melancholy, fear, or fury appear. He gets double vision (diplopia).

Fourth stage: He cannot keep himself on his feet or walk. Gross intoxication and alteration of his motor and mental behavior. Loss of the notion of time and space (he does not know who he is or where he is). Vomiting and incontinence.

Fifth stage: State of unconsciousness; the vital functions get slower and slower until he is in a coma. His heart or breathing may then stop.

(Data compiled by Dr. Alberto Cormillot and Juan Carlos Lombardini.)[28]

The fact is that alcoholism gradually provokes psychological, physical, and behavioral changes, all related to others, such as family, social, and work relationships.

Here is a summary of these changes:

Psychological Changes:

Phase 1:   A feeling of guilt about the way he drinks, greater irritability; he begins to lose his memory; a preoccupation with the supply of liquor; the liquor becomes a necessity.

Phase 2:   Almost total loss of control over his alcohol consumption; ideas and feelings of being persecuted; "everybody is against me;" self-pity; he deceives himself; very low self-esteem; suicidal ideas may appear; an increased feeling of guilt.

Phase 3:   Depression; loss of the sense of reality; a process of depersonalization; hallucinations; distorted perception, thought, and judgment.

Physical Changes:

Phase 1:   He drinks to reduce states of stress or bodily tension, thus increasing his tolerance to alcohol.

Phase 2:   Almost permanent intoxication; a reduction of his sexual impulse; a loss of appetite; deterioration of his health.

Phase 3:   Acute and chronic deterioration of his health; trembling; malnutrition; weakness; organic disorders; loss of appetite.

Behavioral Changes:

Phase 1:   He increases the frequency with which he drinks and spends more time drinking socially.

Phase 2:   Alcoholic amnesia; compulsive drinking; sharp drop in his yield at work; a morning drink; drinking alone; notorious drunken behavior; chaotic handling of money; aggressive behavior; could have fantasies about or attempts at suicide.

Phase 3:   Total lack of interest in food; he lives for drinking; he will drink any type of alcohol including those which are used for diverse purposes; a possibility to die as a result of accidents or suicide.

Relations with Others:

Phase 1:   He makes promises to give up drinking; the excuses for social inconveniences begin; difficulties at work begin: absenteeism, loss of efficiency, frequent arguments.

Phase 2:   He denies or conceals the amount that he has been drinking; a marked deterioration in family relationships; his spouse takes on more responsibilities; he may lose his job; he justifies drinking with less credible excuses; gets into debt; increases his social isolation; mixes with others only for drinking.

Phase 3:   He becomes isolated from his family and friends; there is a break-up of his marriage; he avoids the people who want to help him.

It is commonly held that alcoholism is an illness and not a vice or a moral problem or merely just a weakness of character, which seems excessively indulgent. "Vice" means: "over-appetite for something that incites one to use it to excess," while to "vitiate" is interpreted as "to damage or corrupt physically or morally," all of which occurs in alcohol abuse. I believe that an illness is something that cannot be controlled, something that the individual cannot avoid, not even with the intervention of will and his inner determination, and none of this is so in the case of alcoholism.

The underdevelopment of the "I" and the atrophy of the character and will power are the mothers of all vices, for the individual in this case has a minimal degree of control over his appetites and passions and becomes incapable of resisting them. There are many causes that can incite a person to drink: family and social conditioning, shyness, insecurity, stress, entertainment, an inferiority complex, repetitive participation in social events at which there is alcohol, escapism, neurosis, a childish personality, frustration, solitude, fear, etc. However, the fact is that drinkers are generally people with childish features who have failed to develop their character and will and therefore lack the necessary discipline and self-control to stop drinking or to only drink small amounts.

I believe it would be more constructive to consider alcoholism as a moral and spiritual problem rather than as an incurable illness.

Maybe society has taken the wrong way in trying to understand why alcoholics drink to excess. It would be more productive to know what kind of individuals are those who refrain from drinking, or who drink moderately, or who are immune to this vice, or others.

Certainly, there are hundreds of different causes that make an individual a non-drinker, and perhaps none of them is the individual's voluntary action but rather some sort of adversive programming, such as may for example occur with the children of alcoholic parents who have suffered greatly as a consequence of alcohol in childhood, or people whose religion condemns alcohol, or sportsmen bent on high performance, naturists, vegetarians, or people whose lifestyle has kept them at a distance from the incitement to drink.

What seems improbable to us is to visualize an individual with high moral and spiritual qualities who falls into the vice of consuming alcohol. Spiritually developed people not only can keep themselves away from alcohol excesses, but also from any other immoral or unethical vice or type of behavior. What is the reason for this? Simply, that by means of self-discipline, they manage to have a mature, adult "I," together with a vigorous character and a finely tempered will. In other words, they are people who increase or achieve their development, who are no longer incomplete, which makes them strong, conscious, and stable.

The success of "Alcoholics Anonymous," a voluntary institution of ex-alcoholics whose aim is to try to help those who have become dependent on alcohol, is due to the fact that they consider that alcoholism is a spiritual problem for the alcoholic, and that they are emotionally damaged because they drink to compensate for their incapacities. Their self-treatment consists of twelve steps, among which the following are the most relevant: each member admits that he cannot drink alcohol and abstains from it completely; he believes in a higher power that can regenerate him; he takes meticulous stock of himself; and he commits himself to helping other alcoholics.

What we call "emotional damage" does not usually occur in the individual who manages to have solid moral and spiritual values, for integrity, purity, love, and harmony are sufficient to reject negative emotions or to repair the damage caused by external aggression. We will never see a spiritual individual who has vices, for one negates the other.

When a person has already been damaged or wounded by life, he may in any case repair the damage or heal his moral or emotional wounds if he sets aside his egotism and seriously confronts his own spiritual development. One should recall that "egotism" is not only a lack of charity, but rather chiefly represents an *immoderate, excessive love of himself (love for the self of the personality, not that of the spirit)*, and that it makes a person pay too much attention to his own interests, without caring for the interests of others. This, then, is what the alcoholic has to do: to not make the egotism of the personality the center of himself in order to give a higher significance to his own existence, so that he will not need "to expel" alcohol from his life for it will merely run over him like a drop of water on a glass.

Obviously, there are many different levels of evaluation of one's own existence, in accordance with the heights a person attains in his spiritual development, from the humblest to the most sublime. A mystic or religious devotee would not be able to compare himself with a saint, but he will also be on the path to transcendental experience.

Surely, "Alcoholics Anonymous" offers affection, understanding, fraternity, and human warmth to its members, who, once they have controlled their addiction, revalue their own lives by acting as helpers to other addicts. The habitual drunkard is generally a self-indulgent individual who pities himself, and who at some moment, instead of confronting reality, chooses to evade that reality through drinking. There are times when they behave more sensitively than others, not being able to efficiently disguise or deny certain realities that impress them, as if there were a malfunction in their self-defense mechanisms, which probably find an extra reinforcement in alcohol.

The tendency to alcoholism begins with any wrongly interpreted painful experience, an experience that is not assimilated or confronted, which leads to self-pity, self-indulgence, and low self-esteem. Thus, the drinker learns the wrong way to face anguish and pain by denying it, pitying himself, and fleeing by going back to childish levels of development. A vicious circle is thus progressively established in which the individual returns to drinking in order to calm the anguish produced by painful situations, thus evading confrontation with realities that, if they were honestly processed, would make him evolve. As this does not happen, the anguish returns and, after it, alcohol with the consequent self-pity and deterioration of self-esteem.

During an alcoholic bout, the drunkard begins by fantasizing with those who share his habit, telling them about his sexual prowess, supposed heroic deeds, or spinning all manner of lies that show how noble, important, or brave he is. After this stage, he usually ends by weeping with loneliness and anguish, a cycle that is normally repeated each time he drinks in excess.

Generally, people who are prone to alcohol and mental and emotional problems are very dishonest as regards confronting reality, and their daily life is based on continual self-deceit that progressively deteriorates their contact with reality. They are beings who constantly "accommodate" the truth to their own requirements, by creating a mental map of the world that justifies their own faults and shortcomings, dispels their fears, and which promises the fulfillment of their fantasies of power and the accomplishment of those desires that are most appealing to them.

As a logical consequence, this lying to themselves leads them to deceive their fellows, albeit unwittingly, so that communication with both themselves and other people is profoundly deteriorated.

Alcoholism, as any other form of drug addiction, is a moral fault by the fact that it attacks the integrity of the carnal wrapping of the spirit, the vehicle that one must safeguard to maintain intact the possibility for individual evolution. Drunkenness is one of many ways of eluding this duty imposed by Nature and the Creator, for in our Universe, everything that does not change and transform in accordance with the requirements of life, ends by decaying and dying without having attained its evolutive purpose.

One has to accept that individual evolution totally depends on one's capacity to honestly and squarely face inner and outer reality, in order to draw the quintessence from daily experience and profoundly understand the lessons of life. There is no other means of genuine spiritual perfection than that based on abandoning all illusory mental maps to bravely submerge in authentic reality, for it is there that we shall find our own inner essence, and behind it, the Creator. This is the true purpose of life and he who fails to comply with it may consider himself a failure, however rich, intelligent, famous, or powerful he may seem, and he will have to repeat the lessons of life time and again until he catches up with his own destiny.

From the point of view of divinity, it is one of man's duties to preserve his own existence, which of course is not restricted to merely surviving but means living in a higher way, and this means *completing oneself and evolving*. As far as society is concerned, it fully recognizes the damage caused by alcohol, for a clear relationship has been traced between the consumption of alcoholic drinks, delinquency, family violence, and traffic accidents.

The moral degradation many addicts reach makes them atrociously maltreat children, an unjustifiable act of appalling cowardice, because they are defenseless beings. In fact, the damage that alcohol could produce in the addict's body and brain needs to be accurately measured.

Malnutrition, anorexia, gastritis, cirrhosis, pancreatitis, alcoholic epilepsy, mental disorders, alterations of the memory, Wernicke's encephalopathy (difficulty in concentration and slowness in answering questions), delirium tremens, and alcoholic dementia are all strong probabilities in the life of an addict.

All these disorders are organic but there are others that come under the heading of functional disorders, such as *pathological jealousy and paranoid hallucinations*. Because of its striking symptoms, *delirium tremens* is one of the most dramatic disorders a man can suffer. Below is a brief description by Neil Kessel and Henry Walton.[29]

> For the victim, each conscious moment is of extreme fear. The dominant characteristics are fear, agitation, and great bewilderment; disorientation and the most vivid hallucinations. Delirium tremens begins from 2 to 5 days after abandoning very excessive drinking . . . there will usually have been at least ten years of excessive drinking before the first attack.
>
> The symptoms are spectacular: the victim feels great restlessness and agitation. In a hospital ward two or more people

have to hold the patient down in order to get him into bed, despite the fact that he is weak. He is never still, tosses and turns endlessly, constantly jabbers and goes from one person to another and from one subject to another at the slightest cue; he is fearful and often shouts out greetings or warnings to passers-by. His hands wave around in an uncontrolled way and he clutches the sheets; the delirious patient continually tries to pick imaginary objects off himself, shining coins, lighted cigarettes, cards, or bugs. The prey of ever-changing visual hallucinations, the alcoholic hides his face so as not to perceive the objects, animals, and menacing men that attack him.

A dreadful apprehension prevails in the patient that chiefly arises from his wrong perception and representation of his surroundings. The victim feels that he is being threatened from all sides and possibly will fight to halt his attackers.

There is no need to go into the hallucinations: their presence is obvious. Patients respond to imaginary voices and react to imagined visions. In particular, they see small objects that move quickly. They traditionally describe rats and mice, but often these animals are more ominous: large black flies that buzz into their faces; cats that come to scratch them. Sometimes the hallucinations are even stranger: "suitcases with zippers that bite the legs" said one patient. At times fear turns into resignation: "I know you're going to kill me so do it now once and for all."

I have included this description so that readers can get an accurate idea of the horror an excess of drink can lead to, and so that they may also understand that the vice can be overcome to the extent of the individual's personal and spiritual development. Higher moral conduct is no more than the spontaneous behavior of a spiritually advanced individual. Immorality and vice are the logical consequence of a lack of elevated spiritual values.

We should recall that, according to ancient Greek philosophers, "he who understands virtue can never be immoral or
vicious." The most serious problem is that, as genuine spiritual development is not a cultural subject, there is no real
interest in virtue or values, for the cultural concept of spirituality is not based on the vertical ascent of individual
consciousness. Nobody understands where such an evolution
might lead.

The path of religious devotional spirituality is well delin-
eated, but very few know that there is also a secular path of
spirituality, of a philosophical and scientific nature, in which
individual perfection is a technical/mystical matter.
Culturally speaking, spirituality is equivalent to *goodness,
humanism, music, painting, and works of charity,* none of which,
of course, can ensure the individual's true spiritual development.

Scientific and cultural triumphalism likewise discourages
people from the spiritual path because the impressive
advances of science and technology cause a general sensation
that we are on the right path and that we do not need
anything else. The fact is that our path would seem to be
rather one *of moral and spiritual involution,* together with an
accelerated intellectual, scientific, and technological advance.
This is not a very promising combination for the future of
Mankind.

Materialism

This is a philosophical doctrine that only acknowledges
the substantial reality of matter, on which all of existence
depends. There is no supernatural existence according to
materialism and therefore, there is no need for a final cause or
an ultimate goal, or for any intelligence to explain the

Universe and Nature. The logical consequence of materialism is the immoderate valuing of wealth, the pleasures of the senses, and the satisfactions of the body, with excessive importance given to physical appearance and material power, to the detriment of everything spiritual. Really, nothing more could be expected of the species *Homo sapiens*, because of his scant evolutive distance from the animal and on account of the fact that his instinctive behavior is still controlled by an animal brain, the paleocortex, or "old brain."

Our history to date is an impressive repertoire of crime and violence. The last world war alone left 40 million dead. It is of no concern what rhetoric is used to dissimulate or justify this, the fact is that such a situation can only be possible among inferior beings, beings that are very close to the animal. Savagery, brutality, violence, cruelty, and corruption are neither proscribed nor excluded by the advance of civilization or by scientific and technological advances, nor by the fact that there are examples of charity and goodness that are worthy of imitation.

Materialism is no more than a clinging to four legs, a tail, and a hoof; it is the inner identification with one's own animal nature that only acknowledges the law of the jungle. All this, plus an additional aggravating circumstance—that the pure animal is clean and transparent in the sense that no perversion whatever can be attributed to its behavior. It does not drink, smoke, is neither cruel nor sadistic, does not take drugs, does not destroy for pleasure, and does not know what hatred is. Man, on the other hand, is a corrupt animal that, as his past and present record shows, can reach limits of perversion that a naïve brain would be unable to imagine. Really, he cannot get his feet off the ground, and even when he is standing upright, his instinctive nature leads him to be a mere instrument of his animal appetites.

Food, territorial struggles, reproduction, the preponderance of the herd, competition for power between the dominant males, and the preservation of the species, are all predominant preoccupations of Mankind.

Materialism is an involutive attempt so that man can make himself content with being an animal without endeavoring to cut the umbilical cord that ties him to the collective soul of the simian, which remains alive in his unconscious. This is, naturally, all couched in convincing justifications and explanations.

Scientific advance, technology, humanism, art treasures, and culture all become elements to prove "how far we have come as human beings," whereas any confrontation with the dark side of the species is waived aside. Man makes himself up extraordinarily well in order to hide his hoof and tail, making himself appear as a prodigious conqueror of Nature. This is not difficult, for man's material work is impressive: huge buildings; gigantic bridges; dams; all manner of mechanical artifices; machines that fly; artifacts that try to imitate the human brain; new medicines and advanced medical technology; standards of comfort that could not be imagined a few years ago; bioengineering; and a myriad of other things.

Parallel to all this, there are nuclear artifacts, chemical and biological weapons, war, destruction, famine, massive intoxication by air pollution, depredation of Nature, drug trafficking and consumption, corruption, cancer, AIDS, brainwashing, mental slavery, terrorism, delinquency, the oppression of minorities, loss of personal liberty, confusion of the male and female roles, perversion of all kinds, a lack of higher values, and subtle, hidden tyranny in politics.

Do not be deceived: we are intellectually developed but our intelligence is easily subjected to diverse "persuasion techniques" in advertising. We are defenseless before psychological warfare and other weapons of control of public opinion. We get along very well in the material world, but are totally devoid of any possibility of attaining a higher individual consciousness. "The being" is a mere abstraction for us, for we live for the image, by the image, and in terms of the image.

Prevailing materialism makes us believe that our salvation lies in machines, and that anything can be achieved through them, and this is why we are convinced that our body is just a machine that is more complex than the others. For many, we are merely thinking and sensing bodies, and there is nothing beyond this. How could there then be any higher moral behavior among those who believe themselves to be the offspring of material chance and suppose that the mind is no more than an organic subproduct?

Excessive attachment to the belief that only what can be seen and touched is real has caused more immorality and lack of ethics than anything else. Nevertheless, one must be fully aware that materialism is no more than a superstitious belief.

Even science has its own superstitions, beliefs it considers to be immutable, in which it deposits a blind faith, refusing to accept what it cannot apprehend through the limited observation system of the researcher, and then usually forgetting that he only looks within the limits of his own level of consciousness and never above it.

The absurdity of the materialistic stance is obvious if we listen to what Carlo Rubbia, Nobel Prize winner in 1984, says:

> The relationship between quantums of energy (photons) and particles of mass (nucleons) is roughly a thousand million to one ($9.746 \times 10^8 : 1$).

This means that visible matter is no more than the thousand-millionth part of the actually existing Universe, and that is exactly the portion of reality that materialists accept. In all truth, matter is no more than the transitory expression of an energetic condensation, that may once more disintegrate at any moment. I would even dare to think that man's mind possesses the total memory of the Universe in a latent state, and that materialism is equivalent to a conceptual state having a limit as exiguous as the thousand-millionth part of reality. Thus, the transcendental values of the spirit are usually light years away from the everyday ideology of materialistic man. Of course, this category includes many who, in an attempt to whitewash their image, declare and even believe themselves to be humanists, but act under the total dominion of their passions and the pulsions of the paleocortex.

Materialists hide their heads in the thousand-millionth part of reality, and ignore that there is an archetype of genuine spirituality, beyond falsifications and mystifications, and over and above the arbitrary separation between matter and energy, that is waiting to be incorporated or emulated. Like this, by closing their eyes to this latter opportunity, they can either openly or covertly give free rein to their animal impulses. Furthermore, there are filthy hands that make the greatest efforts to disqualify, discredit, deform, or distort the fact that the individual is a spiritual being who, because he is a fallen being, lies a prisoner of matter. These filthy hands do not take into account that this prisoner can recover his intrinsic condition by cultivating his own latent faculties.

In order to conceal the splendor of the spirit, people are hypnotized through television, computers, and video games. They are given artificial substitutes for all that is true and real; the genuine is falsified so that they do not awaken, but merely continue indefinitely as prisoners of successively more exciting fantasies. As genuine love is scarce, whimsical models are invented that abound in the cinema and on TV.

The romanticism that leads to marriage is replaced by sexual consumerism, and it, in turn, is replaced by the idealization of masturbation as "therapy."

Sensitivity is substituted by hysteria; peace by passivity; strength by violence; beauty by the grotesque; social commitment by monetary donation; manhood by genital prowess; femininity by clothes and makeup; equal opportunities by the social leveling forcibly implemented by the State; fraternity by food and alcohol as social events; tolerance by cowardice in defending one's own rights; love for one's children by the parents' need to turn them into images of themselves; democracy by "democratitis"; liberty by licentiousness; true music by noises with high levels of decibels. Information becomes brainwashing; the State, a tyrant; the president, king; public servants become the masters over citizens; justice becomes a matter of who has more money or political power; the valuable becomes what glitters brightest; the most important men are usually really insignificant; those who are truly important are ignored; the mass media become elements of pressure or misinformation; language becomes words with an adulterated semantic to suit everyone's convenience; noble sentiments become outdated; the shameless become models people want to imitate; sexual perversion becomes "alternative behavior;" communication between people becomes the "phantom contact" (between images); people become useful or useless things; delinquents, become victims, and so on, ad infinitum.

Virtual reality will displace true reality and man will become more and more distanced from Nature and his own divine spark. There is great religiousness and faith amidst the materialism around us, albeit not in a true, unique God but in the utilitarian map that each creates with respect to divinity. It is in this way that a mental image of divinity is naively manufactured in accordance with man's material needs.

When one's own sins become unbearable, Jesus Christ is invoked to relieve these sins by burdening Himself with them, or there are prayers to a certain saint for one's most pressing desires to be satisfied.

There is not much difference between the primitive native gods of water, rain, the harvest, or fertility, and the use people try to make of divinity at the service of human materialism.

Angels have become fashionable as servants to human voracity and frivolity and people suppose they abound, that they are continually visiting Earth and are eager to intervene in human existence. And just why are people interested in angels? Is it perhaps in order to imitate them in their divine humility, love, and service, or is it to indiscriminately ask them for the most selfish material gifts and the satisfaction of the person's own animal lasciviousness?

Atheism has spread through the world and is usually the most obvious projection of a loss of faith in oneself. The atheist does not believe in God because he ignores his own divine spark. He denies the divinity because he knows that he is unworthy of trust and respect for he knows the insignificance of his own inner dimension; he mistrusts because he perceives the magnitude of his own maliciousness.

Others who are more profound refuse to accept the image of God cast in man's image and likeness, without leaving open the opposite possibility that the Creator may have made man in his own image and likeness, albeit made only as his "rough work," so that he who wishes to recover his divinity may have to get down to the great work of completing himself, an ordeal greater than the labor of Hercules, the noblest and most transcendental undertaking man can begin on this earth. The opposite possibility is to remain incomplete, that is, in a larval state.

Thus, the human being has only two real options in life: either to remain in a larval state or to attain the spiritual metamorphosis that will enable him to fly to the Creator and discover his own origin. Anything that does not fit in with the foregoing is a mere masquerade designed to disorient people to the benefit of the great horned one.

The species *Homo sapiens* in its present state is clearly larval, and true great men have only managed to be so through arduous inner work that meant their attaining real individuality by committing themselves to the great work of completing their own human condition. This is a very serious matter, for there are no other options from the point of view of evolution.

Nature cannot be deceived, and those who play frivolously at "candy-coated" spiritual perfection, that is, one that pleases their own personality, will only manage to be larvae that played at self-fulfillment without taking it seriously and thus failed to attain their desired evolution. This is not that unpleasant, because, as a larva does not know what it means to have wings, it will be content with its own condition and will not have any ambition for anything else. However, in order to continue its daily existence passively and contentedly, it has to pay the price of avoiding any true mirror that could reflect the humble vision of its restricted, authentic worth. It means blindly adhering to a culture at the larval stage; practicing larval love and limiting oneself to the thought and conduct typical of one's real condition. The caterpillar and the butterfly are symbols of man's conceptual capacity, at the same time as they mark the difference between living by dragging oneself over the ground or by viewing a far broader reality from the heights. The emblem of the winged sun, typical of the Egyptian religion, was a reminder of the spiritual metamorphosis to which man could aspire.

The materialist stubbornly ignores his chances for spiritual evolution, and as long as he continues to do so, he will inevitably be surrounded by a certain aura of fatalism, for the law of probability shows that it is most likely that he will indefinitely continue like this, arrested at the most primitive level of human life: the larval condition.

This explains why morality should be obligatory, for the larva-person is incapable, by his own discrimination, of consciously and voluntarily assuming a pattern of higher behavior that implies sacrifice and effort. However, that above-mentioned obligation debases the principal requisite demanded by all moral systems, that is, that it be accepted freely and voluntarily by the individual, without any kind of coercion. Nevertheless, for it to be applied *en masse,* there is no other solution, for it is infinitely better for people to behave properly out of obligation, than to give themselves up to vice and corruption by making use of a misunderstood liberty. Indeed, it should be quite clear that there is no spiritual merit in behaving well through a material impossibility to do otherwise and that the individual's authentic moral triumph lies in freely adopting virtue because he understands what this really means and acts correctly out of an inner conviction of the goodness of genuine supreme good and not because some sort of law forbids him to act wrongly. Of course, I am discussing here those who are not prisoners of the rigid paradigm of blind materialism.

As for atheism, it is obvious that he who supposes that he is a sincere believer but continues to act in life as if the Creator did not exist, and merely practices a ritual type of religion of an external nature, is just as much an atheist as he who denies the existence of God.

There are many who, like "bleached sepulchres," project a luminous moral image but possess a corrupt inner world.

They lie a bit, steal a bit more, deceive many people, trade in the misfortune of others, and accommodate morality to the taste of their selfish personality, practicing charity to satisfy their feelings of guilt and not out of inner goodness; all this as if they could cheat God, or as if He did not exist and did not know what they were in fact doing. There are many who pay lip-service to the Creator and at the same time deny him through their actions. And who is the authentic God? The God of the Catholics, of the Protestants, of the Orthodox, the Muslim, the Buddhist, the Shintoist, the Hindu, or of others? Because there is really only one God, religion is an attempt to define the Creator in accordance with the cultural and historical conditions in which each belief originates, so that all speak of the same God but use a different language.

At ground level, the Earth appears to be manifold, but from outer space, it is clearly shown to be unified. It all depends on the height of the perspective from which it is observed. There are many who have tried to show somehow that God exists, but in fact this conviction can only be attained in very special, variable eventualities. In the first place, the person who has grown up in a religious or believing family usually believes in God. The person who moves in a social sphere of believers also believes in God, as well as the person who has been guided by a priest, or one who considers it to be in good taste, or the one who is influenced by a majority who say they believe. At another level, there is the person who, having suffered greatly or lived through very harsh experiences, has at some time felt a sort of inner revelation in the form of a certainty as to the existence of divinity. Finally, there is the person who, on account of his spiritual development, profoundly understands that the Creator exists, for He is revealed through the individual's divine spark, so that he will try to adjust his behavior to the whole divine mandate of evolution.

The fact is that God fully shows Himself only to those who elevate themselves above their own weaknesses to attain access to transcendental states of consciousness, which is only possible in individual experience.

Once more, I would insist that ethical and moral behavior, in its purest form, only occurs spontaneously in those who have attained genuine spiritual development, beyond the myriad falsifications that abound like mushrooms. It is not necessary to speak to truly spiritual persons about morality and ethics, for these are part of their intrinsic nature, and this is what Mankind really needs.

In order to re-moralize the world, people's spiritual sphere has to be developed, but this has to be the result of an absolutely free individual decision based on a concrete concept of a technical kind and not on the subjective beliefs of people with good intentions, however respectable they may be. The mere attempt to implement a consensual cultural option to spiritualize people would give rise to interminable Byzantine discussions as to what should really be considered as spiritual, so that the only feasible and immediately available path is for each individual to feel or understand the need for spirituality, to get down to work on the initial task of struggling against his own vices and defects, of making himself superior to his passions, of tempering his will and character, of overcoming himself and practicing all virtues, for when he manages to do all this, what genuine spirituality really is will become quite clear to him. Is this a hard task? It is far easier and more productive in the long run than remaining indefinitely without evolving, immersed in a larva-like existence.

This type of virtuous spirituality, beyond personal, political, or religious convenience, can only be attacked or rejected by those who openly or covertly defend immorality and corruption. Those who make these attacks thereby reveal their true intentions, since no evil can exist in the spiritual perfection of an individual.

One of the singular effects of individual evolution is that the individual attains full inner liberty, which might be one of the most precious gifts for the 21st century man. Obviously, because of this cerebral independence, man becomes "non-manipulable," so that it is predictable that all those interested in manipulating people, either mentally or emotionally, will tenaciously oppose individual spiritual development.

Unfortunately, our economic system requires a progressive increase in consumers, and these have to be "persuaded" to buy without leaving them an appreciable margin of real personal choice. However, one must have very clear ideas about this problem in order to truly know why there is the moral decadence we can see around us and how a solution can be found.

Materialism, superficiality, and frivolity usually go hand in hand, and this is why we have become accustomed to knowing only an infinitesimal portion of each person. We are only able to perceive the image they project, know what they do for a living, what things they possess, how old they are, what they look like, and what qualifications they have, and we use this scant information to label an individual, thinking that, "that is who he is."

Just think that the part we manage to see and perceive of an individual is perhaps less than the thousand-millionth part which is matter in relation to energy. In fact, we know nothing about his inner world, his hidden desires, pains, sufferings, and ambitions. Not even the individual himself knows much about himself. Thus, people relate more than anything at the bodily level, for they take the body as their own identity and encloister themselves within the narrow limits of matter in this way, without suspecting that their own energetic totality is proportionally equivalent to the total space of the planet Earth, while the city of Philadelphia is equivalent to the material limits of normal human consciousness. The part of our person and of our fellows that we know is *one,* and the portion we ignore, is *a thousand million.*

As the greater part is invisible, it is denied by materialists, as if people's thoughts, yearnings, desires, and feelings did not exist because they are invisible. The fact is that as they are mostly invisible, we live in our infinitely tiny material part, and so identify with our body that we believe it is *what we are.*

The foregoing in no way corresponds to supernatural elaborations, but to reflections on a concept of current physics. I am convinced that unless people understand that our material bodies are merely a vehicle for the manifestation of our real beings, there can be no freely chosen higher morality that is part of people's souls and not of their mental obligations.

The true genesis of our problem lies in the fact that the process of manifestation of the real being is a matter of evolution, and this development is often thwarted, prevented, or disdained, for man has swerved off his path of evolution to center on the conquest of the material instead of an inner metamorphosis, which is the true cause of the crisis of transcendental values; material hyper-development and spiritual subdevelopment; a disproportionate preoccupation with comfort, luxury, and material power; and a total abandonment of what we really are. In all truth, each day we have more and are less. We cannot perceive that we are *spiritual beings trapped in a material body.*

To Expect Without Deserving

It is a malignant disease to believe that just because we exist, and without any further merit than this, we have a right to all the material or spiritual goods of this world. Just because we are poor, we feel wretched when we compare ourselves to the rich, and if we have failed where others have succeeded, we believe we are the victims of unfair discrimination. At no time do we analyze our own merit in the proper sense to establish what training we have, how qualified we are, or what we have really done to achieve what we desire. Neither do we stop to consider the academic degree or standard of training, skill, intelligence, or industriousness of those who are successful. We are convinced that the world is like a huge cake and that if we exist we must have by decree what others have, regardless of individual effort.

Unfortunately there are many who feel wretched at the happiness of others or attacked by the material possessions or personal qualities of some people. To aspire to something when one lacks the merit to deserve what one desires is such a common moral fault that it has already become part of people's normal character.

Each feels himself to be *worthy, good, and deserving,* and when his life is not fortunate enough he is sure that he is the victim of some atrocious injustice, and that what he lacks has been stolen from him or usurped by others. Who are these others? Anyone chosen by a person who feels unfairly discriminated against; for Salieri, Mozart was to blame; for the colonizers of the American West, it was the Indians; for Brutus, Julius Caesar, and thus we find other countless cases it is preferable not to go into in order not to hurt people's susceptibilities. Each considers himself to be *good* and usually identifies as evil all those who hold adverse or different positions to his own, or those who possess goods that have been denied him. The world is full of personal demons, born of false deliriums or overblown individual merit and the contrast between these things and effective reality.

The virus of envy is encouraged by numerous organized groups that try to convince people that the world will only be fair when there is absolute equality. Naturally, this means for such people that *any dissent will be suppressed to level all within a docile and manipulable homogeneous mass, they themselves remaining on the margin and administrating this servile, domesticated equality to their own profit.*

We know that necessarily, equality through revolution or decree would have to be "downwards" and very unlikely "upwards." The fact that there is a wrong notion of equality makes people infected with envy think that the world is unfair and that one needs to take from those who have more, without discriminating as to their merit or lack thereof. As the consumer market multiplies at vertiginous speed, the offer of diverse goods increases people's lackings artificially, so that each day they feel more relegated or marginalized, for at the unconscious level they suppose that it is normal to have everything of value that the market offers and that it is an unjust situation not to possess it. Most criminals do not possess the notion of individual merit, and thus, they believe that by stealing from those who possess more than they do, they are fulfilling an act of justice.

Why is man so prone to these insidious manipulations of his own brain? This happens because, instead of concerning himself with knowing reality, he keeps justifying his vices, faults, or shortcomings, or blindly accepts the beliefs that best fit his own passions.

A concept of fetal happiness has also become popular, in which the world should be at people's service to satisfy all their needs without any effort, a goal that is pursued as a highly desirable one. For high level criminals, wealth is an easy goal within their reach, it being sufficient for them to steal or plunder it without any kind of moral barriers.

Easy success and wealth are the prime ambition of the immoral and weak in character who cannot in their inner world establish any relationship between cause and effect— between being successful and working hard, patiently, and honestly.

Most people complain about their own situation, bearing in their hearts the bitter taste of some sort of social injustice that supposedly prevents them from attaining their desired success. Those who complain most are usually those who least deserve to, and they are usually lazy, indolent, aggressive, envious people.

The most serious damage caused by a desire for success without personal merit occurs in young people who massively receive messages of "easy success" that lead them to the irremediable frustration of their yearnings.

"Earn money without effort" or "succeed easily" are the favorite slogans of the idle in marked contrast to the reality of life that makes one work hard and honestly if one wants to achieve a prosperous situation and really be successful. This concept should of course include the individual's spiritual perfection, for otherwise it would only be a position of materialistic privilege.

Unfortunately, there are many who, intoxicated by unreal messages, hate hard work and long-term planning, living illusorily in terms of a fantastical idea of success.

Why do they reject organized effort and hard work? Because, in some way, they have not been able to mature in order to transcend the stage of fetal narcissism, and are victims of their own childishness that leads them to make irrational demands on society. It would seem as if their head, their stomach, and their heart still remained in the womb and demanded that the State, society, or the Church should become surrogate mothers, this being a false hope that these institutions usually encourage. Fetal life is in fact an experience absolutely devoid of effort or merit. The fetus lives a parasitical existence and does not even make an effort to feed or breathe.

I believe that most people's concept of happiness is related to fetal well-being and certainly a great majority have psychic fixations at that period expecting similar circumstances in life to those of their existence in the womb, without thinking that they must now earn their own keep and happiness.

Comfort and material well-being encourage these irrational demands and thus the frustration and resentment caused by not being able to satisfy them. Occasionally, one resorts to illicit means to attain what one desires regardless of the golden rule of honesty, merit, hard work, and sustained effort.

The quest for what is easy, and the refusal to pay the price that everything we wish to attain costs, is a projection from our inner fetus—a parasitic demand of what we ourselves were when we still lived in our mothers' wombs.

It is deplorable that a certain type of cinema should so abundantly show the myriad ways to break the law to obtain easy money, for this type of story is often used as an example for delinquency.

Likewise the advertising we are exposed to, as I said above, offers a golden version of existence with lots of fun and little effort, an image that profoundly penetrates in our minds to mix reality and fantasy, to make us expect everything to be easy and feel frustrated when we cannot rapidly achieve what we want.

There is an immoral conspiracy of silence as to the fact that fulfilling our legitimate desires depends exclusively on our individual work and individual merit, and that we do not have to ask permission from anyone to honestly obtain what we desire. On the contrary, people live in constant hope of a stroke of luck or a gift from the government, or else come to the conclusion that what they lack has been snatched from them by privileged groups, and that there is no other solution but to recover it by force or violence.

Because of this insistence on showing that "we are all equal" or that "we must achieve equality," we indiscriminately reject any inequality between people in the supposition that our natural or ideal state is that of generalized homogeneity.

In this way, we forget that individual differentiation is the basis of evolution, for it is not a question of masses, but something that requires each individual's free decision. It does not matter how often we equalize people by force; they will very soon all be different because of their individual effort. It is natural that progress and liberty are bothersome for those who seek to control the masses in order to use them to their own ends. There is no doubt that there have always been supposed public servants, leaders whose true desire is really to "be served by the people," which is typical of brute or "incomplete" human nature.

Will Durant presents history as a fragment of biology and says that man's life is a part of the vicissitudes of organisms on land and in the sea. He writes:

At times when we stroll alone through the woods on a summer's day, we hear or see the movement of a hundred species of beings that fly, leap, wiggle, crawl, or burrow. These surprised animals flee from us; the birds fly away; the fish separate in their flight upstream. Suddenly, we realize to which dangerous minority we belong in this impartial planet, and for a moment, as these diverse residents clearly show, we are circumstantial intruders on their natural habitats. Therefore, all man's chronicles and achievements humbly submerge in the history and perspective of a polymorphous life; all our economic competence, all our struggle to join forces, all our appetites, loves, pains, and wars resemble the anxieties, couplings, struggles, and sufferings, hidden beneath those fallen tree-trunks and leaves, in the waters, or in the bushes.[30]

According to Will Durant, we are all born unequal, and inevitably have to submit ourselves to a process of selection in the struggle for life, in which some succeed and others fail, inequality increasing with the complexity of civilization and freedom, for freedom and equality have sworn eternal enmity to each other, and in order to favor the latter, the former has to be limited.

We cannot close our eyes to the evidence that survival and progress belong to the most capable and that supposed, oft-mentioned equality is a utopia used as a tool with which to manipulate the masses, as occurs with envy, since this and the belief in equality usually go hand in hand. Envy is used to reject inequality, making people believe that the superiority of others has been obtained illicitly, so, in order to equalize things, they have to be either destroyed or enslaved.

We do not stop to think that all living persons, however wretched they may seem, are superior to us in some way, having the advantage over us in some quality, which could be good health, astuteness, physical strength, a lack of stress, manual skill, or the capacity to survive, or perhaps they surpass us in internal qualities such as peace, modesty, tolerance, and virtue.

The same occurs with regard to animals, for man cannot live underwater; he lacks the strength of the elephant, the majesty of the lion, nor can he fly like birds do.

There is not one being that in some way does not surpass us or that does not draw some advantage from its apparent weakness or lack of resources. The syndrome of expecting without deserving is also manifested in the relationship of the couple in which in an endeavor to be loved, the man carefully examines the woman he is interested in to perceive her qualities without doing likewise with himself in the supposition that he possesses outstanding qualities, so that if he is rejected he will disqualify the person who does so, try to show that he has been misunderstood, or blame the failure of the romance on third-party interventions.

The desire to be loved without bothering to love first, to demand without giving anything, to ask for friendship without being friendly, or to ask for justice without deserving it, are all typical of this syndrome of demands. This moral disorder brings with it a marked inner insecurity, for in some way the person affected perceives that his repertoire of qualities or merits is exiguous concerning his ambitions, so that he has to continually boast or show off about his own capacities in order to reinforce his shaky self-esteem.

When we project this matter onto the world of business and commerce, we continually encounter businessmen who fail because they have unwittingly attempted to obtain profits which they do not really deserve because of their poor training, improvisation, lack of industriousness or sacrifice, or insignificant level of inner commitment to their work.

Something similar occurs in the world of work. There are too many people who try to earn what they imagine they deserve in their minds, in the conviction that their employers do not wish to pay them more out of a mere desire to exploit them. Of course, they do not stop to analyze their own qualifications, that is, to determine the concrete reasons that the company they work for must have for not paying them what they want.

There are people who are unhappy on account of their meager wages, or if they have the bad luck to be fired, think that there has been a great injustice done to them. Even though this may be true, it often happens that these persons, unfortunately, do not comply with the necessary demands to meet the requirements of their jobs, or else the companies have to cut down expenses or make changes due to the ever variable dynamics of business.

For example, would one dismiss an employee one needed if one was a company owner? Of course not, but if one did not need him, how could he be kept on when money is the only way a company can meet its obligations?

The selection of the fittest operates mercilessly in the labor and business market, and he who is not efficient is usually replaced by other, better workers. There are some who will never be short of work because of the outstanding qualities they possess, these most likely being the result of a voluntary development and not something he was born with.

When the distribution of wealth in certain countries is analyzed, the subject of social injustice inevitably crops up when the difference in income between rich and poor is proven.

I believe it is a serious mistake to try to solve this problem on the strength of specific economic policies, when what should be done in the first place is to give more opportunities for all people to develop, be educated, and enabled in order to increase their talents and skills, to thus attain privileged posts on the labor market, and at the same time, it would mean a huge contribution to the country's wealth. There seems to be a persistent interest in hiding from the poor the fact that all wealth or prosperity lies within each person and that each one is free to develop this precious vein. People insist *ad nauseum* that poverty is a problem that affects certain social groups that would be irremediably doomed to continue in this plight were it not that a messianic State managed to reestablish the balance of social justice. As usual, the principal one who is disregarded or forgotten is the individual, the subject, the person himself, who is the fundamental unit that makes up any social group.

If the family is the basic nucleus of society, the individual is of the family, and it is precisely he who has to understand that in order to overcome poverty, he need ask permission from no one, for he can get down to work at it right now. To this end, it is enough for him to understand and accept definitively that the basis of all wealth lies in the development of a person's inner resources, and that material prosperity is a mere reflection of the inner capacity of each one. Let that individual decide right now to take his destiny in his own hands, taking responsibility for himself without waiting for the charity of the government in power, struggling and disciplining himself to be more and more skilled each day, training himself in highly specialized jobs, administrating his own life efficiently. However, in order to do this, he must bring about a total change of mentality and must stop living expecting external aid but begin by helping himself and taking care of himself, developing his own capacities to a maximum. If possible, he must find out in detail about those people who, having been born in humble homes, managed to attain success by their own means. He must take note of how they did it, what kind of life they led, what their everyday life was like, what passed through their minds and hearts. He must at heart be convinced that one can succeed despite being in a disadvantaged position.

In this world of inequalities, there is nevertheless the total equivalence of opportunities as far as people's spiritual possibilities are concerned, for anyone, no matter what their condition, race, class, or color, can set out on the path of perfectioning.

However, very few understand that spiritual development does not mean to privilege one area to the detriment of others. It is not a case of the individual devoting himself to a mystical, contemplative existence to neglect the material world. There can be no such divorce because both spirit and matter are formed from the same type of energy.

Spiritual development means to place within the *being* what is normally centered in the personality. Therefore, it entails growth from within outwards and not the opposite.

This process inevitably leads to an elevation of consciousness and to the possession of a truly mature, adult "I." Under such conditions, the individual can forge his own destiny because he becomes progressively more suited by observing reality as it is, regardless of subjective appraisals, to thus attain an inner strength that he can use to achieve a sort of total success with the exact proportion of spirit and matter. In this way, he may at a given moment come in time to *deserve without trying,* that is, to accumulate merit.

The foolish, ambitious man aspires to thousands of things that he neither deserves nor needs; the wise man accumulates merit so that things, persons, and events come into his life that can lead him to encounter happiness and the supreme good. If we wish to act in accordance with higher moral laws, *we should moderate our expectations until they coincide with the magnitude of our merit but never exceed it.*

Let us accumulate merit by carrying out spiritual works that entail an impersonal ideal for the benefit of Mankind. However, let us also take care not to get ensnared by the vanity that affects so many who deceive themselves into believing they are doing something for others in circumstances in which they act solely to inflate their own images.

Ten Moral Rules

1. To prioritize personal objectives, establishing that the first fundamental obligation is to oneself, for only by fulfilling oneself as a complete, higher human being can one give back anything of value to the world and to people.

2. To commit oneself to good and swear loyalty to one's own spirit.

3. To confront one's own dishonesty.

4. To put oneself emotionally in the place of others, learning to understand and tolerate one's fellows.

5. To have dominion over oneself.

6. To come out of one's own burrow. To leave the narrow mental grid in which we take refuge and open up to other realities.

7. To develop will power and temper the character.

8. To live in harmony with Nature.

9. To practice the law of egalitarian equivalence.

10. To mistrust appearances and force oneself to find more profound truths.

To Prioritize Personal Objectives

One must understand that there is one true reality of an objective nature and another subjective and false one which is accommodated to the individual's illusory expectations. We are, of course, so accustomed to living in accordance with a personalized version of the world, one born of our own labyrinthic process, fantasies, and personal dreams, that we cannot suspect there exists an impersonal, more profound, and concrete reality born of the energetic interaction between man and Nature. The false reality we take as true originates in the mental limitations typical of the very low level of development of our consciousness, due to the fact that we are incomplete.

The anguish, pain, and suffering we encounter in our lives emanates from the fact that we are "fake men," that is, men whose instrument of perception cannot differentiate between fantasy and reality, dreams or wakefulness, so that only too often we violate or contradict the laws of Nature and receive the corresponding punishment.

Mankind's most urgent concerns are not based on factors alien to his control, for they entail problems of perturbation of the higher faculties of the mind and affect almost the whole of the world population. These problems are derived from the lack of a human consciousness that can be developed by personal effort. The lack of this precious capacity is the origin of most of the miseries and flaws that affect man.

People make the serious mistake of seeking prosperity and defining the quality of life by centering almost exclusively on material factors, basically on the possession of an income commensurate to the average aspirations, thus violating natural inequality and ignoring individual freedom to choose one's own objectives. It would seem that there is an attempt to increase people's income not with the humanitarian intention of satisfying their basic needs but chiefly to turn them into superlative consumers with the aim of enabling the capitalist system to attain its maximum profit.

There are countries whose governments turn the struggle for the redistribution of wealth by decree into their goal and banner, arguing that social inequality is the source of injustice and suffering, and others will try to achieve the same by means of revolution, forgetting that, as Will Durant says, the concentration of wealth is the natural result of human inequality, for as practical capacities vary from person to person, most of these capacities are, in almost all societies, concentrated in a minority of men. The concentration of wealth is the natural result of the concentration of capacity.

Let us once and for all understand that the only real revolution is that which develops people's capacities and that redistribution by decree is a mere palliative designed to yield political dividends to a certain party rather than to raise the standard of living of the people.

Why do we not direct our efforts to the development of people's capacities? I believe this is due to the fact that neither the most able nor the least skilled want this; some, in order to avoid competition; others not to lose votes; and even others so that consumers keep on being obedient. The discourse of social justice is hypocritical at heart, for the only genuine social justice is that which can be attained through the individual freedom of those who are properly trained to achieve success.

One must understand that this type of training does not mean educating, but far more than this. Education is generally biased and dogmatic, and invariably acts to program people's brains through patterns that emanate from dominant social groups without the pupil ever having the slightest opportunity to freely and consciously choose, for he only chooses compulsorily in accordance with the information that has previously been implanted in his brain.

While it is true that education broadens the individual's cultural panorama and trains him professionally, it would likewise be fair to admit that it also programs him rigidly within ideological and behavioral patterns, limiting his conceptual and creative capacity. It would be no exaggeration to say that, as far as creativity and mental liberty are concerned, *"to educate is to limit,"* at least in accordance with the style of education most in fashion in the world today. In each person's mind, the world is as it was implanted in him through the education that he received, and this message is already tainted with the political or religious tone of both parents and State, who favor certain educational patterns and forget others.

We are taught to see only a narrow segment of reality, and from this emanates the lack of solidarity and comprehension between people, for each defends the tiny bit of truth that has been infused into his brain, thus making it impossible to express the high level of perspective that accompanies the possession of a broader, more profound reality. This high level of perspective is indispensable if we wish to have a world united by higher values. Man's only true liberty is to make himself superior to his own cerebral programming, surpassing himself to make the information carried in his neurons pass over into the discriminatory crucible of higher vigilic consciousness, thus genuinely managing to "choose in conscience," that is, by the grace of the lucidity that emanates from the highest inner judgment.

This is man's most important moral imperative; it is the only valid recipe for inner growth, human evolution, and true social justice. Let us open our eyes: there is social justice, and we only have to take it, to make it operative. This lies in the opportunity for individual spiritual development, the source of all good and value. However, in practice this does not work, because there is a conspiracy of silence to conceal or discredit this option in order to keep the human race in the slavery of ignorance and superstition. People are brainwashed to such an extent that they want to live in terms of consumerism and pleasure, and this leaves them no space to perceive the contradictions of their lives.

At all costs, there is an intent for many to be obliged to work free for more than a hundred days a year in order to be able to pay their taxes, and this is never questioned, nor is there any clear proof as to where the State really invests this money. The intent is for man to continue to docilely pay usurer's interest for loans which he does not really need, for he could get this same money by saving; for women to be limited to only wanting to have children and bring them up as the chief goal of their existence, so that they have neither time nor any desire to broaden their human possibilities to complete themselves spiritually and to have to content themselves with passively accepting their role of wetnurse; for the poor to think that their lackings are due to the existence of perverse rich men and not to differences in individual capacities; for all to believe that, if there is poverty, it is because the system to create wealth has not been discovered, and that there is no consensus as to how it should be distributed.

Will Durant says: "In progressive societies the concentration [of wealth] may reach a point when the strength of numbers of the many poor, rivals the strength of the capacity of the few rich; then an unstable balance generates a critical situation, diversely confronted in history by laws that make a new distribution of wealth or revolutions that distribute poverty."

There are many who, in a mechanized, repetitive way, combat human inequality by giving this concept a pejorative meaning based exclusively on the level of people's economic income, without considering it as a logical consequence of individual merit or demerit, silencing the fact that anyone who seriously decides to, can, in countries with an acceptable economy, manage to attain an economic situation that will allow for a satisfactory quality of life. However, to this end, one has to devote one's efforts to working honestly and efficiently, forgetting the excess of money that others have, thinking only of that which one can obtain oneself.

Other sectors attempt to impose the model of a materialistic society, one opulent in material goods but devoid of higher spiritual values. The contingencies of everyday life are overly criticized because people do not understand that any spiritual development, the purpose of our terrestrial life, needs individual exercising in continual, arduous struggles or confrontations with the problems inherent to being alive. When we deprive people of this opportunity, we prevent them from developing and end by incapacitating or invalidating them, turning them into social deadweights, and this is precisely what happens in certain places in the world. An excess of comfort, state overprotection, and tendentious informational saturation may make us mentally handicapped as far as our level of awakening and higher consciousness are concerned.

Our instrument for knowledge is deficient and functionally perturbed, but no one is really interested in the fact that the human being can develop himself, for people prefer him to be a domesticated consumer. For this reason, numerous myths are created that are all accepted passively without being questioned by the mere fact that they are incessantly repeated. It is a simple matter to hide true things *en masse* because anything that is generally and incessantly repeated comes to be accepted without question.

One of these myths is that of human inequality when people try to attribute it exclusively to socioeconomic factors, regardless of the differences in individual talent and personal effort. This is usually how attempts are made to dictate protectionist laws to favor the less fortunate sector and thus enable them to rise to the same level as the rest. This is just as contradictory as if, within a system put in place for corporal growth, short people were protected by obliging the whole population to walk permanently hunched over so that the shorter people did not feel debased, thus saving them the painful effort of growing, but condemning them forever to be short. To strive to shrink those who stand out in a group, would seem to be one of the primary desires of the mass, perhaps because the ones who stand out resist attempts at total homogenization. One should put an end once and for all to the myth that inequality implies social injustice, and stop idealizing the weak as a worthy model to emulate, accepting instead the challenge to become beings with a strong will and character, albeit sensitive and solidary.

Equality of opportunities really exists and is based on the inner development of each individual, which leads to a growth from within outwards. The total process of human-izing people makes each individual's latent capacities emerge by virtue of a faithful vision of inner and outer reality, which acts as the most powerful pedagogical and evolutionary tool there can be. Man's essential development is adulterated and paralyzed due to the multiple and continuous distortions of reality, which make him live in a mythological, unreal world.

Just like birds, people build the nest of their "I" around their own fears, desires, and fantasies, and once they have finished this task, they merely rest in the comfort of their mental dwelling. This nest is called personality and controls the individual's existence to the day he dies. Its most harmful function is to systematically conceal reality in order to combat or avoid the anguish of the "I," to this end resorting to the well-known psychological defense mechanisms.

One never asks whether there is something for us outside the personality, what it might be, what effect it might have on one, and how to reach it. The fact is that beyond the personality there is the door that leads to spiritual perfection, the basis for genuine happiness, but only very few have the courage to cross this threshold.

I sustain that all people have the same opportunity for spiritual development, and that this kind of progress corresponds to what should really be the individual's normal development, if this development could prevent the obscuring and accommodation of reality. By spiritual development, one should not understand a religious or devotional process, but rather the type of behavior that the Creator expects of man, which is the true evolution of his immortal consciousness.

The access to the path of evolution is within people's reach right now, and to follow it is a matter of simple individual decision, since no one can stop the person who freely chooses it.

The problem of inequality proves nothing more than that we can reach higher, that nobody can stop us, and that we can grow to the same extent as our effort and purpose. We have no need to ask permission from bureaucrats of whatever kind to begin our spiritual growth, which really corresponds to the blossoming of the individual's latent capacities. Anyone, even those who have not had access to education, can become self-taught at a level of wisdom that nobody could imagine, a capacity that undoubtedly would wipe away all possible marginalization or social discrimination with one stroke. As for our possibilities of evolution, we are all equal and only need to understand this fact and get to work on it.

Really, true success in life, with respect to our relation to God and Nature, is measured by the parameters of spiritual perfection and not by material goods or social prestige. It is *to be* and not *to have* that counts. Social success often goes hand in hand with a total failure in evolution, that is, the irremediable frustration of individual destiny with respect to divine and natural requirements; this, of course, without the individual ever realizing this painful, irreversible misstep unless this occurs at the moment of his death. The worst type of marginalized individuals are those who, through their own decision, indifference, stubbornness, or blindness, deprive themselves of access to the supreme good, the root and trunk of true happiness, preferring instead to be devoured daily by their own illusory fantasies.

No matter the magnitude of his credentials, whether financial, professional, or social, the individual who has not set out on the path of spiritual development will continue to be a failure and his own inner intuition will make him perceive this fact and thus prevent him from being happy. To be successful in life is to succeed on the path of evolution, the supreme challenge of Nature.

It is obvious that the social parameters used to measure personal success or failure are whimsical, limited, biased, variable, and circumstantial and are generally restricted by whether or not one attains a personal situation of privilege or social admiration. However, people forget that society is sick and its approval or admiration of certain types of behavior has no greater value than the expression of the convenience of a dominant class or culture at a given moment and place. For example, the ultimate ambition for most people is to dominate and control their fellows, whereas for only a few, it is more appropriate to master themselves.

If we wish to be really successful in life, we have to understand and accept that the first, most important duty of the individual is to himself, and that it concerns his own evolutive development, a divine mandate that one has to obey if one hopes to "do right" in life and keep on the right path.

Unfortunately, whenever we speak of Mankind, we inevitably mean a species that has gone astray, that at some moment lost its way, and which marches towards the cultivation of sensorial pleasure as its goal, letting itself be won over by the pride typical of those who, because they lack self-criticism, believe themselves to be far better than they really are.

The tiny segment of Mankind that still preserves a certain mental lucidity, in the sense of a faithful vision of a broader, more profound reality, is a minority whose qualities, rights, and opinions are systematically ignored or disqualified by the mass, and any attempt to join this cluster of clearsighted minds is immediately punished with social reproval for the mere fact of trying to detach oneself from the general homogeneity.

However, one must be quite clear that whatever the opinion of certain unconscious people, there is no other way to offer anything really valuable to the world that is not through a previous development, until one has completed oneself as a genuine, real human being, with the inner judgment, wisdom, tolerance, and criterion that corresponds to an individual who has achieved his higher fulfillment.

Once this conviction has been accepted and the corresponding decision is taken, no one and nothing can stop the process of evolution or prevent the results from being spread among Mankind.

To Commit Oneself to Good and Swear Loyalty to One's Own Spirit

In order for our own acts to be coherent and for us to act most appropriately, we have to decide to undertake a complete commitment to good. If we do not do this, we shall accumulate a long list of wrong acts and only a very short one of good deeds. Good and evil are cosmic forces of a universal nature, and in some way we connect to either the luminous or the obscure aspect of the energy of the Universe. If we remain under the boot of the dark side of the force, we shall be committed to evil, and it will use us as instruments to express itself, making us become a part of evil. If on the contrary, we are committed to good, we shall be with the light and truth and shall follow the path of evolution. To this end, we must have certain immutable parameters to show us what is good and what is evil. We cannot remain in the simplistic belief that good is what gives us pleasure and favors our material interests.

For the snake that devours a chicken, this act is good, whereas it is evil for the bird. Depending on our stance, our classifying of good and evil will be quite variable and arbitrary, and we shall quite easily identify with one or the other of the two aspects of this duality. *This is why we need to visualize good as something so elevated that it transcends petty personal interest and is raised to the sphere of the spirit. Undoubtedly, supreme good is everything that enables the individual to awaken from daily environmental hypnosis to evolve towards higher states of consciousness.*

Evil on the contrary is what keeps man's attention captive to the alienating influence of the external and inner environmental hypnotic panorama, the former originating in the continual multiplicity of stimuli and the latter in the uninterrupted autonomous activity of cerebral information which, as it is not subordinate to the "I," dominates and controls the individual through his thought, binding him to the specific programming modality that has infiltrated subliminally into his brain, depriving him of any faithful vision of genuine external or internal reality, and thus preventing him from fulfilling the Creator's mandate of evolution by thwarting the pedagogical aim of existence.

The human being's mental slavery arises from the impossibility to free thought from the uninterrupted wave of internal and external stimuli that capture his attention, thereby provoking a continuous state of semi-hypnosis, a condition in which the individual is only able to be half-aware of his own situation. In this case what I call "semi-hypnosis" is to remain at a certain level of sleepwalking, without this being noticed by either the person affected or by those who observe him, and without the individual's normal behavior being apparently affected. Really, the individual is deprived of contact with genuine reality, a phenomenon that affects the whole species, and that one can only transcend by means of long, patient individual training.

Technically, this mechanism is translated into a deficient state of awakeness with a considerable broadening of the segment of subliminal perception and a great reduction in perceptions that happen at the threshold of consciousness. In this way, what the individual sees, thinks, and feels is contaminated by the oneiric fantasy that affects his mind.

Continued subliminal perception means the accumulation of *cognitive trash* that makes us take as real our own fantastical, distorted representation of authentic reality. Because we are in this state, the development of our essential "I" is atrophied and we deprive ourselves of what we call *spiritual development and evolution* which, if they are to be carried out, require an augmented perception of total reality.

Therefore, *good* for both men and women of any condition, race, color, epoch, or place is anything that enables them to awaken in order to complete themselves as human beings, and to attain the spiritual evolution which the Creator expects. If we reflect on this paradigm and understand it in depth, we shall conclude that the individual's highest moral imperative is the development of his spiritual consciousness and that only in this way is it possible to attain happiness and to gain access to supreme good.

Alas, good intentions are not enough to attain spiritual perfection, since we have to confront anything that motivates us to obtain what we want regardless of the moral rules that seem to hinder our purposes, for example, the one that says that the only fruit we can take legitimately is that generated by our own painful, sustained, personal effort. The animal passions continually press us to make us forget love, tolerance, and respect for others, and often lead us to lose our self-respect and dignity. For the struggle against the passional temptations to be successful, a perfect inner clarity is required which will enable us to evaluate what we wish to attain at each moment and what our struggle is based upon. It is as if we had joined a sports club and our essential rule were never to forget the color of our shirt and the team's ideals.

When we possess inner clarity, the struggle moves more in our favor, because we do not let ourselves be so easily confused, as occurs in mythical stories in which an individual is tempted by the devil, and the goods that the devil offers him makes the victim forget who the devil is and what he is really seeking by such actions.

Inner clarity prevents us from being blinded with expectations of an imminent or apparent good, and gives us the strength to sacrifice this mirage for the sake of a real and greater good.

In order to swear loyalty to one's own spirit, it is essential to understand that it corresponds to our authentic being. We are spiritual beings incarnate in material bodies, and our true identity (the being) is divine and not human. If this cannot be realized in everyday life it is because the spirit, our true being, remains incapable of manifesting itself because of the rigid control the body and personality exert over the mind and psyche.

The personality, which is the individual's social "I," is what controls his conduct, preventing the being from expressing itself on account of the antagonistic nature of these two identities; one social, the other divine, and each with diametrically opposed purposes. One of them, the personality, only seeks the survival of the species, whereas the spirit endeavors to attain transcendental evolution of an individual nature that brings the individual close to the source of his own origin: the Creator.

The social "I" may be considered as a false "I," in the sense that it *represents something that does not belong to the individual,* a forcible superimposition of the social entity over the individual "I," which is assimilated by the former. In this way, *the individual comes to be what he in truth is not,* and his intrinsic essence is snatched from him or denied him, so that he comes to live in order to please the mass and comply with the goals of the species, but not to fulfill his own.

If I ask "Who am I?" I would have to acknowledge that, "I am my own spirit," that is, "I am me," in order to refer to my intrinsic condition.

The wretchedness of terrestrial life lies in the fact that my authentic "I" remains in semi-exile from my material existence, and is united to it only by a fine thread, unable to fully manifest itself through the instrument of the body, whereas the personality makes up a "false I," a social graft that the individual takes as his true identity.

The glory of terrestrial life lies in the fact that there is a chance for all human beings to make their own spirit (what the individual essentially is) manifest itself through the material body. An individual only becomes truly spiritual if the being, that is, the spirit itself, takes possession of the corporeal brain and turns it into the authentic governor of this microcosm.

To swear loyalty to our own spirit means to acknowledge our own hidden divinity, a divinity that is prevented from acting because it is fettered to matter; so that we must be committed to achieving the spirit's freedom by overcoming the passions in order to take control of ourselves.

Man's most intimate, subtle suffering emanates from the sublime sadness of the divine spark when it cannot gain access to the material reality of the body that belongs to it. When an inexplicable sadness appears amidst pleasure, or despite pleasure; on every occasion that our joy is suddenly clouded without any apparent reason and melancholy or nostalgia reign; when we are not satisfied with what we have; it is the message of the spirit that manifests its silent voice in this way.

It is typical of highly animalized individuals to remain indifferent to this voice, but any individual who respects himself has a primary duty to carry out the heroic deed of rescuing his own spirit from its condition of passive dependency, to crown it as the sovereign of the little universe which is the corporeal, physical man.

In order to fulfill his purpose, he will have to confront many obstacles, trials, and temptations, because the material world is more a kingdom of shadows than of light, and all those who serve dark interests will try to prevent him from complying with his sublime purpose.

Common man cannot forgive clean, elevated beings because they are usually true mirrors that faithfully give back without alterations the reflection of those with whom they interact, stripping off their masks and displaying the falsehood or imperfection hidden beyond their sparkling images.

The oath to one's own spirit has to be renewed daily, for one must remain faithful to its interests, which are virtue and the supreme good.

I would once more repeat that only the practice of the highest human virtues can lead us to continued happiness and authentic good, a condition to be definitively attained by those who comply with the process of evolution to recover their intrinsic essence and then continue to raise themselves to progressively higher states of consciousness.

Virtue and spirituality are not antagonistic to pleasure and material enjoyment; they only move, regulate, and subordinate them so that, now pure and clean, they will be at the service of the spirit and not of the animal part. When it is the spirit that moves and controls the individual's conduct, he can do no evil nor act immorally, because he keeps strict respect for virtue, good, and the harmony of Nature. That does not mean that he should deprive himself of conscious, clean, and controlled pleasure.

It is not rare in many cases for certain sins of the flesh to be defined as such, not because what the individual does is sinful per se, but because of the filthy and depraved way in which he does it, or by the fact that what he does goes against life in some of its manifestations.

It is not by fleeing from temptation and sin that we shall become virtuous, but by confronting and overcoming them.

The dual nature of man's identity (spirit/personality) is the origin of his inner conflicts, for despite the fact that the spirit is his intrinsic essence, at the material level it is overcome by the personality that prevents him from expressing himself. In this way, one must keep quite clear that to swear fidelity to one's own spirit means, in the first place, to safeguard the interests of the being, freeing it from the social prison in which the personality has encloistered it, and this entails a whole process of revision and purification of one's own mind. This process should be carried out at an augmented level of awareness, in order to discern to what extent our conduct is our own or whether it emanates from sources alien to our genuine "I."

The being needs to manifest itself properly through the vehicle that houses it: the physical body. The body, however, is managed by a brain in turn controlled by the personality whose structure is mechanically automatized in accordance with the behavioral patterns inserted into it. The aim of the personality is to suit the individual's behavior to social requirement, and act as a shock absorber between the "I" and reality. It is the filter that comes between the two and that conditions perception to its own structural style. This is why the individual "I" is invaded or colonized by the collective psyche of Mankind. It thus becomes rather a mechanized "we" whose center of gravity is not within the individual himself, but in the mass, so that the individual's behavioral goals will be inevitably limited to the survival of the species and passive acquiescence to social messages, among which of course there is no possibility of evolution as an individual challenge.

The basic impulse of the personality is to keep the individual correctly adapted to social norms, which leads us to acknowledge that this means acquiring not only the achievements of society, but also its deficiencies, the most serious of which is ignorance, in reference to the spirit and to evolution. This means that, for the moment, we are doomed to follow a path which, instead of pursuing a goal of evolution, has as its aim the increase in possession of material goods and the increase of comfort and sensorial pleasure, which are interests quite alien to the needs of the being.

People generally keep themselves in submissive obedience to the personality, for they ignore the possibility of acting otherwise, and would never suspect that what they take as their true identity really corresponds to a graft that comes from the collective psyche of Mankind. The individual does not understand that by defending what he takes as his own ideas, feelings, and patterns of behavior, he is really privileging what is alien to him, to the total detriment of what is his own, through a process of confusion between what is intrinsic and what is alien.

When are intangible goods such as knowledge or ideas really "mine?" Perhaps, when my mind is passively colonized by them? Of course not, for in this case I would be a mere bearer of autonomous information, and this is what happens to most of people's mental content, their brains limited like sophisticated recipients to be the depositories of information, ideas, and knowledge they neither understand nor control, but which act by completely determining their behavior and hence their whole life.

When we imitate what others do, we do not appropriate it; it is "it" that appropriates us, and the more we imitate, memorize, and passively learn, *the less we shall be in relation to our being.*

When we consume the products promoted by advertising, we do not take charge of them; it is the advertising message that takes possession of our minds. To swear fidelity to our own spirit means to acknowledge our true identity; it means to separate the "I am" from the ordinary "I" with which we function every day, in the understanding that if we remain imprisoned by the rigid demands of the personality, we shall be doomed to be mere cogs in the huge machinery of the species.

If we commit ourselves to the "I am," we have to act in consequence and decide to "be good," that is, to do anything that, in accordance with the absolute definition of good, enables us to awaken from the environmental hypnosis in which we live, a mortal lethargy that prevents us from truly perceiving reality and consequently from individual evolution.

The personality continually struggles to keep us within inflexible schemas that do no more than promote the deficiencies or impediments that prevent our mind from experiencing the state of awareness.

It is important to consider that the "I" of the personality is substantially egotistic and unable to avoid being self-centered, because it suffers from an incurable voracity.

The "I" of the spirit, on the other hand, is impersonal, that is, it is not tainted with any of the material appetites and interests that commonly afflict people. It is not affected by the passions. It is not committed to what pretends to be good nor is it against what appears to be bad; it observes everything from the profound serenity and peace of the celestial heights, and can therefore invariably act in accordance with transcendental values and ideal virtues, ever united to the supreme good.

If this vision might seem totally removed from man's crude reality, it is not my fault. We all have a spirit, that is, "we are spiritual beings in transit" who for the moment are housed in a material structure, but our ignorance and blindness lead us to ignore our being, enclosing us within the personality. The first step to perfection consists in acknowledging our own true spiritual identity, in order to rescue it from the clutches of those impediments that prevent it from manifesting itself accordingly. To this end, however, it has to be freed of environmental hypnosis in order to enter intensified states of awareness, the compulsory threshold that marks the beginning of the genuine path of spiritual perfection. Without this fundamental requisite, no real progress is possible.

To Confront One's Own Dishonesty

The only type of lack of honesty we perceive is that of others but never our own. We are expert masters in the art of self-deceit and maybe most of our behavior, beliefs, thoughts, and feelings are of a different or opposite nature to what we think they are. A feeling of compassion may be the mask of the vanity we experience from the position of superiority we adopt when we pity someone. Charity may be the distorted expression of a feeling of guilt; hate, of rejected love; envy, of the distortion of love and admiration we feel for someone; moral intolerance, of the perception of our own ethical failings.

We rarely use higher rationality to analyze our own acts or those situations in which we are involved. On the other hand, we resort to covering up our desires and purposes so as not to feel ashamed of them. We are experts at sugar-coating our actions so that our true motives, that we harbor inside, remain hidden from our fellows and our conscious thought.

This elaborate strategy enables us to act incorrectly, appropriating what does not belong to us, lying, cheating, swindling, or killing, while at the same time we keep inside the sensation that we have not, at any moment, strayed from the correct path. Many of us often lie to get what we want; we lust after our neighbor's wife; break the word we have given to others; live amid hypocrisy, pretense, and covert illegality; but we generally endeavor to shine forth like white doves, which requires continual, indefinite lying to maintain this image before other people and in front of ourselves.

We are terrified of acknowledging that there might be something evil, filthy, or twisted in our hearts, which often obliges us to feign a complacency, tolerance, friendship, or sympathy we do not really feel.

Hypocrisy dominates our existence, and we stubbornly deny our personal defects, assuming that we have none. We fear those who tell the truth because they disrupt the system and show us up. We sympathize, on the other hand, with lukewarm, sugary hypocrites who take no responsibility and commit themselves to nothing but always keep within an ambiguous undefined position in order to avoid criticism. We like to label ourselves as noble, good, generous, brave, and sensitive, and believe that we act consequentially.

We want a world adaptable to our own psychological makeup, and when we encounter realities that do not please us or that perturb us, we resort to elaborate mechanisms of self-defense to deny them, repress them, project them, or turn them into their opposite, all of which requires extraordinary, sophisticated mental juggling tricks in order to lie while at the same time remaining convinced of our own sincerity. Lying is reinforced by means of people's mental monologues, in which, in a sort of inner conversation, they talk about their own situation and the role they have to perform in the diverse events of everyday living, endlessly thinking with the aim of reinforcing their own image, inventing elaborate justifications for the failures and unseemly actions that compromise their self-esteem, rationalizing their whole existence in order not to confront internal or external reality.

These thought patterns probably begin in childhood, when the child breaks some valuable object and has to think up some explanation that will free him of responsibility before his parents and thus blame others for what has happened. If he succeeds and this situation is often repeated, he discovers an efficient tool to get away with things and avoid guilt. Maybe this is one of the ways in which a mechanism of dishonesty gradually forms in the individual. In addition to this, the child may also discover the lies his parents tell other people, rapidly figuring out that their aim is to derive some benefit from them. Thus, diverse, more or less serious forms of lying are born, to create a totally false story, distorting what really happened by concealing part of the truth or by blaming others for what has happened. Little lies at school that are apparently inoffensive, that perhaps concern how important one's parents are, or the adventures and activities one has supposedly shared with them, make some children gain popularity and admiration from their companions. All the mechanisms of deceit that achieve their aims gradually become permanent patterns of behavior, resulting in a dishonest lifestyle.

As there is no limit to dishonesty, an individual may, by making use of it, ascend the highest peaks of cultural, economic, or political power, nevertheless remaining totally convinced in his inner world of his own rectitude and honesty. These people are rarely discovered once they have attained sufficient social prestige, because, as they are idealized by the mass, they are kept protected and beyond any suspicion.

The word *dishonesty* tends to suggest situations of a delinquent nature, but I am using it basically in its first meaning to define a process of self-deceit through which covert aims of a manipulative kind are achieved by illicit means, without apparent bad intentions, since to the extent that the individual lies to himself, he spreads his deceit to the people around him.

In its second meaning, it refers to any unconscious falsifying of the truth of one's own acts, which enables the individual to safeguard his image and avoid blame when he makes mistakes or behaves wrongly or in an unethical way. In this case, by means of dishonest mental manipulations, he blames third parties for his failure and convinces himself of the truth of his allegations, or else denies that he has acted incorrectly.

There are other cases in which the individual repeatedly fails in some area of his life because he adulterates or unconsciously reduces the magnitude of the problems he has to face in order to succeed. He will thus slip into triumphalism, an exaggerated simplism, an overevaluation of his own capacities, or a blindness to or disqualification of the obstacles to be encountered in the situation he has to handle. For example, there are people, too anxious to be successful in the world of business, who will act imprudently, without counting on reliable information or sufficient capital, driven by the premature visualization of their expectations of success, spending money in advance from earnings that will be hard to obtain. Moreover, such people refuse to listen to those who, out of their greater experience, offer to advise them properly. They really do not wish to learn of anything that may block, perturb, or delay the fantasy of success and happiness they have shaped for themselves beforehand. This not only occurs in the professional, business, or lucrative fields but also with regard to relationships within a couple. It often usually happens that, in order to make a positive impression, people will dramatically falsify their own images when they want to seduce somebody, and this is the concrete reason for many failed marriages, for each day it becomes progressively harder and more laborious to continue projecting the adulterated image successfully. The individual's supposed qualities clash with stark reality and the moment of truth will inevitably come when the couple will have to accept the real worth and capacity of each.

There is also another type of self-deceit which Theodor Reik discusses in *Love Viewed by a Psychologist*,[31] and this is the projection of the idealized image, which, in the case of the woman, for example, means centering all her fantasies and expectations about love on what she thinks should be the ideal man, to project them onto a neutral individual whom she uses as a mere backdrop or hanger on which to hang her own idealized image. Once this process has been carried out, she will only have eyes for her own projection and will be blind to the individual's real qualities. With time, the situation will come to a crisis, for reality makes it hard to keep up the fantasy, and there will come a moment when she will inevitably recover the idealized image she had projected, with the consequent disillusionment this brings.

At bottom, dishonesty means *a malicious and biased adjustment in the way we structure the reality of the world by means of the arbitrary elaboration of adulterated mental maps in order to accommodate them to the fantasies, fears, and failings of the individual.*

In this way, innocent windmills can represent veritable monsters for them *(projection)*. On the contrary, a ferocious lion can be visualized as a meek lamb *(denial of danger)*.

It is the mental adulteration of reality that I call *dishonesty*, to express the fact that the individual does not adapt his conduct to objective reality, shirking the effort this entails, on the other hand rationalizing life and its events in accordance with a criterion of obstinate self-indulgence, ever seeking dishonest shortcuts or *unconscious mental arrangements* in order to achieve his objectives, which seldom are those that he himself believes. The root of dishonesty lies in the *substitution of objectives*, in changing the real one for other apparent ones.

This is explained by the fact that the great majority of unconscious pulsions are *immoral*, in the sense that if they flowed freely they would openly violate the chief ethical and moral principles, which is the reason why they are usually repressed. However, a part of them crosses the barriers of moral consciousness, disguised as honest purposes. This is why many good intentions are subterraneously eroded in an underhanded way, and the individual ends by "wanting without wanting," deceiving, swindling, or harming others, but in such an elaborate way that it is no simple task to prove it. Most likely the author of such machinations will continue to be indefinitely convinced of his own honesty. We shall be able to understand such manipulations better if we consider that the individual cannot bear *to appear evil to himself,* so that he must at all costs convince himself that his motivations are clean, however sordid they may really be, with the aim of keeping his own image clean and shining. The individual has to believe he is good even though he is an inveterate criminal, so he will arrange things, using all the artful accommodations of his inner reality, to justify his acts, either by denying them or by blaming others for them. The dishonest person is a trickster of life; a cheap, idle swindler who will ever seek the easiest path, but in the end will be the victim of his own manipulations. Unfortunately, the greater part of Mankind ends by becoming involved or ensnared in this game.

There are various ways to promote dishonest beliefs, such as: the myth of easy money, political utopias, the desire to make everybody equal, the belief that truth is in the majority, gambling, drugs, alcoholism, sexual perversion, violence and delinquency, pretending to be a victim or deliberately seeking to be one, feigning the struggle for life, and the distortion of love.

The invention of electronic devices to simulate virtual reality is in no way a novelty; the great majority of individuals who from remote antiquity have made up Mankind have invariably lived in the virtual reality of their own minds, detached from genuine existence. In this way, as some thinkers say, there is no Universe but a *Multiverse,* for each person has his own mental map of reality. This is not, as might be thought, a happy circumstance related to the diversity of opinions necessary for democracy, for example, but the sad proof of human blindness in which each, instead of contemplating the world with a profound gaze designed to learn its truth, limits himself to remaining in the sleepwalking state of the exclusive contemplation of his own mental delirium, projecting these pictures to paint the world, to then confuse the made-up with the real structure.

Generally, what we call *failure* merely refers to diverse forms of self-indulgence *(dishonest manipulation)*, in which the individual, instead of making an effort to attain the desired goal, simulates that he is almost within reach of it, so that he will not take any of the necessary steps to effectively fulfill his intentions. True effort, to be successful, should consist of equaling the magnitude of one's perseverance to the dimensions of the obstacle that has to be overcome. The *simulation of effort* is the dishonest attitude of pretending that one is struggling to win the battle, when really one is more concerned with keeping oneself away from its hardships, so that generally, failure will come in such situations, after which the artful manipulator will adopt the stance of victim, bitterly bewailing his misfortune.

Each comedian has his own style, and there is no limit to the creativity of the human comedy. The most pathetic thing about this case is that no one realizes that instead of *living in the real world, he is acting in a theatrical performance.*

There are millions of hypochondriacs who have somatized their own delirium, and no fewer who are dispossessed, solitary, abandoned, failed, embittered, and frustrated. Most of them share a dramatic fate: they have never managed to find the entry to the real world. Their bodies live on the material plane, while their minds are in virtual reality.

True morality is the supreme science of life, which, by enabling us to act honestly, confers on us the power to carry out our plans in Nature *(honesty is to act by always respecting Nature)* to make body and mind coincide in the same reality. When we achieve this goal, we are ready to attempt the next stage, which is coincidence in the same space-time of the body, the mind, the emotions, and the spirit. If that moment arrives, then the individual is truly spiritual and is already ascending along the path of evolution.

To Put Oneself Emotionally in the Place of Others

Empathy is a psychological expression that among other things *denotes the capacity to put oneself in the place of others and share their feelings*. This facilitates understanding of the emotional life of others, an essential requisite for a fruitful, happy interpersonal relationship. It is our own inner maturing that enables us to understand other people, which does not necessarily mean sharing their points of view or becoming accomplices to their mistakes or inconsistencies.

The recognition of people's right to make mistakes makes us more tolerant and disposed to fraternal solidarity. It enables us to understand, too, that this favorable disposition does not include taking over the mistakes of others, which would mean depriving people from confronting the consequences of their errors and violations of moral law, thus preventing them from receiving the corrective lesson from Nature, so that we would be thwarting their chances of evolution. One of the most important consequences of practicing empathy lies in the destruction of egotism, which causes one to be self-centered in reference to one's own "I."

The best recipe for overcoming narcissism and its consequences is to preoccupy oneself more with others, not necessarily through charity but through an integral respect for their human condition. Each demands that the rest understand him and take on his own emotional attitude, living in the belief that people are obliged to support him and accept him. However, at no instant does he see that the correct position is just the opposite one, and that it is the individual who must make an effort to understand others, even though he may keep a hope in his inner world that it will be reciprocal.

Generally, we are full of demands on the world and people, and very often feel frustrated or annoyed because others do not think or behave as we do. We always demand, without realizing it, that the world love and understand us, without admitting that this is something that has to be earned, by first inverting the order of things and by giving what we would like to receive.

Social sensitivity, however, is something far more complex than doing charitable works and helping people because we sympathize with them. *One has to know what kind of aid to give people, "whether we should give them fish or teach them to fish."*

If we are incomplete, we shall have to restrict ourselves to charity, in the knowledge that this will always be insufficient and rapidly perishable, so that our sphere of action will be very restricted. Nor do we ever know whether we have made the right choice, that is, if we have been magnanimous to people who really deserve it. This is of great importance, because if we help people who do not deserve it, we shall be doing them harm by preventing them from waging the battle corresponding to them and from developing their own strengths, so that our work will be lost like a drop of water in the desert.

When we empathize with someone, we put ourselves emotionally in their place, understand them, sympathize with them, or we justify their actions.

What happens to those who we know have not only acted wrongly, but who also are devoid of the slightest personal merit? Is it fair to indiscriminately help or to be in solidarity with both the guilty and the innocent? Of course not, for if we support a person guilty of immoral acts, this would be the same as covering up for a criminal: we would become his accomplices, and by doing so would be acting unfairly and putting society at risk, since we would be favoring or reinforcing an individual who habitually damages it.

Likewise, the only hope for moral salvation for the person who has behaved wrongly depends on him receiving fair punishment for it, which does not ensure his redemption, but at least gives him the fair chance he needs by placing him in situations equivalent to those he has caused his victims, which is the only way to appreciate the magnitude of one's own faults. After natural punishment, it depends on the individual's inner attitude to either take advantage of the lesson or not, for rebellious pride may lead him to an even greater moral disintegration. In any case, if we bear the sufferer's cross by being unconsciously driven by our own vanity, boasting that we are the Messiah, we shall be blocking Nature's corrective pedagogical process. In fact, life continually and covertly punishes those who break the harmonious laws of egalitarian equivalence by taking what does not correspond to them or by taking it in excess.

The wisest and most profound way to empathize with people is to first commit ourselves to our own spirit, our true being, by getting down to work to attain our inner development to thus obtain a double aim: individual evolution and the contribution to society of the complete individual we shall become, with the capacities this fulfillment brings with it.

The complete, fulfilled man can become the guide and shining light of the world, contributing to Mankind the spiritual food it so badly needs, *teaching people how to "fish," so that they feel the joy of being able to satisfy their own needs without having to beg for charity from anybody.*

This type of empathy is in all truth far more laborious and profound than giving money as alms, because it requires years of previous work on oneself. However, its fruits have a future projection of extraordinary, vital importance, because those who gather them will in turn become a source to propagate the spiritual message.

Those who fulfill themselves spiritually really are a moral reservoir of Mankind, even though they may be misunderstood or attacked by narrow-minded people who are unable to assess their value. One must bear in mind that it is licit to make common cause with people without necessarily being in agreement with their behavior or ideas. To understand a person does not mean to cling blindly to his thoughts, acts, and feelings, nor does it mean justifying his mistakes or faults, *but to understand the profound motives for his conduct.* In this way, it may quite well occur that if an individual complains that we do not understand him, the truth may be just the opposite: we understand him only too well; the unethical nature of his acts and the dishonesty on which they are based are revealed, so that we refrain from supporting or justifying him.

One of the fundamental causes of popular discontent and people's unhappiness lies in the fact that, due to international campaigns or messages of a diverse nature, probably from religious or political origin, people believe they have innate rights to possess all that is tangible and intangible that this world has to offer, and dissociate this belief from the concept of individual effort or merit. This is why, when they confront the harsh reality that in order to achieve what they want, they have to work hard, honestly, and perseveringly, they are often overwhelmed with distress and frustration. The lives of those thus affected often drift towards extremist political ideologies, antisocial behavior, rage, envy, and resentment—a bonfire that is regularly stoked by sources with a vested interest in keeping up social agitation. All living beings have to earn their right to exist, paying for it in some way, except parasites, who seem to belong to the dark side of the universal force.

People's right to possess certain things must necessarily be based on individual merit, and any system that excludes this obligation will be a perverse regime in which there is neither reward nor punishment.

The desire for solidarity should not make us commit the error of believing that injustice is being done to certain persons or groups, without first having carried out a profound analysis. Really, injustice only exists as regards man's actions, but not at the level of Nature, whose supreme law is the search for harmonious equilibrium.

The nearest thing to brotherly love is empathy, but one must consider that the true way to help a person with his problems is to teach him how to develop his own capacities, and not to practice indiscriminate charity, which is an affront to the dignity of those who could probably be perfectly capable of growing and developing themselves. It is every healthy person's duty who is in full possession of his mental faculties to discover and increase his higher capacities before setting his hopes on institutional, state, or divine charity.

Unfortunately, there are many who, having become accustomed to subsisting through someone's generosity, have no wish to make an effort to comply with the mandate of earning their bread with the sweat of their own brow. If the State really wished to help the needy, it would have to create schools in which children would be taught to discover their own latent faculties. Classes in which, instead of merely stuffing the brain with theoretical information, means would be implemented so that each could grow for himself, thus becoming self-taught as to the capacities of his own spirit and consciousness.

We should never forget that the chief source of our misfortunes comes from the fact that we act like mentally castrated beings, for culturally, the concept of "higher consciousness" has been eliminated or ignored. It is an even more valuable faculty than intelligence, however, since it is what gives sense and meaning to it. Thus, we only use the least important portion of our instrument of knowledge: the gathering and filing of data, so that our limitations come from this precise circumstance. Intelligent men, deprived of intensified vigilic consciousness, lack the inner judgment or higher discrimination needed to give profound meaning to information, and this is Mankind's "normal" condition. Those who, having become disillusioned with life and pessimistically complain that "it has no purpose or meaning," are not wrong, although they ignore that this only means their own lives, due to the inadequate mental disposition in which they place themselves. They are right to complain of injustice and discrimination, for they cannot in their own minds perceive the hidden or unnoticed forms in which life acts to mete out justice by either rewarding or punishing.

We can only discover the meaning of existence in the interior of our minds, which unfortunately have been trained only to accumulate information and not meaning, for this is exclusive to higher vigilic consciousness, which is not an innate faculty.

Empathizing with people should be based on the conviction that, generally, "people are good," that is, their wrong behavior is the result of ignorance, anguish, or alienation caused by external messages of dubious moral intention. However, we should not close our eyes to the evidence that there is an important sector of human beings who do not deserve to be considered as such, on account of the corruption that weighs upon them and the intrinsic perversity of their acts. Against everything that preachers of equality say, I believe it would be more judicious for society if people did not have the same rights and, in some way, those held by individuals who are closer to the animal than to man were limited, of course, leaving a chance open for them to be socially redeemed, in accordance with the merits observed in each. Otherwise, we should never be able to establish a relationship of cause and effect between "rights and prerogatives" and "obligations and duties," and people would not understand why they should act morally, for one and another (the moral and the immoral) would be rewarded with similar attributions and rights. In any case, beyond these remarks, it is our moral duty to try our utmost to understand and tolerate our fellows, which in no way entails the obligation to approve or justify their acts. For the rest, if we act in this way, we shall not only contribute to making the world a better place, but shall also sow our own success and happiness.

To Have Dominion Over Oneself

If we really want to act in accordance with higher ethical principles, we have to be the owners of ourselves and be able to withstand the negative impulses and emotions that tempt us to behave in morally inadequate ways. The person who is at the mercy of his passions cannot be virtuous, for virtue invariably demands a profound self-control so that the will can withstand the myriad temptations of everyday existence.

Good and evil have become diluted to the point that they have become totally ambiguous and adaptable concepts, which makes it harder to commit oneself to good, for the pleasurable and pleasant would always seem to be positive, and displeasure, negative.

Attaining proper self-control should not be a whimsical choice for modern man, but a fundamental imperative for him to behave in a more refined way. It is supposed that civilized conduct should preclude any type of barbarism or violence, yet instead of diminishing, it tends to increase day by day. Each real or imaginary offense received is usually paid back with greater affront, which often leads to conduct that runs counter to the concept of Mankind's progress.

Really, we behave like *civilized barbarians,* and this contradictory mixture is what prevents people from understanding one another, for each is moved by the sway of his passions and not by his higher rationality. Unlike animals, what characterizes man is that he can control or repress his instinctive impulses. Unfortunately, there is not a lot of educational information with regard to this subject, and the scant amount that exists is usually criticized or hidden by those who are committed to the dark side of the universal force.

I have often wondered whether it would not be preferable for schoolrooms to shape "moral citizens" instead of learned persons, giving greater importance to self-knowledge and the discovery of one's own potential than to the study of physics, mathematics, chemistry, or history.

Our culture is really an anti-culture, in the sense that it limits, ignores, or represses the development of the truly human capacities, privileging those that imitate computers or machines, such as speed in informational associations, mechanical behavior, swift, automatic reactions, the indefinite repetition of the same activity—all of which serve to create patterns of non-evolutive behavior. Really, man's concept of education resembles more and more a computer process than the higher perceptiveness required by a conscious, sensitive being. We are culturally programmed in our classrooms, but are never taught mental hygiene, control of negative emotions, dominion over ourselves, and the development of character and will. An automated system treats us like machines that accumulate information, the object of which, beyond any idealization, is to turn the individual into an obedient consumer of material and intangible goods.

The mandates implanted in our brain prevent us from behaving freely and spontaneously, for we are always dominated by powerful forces, such as submission to state authority, ideological bondage, and absorption and fusion into the will of the masses.

They condition our minds to make us simple appendices of the social psyche, stratifying and petrifying our personality to the point of preventing any spontaneity, turning us into biological machines with automatized behavior. In order to elude this evidence, we argue that our feelings prove we are sensitive, and are proud of this condition. However, we refuse to acknowledge that our emotions are absolutely stereotyped and repetitive and that they are invariably activated by the same detonators, which can be classified and typified to the point of making it hard, if not impossible, to encounter free, spontaneous emotions. We boast, perhaps, of being compassionate, sensitive, friendly, generous, understanding, and sincere, and do not realize that if this were really so, it would probably be to our regret for we would have been programmed to such an extent, and our conduct would not be the result of exercising our will and free choice but merely of previous conditioning.

Sociable, friendly, joyful, and talkative people, such as those who are the life and soul of any party, are usually classified as "spontaneous" on account of the ease and speed with which they express themselves. However, genuine spontaneity is not that which is born of ease and speed in automatized behavior, but of conscious, deliberate behavior which tends to be slower or measured.

What has been formed by neuronal associations, which always react automatically to the same stimuli because it is the fruit of cerebral programming, is not at all spontaneous, although it gives rise to swift reactions and responses. Extreme intellectual agility does not reflect spontaneity but, on the contrary, is the result of an overwhelming programming that is manifested with similar speed to that displayed by the processor of a computer.

The only thing that is spontaneous is that which has its origins in non-automatized behavior, that is, through cerebral processes of higher awareness which, by surpassing the limits of the program, can lead to *conscious behavior* that always springs from the individual's free deliberation.

What is commonly termed *spontaneous*, is the fruit of an automatic impulse and not a momentary creation, whereas the truly spontaneous is something born from an area in the individual, that in some way is beyond what can be programmed; this is only possible through the aid of the vigilic will power (will power exercised in a state of higher awareness). The spontaneous invariably emanates from a higher volition, but this faculty is neither innate nor easily acquired, but is the fruit of a process of long, gradual inner work. What really makes us human is our capacity to behave spontaneously, that is, beyond the limits of cultural and environmental conditioning. This concept might sound ominous and be interpreted as *something savage and not based at all on discipline or control*, whereas it is precisely the opposite. *"Beyond culture"* means *"in a form higher than it,"* that is, in a manner that is qualitatively and intrinsically more elevated.

Yet, what could be more important and valuable than culture? Simply, spirituality. I do not mean the religious concept or that which is synonymous with charity, goodness, generosity, sensitivity, or brotherly love, but the primitive meaning given to it by the Greeks, Egyptians, and ancient Chinese philosophy, as an evolutive science that enables man to increase his inner Humanity to proportionally reduce his animal part, that is, to *humanize the species.* At a certain point, this knowledge was intentionally obscured and then lost, resulting in a general ignorance of it. What is known now is mainly a bad, capricious imitation of previous, successive falsifications.

Original wisdom consisted of diverse disciplines designed to overcome oneself and to take charge of handling one's own consciousness, with the aim of returning to the original source from which we have emanated: the Great Spirit, or God (the origin of our divine spark). That return was achieved when the full coincidence of the spirit and the spatial and temporal reality of the mind and physical body was able to be attained.

The belief in the need to master oneself comes from the conviction that we are not really the true masters of our own acts. In fact, our brain belongs to the mass media; our heart, to the emotions which are automatically activated by the previously mentioned causes; our sex, to the self-preservation impulse of the species; and our body in general to the State, for we cannot dispose of it freely.

Really, we are dominated by our own passions, which prevent us from making the free choices we believe we have. In its true sense, this does not mean doing what the personality wants, which is the mere prolongation of the social psyche, but what our authentic "I," our spirit, which is the being, wants.

If we are slapped across the cheek, the personality obliges us to respond with greater aggression, but the spirit, should we consider it the right thing to do, would permit us to *turn the other cheek.* Note that I say "should we consider it the right thing to do," since this act must come from the higher rationality of inner judgment as an act of will, and not as an automatism, for then *we would always turn the other cheek,* and this would be as wrong as never turning it. Any kind of higher behavior, both with ourselves and with others, implies keeping a discipline by which one can in fact control one's instinctive impulses.

A demonstration of skill in self-control should be one of the chief requisites demanded of a person if he is to be considered civilized, for otherwise he would always be prone to giving in to the impulse of his inferior appetites.

The person who does not control himself is just as dangerous as the one who carries a weapon without being qualified to do so. By self-control, I do not mean merely the ability to behave in a socially acceptable way, nor do I mean repression, but mainly the capacity to dominate oneself when one is under internal or external stress, a fundamental requisite for adequate social coexistence. He who has this power cannot only turn the other cheek if he feels that it is the right thing to do, but can also keep himself free of vices and detached from the passions that commonly afflict people.

Man's higher behavior comes from the voluntary, conscious control of his acts, impulses, thoughts, and feelings. As is only logical, this discipline must be based on higher values and be at the service of them, being governed by the most elevated ethical norms. He who responds to an aggression with a greater one gives in to an instinctive impulse, whereas to turn the other cheek, one needs a previous process of self-control and serious, profound reflection, giving rise to an inner adjustment by which one can perform an act that is alien to the common program of the human being.

To keep within the limits of the normal conditioning society enforces on man entails no great effort, whereas to carry out a *conscious act*, in the higher sense of this expression, demands a higher character and will that will enable one to overcome the inertia of habitual behavior.

This is the reason why moral indoctrination, however valuable it might be, has minimal transcendence on people's daily behavior, since despite people's good intention, they very often end by behaving immorally or sinfully because they do not have the necessary force to withstand temptation, as moral vigor does not come from intellectual consideration but from an individual will power that has been patiently forged by the turmoil of the myriad battles of life.

The individual's ethical and moral level is founded on a strong character and a developed will power that allow him to control himself. Unfortunately, in classrooms, one is not taught the arts of life but merely general culture and the knowledge one needs to earn a living. We are not taught how to develop our will power, control our thoughts, or sublimate our negative impulses and emotions. It would seem that everything that could promote the development of the latent inner capacities had to have been carefully eliminated by the hand of some mysterious censor. Or perhaps, cognitive desolation is so widespread that no one can perceive the importance of inner growth, so that everyone devotes their efforts to the cultivation of the body and the image, which, as they are confused with the being, are magnified in order to increase the sensation of being alive.

Imagine how terrible the world would be in which school-children and students continually lived in a state of hypnosis, and were not warned of the state that afflicts them because their teachers, wise men, authorities, and other people in power were in the same conditions as themselves; a world in which the great majority was cut off from its higher rationality, thus being prevented from behaving in a truly elevated way.

Is our world in this state at this moment? There is nothing to show that reality is any different. The comforts of modern life have brought about an enfeebling of will power and paralysis of the character. The great majority seek the easiest way to avoid sustained effort, ever pursuing easy gain, or to join majorities so as not to take responsibilities, blindly adhering to any belief in order not to be obliged to think, letting oneself be swept along by inertia, vulgarity, and conformism.

The dominion of oneself is not only the key to becoming virtuous, but is also the key to success in any of its forms, since it is usually the result of a long process of organized effort and not a matter of good luck. It is what enables one to persist when most no longer wish to carry on, when the will power flags or when one is overcome by discouragement or frustration. It is the force by which we can become virtuous and keep ourselves clean and transparent.

It is also that which gives us the necessary inner generosity to forgive our enemies and be tolerant with those who wound us. It is anything that makes us postpone a violent or inadequate impulse, so that we take the necessary time to reflect and reach a mature, conscious decision.

It is like being able to count to a hundred, or to ten thousand if necessary, before doing what we viscerally, instinctively, or emotionally desire, taking time for tolerance, love, and inner harmony to come between us and any foolish act.

To Come Out of One's Own Mental Burrow

The mental burrow is a narrow conceptual grid in which we position ourselves to structure the world and which, as happens with animals, becomes a refuge from anything that seems a threat, at the same time as it becomes a rationalizing tool to justify failure.

It is as if life were a huge math notebook in which each little square represented a module of reality, that is, a tiny part of total reality.

The narrowness of the limits of this minute portion enables us to take refuge in a mental space that is familiar, makes us feel at ease, and offers us a tranquilizing sensation of being safe, with everything under control. As a result, we disregard any reality, however rich it may be, that does not correspond to our scant conceptual map. This "grid-like" lifestyle affects the great majority of Mankind, for the reduced nature of the mental space each occupies gives an artificial sensation of power and tranquility, although at the same time it engenders fear of surpassing its limits.

The conceptual territory we occupy is so small that it gives us a feeling of increased personal importance, for we perceive that our "I" takes up most of the psychological space around us, the grid, which we wrongly confuse with the entire world.

Fear of the unknown makes us cling to our tiny dominions, within which we think we are experiencing life, but do no more than move within our own mental map that has been created in accordance with the conflicts, desires, and fears that afflict us and not on the strength of genuine reality.

It is as if each individual re-created the world to his own dimensions within the confines of his own thought, in order to take control of the forces that compose it, even if only in the imagination.

These maneuvers cause a sort of cognitive and emotional myopia that reduces and limits our chances of success, prosperity, and happiness, at the same time as it restricts and deteriorates the individual's conceptual capacity, for he usually confuses his internal reality with the external. In this way, he will demand a treatment from people in accordance with the magnitude of how important he thinks he is, dazzled by the apparent extension of his "I," an illusion derived from the tiny mental space that constrains and limits it, which by contrast causes a deceptive sensation of the greatness of one's own identity. It thus happens that each individual lives in a veritable virtual reality, depriving themselves of knowing life as it really is, and refusing to comply with the pedagogical purpose that life has for people, which is thwarted in this case by narrow-mindedness.

The aim of life is to grow and evolve individually, which is the most profound form of transcendental ethics. To elude this obligation implies an attack on the evolutive order of Nature. It is as if a university student decided to limit his efforts to the study of botany and closed off his thoughts to any other subject, only in this case it is the university of "real life," and the price we pay for failure is the restriction of our quality of life and the loss of the option for evolution. To open our mind to broader, more-profound realities is an ethical and spiritual obligation, for if we do not do so we thwart our own evolution, frustrating the immense human potential we bear within ourselves, thus depriving society of the significant contribution it would mean for us to share this wealth with others.

The world is full of mentally handicapped individuals who could be giants if only they dared to come out of the mental burrow in which they seek shelter.

People ignore the true capacities of the human mind and consciousness, so that they are unable to assess the magnitude of their limitations, which probably allows them a passive conformity with their own lifestyle.

I accept the proposition that man should be free to be mediocre if that is what he wants, and this mediocrity should be respected, but human sympathy bears no relation to the workings of Nature, which pitilessly punishes those beings who refuse to keep in step with the changes of life.

Anything that does not evolve becomes petrified or destroyed. However, one must be careful not to confuse *evolution* with *modernity*, for this latter is only too often a sophisticated form of barbarism.

True moral rules are not arbitrary or capricious commandments, nor are they mere prohibitions or recommendations, but the conscious, harmonious adaptation of man to Nature, which contains and conditions him. We are conscious of only the most rudimentary, coarsest, or roughest of its forces, such as rain, cyclones, volcanic activity, photosynthesis, and the laws of present-day physics. On the other hand, we know very little about the forces of Nature that are hard to detect because of their subtlety, but which function even if we do not believe in them. The possibilities of human magnetism, electric fields as a basis for life, experience in states of higher awareness, the feedback of cause and effect between man and Nature, the existence of energy faster than light, the creation of an intermediate substance between matter and energy are all more-profound realities that science will one day accept, and perhaps the moment will come when ethics and morality are what they really should be—the science of living wisely.

However, to this end, man has to take the first step: he has to abandon the narrow paradigmatic egg in which he hides, to come out of it and experience life beyond his own superstitious beliefs. The world is divided between the dogmatic and the skeptical. In the theory of knowledge, dogmatism is in the first place understood as the position of naive realism that admits not only the possibility to know things in their real essence, but also to know the effectiveness of this knowledge in daily life.

Skepticism as a philosophical doctrine of knowledge in its theoretical aspect sustains that there is no stable knowledge, nor can there be any absolutely sure opinion. Comte states:

> Dogmatism is the normal state of human intelligence, which tends towards it, on account of its nature, continually and in all ways, even when the intelligence seems to be furthest removed from that dogmatism. This is because skepticism is no more than a state of crisis, the inevitable result of the intellectual *inter regnum* that necessarily arises whenever the human spirit is called to change its doctrines, and at the same time, the indispensable means used, either by the individual or by the species, to enable a transition from one form of dogmatism to another, which is the only fundamental use of doubt.

In his everyday life, man is alienated by dogmatic beliefs of all kinds, and the expression "dogmatism" is normally used pejoratively. Skepticism has also led to *cynicism, materialism, atheism,* or *total impudence or incredulity.*

Some blindly trust their own beliefs, and others do not believe in anything. In order to understand the problem of knowledge, one has to accept that, if it is to be truly stable and secure, it must emanate from cognitive perception carried out in states of higher consciousness, which include heightened awareness and meaningful experience, in the sense of transcending mere information to reach through to the quintessence of knowledge.

The vulgar type of learning that is carried out in a state of "half-sleep" (the common condition of human consciousness) is what gives rise to unreliable and untrustworthy information, for it occurs without a prior training of the instrument of understanding, a knowledge which originated in the remote past and which is now lost.

Personally, I like and consider accurate the following definition of *dogmatism:* "a doctrine that considers knowledge as the spirit taking possession of reality as it is."

This is an intuitive and profound description, because it neatly expresses the operational means man should observe in order to apprehend reality—*taking possession of it by means of the spirit.* Let us consider the spirit as the divine spark or man's immortal being, as the true "I" or what we really are, of which the physical body is no more than a passing carnal dwelling place.

When, through the right kind of work, the individual makes the physical body, mind, emotions, and the spirit coincide in the same space-time, he attains the summit of the current possibilities of evolution of his *consciousness* and is then able to contemplate reality as it is and thus gain access to total truth, which at this level is just one truth. Then, overwhelmed by the majesty of the Universe, the aspirant to perfection, in order not to be blinded, must take refuge in modesty and insignificance, by acting as if the magnitude of his ignorance continually grew. It is at this moment that universal morality will have fulfilled its transcendental purpose, which is to harmonize the individual with the music of the spheres so that by being tuned in to the divine metronome, he may consciously integrate with the sublime plan of cosmic life.

No one is obliged to proceed in this way. To live with one's head in the sand or squeezed into one square inch is quite valid and that decision can be respected, but it is very important for one to know that one has other options for development.

Developing Will and Tempering the Character

Common people generally remain at the mercy of life and pray for winds that will favor their own plans in expectation of a stroke of luck, or they entrust themselves to their favorite saint. They invariably set their expectations on favorable external circumstances that may help them satisfy their needs.

There are many who implicitly admit that they are incapable of carrying out acts that require the necessary will power to make painful efforts.

Generally, we are beings with a softened, fragmented, or deficient will power, this being the reason why we continually seek an easy solution or the quickest, easiest way out. We are forever imagining ways to find shortcuts to achieve what we want, for we are intimidated by hard, patient work. We do not have the strength to rid ourselves of what we do not want to have, nor to achieve what we need, so that we are eternal seekers of solutions from the outside world that seduce our fantasy or naïveté.

There are, for instance, many obese people who are not able to control their appetite; smokers who heedlessly poison themselves; vicious people of various kinds who are enslaved to their unbridled passions; mediocre people who languish in dreams of a better tomorrow; shy, apathetic, idle people who cannot succeed in life; those who are puppets to their own passions; in summary, all those who lack the will power to achieve what they propose.

One must understand that on the one hand, immorality is a cultural problem, and on the other, an underdevelopment of will power. In fact, one cannot behave in a truly civilized and ethical way if one lacks the necessary will power to control one's baser appetites and instinctive pulsions that continually emerge from the unconscious.

The apathetic, among whom I include most of Mankind, which I will justify later, cannot postpone their present impulses to choose a future benefit of greater worth. The capacity to substitute the imminent impulse for a far-off reward undoubtedly requires will power.

Current culture, unfortunately, promotes rapid and easy gain, so that, seduced by these sirens' songs, people catch the moral disease of desiring narcissistically, supposing that to have what the consumer market has to offer in tangible and intangible goods is far easier to obtain than what happens in reality, so that with the passing of time they become full of envy and frustration. Their babyish part, which remains introjected in them, leads them in some way to expect their desires to be granted in a similar way to what would happen if they were still in the womb, that is, easy and immediate gratification.

All this is because the expression *will power* does not exist in their mental dictionaries, since they blame everything on luck or on a certain type of supposed, obscure, congenital personal merit.

There are those who think they have great will power because they carry out great physical activity or work long days, but the fact is that anything that is done out of an obligation to comply with one's duty, to fill an empty stomach, to satisfy personal ambition, a desire for revenge, or to appease narcissism, does not emanate from will power but from an attempt for corporeal and psychological survival.

It is will power that has to act when we want to achieve something that requires going against our instinctive appetites or impulses, or on those occasions when we set out to do something that is dispensable and does not relate to any imperious vital need, for example, the case of an individual who can survive perfectly well with his current salary but aspires to earn double, or of a mediocre citizen who tries to become an important person, but who would have no serious problem in remaining as he is at present.

The instinctive appetite that drives us to move mountains to satisfy a desire for revenge, for example, is not will power. Will power is the conscious, non-compulsive pushing of the "I," that can enable man to act virtuously, endowing him with the strength to withstand temptation and sin, overcoming the adverse circumstances of life.

Character is the set of inherited or acquired qualities which condition each individual's behavior. Qualities are each one of the circumstances or characteristics, either natural or acquired, that differentiate people or things.

What most abounds in our species are people of a passive character who *passively allow environmental circumstances to stamp on them the fashionable attributes of the moment, thus modeling a false, artificial "I" which displaces the one that belongs to the individual himself.*

These people are extremely weak, for most of their psychic content is alien to the genuine "I," making up a replacement identity, a sort of graft or patch, which has the interests and motivations typical of the circumstances that cause it, and not those which legitimately correspond to the person thus affected. From this point of view, the human being's level of alienation is incommensurable, and the motivations that move him are usually quite alien to his inner desires, so that he will drift to diametrically opposed or noticeably different goals.

In the depths of most people's being, there lies a frustrated, sad creature that senses that the plot of his own life has been arbitrarily imposed on him, forcibly and without consulting him, so that in the depths of his soul there beats a desperate impulse for liberation.

It is habitual for people to act *despite themselves, against what they really desire,* and generate an inner contradiction that holds back, retards, or weakens the projects they had planned to carry out.

The weak-natured man is far removed from a fully shaped person and perhaps will never become one, much less behave in a morally acceptable way. The fact is that to become a mature, optimally shaped person requires a state of higher awareness as a prior requisite that will enable one to stop interacting mechanically with the environment. *This means to avoid being abandoned by one's psychological "I,"* as occurs in hypnosis, a process by which the hypnotist takes away the individual's "I." The same occurs in environmental hypnosis when the individual *loses his notion of identity to mentally fuse with whatever catches his attention.* The "I" invariably follows one's attention, and wherever the latter goes, the former will follow. Really, man's daily experience is carried out in a continual state of identification and only very occasionally will he, for a brief instant, contemplate the splendor of his own essential selfhood, even though he might not be aware of what has happened. This is one of the great obstacles to the development of consciousness and character, for the individual fuses with external messages and stimuli, temporarily becoming part of them. This is the reason why his critical and discerning functions are annulled, and he passively accepts the messages with sufficient suggestive power, which happens, for instance, with those that come from sources of very high authority or social or academic prestige. In this way, *instead of creating the experiences he undergoes, he is passively shaped by them, becoming a mere appendix of their conditioning force.* The most dramatic consequence of this is his incapacity to behave in a truly conscious way, that is, in a state of higher awareness that enables him to freely and independently vary, choose, or create the most suitable patterns of behavior, whereas he has to content himself with being a passive executor of the mandates of existential circumstance.

Obviously, this mechanism prevents one from developing the higher qualities of character, which first means freeing the "I" from subjugating environmental influences, a discipline that is by no means easy to execute. The character necessarily has to be forged in the school of life, for one has to continually confront one's hardships and obstacles until they no longer upset one or make one lose one's inner balance, but on the contrary, they may become the most powerful nutrient of the strength of one's will power.

Diverse problems may be a source of either vigor or weakness, depending on how we process such experiences. When we learn to keep calm amidst a storm, to respect everyone's rights, to remain serene through both success and adversity alike, to not let ourselves be impressed by appearances, to avoid self-pity and self-indulgence; to be flexible like the willow in the storm, when we are able to remain firm and stable in the most varied, difficult situations by keeping our inner virtue and transparency intact—it is because we are being successful in the shaping of an optimized character, and are therefore in the best position to behave in accordance with the highest moral patterns.

Those who elude the challenges of life, or pass through them lukewarm or passively, are doomed to have a weak, rickety character, and a will power that is atomized in the face of multiple external demands.

Will power is very often confused with the power of the passions, in the belief that an individual possessed by ambition, covetousness, or hate, and who displays a power that terrorizes or overwhelms the masses, has achieved this through his will power. However, what is certain is that all those who obey the dominion of their baser impulses and passions do so despite their will, since we can only conceive of will in its true meaning as a power that is at the service of the spirit and of good, and never as a destructive force.

He who attempts to develop his will power with the aim of subjugating his fellowmen, violating their rights, or snatching their belongings from them, will be cheating himself and sowing the seeds of his own destruction, for whatever he takes "by will" really corresponds to the intensification of his basest animal impulses, so that his behavior will gradually drift towards a subhuman condition.

There are many people who seem to have a "very strong character" and who usually find it easy to get on in life, but who are really motivated by the rapacity of their animal instinct and are totally lacking in ethics and moral norms.

This phenomenon contrasts with the case of shy, apathetic individuals who are nevertheless peaceful and honest and who usually behave correctly, but lack the force to do important things in life.

This is why we paradoxically encounter "bad" fellows (in the moral sense) who have strength, and "good" ones who lack it. This contradiction can be seen even in the cinema and in literature when the villains seem to have unlimited cunning with which to easily deceive their just but foolish victims, who are usually weak and indecisive. This helps us to understand the true nature of will, as opposed to animal passion. This latter is merely the expression of man's animal instincts, which requires no effort at all from the protagonist.

Will power, in its highest meaning, corresponds to a power that has been consciously and voluntarily developed with the primordial aim of overcoming oneself (the self of the baser nature) to behave virtuously and resist immoral temptations.

When an individual manages *to possess himself or master his own person,* he has to muster all his energies and yoke them to the mandate of his "higher I" (the "essential I," as opposed to the "social I"), which frees him from the passions and makes him master of the capacity to oppose the forces of disintegration and chaos. Before, he only knew *to desire,* but now he has learned *to want,* so that he is in a position to fulfill all that he sets out to do in life, if, that is, he has the necessary previous merit for it, which includes, not only the personal capacities he may have attained, but also his level of impeccability in the effort he has made.

The traditional but discredited saying, "where there is a will, there is a way" becomes a reality when, after one has understood the difference between desiring and wanting, one forges ahead and keeps to a specific purpose with the power of true will. This latter is not born of mere desire or intent, but of patient, sustained sacrifice and effort, so that it is not suitable for the inert who are not willing to sacrifice their everyday ease and have to content themselves with the crumbs life throws at them. It is not for those who are weak out of their own choice, having chosen this approach to feel protected or sheltered by society. It is for those who, having tired of testing out diverse formulae for success, have become disillusioned with the unreal fantasies offered by the consumer mentality (obtaining something fast and easily), and are ready to try out the path of sacrifice and asceticism, which at times entails *blood, sweat, and tears,* an insignificant price to pay in view of the sheer number of goals it is possible to achieve.

There is a great deal of confusion as to what is ascetic, because it is invariably identified with strict religious disciplines that imply a renunciation to all earthly things and carnal pleasures. The fact is that such practices in their true meaning seek to act as an aid to yoke the bodily appetites under the control of the "I" and the spirit, so that the spirit can manifest itself in the corporeal reality of the present moment, participating in healthy pleasure and discarding the impure.

The possession of material goods, like the experiencing of different pleasures, is an inappropriate act when it subjugates and alienates the "I," but is not a danger when it is at the service of the spirit and when such pleasures are pure and healthy.

Only he who has tempered his will in a higher, profound way can choose freely and voluntarily to deprive himself of apparent or lesser good in order to choose the supreme good: the uninterrupted happiness of a stable, peaceful inner world. Heaven does exist. It is our inner world once it has been worked upon, sublimated, and quintessentialized. It is where God is represented by the divine spark we all possess, but we have to enter this heaven while we are still alive and not after we have died. This is the supreme reward of the transcendental morality of Nature, for when we enter this inner heaven "everything will be given to us as a matter of course."

LIVING IN HARMONY WITH NATURE

Nature is the intelligent cosmic-whole in which we live and are inserted, and if we intend to lead a full, prosperous life, we have to respect its laws. This is morality in its most profound sense. The following are some of its mandates:

- Do not hate.

- Do not be resentful or envious.

- Do not try to get what you do not deserve.

- Do not take on a sex that Nature has not given you.

- Do not deceive thy fellow man nor thyself.

- Do not delight yourself erotically with your own person.

- Do not insult or defame your fellow man.

- Consciously respect every form of life.

- Respect the rights of all human beings, whatever their class, ideology, race, or color.

- Love your own spirit as an emanation of God upon Earth.

- Respect and help the elderly.

- Practice the highest transcendental virtues.

- Love your homeland and have the most profound respect for all countries in the world.

- Repudiate all manner of perversions.

- Condemn all forms of unnecessary cruelty.

- Fight to defend human dignity.

- Condemn all forms of exploitation.

- Strive to the utmost to evolve spiritually.

- Have an impersonal ideal to the benefit of Mankind.

- Shun hypocrisy.

- Do not do unto others as you would not have them do unto you.

- Close your ears to morbid gossip, scandal, calumny, and cursing.

- Take care of and respect your body because it is the dwelling place of the spirit.

- Be active, swift, and diligent in the fulfillment of your duties.

- Sow only what you want to reap; he who sows winds reaps tempests.

- Respect Nature in all her manifestations.

- Purify your speech and never pronounce anything you may later regret.

- Refrain from hurting anyone through your words.

- Raise your own level of awareness.

- Commit yourself to good and swear loyalty to your own spirit.

- Always defend truth and justice.

- Practice solidarity with those who are unjustly oppressed.

- Always keep your word of honor.

- Repudiate pornography and any type of morbidity.

- Keep yourself from the envy and resentment of the embittered.

- Harmonize with all people and do not create emotional quarrels with anyone.

- Make an effort to remain imperturbable in the face of insult, injury, and calumny.

- Free yourself from your negative feelings and thoughts.

- Practice love for yourself, for others, and for all forms of life, but do so with reflection and not mechanically or indiscriminately.

- Accumulate merit in your life and you will be rewarded.

- Never commit unjust or dishonest acts because Nature returns the equivalent of everything that penetrates through to her.

- Do not be proud or vain because you will blind yourself; try to be insignificant but conscious of your powers and capacities.

- Give thanks daily to the Creator for what you are and have.

- Do not be intimidated by the apparently evil or cling to the apparently good.

- Be joyful, optimistic, and positive; laugh very often.

- Use sex without allowing sex to use you.

- Do not waste time trying to foresee the future, for you are able to write your own future.

- Flee from self-indulgence and self-pity.

- Do not worry about the defects of others, just take care of your own.

- Fight to create and maintain the higher union of the family, but take care to maintain your own identity.

- Try to lead an austere, sober, and orderly life.

- Master yourself so that you may keep peace in your inner world.

- Avoid depression and sadness because they are a source of self-pity and negativism.

- Do not complain; you have what you deserve to have. If you want more, then deserve more.

- Take responsibility for your own life and all your actions.

- Confront problems and do not run away from them.

- Love the truth and reality as you love yourself; do not lie to yourself.

- Be just and impartial.

- Flee from drug addiction because it is the devil's bait.

- Respect the law and be a model citizen.

- Do not be blinded by apparent good.

- Be careful when you ask for divine justice, for what you think you deserve may be taken from you in a greater proportion than has been taken up until now.

- Respect and you will be respected; love and you will be loved; steal and you will be robbed; lie and you will be deceived.

- Respect universal law and you will be rewarded.

Do these seem like too many rules? In reality, they are not too many and many are missing, but these will be discovered after practicing those given here. One must consider the magnitude of the reward one can attain by respecting and correctly using the morality of cosmic nature, which leads to the supreme good and uninterrupted happiness.

The above list is not a mere set of recommendations; *it is a compilation of certain types of feedback of little-known, subtle energies between man and Nature.*

These forces, albeit ethereal, are quite material and physical, and are not strange energies that can be attributed to supernatural phenomena. *I refer simply to the pulses of photonic irradiation generated by people's actions, thoughts, and feelings, which leave their physical bodies to immerse themselves in the Universe at a speed at least equivalent to that of light.*

The physical mechanism of morality refers to the essentially feminine condition of Nature, which, like a cosmic womb, conceives the pulses of photons that emanate from people and that bear the vibratory information of their particular passions, in order to give back to them the equivalent of what came out of them. The human being is immersed in a holographic Universe in which each particle contains the memory of all, and man's body is the microcosm in which diverse universal phenomena are reproduced.

Each individual is connected by invisible threads to the totality of the Universe, and what he deposits vibratorily into the creation is returned to him, increased.

Morality is no more than the relation of cause and effect of the eternal vibratory and energetic process between the individual and the Cosmos, in which, irredeemably and inevitably, "the one who does is the one who pays."

Nature does not forgive in the sense of settling an account out of goodness or pity, because if it did so, it would destroy itself by going against its own rules. Anyone who acts in a criminal, immoral way, or contrary to the universal ethics of Nature, will fatefully receive his just deserts, that is, he will punish himself by the fact of having violated the law of universal harmony.

We are seldom aware of this, because we do not relate the events that take place in the present of our lives to moral behavior observed in the past, and believe that the diverse personal events merely obey fate or pure chance. *The fact is that we reap what we sow, and if we want a better life, we have to sow superior seeds.*

Those who try to mock or disqualify such laws when they hear of them will not be able to avoid continually receiving the fruit of the pulses of their habitual photons. One must understand that as this is a matter of Nature, there is no repentance or good intention that can be used to this end, but only one's good or bad actions will be counted.

What makes it difficult for us to perceive this type of natural justice is the fact that badly behaved people at times seem to be quite successful, but one must accept that it is not possible to slip into mere simplistic views when a specific cause and its possible effects in an individual's life are analyzed, for in order to predict the future one would have to handle a large number of causes, as they are interrelated and influence each other.

A man who has done wrong will never be forgiven by Nature, but will be able to do something to soften or diminish the effects of his wrong actions, by devoting himself to charity and good, helping his fellows anonymously. It is something like an individual who sowed bramber berry, this being a plant that smothers and kills off other plants, and when he realizes his mistake tries to kill the bramber berry, and when he sees that he cannot, decides to sow wheat elsewhere, which, once it has been ground into flour, will serve to make bread that will feed the hungry.

The most that one can aspire to with respect to the evil we might have done in the past is to diminish its effects by devoting ourselves to doing good, for Nature will give back both kinds of photonic pulses equivalently. One can only be truly successful in life if one scrupulously respects universal harmony.

I refer to the total, lasting success obtained by he who effectively manages to tread the path of ascendant vertical evolution marked out by the Creator, thus making spirit, body, and mind coincide in the same space-time. This means that by having truly attained his spiritual perfection, which is the ultimate purpose of our corporeal existence, he is also free to decide his material circumstances to a great extent.

Let us recall that *he who reaches heaven will have everything given to him as a matter of course,* being able then to freely choose the plan of his own existence.

Any success that does not include spiritual fulfillment is merely apparent, volatile, and perishable, whereas the world of the spirit is immortal and transcends space and time because it is the plane on which life has been created. The best investment a person can make in life is in spiritual development, for it is something that is never lost and instead of diminishing in time, it increases. Material possessions, fame, honor, glory, and pleasure are all grains of sand scattered by the winds of time, and the most they can last cannot exceed the scant span of our corporeal life.

In order to better understand the moral rules of the Universe, we shall briefly analyze some of the commandments expounded above.

Do not hate (because if you do, your own hate will come back to you a hundredfold). Hate is an energy with a destructive intent, which stamps its informational vibration on the magnetic fields of he who experiences it, and its emotional intensity acts as a protective force to the pulses of photons of a dissociating, fragmenting type, which, in due time, will return to the source that emitted them with an intensified destructive impulse. In this way, the one who is not able to control his own hateful nature must be conscious of the huge price he will have to pay for it, which is the deterioration or destruction of his own life, his physical or mental health, or his most cherished illusions.

Do not try to get what you do not deserve (because you will be trying to commit a robbery). The law of egalitarian equivalence says that we must pay for everything we want to have, and that to aspire to something that one does not deserve is similar to robbery, and the one who robs will soon be stripped of other things when the natural balance he has broken is restored.

Do not delight yourself erotically with your own person (because you will increase your selfishness and Nature will be like a selfish stepmother to you).

Do not insult or defame your fellow (insult and you will be insulted, slander and you will be slandered). He who lets himself be led by his negative temper, and defames or insults his fellowman will receive the same garbage which he has projected a hundredfold.

Respect and help the elderly (and you will be helped in your old age).

Repudiate all manner of perversions (because perversion is antinatural and Nature, in many subtle ways, destroys what is not adjusted to the harmonious parameters of life).

Do not do unto others as you would not have them do unto you (do not do to others what you do not want Nature to give back to you multiplied).

Raise your own level of awareness (which will enable you to act more consciously and ethically).

Always defend truth and justice (and Nature will give you her support).

Free yourself of your negative feelings and thoughts (in order not to attract the equivalent, multiplied).

Respect universal law and you will be rewarded (live in harmony with Nature and you will attain the supreme good).

Reflection on these precepts will enable one to understand that the human being is eminently creative, albeit unable to qualitatively control his own energies, which are projected out into universal space and then, after a certain time, return to him to influence his life positively or negatively, in accordance with the type of vibration of the force that was originally emitted. In this case, what least interests us is the fact of whether or not we believe in this explanation, for one does not need to have faith in Nature for it to carry out its own mandates, and it will not refrain from acting simply because one doubts its effects.

People will inevitably continue to receive the consequences of their own acts, being rewarded for those that fit in with universal harmony, and being punished for those which are discordant and destructive. This occurs not because God bothers to punish or reward each one, but because the rulebreakers punish themselves, for by violating the established rules, they disrupt the equilibrium of Nature, and this has to be reestablished by neutralizing the transgressor.

Morality is profitable, for the best "deal" (the superlative investment of one's own time and energy) is to behave virtuously, respecting the transcendental values that sustain life in the Universe.

Acting in Accordance with the Law of Egalitarian Equivalence

In principle, this means acting in accordance with what is just, beyond personal sympathies or convenience, by objectively respecting one's fellows' rights and the rules of Nature, adjusting what one gives to what one intends to receive. In order to comply with this very simple precept, one requires a fully developed inner judgment that enables one to see oneself correctly and objectively, for usually, the individual has an inflated concept of his own worth at the same time as a manifest blindness to his own defects, so that he cannot carry out proper self-criticism or accurately assess the magnitude of his real merit.

Faced with a vision of an imminent good, the individual is usually blinded by ambition and is unable, no matter how hard he tries, to evaluate if what he has given previously, that is, his merit, has enough value for him to take what he intends without provoking an imbalance in Nature.

The great majority of people live with a recurrent sensation that they suffer injustice, in the sense that their merit by far surpasses what they have managed to take from life, a conviction that usually has no rational basis but which obeys a vain overvaluing of themselves that has been carried out in a totally unconscious way. The individual believes he has certain rights and this leads him to pose unconscious demands, which, as they do not give him the expected satisfaction, easily lead him to a life of frustration, unhappiness, and resentment.

These beliefs are fertile ground for the "engineers of envy"[32] (from the book *Equalitarian Envy* by Fernández de la Mora) to promote discontent and social resentment, by using communicative conjuring tricks so that the concept of prior merit based on work and personal effort vanishes and is substituted by a sort of superstitious conviction based in some supposed birthright or popular justice. Thus, even the laziest or most negligent supposes that, just because he is a member of a political or trade union collective with a certain amount of power, he has the right to enjoy the same level of well-being as any other, more efficient, more hard-working and better trained individual. When the rules of the game of life are not clear, all manner of confusions, frustrations, and apparent injustices take place.

One of the most significant norms of existence says: *as much as you give you will receive.* What happens is that people usually exaggerate the amount of their own effort and the qualitative importance of their personal talents, which almost invariably leads them to the subjective sensation that *they give a lot and receive very little.* However, when this situation is observed more objectively from outside, one realizes that very often the little that the individual believes he is receiving is already excessive when compared with the inefficiency, carelessness, lack of training, or negligence he displays.

Voracious egotism, a lack of objectivity, proceeding according to what suits one's own convenience, narcissism, and a lack of generosity all provoke a continual breaking of egalitarian equivalence, which is giving something of value and receiving something in proportion.

People refuse to respect the concept of what is fair, and manipulate this measure in order to tip the balance dishonestly and forcibly towards their own favor. There are very few who are willing to give something of real value without intending to receive a considerable amount of profit or a disproportionately higher one, and, as the market of supply and demand has its own adjustments and regulations, there are many who experience great frustration that usually results in claims of injustice, rage, resentment, or envy.

On the other hand, the continual multiplication of the offer of new, varied merchandise and goods induces consumers to voracity, and the consequent attitude of rebellion against the need to pay for what one wants. The apparent ease with which people become wealthy and the ignorance of the magnitude of previous work that well-off people bear on their backs, contrasts even more with the deficiencies of those who have not been successful, thus increasing the belief in social or divine injustice. People ask for justice merely because they lack something, generally disregarding any analysis of their own worth in the sense of assessing whether that worth is really equivalent to the magnitude of the desired object.

Within each individual, there is usually an unconscious, surreptitious belief that he or she possesses some sort of decree or privilege bequest by divinity, an inner possession that makes that person extremely different, unique, and special, giving one the right to claim special privileges.

In sum, there are many varied justifications that lead people to manipulate or scorn the balance of Nature, eluding the obligation to pay an equivalent price for what one intends to attain or possess. There are those who, having fallen into the immoral temptation of cheating on the payment, only too late in their lives discover that this is not possible, for what they thought they had achieved in the end became merely a cruel joke, like a mirage of an oasis in the desert.

When we act immorally, we are only supported by our own selfish arbitrariness, and we lack strength, but when we act in accordance with universal structural rules, we are firmly, securely, and transcendentally supported by them and can enjoy the power that acting according to justice offers us. Whenever we try to cheat the payment demanded by egalitarian equivalence, Nature will sooner or later act contrary to our deeds, in order to cancel out such arbitrariness and thus reestablish universal equilibrium. Rogues, crooks, and delinquents seem at times to get away with it, but they will always fall under the cosmic millstone that will grind them into dust scattered by the wind.

Let us never fall into the temptation of flouting the required contribution we have to make in order to achieve what we want. On the contrary, *let us accumulate merit* just as others hoard money in the bank, for individual merit is what will enable us to always act in accordance with the legality of cosmic nature. Let us learn to pay happily; the measure of our deprival will be equivalent to our tightfistedness, whereas prudent, balanced generosity will bring us a continual state of individual merit that will make us fit to carry out our aims naturally and harmoniously.

It is a fact that a very considerable sector of the human race has the soul of a thief, in the sense that it believes that to violently or dishonestly appropriate the goods of others is an act of justice rather than illicit usurping. These same people make dishonesty a normal lifestyle and pass as respectable citizens while their fraudulent machinations remain concealed. It is obvious that all those who fall into the game of dishonesty will cynically flout the concept of egalitarian equivalence, or perversely believe that in their case they are properly applying proportionality between prior merit and the reward pursued.

Absolutely everything an individual wishes to achieve has its price and has to be bought and paid for, either with money or with an equivalent effort, and there is no way to avoid this obligation.

The snares entailed in this are on the one hand based on mental manipulation designed to disqualify or devalue the worth or price of what the individual wants to acquire, or else to overvalue his own merit, all of which is really aimed at craftily defiling egalitarian proportionality.

One must consider that the laws of the Universe are fundamentally mercantilistic. We all have to pay for existence in the sense that we pay back Nature for our own creation. Everything that interacts in the Cosmos obeys a sort of barter through the exchange of goods or natural values for which one pays in proportion to their qualitative quantity.

Groups that are interested in manipulating the masses have for a long time been profusely divulging the demagogic notion that there should be things that must be gratis, a concept that does not exist at the level of Nature or social reality, and that was invented with the sole aim of provoking agitation in the masses in order to cash in on their discontent.

The mass media and advertising, as I have said in previous chapters, also covertly try to make us see that we can quickly and easily obtain the goods we desire by merely asking for a bank loan. The interminable and varied repetition of these types of messages adulterates the principle of egalitarian equivalence in our minds, because it ends by convincing us at the unconscious level that it is easy, simple, and quick to have the goods we intend to get. As is logical, when we see that this is not so in practice, we assume we have been the victim of some cruel joke or degradation. In some way, the human being came to believe that life should be easy and that when this does not happen it is because some wicked being is interfering with his existence.

There is a syndrome of adoration and faith in which everything can be obtained without effort, which is a neurotic disposition of the consumer who expects that everything has to be expedient, attainable, comfortable, and without obstacles. Very likely this attitude was born at first through observation of Nature and the apparent ease with which plants, trees, and flowers appear, or the proliferation of animals, birds, and insects. The fact is that man, unlike animals and vegetables, cannot count upon the protection of Nature and, therefore, has to "earn his bread by the sweat of his brow," as the biblical mandate says. As is only logical, this precept does not correspond only to what we have to do to obtain our daily sustenance, but also to all the tangible or intangible goods we wish to acquire. "To earn one's bread by the sweat of one's brow" is, as we can understand, a mandate that means paying the price of the goods and values we intend to have. One of the inherent realities of the mere fact of being alive is that existence is an uninterrupted succession of problems that have to be confronted, and the time and effort spent in solving them is the currency with which Nature charges for the goods she supplies.

As is logical, the more important, scarce, or valuable something is, the higher the price we have to pay for having it, and we must accept this in our hearts if we intend to be successful in life.

If we always pay joyfully in advance for what we want, life will be like a loving mother who pours the most beautiful and important goods of life over us. If we are stingy, Nature will be a cruel, stingy stepmother from whom we will always have to beg a crumb of bread. In reality, the human being usually inverts the order of factors in this type of thing, by thinking of *receiving* before *giving;* he needs to have money in advance before starting to work, to receive love from a partner before thinking of loving, to seek *to be understood* before *understanding,* to receive affection and friendship without previously giving it.

Resentful people believe that the world owes them something and that they are victims of injustice, this being the reason why they are usually embittered and mean. With such an attitude, they are really digging the grave of their own expectations, for Nature will give back to them an equivalent amount to what they have sown in her.

Vicious and corrupt people irradiate into the Universe pulses of photons that bear the information or vibratory mandate of their own aberrations, which will come back to them a hundredfold at some time, provoking the decline and unhinging of their lives.

Seeking More Profound Truths

There are many times in life when we seem to have "reached the bottom," in the sense that we feel frustrated, unhappy, or discontented with our own limits. On the one hand, we shut ourselves into a small mental space in order to feel protected, and on the other, a sensation of smothering oppression invades us in the face of the narrow limits that surround us.

The most desirable lifestyle for many people would seem to be the one that best allows for superficiality, frivolity, and banality, albeit carefully concealing these defects with touches of profound thought learned by heart from magazines and popular texts.

The outside world has become so powerful and seductive, thanks to that which consumerism offers, that it has finally emptied people's souls and annulled their higher rationality, for they have forgotten how to think for themselves, amiably confusing "what stirs in their neurons" with their own thought.

In reality, very little or nothing is left to the individual of what is his own—conditioned, alienated, possessed, fragmented, confused, and overstimulated as he is by a fake civilization, directed by enlightened barbarians who are illiterate in the field of consciousness and learned in informational knowledge. These cybernetic monstrosities are the result of an imitative, memoristic, alienating, and dehumanized educational system that ignores what significant learning is and that is only concerned with the massive production of *consumer-citizens*, electronic men whose minds docilely and passively lend themselves to receiving the communicative informational implant most suitable to the system or to the most dominant power groups.

To obtain a true individual mental identity has become a herculean task, for the individual has become food for the masses which absorb him, process him, digest him, and assimilate him to the collective interest. At the same time, he has also become a passive container for the millions of communicative messages which continually bombard him with the aim of convincing him to buy such and such a product or join diverse ideologies.

The state authority, for its part, tirelessly presses the citizen to become progressively more cramped by means of laws that impose a greater density of population, which significantly deteriorates people's quality of life as it increases, thus considerably raising the level of stress, anguish, pollution, mental disorders, and depression, thanks to erroneous government planning that often puts the economic interests of large companies before the citizen's welfare.

Man's inner space is also reduced more and more, smothered by the inordinate influence of the mass media, advertising, ideological indoctrination, and the progressive, overwhelming demands and prohibitions the State imposes on citizens.

The first impression that springs to mind when reflecting on our civilization is that of watching a children's film or a cartoon. The most childish explanations are universally accepted and nobody doubts them, whereas the most profound and obvious truths are subjected to discredit and scorn.

We are told that we are highly civilized, but we continually need to manufacture more sophisticated and powerful weapons; that we are free, when we really belong to the State and the universal financial system. We work for the former for free for almost half the year in order to pay our taxes, and the rest of the time we are kept busy generating the money we need to feed the financial entity that lends us artificial money to incite us to consume. The little space left to us is completely filled with the morbidity and vulgarity of television and the considerable flow of covert political indoctrination, while the full arrival of virtual reality is yet to come, which will vertiginously accelerate the spiritual decline of Mankind unless a miracle occurs.

Never in history has man been less master of his mind than at this moment, and hence more enslaved to alienating external influences. In order not to see reality, people take refuge in puerile religious beliefs or in cynical, materialistic atheism. Some evade reality through drug consumption, or drunken, genital, or gastronomic orgies, while others prefer to stupefy themselves with video games or fragment their "I" by fusing with mass collective organizations. The less fortunate drift towards envy and resentment to devote their lives to openly or covertly hating in order to feel something that fills their hearts, even though it may be negative.

Paradoxically, the individual lacks inner space and, even though he is continually empty, he desperately seeks something with which to fill this inner void. As long as the individual believes that the consumer market, with all that it entails, can in some way satisfy the needs he feels, he will remain enthusiastic and expectant, and when something fails, he supposes that there will always be new, fascinating possibilities. However, the time almost inevitably comes when he has to accept that he is not happy, and that what the market has to offer him will never fulfill his true inner expectations.

Only a few fortunate individuals undergo this experience while they are still relatively young, which enables them to ask for a second chance that offers them the possibility of righting their course, whereas the dreamers arrive at the point of being shipwrecked on their own illusions almost at the end of their lives, when there is no time left to seek better paths.

There are others who, because they perceive that they are not happy, fill their lives with material possessions or struggle for relevant positions to feel that "they have something of importance," without realizing the dramatic difference between having and being. The former merely concerns the corporeal and psychological voracity of the individual, which is an ephemeral and circumstantial situation, whereas the latter corresponds to the immortality of the being, which is our true, profound identity that originally emanated from the Creator.

The aim of this moral rule, as regards the need to see more profound truths, is to save people from the negative consequences of the inevitable experience of disillusionment and emptiness in their lives. It aims to save them from discovering only too late that they have been used for ends totally alien to their own, thus cruelly dooming them to go through life pursuing fascinating illusions they will never reach. Even if they are attained, they dissolve like soap bubbles, with the same cycle being repeated time and again. As one will understand, the true purpose of this mechanism is to promote consumerism so that the individual will not perceive the immense emptiness of his life, thus moving him away from any chance of inner development that might lead him *to know the higher levels of the being, to evolve in accordance with the Creator's mandate.*

This raw analysis of people's limitations does not obey any apocalyptic view of life, but rather obeys the real fact of the progressive dehumanization we are suffering as a result of the destruction of the space of the individual's inner freedom.

This individual is dazzled and overwhelmed by the mirage of the various "candy-coated" versions of life which are intended to convert him into the mental vassal of a system that coldly exploits people in a thousand different ways, despite its humanitarian disguise. It does this at such an efficient level that people do not realize it nor do they want to, because they are hypnotized by the siren songs of the consumerist message that floods their brain.

When I speak of consumerism, I naturally do not mean the mere commercial event of buying the goods with which we are all familiar. *Buying is, first and foremost, the internal acceptance or acquisition of something because we have been persuaded that we need it or that it is good for us.* In this way, as obedient consumers, *we buy* the widest accepted historical view of the world, *we buy* the lifestyle we lead, the religions we believe in, the Presidents who rule us, the beliefs in vogue, and the most popular celebrities, and in time, end by being convinced that what we have acquired corresponds to our own identity and ideals.

The natural consequence of all this is the progressive denaturalization of the individual who moves further and further away from the inner roots of his genuine "I," obliged to lead a false existence that under such conditions brings about the annulment of his vital and creative impulse. Only the discovery of a more profound reality can save the individual from his own frustration and failure.

Let us remember that *true success* has nothing to do with the individual's material achievements (although it does not exclude them), but it does have everything to do with evolutive victory, with the fact of entering and maintaining oneself on the ascending path of the elevation of individual consciousness, thus fulfilling the Creator's designs. Whoever does so is successful, no matter what his momentary social condition may be; he who does not achieve this, despite his fame, prestige, or fortune, will fail within the intelligent schema of Nature.

When evolution occurs, it most certainly implies the triumph of morality, for the individual will be incapable of behaving immorally, since he will understand and love the essence of virtue and what it means.

I believe that moral recipes are of no more use than friendly recommendations that can be either taken or left behind, this latter being the most probable case since it corresponds to the line of least resistance, like a rock that rolls down a hillside, whereas the path of virtue demands will, comprehension, patience, courage, and an intensified state of awareness.

It is very hard to convince people to act more ethically if they do not feel a sort of "inner calling" that implies getting a glimpse of a tiny bit of understanding, for they merely end up by choosing the easiest alternative—to roll down the hill, joining all those who will be their fellow travellers in the search for pleasant mirages that put the individual to sleep, thus remaining passive while being devoured by the insatiable Chronos, the father of the gods.

Higher ethical behavior can only be attained by understanding that the Universe is managed by a harmonious master plan, which we have to tune into if we wish to attain supreme happiness and well-being. Genuine morality corresponds to the norms of harmonization with the Universe and Nature, so that he who carefully observes its laws will always be successful, this being considered, in its greatest sense, as the supreme achievement of evolution to which a man can aspire.

People fail and suffer when they do not respect the consonance of Nature, but unfortunately, they do not learn from this, since they ascribe their tribulations to causes alien to the real ones.

Reflection and then comprehension of profound truths is the only thing that can induce elevated ethical behavior in people, but the unbearable banality of popular subculture makes the search for truth undesirable and improbable. On the other hand, highly cultured individuals are usually so steeped in the infallibility of science and culture that the magnitude of their own egos provokes in them persistent and incurable blindness. Really, there is nothing worse than empty, pretentious intellectuals who are convinced of the perfection of their own instruments of knowledge, adoring their own ideas as if they were gods. Totally programmed by the environment in which he was educated and in which he moves, the intelligence of each individual is captive within the paradigm of the cultural, ideological, religious, or political collectives in which he is inserted, and fears opening himself up to real analysis of unprejudiced, profound truths or realities as he would fear the devil.

Without any true interest in understanding, people only seek to believe in something that coincides with their own deficiencies or justifies their vices and defects, taking moral rules as a mere cosmetic veneer that magnifies or whitewashes their image. This attitude condemns one to failure, even though the star of social success may seem to shine with splendor.

If we stop to think about the human being's life, we shall realize just how tremendously important it is for him to understand the laws that regulate the equilibrium of the Universe, since, as a living being inserted within the intelligent system of Nature, he is submitted to similar regulations, and his happiness or misfortune depends on his observance of them.

Right from antiquity, man has intuited that there is a mysterious relationship between his own destiny and the Universe, and has tried to seek an explanation in the stars for the vicissitudes of his life.

Astrology is perhaps an attempt to relate man to the stellar whole around him, in the supposition that celestial bodies in some way have influence over the human being. Transcendental moral teaching shows us that cosmic space is full of a sort of subtle, imponderable energy that the ancients called *ether*, the existence of which, despite the fact that it has not been proven by science, could open up a possibility for us to understand the way in which light, heat, and other types of energy are transmitted, as likewise the mandates of Nature that balance out the interrelation between these bodies and living beings.

If the stars do in fact influence man's life, one needs to accept that the opposite is just as possible, that is, that men's actions have the corresponding influence on their stellar environment.

The true origin of wars could perhaps be due to the stellar famine caused by a sudden imbalance, a cosmic appetite that needs to absorb the huge energy mass of pulses of photons generated by the effort and destruction of war, in order to establish its harmonious proportions.

I must confess that when I think of "man" I am not restricted to *Homo sapiens*, for I believe in the existence of a "universal man," an archetype fashioned in the image and likeness of the Creator, not in the sense of corporeal form, but of the structure that governs his life.

It is quite possible that, regardless of physical form, which is the product of the particular vital conditions of a planet, there may be men in diverse parts of the Universe, who, in accordance with their evolutive age, may be more or less advanced than *Homo sapiens.*

Universal man is in a feedback loop with cosmic Nature, and morality, in its profoundest sense, is the set of laws that governs the structural harmony of the Universe. The acceptance of these possibilities is only possible for people who have been able to enter into their inner silence. This inner silence is able to be found if we can dehypnotize ourselves from the suggestive environmental stimuli, achieving thus through a profound introspection, the possibility to look at the inner universe where the truth of everything resides.

The most profound of all truths is total, absolute reality, that is, the way in which Nature maintains life in the Universe. Science has studied the material part accessible to man's bodily senses, but has not yet penetrated knowledge of the most profound laws of existence, as far as the mechanism by which everything is harmoniously interrelated in the Cosmos is concerned. *Science is ignorant of the structural laws that are the foundations of the Universe,* since these can only be apprehended in states of higher consciousness.

Science cannot explain how a man who feels true love in his heart by this very fact gains access to a destiny higher than that of the individual who hates, due to the fact that Nature gives back to us the equivalent of what we sow in her.

Science cannot explain natural law, as opposed to the justice of man. For example, it cannot perceive that most married couples live in a state of concubinage, in accordance with natural law, for what makes a marriage legitimate is genuine love and not an imitation of it, nor a legal or religious contract, and that without true love, the married couple does not exist. Science fails to see that the great majority of the Universe is immaterial and invisible, and that matter is only one tiny part of its total structure. Science can go no further than the men who discover its knowledge and these men, even though they may be geniuses, are common men as far as the development of their consciousness is concerned, since their instrument of knowledge (mind) has not been worked upon in order to gain access to higher vibratory states that permit a vision of subtler energies than those we normally know.

This is the reason why the wisdom of Nature has not become a cultural knowledge, since it requires the individual to first awaken from environmental hypnosis to then later proceed to intensify his level of awareness and learn how to think and perceive from these higher levels.

When that experience is shown to those who still remain in a state of half-sleep, which is common to the whole species, they cannot understand it because of the oneiric limitations of their minds, and in order for them to understand, they would in turn have to elevate themselves to the level of a higher reality, which is really of no interest to them. There is a very large group of people who seem to be captivated by this subject, but who cannot refrain from projecting their own fantasies, ending in their delirium by visiting remote planets or conversing daily with the angels. Of course, these are the ones who usually disparage this subject. This is the risk entailed in speaking of profound truths. Some reject them as if they had been bitten by a viper, which shows that they were touched by them, and others cling to them, not because they have either understood them or are really interested in possessing these truths, but in order to distort them to fit them into their own dreams and delirium, thus justifying their own deficiencies and superstitions. The truth is inevitably elitist, not because those who can possess it, monopolize or conceal it, to reveal it only to the people they prefer, but because a process of natural selection makes only a select minority interested in knowing it and willing to make an effort to this respect.

The rest prefer to remain inert in the concepts that are familiar to them and refuse to open themselves up to vaster, more profound realities.

Carefully Examining the Legality of Nature

In order to go deeper into the notion of "justice," one has to know if it is possible to specify which acts of the human being are or are not just, in accordance with the legality of Nature.

Within this environment, it happens that man cannot arbitrarily invent rules that entail a contradiction of Nature because there will inevitably come a negative reaction that will deteriorate or destroy his purposes. For example, this happens in the case of marriage, in which there is often a conflict between human and natural legality. The aim of the marriage contract is to legalize a couple's union, but as it usually does not respect natural legality, it ends by being false, arbitrary, and capricious. In fact, the only valid reason for a man and a woman to marry is genuine love, which in these times of imitation and falsification is usually very rare. Thus it is common for people to unite for something that seems like love to them but which only too often turns into an exchange of mutual aspirations.

The concrete fact is that, for Nature, only a couple united by true love and not by a passing attraction is a *marriage,* whereas for society it only means two beings of the opposite sex who are linked by a legal contract, both with the good intention of loving but generally ignorant of that profound, genuine love that transcends personal, selfish interest and that is immune to the internal and external vicissitudes of life to attain perfect complementation within the harmony of Nature.

It would be futile to ask who is right, whether it be man or Nature, since Nature has always been here (and everywhere) and will not go away, whereas man, according to his evolutive age, is still a babe in arms. Likewise, Nature is unitary and fills the entire Cosmos and all that is contained in it, while the man that we know is merely a grain of sand that clings to a minute pebble in space, just one more among millions of other living beings.

No matter whether man believes or not in the designs of Nature, Nature will continue acting as it has always done and will continue doing.

This is how man repeatedly comes into conflict with the natural through the arbitrariness of his own acts, and there is no need to be very clever to foresee who will be most harmed.

Arbitrary marriage (without true love) must invariably pay for the fruits of its deficiencies with frustration, disillusionment, and disappointment. Finally, children of such a union will be innocent victims of their parents' naïve incompetence. In the eyes of Nature, it is quite possible for a couple to live together without being married and yet have a perfect marriage, as a result of their being united by genuine love, whereas another couple, despite the fact that they have complied with the law of man, will live in concubinage. In order to understand this, one must realize that man feels himself to be the conqueror and master of Nature and continually tries to subjugate her, at least externally, without realizing that it is really he who is a servant to the force that he intends to manipulate. And this is so because he usually believes that Nature is a blind, unbridled force that has to be corrected and channelled to comply with the designs of human beings, whereas the fact is that this is just one more of the great narcissistic fantasies of the species. Nature is indomitable, and the most one can aspire to is to live in harmony with her. The case of Nature's manifestation of herself in the interior of men is very different, and this refers to our own internal nature, which is our moral duty to master, sublimating our appetites, instinctive impulses, and passions, since only in this way can we attain mastery of ourselves, an indispensable requisite in order to act ethically. I believe that one of the most interesting points on this subject refers to determining which acts of man respect natural legality and which lie outside of it.

There is a golden rule that states the following: *Before Nature, all actions are licit if they are carried out by a human being who, having achieved spiritual perfection, reaches the peak of man's possible evolution.* This refers to the individual who, through long work on himself, manages to make his body, mind, emotions, and spirit coincide in the same space-time, the moment when the spirit manifests itself through the corporeal brain to gain full access to the present reality.

This is how the spirit begins to express itself through the thought of the body that contains it, speaking through its mouth and using its hands, purifying everything it touches with its high irradiation. The emotions become spiritual, and everything that is done, felt, or said originates from a point firmly based on the legality of Nature, so that it is not possible for it to carry out arbitrary or inharmonious acts but only those which in some way coincide with the forces that maintain the universal structure.

Common man is an anarchic being, for he does not have a unique "I" to govern his psychic system, whereas the truly spiritual individual, in the sense of technical efficiency, is a harmonious being who fully respects the higher laws of life.

The corporeal individual is arbitrary; he wants what he does not deserve, acts immorally, and does what is not just. Spiritual man adjusts his behavior and desires to the harmony of the Universe, so that he has the right to do everything he wants, in accordance with the law of egalitarian equivalence. As is obvious, this individual cannot do evil or act immorally, since he has sworn loyalty to his own spirit that has emanated from the supreme light which is the opposite to the kingdom of the shadows. This individual will always keep to the comprehensive ethics that emanate from the inner judgment that comes from the spirit, which will inevitably respect what is just. Spiritual man will never violate people's true rights, and will give to each what he deserves.

In the eyes of many people, this portrait would seem to define an unjustly privileged individual, who in some way would not be affected by prohibitions that affect common men, for in accordance with the foregoing, *this individual may do what he wants, unlike others who would seem to be precluded from this privilege.*

The truth is that to do what one wants, with no more limitations than to respect one's fellows' rights and those of Nature, is not a privilege but a huge responsibility, for it means consciously accepting the effects of all the causes one sets in motion, that is, being ready to receive what life gives back in virtue of what one sows.

Common man is almost invariably *outside the dictates of natural law,* for he does not respect the harmonious moral rule of the Universe. He wants what he does not deserve, is dishonest with himself, acts unjustly, does not respect people's rights, sows hatred, resentment, and envy, is mastered by animal rapacity, abuses the weak, does not take responsibility for his own acts, continually lies, lives for his image and in the service of hypocrisy, does not possess true individuality, steals whenever he can, and is a mentally limited being because he cannot see reality as it is, but navigates through life like a true sleepwalker, stripped of any moral compass, and with no other course than that marked out by his own passions. All this is so, if one dispenses with the hypocritical and biased view when discussing these matters.

Common man is neither poor nor anonymous; he is the individual who turns himself into the mere continual repetition of the social model, without any inner identity or characteristics of his own; the psychological cloning of infinite previous imitations; a hollow, empty individual who is a mere projection of the collective psyche of the world.

Ambitious people often believe that the ends justify the means, thus intending to trample over any rule or person who stands in the way of their plans. In order to better understand this important matter, let us take a look at a brief list of "typical situations" in which the protagonist acts outside the natural law:

- One who endeavors to achieve something which he does not really deserve, due to his lack of moral quality and the scant effort he makes. Thus, what he wants to achieve is "not appropriate" because it is illegal as there is no egalitarian equivalence, that is, the individual's lack of merit by far surpasses what he wants to obtain.

- One who lies in order to achieve some personal advantage.

- One who deceives himself, making his behavior fraudulent.

- One who arbitrarily tries to impose his own opinion on that of others.

- One who does not respect his fellow mans' rights.

- One who has an image that does not correspond to his true condition, and who uses it to manipulate his fellowmen.

- One who is dominated by his baser passions and tries to carry out immoral desires that are born from them.

- One who is hypocritical.

- One who has dirty unconscious motivations, even though he is not conscious of them.

- One who tries to *take without giving.*

There are other situations in which the individual is not merely outside legality but is in fact *a delinquent with respect to the laws of Nature:*

- The corrupt judge.

- The corrupt policeman.

- One who deceives people with his demagogic discourse.

- The statesman who does not aim to serve the people, but rather his own power and profit.

- The corrupter of minors.

- One who acts perversely against Nature.

- One who adulterates food or medicines.

- One who traffics in dangerous drugs.

- One who, regardless of people's mental privacy, brainwashes them in order to control their behavior.

- One who lives by exploiting his fellows through usury.

- One who spreads pornography among minors.

- The professional swindler who, by cheating a customer, jeopardizes the customer's personal security, his goods, honor, freedom, or life.

- One who uses calumny to attack people's honor.

- One who trades in others' misfortune.

- One who jeopardizes the security of a country, or who seriously endangers world peace.

- The public servant who jeopardizes citizens' security by neglecting his duties.

- One who pollutes the water or air.

- One who knowingly sells counterfeit or adulterated food or medicine.

- One who carries out terrorist attacks.

- One who, without justification, protects, shelters, or forgives terrorism, criminality, and delinquency.

- The perpetrator of unspeakable cruelty to animals.

- One who brings about ecological disasters or covers up the ravaging of the natural environment.

- One who contaminates other people's magnetic fields with his own energetic poison.

These points constitute only a minimal list that serves as an example so that one can understand that very often what is a crime for Nature is not always illegal for man. Of course, this former list could be enlarged considerably, but it is not the aim of this book to offer a code of Nature, but rather to make people understand what this type of crime means. Logically, I have not included many common offenses specified by law, and if something does not appear on this list, it does not mean that it is not a "sin" before Nature.

One of the most important differences between the code of man and that of natural equilibrium lies in the fact that, in the former, a delinquent is innocent until he is proven guilty and sentenced, whereas, in accordance with natural law, "he who does it, will always pay for it."

For obvious reasons, it is impossible to establish what percentage of offenses committed remain undiscovered or unpunished, but a small dose of healthy malice leads me to believe that only a tiny part of all offenses are brought to light, so that the covert wrongdoer avoids the punishment that corresponds to him under human justice.

The same does not happen with Nature, for the offense committed is stamped on the archives of the terrestrial magnetic field, from which the energetic network of subtle wires that cover the whole Universe bear this unbalancing information which provokes, upon attaining its objectives, an adverse reaction that will restore the harmonic proportion. This means that absolutely no offense is left unknown or unpunished, although our limited terrestrial perception prevents us from perceiving or knowing the forms such punishments take.

One must accept that nothing takes place by pure chance, and that one of the most important laws of universal feedback is the one that says that "everything has a cause, and every cause has an effect."

With honesty and patience, it will not be very hard for us to discover the possible cause of the misfortune that may afflict us, as it always springs from our own actions, and on the other hand, we shall also perceive everything that is a reward for our good deeds. If we do not want to reap storms, we have to stop sowing winds, and if we want a fruitful, balanced harvest of spiritual and earthly goods, we have to sow them in the same proportion.

The last point in the list, which refers to the delinquent of Nature, deserves a separate explanation, that is, *"one who contaminates other people's magnetic fields with his own poison."* This refers to embittered, resentful, envious, aggressive, perverse, vicious, destructive, and depressive people who so poison their own magnetic field that they begin to feel smothered by their own psychic feces, so that they seek relief through trying to inject their poisonous magnetism into their fellow men, making them accomplices to their twisted feelings, slandering and insulting those they hate, or thinking up perverse ways to bemire the minds of others, so that in this way they seriously pollute their psychic environment, and feel a passing relief for their own disease-like wounds that heal by letting out the purulent matter they contain.

The range of such pollution is incalculable, particularly in those unfortunate cases which originate exceptionally in public or significant figures whose words have a huge repercussion. Infected individuals will, in due time, also try to pollute others in order to reduce their own anguish.

This epidemic not only affects people's magnetic fields but also their minds, as occurs in the case of ideologies based on envy, hatred, violence, and destructiveness, which affect whole countries, paralyzing their inhabitants' inner creativity and internal wealth, preventing them from adopting an attitude which is constructive, positive, and with a fighting spirit, and promoting the most cruel underdevelopment. Negative emotions create toxic substances in people's organisms, which correspond to destructive magnetic fields. We are poisoned daily in big cities by the magnetic radiation of their citizens and this is the reason for the relief we feel when we leave these polluted areas and go to the seaside, the mountains, or remote places.

Unfortunately, we live in a highly polluted magnetic environment, and only well-trained individuals can keep themselves free of this influence. However, the best remedy to protect oneself from this plague is behaving virtuously, positively, and optimistically, maintaining adequate mental hygiene and a state of inner cleanliness and inner transparency.

All those who pollute individual magnetic fields with vibratory trash are *delinquents* before Nature and will invariably receive their due punishment. Those who infect the mind with messages that incite people to hatred, envy, violence, corruption, or immoral behavior are also in the same category. Once again, I would repeat, *he who sows trash will receive trash; he who sows gold will reap gold* (that is, one who sends out higher vibratory photon pulses).

Personal magnetism, which can be accurately measured, is always charged with the individual's predominant vibratory tone, in accordance with his thoughts, customs, feelings, and actions, as likewise by the influence of his state of bodily health.

The individual who has a healthy, clean, and harmonious personal magnetism is like a living panacea, for this radiation positively influences the people around him, passing on peace and harmony to them. As you may understand, this takes on strong moral connotations, for quite *voluntarily* and *by our own decision,* we become positive or negative sources of photonic emission, meaning that we either purify or pollute the psychic environment around us.

There are places that are saturated with negative magnetic energy, which cause us sadness and sorrow, as also occurs when we are in the company of or in touch with people afflicted by depression. One should bear in mind that the great majority of the species live outside natural law, and this is the reason for their difficulty in attaining peace, happiness, and prosperity.

It is necessary to insist once more that only the individual who has truly evolved can come of age before Nature, that is, one who has attained his spiritual perfection in the terms described above. This individual *has total validity before universal law, for his acts emanate from the will of his own spirit, his own just mandate that is in harmony with the laws of Nature.*

It is of interest to point out here that this is not a prerogative that is graciously granted a person for the mere fact of being spiritual, but by the fact that Nature respects those who are integrated into her own schemata, which are ultimately the structural bricks of the Cosmos.

Human law has carefully crafted a body of codes organized in a tidy, systematic way so as to regulate citizens' behavior, and we must all adhere to them. One must consider that such laws change according to the epoch, and that they also display marked differences from country to country. The code of Nature, on the contrary, has always been, is, and always will be the same—unique, eternal, and immutable— for it emanates directly from the Creator and becomes the basis of life in the Universe. These rules are what show how licit or illicit the level of man's acts are. Any arbitrary action that does not entail a state of higher consciousness in its genesis is illicit, and for this same reason is more suited to an animal than to a man.

Such an act is based merely on an individual's capricious or arbitrary impulse when he intends to do what he fancies regardless of the interests of his living environment, without ensuring that his action has a constructive or positive end, without taking responsibility for it, and without inserting it wisely in the harmonious proportionality of life.

Illicit acts in this case mean that one neither respects nor adjusts to the natural parameters that maintain vital equilibrium in the Universe, which demands continual and repeated natural adjustments in order to keep total equilibrium. It is as if people were continually taking things for themselves illegally, things that do not correspond to them or that they have not really earned because of their low level of consciousness and lack of previous merit. This would bring about a reaction from Nature that would snatch away something else of equivalent or greater importance, according to the transgressor's degree of naïveté or perversity.

This is the case of undeserved pleasure, for example, which inevitably has to be paid for with an equivalent dose of suffering, an experience that any one can see for themselves.

It happens that human beings act arbitrarily as if they were gods, that is, as if they did not have to overcome their own defects, become virtuous, perfect themselves, and evolve, and as if they had all the time in the world to waste on distractions. No one asks before enjoying a pleasure whether he in fact deserves it, or whether it entails an abuse of natural proportionality. Unfortunately, it usually happens that excesses of pleasure are paid for with greater doses of unhappiness, misfortune, solitude, anguish, and degradation. Invariably, undeserved pleasure *empties* the individual and it is probable that the Spartan lifestyle of ancient Greece was based, among other things, on perfect knowledge of this principle.

What is undeserved pleasure? It is that which surpasses a person's level of virtue and consciousness, that is, practically everything we currently consider pleasurable.

The individual begins to acquire personal lawfulness when he stops being a mere bridge between the animal and man and abandons his hybrid condition to become a complete, total human being. People in a democracy attain their full civil rights when they come of age, and consequently a child of 10, for example, would not be allowed to vote, but should he succeed in doing so by cheating the system, he would be doing something illegal.

Similarly, man has to come of age in evolution in order to obtain full natural rights, that is, the recognition of his level of perfection by Nature. It is then that he can act on the mental, emotional, physical, and spiritual plane and attain total legality within the Universe. Likewise, and as a harmonious counterpart, he is also obliged to shoulder all his duties as an inhabitant of the Universe, which implies a huge responsibility.

One of the things that makes it hard to study this subject are the diverse presumptions man makes about his own capacities, carelessly attributing to himself *consciousness, will, free choice, and an elevated human condition,* at the same time as he ignores the need to work on himself to effectively develop the aforementioned attributes.

The expression *humanism,* for example, gives the impression that there are people who, just because they behave in a humanitarian and cultured way, would be worthy of the highest social consideration, so that if there were a learned lamb who also practiced charity, it would get similar esteem. The fact is that the human condition is determined, technically, by the individual's true level of evolution. The truth is that logically, it is far easier to be charitable than to evolve.

Traditional virtues:

- Sincerity

- Honesty

- Fraternity

- Honor

- Family unity

- Patriotism

- Love

- Courage

- Tolerance

- Respect

- Modesty

- Loyalty

- Industriousness

- Patience

- Prudence

- Temperance

- Generosity

- Compassion

- Empathy

- Gratitude

- Good faith

- Respect for the elderly

- Protection of children

- Pacifism

Spiritual virtues:

- Peace and serenity

- Impersonality

- Unitary perception of the Universe

- Coronation of the spirit as the true "I"

- True vision of external reality

- The capacity to attain higher states of consciousness

- The capacity to transcend one's own cerebral programming

- The capacity to grow at the level of the being

- The capacity to know the meaning and purpose of human existence

- A faithful vision of one's own reality

- The capacity to carry out absolutely free, self-generated acts, conceived in an omnipresent, stable, and mature "I"

- The capacity to relate specific knowledge with the total schema of life

- Wisdom, in the sense of meaningful knowledge of life and its elements

- The capacity to access a universal knowledge that is not circumscribed to a specific space-time

- The capacity to evolve individually and in a conscious way

- Knowledge of the moral laws of Nature

- The capacity to individually transcend oneself beyond material existence

- The capacity to overcome the passions

- The capacity to forgive offenses and be tolerant

- The capacity to obtain lasting happiness and the supreme good

- An objective vision of oneself

- Self-knowledge

- Objectivity

- Mastery of thought, attaining the capacity to stop thinking at will

- Sublimation of the libido

- Self-dominion

- Vision of transcendental reality

- Control and modification of one's own destiny

- The capacity to live in the present moment

- The capacity to be unitary

These are some of the traditional and spiritual virtues. The former are the fruit of love and devotion, and the latter are the result of a long process of spiritual training.

We have only three possibilities in life:

1. To live on the margin of virtue, preoccupied only with satisfying our personal passions, without any moral rules to guide our actions.

2. To practice the traditional virtues, which is a preparation for choosing a higher pattern of behavior.

3. To develop the spiritual virtues, which will lead us directly to individual evolution, the goal marked out for the human being by the Creator.

Individual liberty enables us to voluntarily choose our path in life, with the results I have already explained throughout this book.

Note on the use of the word "consciousness"—it has been used in two ways:

1. Consciousness: "A peculiar mode of existence in which there are personal experiences, psychic processes that are immediately experienced by the individual, such as perceptions, memories, thoughts, feelings, desires, processes of will, etc." (the psychological meaning).

2. Consciousness: "It refers to increased levels of awareness which allow access to superlatively superior states of consciousness, increasingly higher than the usual ones" (spiritual-technical meaning).

1. Karl Popper, from an article appearing in *El Mercurio* (Chile: July, 1995).
2. Calvin S. Hall, *Compendio de Psicología Freudiana* (Paidós Publishers, 1997).

3. Bradley R. Schiller, *Essentials of Economics* (McGraw-Hill Publishers, 1994), p. 282.

4. Quoted by J. Bochaca, *La Finanza y El Poder,* Bausp Ed. (Barcelona), p. 9 ff.

5. J. Bochaca, op. cit., p. 20.

6. Pío XI, *Quadragesimo Anno Collecíon de Encíclicas y Documentos Pontificios* (Madrid: 1967), p. 646.

7. J. Bochaca, op. cit., p. 6.

8. Bank of America, *Country Data Forecast.*

9. For a general overview, cf. on this point the book by Daniel Bell, *The End of Ideology* (Free Press, 1960).

10. Cf., for example, the book by the Marxist Nicos Poulantzas, *Fascismo y Dictadura* (Madrid: 1973).

11. Gonzalo Fernández de la Mora, La Envidia Igualitaria *(The Egalitarian Envy),* (Barcelona: Planeta Publishers, 1984).

12. Carl Gustav Jung, *El Yo y el Inconsciente (The I and the Unconscious),* (Miracle Publishers).

13. Elizabeth Badinter, *¿Existe el Amor Maternal? (Does Maternal Love Exist),* (Barcelona: Paidós-Pomaire Publishers, 1981), pp. 67 and 69.

14. Antoine Porot, *Diccionario de Psiquiatría Clínica y Terapéutica (Dictionary of Clinical Psychiatry and Therapy),* (Labor Publishers, 1962).

15. Sandor Ferenczi, *Sexo y psicoanálisis (Sex and Psychoanalysis),* Hormé Ed. (Buenos Aires: 1951), p. 133.

16. Harold Saxton Burr, *Blueprint for Immortality, the Electric Patterns of Life* (London: Nevilla Spearmen Limited, 1972).

17. Paul Le Moal, *Una Auténtica Educacíon Sexual* (Spain: Marfil Publishers).

18. Epictetus, *El Arte de Vivir (The Art of Living),* (Norma Group Publishers), p. 44.

19. Friedrich Dorsch, *Diccionario de Psicología (Dictionary of Psychology),* (Barcelona: Herder Publishers, 1991).

20. Jean Laplanche and Jean Bertrand Pontalis, *Diccionario de Psicoanálisis (Dictionary of Psychoanalysis),* (Barcelona: Labor Publishers, 1994).

21. Theodor Reik, *El Masoquismo en el Hombre Moderno (Masochism of Modern Man),* (Buenos Aires: Nova Publishers, 1949), p. 17.

22. Gabriel G. Nahas, *Keep Off the Grass* (Paul S. Eriksson Publisher, 1990).

23. National Institute on Drug Abuse (NIDA), *The Analysis of Cannabinoids in Biological Fluids* (U.S.A.: 1982).

24. National Institute on Drug Abuse (NIDA), *Marijuana, Research Findings* (U.S.A.: 1980). See also: idem., *Testing Drugs for Physical Dependence Potential and Abuse Liability* (U.S.A.: 1984).

25. Jerome Jaffe, Robert Petersen, Ray Hodgson, *Vicios y Drogas* (New Mexico).
26. Calvin S. Hall, op. cit., same chapter.
27. Jean Laplanche and Jean Bertrand Pontalis, op. cit., same chapter.
28. Alberto Cormillot and Juan Carlos Lombardini, *Beber o no Beber* (Paidós Publishers).
29. Neil Kessel and Henry Walton, *Alcoholismo, Cómo Prevenirlo para Evitar Sus Consecuencias* (Paidós Publishers, 1990).
30. Will Durant and Ariel Durant, *Las Lecciones de la Historia* (Sudamericana Publishers, 1969).
31. Theodor Reik, *El Amor Visto por Un Psicólogo (Love Viewed by a Psychologist)*, (Buenos Aires: Nova Publishers, 1946).
32. Gonzalo Fernández de la Mora, op. cit., same chapter.

APPENDIX

EXPERIMENTAL PROOF OF THE NEGATIVE PHYSICAL EFFECT OF CERTAIN MORAL VIOLATIONS

This experimental work has a purely ethical aim, for in the light of the new concepts expounded in this work, it aims to show how certain moral faults can seriously harm both the transgressor himself and those around him, which takes the problem of ethics to the terrain of biophysics. I particularly mean the harm which the following acts can cause:

1. Sexual relations during menstruation.

2. Masturbation.

3. The perverse sexual relationship of anal sex.

4. Emotional states of rage and destructiveness.

Once I had worked out a suitable working hypothesis, I formed a research team made up of a physicist, an electronic engineer, and a biochemist, who developed their work according to my working methods.

Our research was successful, for it showed without any doubt that under the influence of certain moral violations, the body and the mind generate a sort of toxic energy that perturbs the organism so that it notably reduces its defenses and weakens its physical and mental health. Therefore, morality no longer represents a mere set of recommendations for behavior, but has become what it really is—the flow and reflow of energetic feedback between man and Nature, in which each moral violation means a breaking of natural equilibrium, and its consequent punishment means the reestablishing of this equilibrium.

The following is a brief summary of the research carried out, which took about a year, and which, in order to be understood, requires that one put aside all hypocrisy to focus oneself with a mature, broad, and unprejudiced criterion.

John Baines, 1998.

Measuring the Electromagnetic Energy of the Body in Different Physiological Processes

Introduction

This work of experimental research aims to show that the energy irradiated in certain physiological processes of the human body is of a harmful nature for it. The techniques used and the results obtained force us to rethink our approach to physical reality and therefore to the human being. This is why we have devoted a chapter to the comprehension of the foundations for this new point of view. We do not mean by this that there are contradictions in the classical thought of science, but rather that just the perspective from which things are analyzed has changed, to attain a more global view of them. We will base our findings on experiments carried out by different researchers, in order to establish the existence of this electromagnetic field and to offer an explanation for acupuncture. We quote in full detail the experiments carried out by the German biophysicist Fritz Albert Popp, who experimentally showed that the human body is an emitter and a receptor of electromagnetic energy. In addition, we also mention other researchers who verified Popp's results, thus broadening this knowledge.

591

As these experiments are based on principles of quantum physics, certain concepts of this branch of physics have to be explained. We shall begin by offering a definition of what we understand by quantum physics and electromagnetic energy, and will go into the atom in order to be able to understand that there is a unique field of energy that maintains and defines biological structures, thus permitting an exchange of energy with the surrounding environment. This field of energy is defined with different names, according to the instrument used to measure said field. For example, if we use an instrument that depends on magnetic forces, this instrument will define this energy as electromagnetic. This idea leads us to the fact that everything that exists and surrounds us can be explained from the energetic point of view, for matter and energy are one and the same. Thus each body, both animate and inanimate, sends out electromagnetic energy with a characteristic frequency.

In order to carry out the measurements, we have worked on the basis of the techniques of acupuncture from Chinese traditional medicine, using a piece of equipment called a Vegatest, manufactured in Germany by VEGA, which is certified under the strictest quality and security control, ISO 9001. This apparatus is designed to measure the points of acupuncture electrically (electro-acupuncture). Vegatest was chosen on account of its reliability, as it has been in use in Europe and particularly in Germany for over 30 years. Different doctors who work with this equipment have written diverse publications in which they explain the use and applications of the Vegatest method, among whom we could mention Dr. Stuart J. Zoll, Dr. Julian Kenyon, and Dr. Andreas Bachmann. All these publications have been of great use to us for the development and understanding of this work. The results obtained from the measurements are clearly shown in the graphs, which will be discussed and analyzed in later chapters.

1. Bases of the Experiment

What is understood by quantum physics is the branch of physics that allows us to understand the interaction of subatomic particles through the concept of a field (region of space within which every body is submitted to forces of attraction or repulsion, a zone of mutual influence), so that it is clear that particle and field are complementary manifestations of one and the same thing. It shows us that matter is no more than condensed energy, as Einstein demonstrated in his well-known formula: $E = MC^2$, by which he established that matter and energy are indissolubly linked and interdependent.

As Nobel Physics Prize winner Carlo Rubbia said in 1984, "the relationship between 'quantums' of energy (photons) and particles with mass (nucleons) is approximately a thousand million photons per nucleon ($9.746 \times 10^8:1$). This means that visible matter is no more than the thousand-millionth part of the universe that really exists. The importance of matter is diluted until it becomes insignificant."

According to Dr. Bodo Köhler, in his book *Introduction to Quantum Medicine,* all the processes that occur in our universe can be described from either the material point of view, or from the energetic perspective, but in no case can the other complementary aspect be ignored. Therefore, all things have two sides to them and in order to describe something integrally and in a scientifically accurate way, the other side must always be taken into account.

We are going to give a brief definition of what electromagnetic energy is, and will abbreviate it as EME.

EME is a current of photons that moves through space by means of waves. It has a double nature of wave/particle, that is, the particles can behave as fields of the wave and the fields of the wave can behave as particles, depending on the instrument with which they are observed. It can be considered as a wave of an oscillating electrical field associated to a magnetic field.

These photons move by means of waves at a unique speed in the void ($C = 3 \times 10^8$ meters/second) and vary with regard to the medium of propagation. Electromagnetic energy is what maintains coherence in matter, as explained by the physicist Heinz R. Pagels in his book *The Code of the Universe* (Pirámides Publishers):

> Almost all properties of matter can be understood in terms of the quantum and electromagnetic properties of atoms. The individual particles within the atom, such as electrons, have associated electric fields that keep them in their orbits around the nucleus and are responsible for the chemical interactions of the atoms. If electromagnetic energy did not exist, the atoms would no longer exist and there would be no matter in the form that is known.

If we go into atomic structure, we can see that the nucleus is made up of protons and neutrons linked by nuclear forces and that electrons spin around them in their orbits, linked by electromagnetic forces.

It is known from electromagnetic theory that when a charge circulates through a spiral, it forms a current and thus generates a magnetic field, which is the same as a magnetic dipole or magnet, located at the center of the spiral and perpendicularly oriented to the plane of that spiral. From this, it may be deduced that the electron in the atom generates a magnetic field and that the atoms have a dipolar nature, sending out electromagnetic radiations that are specific for each atom.

If it is understood that a set of atoms forms a molecule, and that these in turn form higher structures such as proteins, cells, organs, and the different bodies, it can then be seen that each living form and each inanimate body sends out a pattern of characteristic frequencies.

This was demonstrated by the biophysicist W. Ludwig, who used a frequency spectrometer and measured certain homeopathic preparations, to discover that each plant sends out its own spectrum.

As we have seen, everything that surrounds us is no more than a concretizing of energy, this in turn being a vibrational matter. We define "vibrational" as a regular, periodical movement that can be represented by a sinusoidal wave. We may therefore say that all organic and inorganic things have a fundamental characteristic, which is frequency, that is, their own radiation.

In this way, we understand that the human body, as an emitter of EME, sends out a characteristic spectrum of frequency. The Canadian biophysicist Bigu del Blanco, experimentally measured the complete oscillatory field of the organism, as can be seen in Fig. 1 (quoted in *Introduction to Quantum Medicine*, B. Köhler, ISBN 3-8243-1242-5, Center for Coordination of Bio-resonance and German Quantum Medicine).

The diagram shows the interferences of all the individual oscillations of the different organs and tissues, starting with a basic oscillation of low frequency of the cells of the conjunctive tissue, to high-frequency tissue oscillations. The spectrum ranges from less than 1 Hz to 10^{18} Hz, with maximum intensity being in the zone of the microwaves.

Figure 1

SF= Sound Frequency
TO= Tissue Oscillations

The Bigu Spectrum

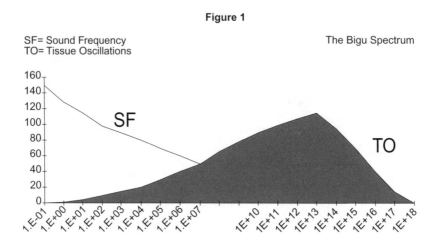

The engineer Simonetton also researched this matter, and his work is quoted in the book *Electromagnetic Fields and Life,* by the Russian physicist A. S. Presman (published by Plenum Press, New York, 1970). After having carried out a great number of measurements on people, plants, and animals, Simonetton came to the conclusion that a healthy person is within a range of frequency between 6,500 and 8,000 Å (Angström), that is 10^{14} Hz, which corresponds to the maximum intensity of the Bigu spectrum.

The German biophysicist Fritz Albert Popp, at the beginning of the seventies, as described in his book *Electromagnetic Bio-information,* pp. 144–167 (published by Urban & Schwarzenberg), demonstrated experimentally that living organisms send out and store electromagnetic energy.

In his study of cancer, he developed the idea that the carcinogenic properties of certain substances did not lie in their chemical composition but were due to the interactions of radiations, so that he constructed an apparatus based on high-sensitivity photo-multipliers with which he could detect the ultra-weak radiations of living cells (biophotons) by carrying out highly accurate measurements on a large number of vegetable and animal cells. The frequency of the radiations sent out were found to be in the whole of the visible, ultraviolet, and infrared spectrum. Popp observed that the field of EME made up of biophotons is the primary factor that directs the vital processes of the organism. This field must be "coherent" so that it will allow for communication and exchange of information between cells. The concept of "coherent" means oscillations of the same wavelength, these being ordered and coordinated waves whose upper and lower peaks interrelate so that they can be placed over one another. The best example of this is the laser, which oscillates with practically only one wavelength and is barely dispersed, even when it is far from its source of origin. Thus, the waves of a coherent field behave in the same way, so that they can transmit information and unite in a whole, cells, tissues, and organs. The living cells constantly send out these types of waves, which are propagated at the speed of light and inform the organism they belong to at each moment of their current state and which homeostatic mechanisms it needs to set in motion, with the aim of maintaining health. This homeostasis can be defined as the condition in which all the organic tissues are in harmony with one another. This harmony is maintained and expressed by ordered, coherent electromagnetic waves. When they become disordered and incoherent, they do not correctly transmit information between the different parts of the organism, and disease appears.

Popp believes in the existence of some mechanism that allows for the maintaining of coherence in the field of biophotons, and experimentally demonstrated that the DNA molecule is a storer of photons and that through transformations in its spatial structure (spiralization and despiralization) it is able to store and emit light.

In order to show that DNA is a storer of photons, he used a chemical compound called bromocaine, which interacts only with the DNA molecule by substituting its bases. By increasing the concentration of bromocaine, the DNA spiral changes, and twists in the opposite direction (despiralization), as shown in Fig. 2. If the DNA can store photons, these photons later have to free themselves in the despiralization phase, which is shown in Fig. 3. There we can see that, to the extent that the concentration of bromocaine increases, there is greater emission of photons, reaching a maximum and then descending, which corresponds to the spiralization and despiralization of the DNA molecule. The three curves indicate the variation the DNA molecule undergoes in a period of one, two, and three hours.

This also corresponds to experiments carried out by the Russian engineer George Lakhovsky, described in the book *The Dark Side of the Brain* by the researchers Harry Oldfield and Roger Coghill (published by Element Books, 1991, pp. 66–71).

Figure 2

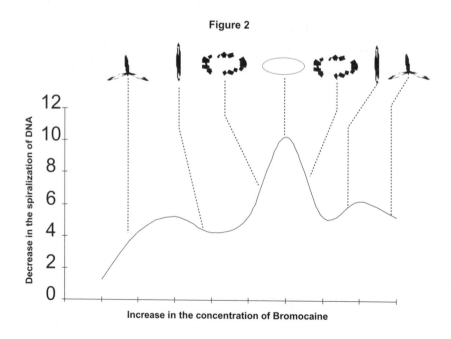

Increase in the concentration of Bromocaine

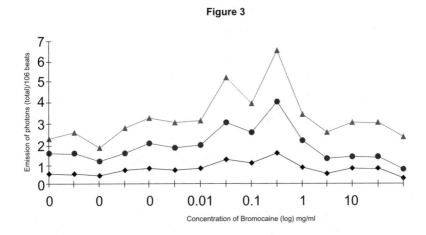

Figure 3

In 1920, Lakhovsky carried out a series of experiments to confirm the existence of this EME field as expressed in the following quote: "The cells which make up the basic organic units of everything that lives are electromagnetic transmittors, capable of sending out and absorbing high-frequency waves. The nucleus of the cells behaves like a microscopic oscillating circuit, just like an electric circuit." (*The Secret of Life*, by M. Aguilar Publishers, Madrid, 1929).

For Lakhovsky, disease is an imbalance in cellular oscillation, beginning by oscillating arrhythmically, until the cells finally stop oscillating and die. In order for a cell to recover, it has to be treated with an appropriate frequency. In this way, he came to the conclusion that the necessary energy to maintain the normal oscillations of the cells cannot be produced in the nucleus, but that it comes from external energy, which is stored in the DNA, just as in a condensor.

Today, it might be said that the existence of a field of biophotons is a proven fact, not only by Popp's and Lakhovsky's experiments, but also by those of other researchers.

In order to continue proving that this field of biophotons or electromagnetic field exists, we shall analyze experiments carried out by Dr. Burr, which are described in his book *Blueprint for Immortality* (published by Neville Spearman Limited). These experiments suggest that the organization of any biological system is established by an electromagnetic field of an electrodynamic complex, which anticipates the physical events that are going to take place within them and points out that the mind can either positively or negatively affect the matter with which it is associated by modulating this field.

In order to prove his theory, Burr used a voltmeter made of a vacuum tube and special electrodes, with which he was able to measure the EME fields in vegetables, animals, and human beings. The apparatus consists of an amplifier with a high-entry impedance (inner electric resistance) so that the changes of resistance in the system did not alter measurements. This instrument has a high degree of sensitivity and is able to register any change in electric voltage, however subtle this may be. It must be stable in order for fortuitous variation to be reduced to a minimum. According to Burr, "these voltages have nothing to do with the alternate electric currents doctors obtain when they measure the brain and heart."

In order to measure the EME of the human body, Burr connected a couple of flower pots to a voltmeter and filled them with a solution of common natural salt, placed silver chloride electrodes inside them and then reduced the potential of the electrodes to half a millivolt, thus ensuring that their voltage did not interfere with the measurement. Finally, he closed the circuit by submerging his left index finger in the left-hand pot and his right index finger into the right-hand pot, and registered the potential generated by his body with a voltmeter.

Burr also measured the EME fields of sprouting seeds, discovering that this field does not have the form of the original seed but that of the *completely developed plant.*

By measuring the electrodynamic field of trees, it was observed that the recordings showed that the fields of the trees varied with the sunlight, with darkness, with the cycles of the moon, with electric storms, and with sunspots. From all the experiments carried out with his collaborators throughout his life, Dr. Burr reached the following conclusion:

> As the field of a living system is an organized model, it must be part of the enveloping or general model of the Universe. It might be argued that the Universe is a field of energy and that all that exists in it is a component part of this total field.
>
> This energy can be measured, has order, and is not a strange, separate phenomenon, but an essential characteristic of the Universe.

It is also of interest to us to describe the experiments of the bacteriologist Otto Rahn, which are quoted in the book *The Secret Life of Plants* by Peter Thompkins and Christopher Bird (Diana Publishers), for they help us to understand the experiment we carried out with magnetized seeds, understanding by this that they received the characteristic EME of each human being in an emotional state of rage, during menstruation, and in the absence of it, as we shall see below in the experimental section.

Professor Otto Rahn was surprised when he noticed that every time one of his collaborators fell sick, it seemed to cause the death of the yeast cells he was experimenting on. It was enough for them to point their fingertips towards the plant for a few minutes to kill off vigorous cells of this fungus. Rahn proved that the human body constantly sends out electromagnetic energy through the hands, the cornea of the eye, etc., as he described in his book *Invisible Radiation of Organisms.*

In relation to the same subject, there are the experiments of S. P. Shchurin of the Institute of Automatization and Electrometry of Russia, as described in the book *The Secret Life of Plants,* in which he showed that cells can "converse" by means of coded messages in the form of a special electromagnetic ray.

In these experiments, two cultures of identical tissues were placed in hermetically sealed recipients and separated by a glass wall. Then, a lethal virus was introduced into one of the chambers, which killed off the colony of cells that inhabited it. However, the colony of the other recipient was totally unharmed. Then, when the dividing glass wall was substituted for one of quartz and a deadly virus once more inserted into one of the colonies, they saw how both colonies suffered the same fate.

What was it that killed the second colony?

As ordinary glass does not let ultraviolet rays pass through it but quartz crystal does, it seemed to these Soviet scientists that the key to the mystery lay here. Then, they used an electronic eye, the power of which was increased with a photomultiplier to register the levels of energy. They discovered that when the vital processes remained normal in the tissue cultures, the ultraviolet light remained stable, but the moment that the affected colony began to fight against infection, the radiation was intensified. In view of this, we can clearly see that there is a coherent field or electrodynamic field of biophotons in living beings, which has characteristic patterns of frequency, which are in a mutual relationship to matter and the environment around them. This enables us to approach the subject of acupuncture and our experimental purpose from a more scientific perspective.

Acupuncture is one of the first methods of bioenergetic regulation, and it is widely known that this healing system is based on locating and treating certain areas of the skin. These areas have been called acupuncture points, through which certain points are stimulated, for example, by needles, heat, light, electric current, etc., to achieve certain effects on the process of energetic regulation of the organism in the sense of a therapeutic effect. The energetic channel that relates a specific point with a certain organ or with a certain functional process is called the *meridian*. According to the tenets of acupuncture, there are 12 meridians, each of which is associated with a particular organ and has a path through the organism, which we will discuss in detail below:

Meridian	Organ	Path
Lung	Lung	Starting from the zone under the shoulder blade and ending in the thumb.
Large Intestine	Large Intestine	Starting at the tip of the index finger and ending at the level of the nostril.
Stomach	Stomach	Beginning above the eyebrow and ending in the second toe.
Spleen/Pancreas	Spleen/Pancreas	Beginning in the big toe and ending under the armpit.
Heart	Heart	Starting in the armpit and ending at the tip of the little finger.
Small Intestine	Small Intestine	Beginning in the inner tip of the nail of the little finger and ending in front of the ear.
Bladder	Bladder	Starting from the inner corner of the eye and ending at the tip of the little toe.
Kidneys	Kidneys	Starting under the foot and ending under the shoulder blade.
Circulation and Sex	Circulation and Sex	Starting in the chest at the level of the breast and ending in the middle finger.
Triple Warmer	Triple Warmer	Starting at the tip of the ring finger and ending in the temple.
Liver	Liver	Starting in the big toe and ending in the eighth space between the ribs.
Gallbladder	Gallbladder	Starting in the outer corner of the eye and ending in the phalanx of the fourth toe.

Acupuncture points are different from the surrounding zones because the skin in them is less resistant.

Popp, like Pribram and other scientists, sustains that information is not only stored in the brain but in the whole body. Memories are stored holographically (a hologram is a tridimensional image formed by the interference of two laser rays, whose chief characteristic is that one part contains the information of the whole). Popp observed in the field of electro-acupuncture that the acupuncture points of the whole organism contain the information of the whole meridian. These points never react individually to electric stimulation, but do so jointly, that is, in combination and interaction with the rest. This can only occur if there is an extremely coherent field of biophotons. The meridians of acupuncture are types of preferred channels of waves so that information can be better transmitted, that is, through purely electromagnetic channels.

According to Dr. Bodo Köhler in his book *Quantum Medicine*, the crests of the waves of the biophotons can represent the acupuncture points. When these waves collide with the body's extremities (feet, hands, ears), they are reflected in these limited surfaces and form stationary waves. Thus, these extreme organs of the body are reflecting zones in which the whole human body is projected.

In the book *Electromagnetic Man* (published by St. Martin's Press), Drs. Jean-Claude Darras and De Vernejoul were able to prove that EME is carried through the meridians. We shall see a brief description of their experiments below. They injected a radioactive tracer (a solution that contains a radioactive isotope, such as technetium 99) into an acupuncture point and, using a gamma-camera (an instrument to detect gamma rays, photons), they saw that the radioactive substance travelled through the meridians at a speed of 1½ to 2 inches/minute. On the other hand, the speed of this substance was much slower in the meridian of a sick organ.

2. Experimental Variables

In order to carry out the experiments, a place was chosen with controlled temperature and humidity conditions in an environment free of interference from electric or magnetic devices. The acupuncture point called lymph was chosen, which is recommended in the Vegatest method, for it reflects the general condition of the organism. Special care was taken that the measuring point could be reproduced, that is, that when pressure was repeatedly applied on the center of the point with the measuring pencil, and at the same pressure, the value of the point kept constant. The starting figure for different people was regulated at 80 u.s. (units of scale), so that they all had the same initial parameter. This can be done with the TP regulator of the Vegatest equipment, which enables one to increase sensitivity without altering the measuring current. Patients must remove any jewelry so as not to alter measurements and the therapist must wear plastic gloves in order not to interfere with the measuring process.

3. Experimental Procedures

The aim of this work is to experimentally prove that:

(a) Menstrual blood has a strong concentration of toxic energy, and menstrual coitus has a poisonous effect on the man's organism.

(b) Masturbation, unlike normal coitus, notably depresses the organic defenses because of the remarkable loss of energy.

(c) Electromagnetic energy emitted by the body through the anus is of a toxic, polluting nature, so that the practice known as "anal coitus" has a notably poisonous effect.

(d) During emotional states of rage and destructiveness, the body produces and radiates poisonous, destructive magnetic energy.

We have used the term "toxic" not as a substance that chemically poisons the organism, but in the sense that it

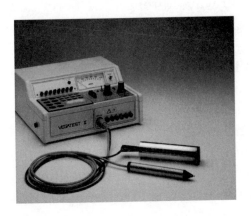

brings about an alteration in the field of biophotons, thus preventing proper transmission of information, which will finally lead to a state of sickness or alteration. In order to carry out measurements of the electromagnetic energy of the human body, we used an electro-acupuncture apparatus called Vegatest, which measures the points of acupuncture. See picture.

Currently, there has been much research on acupuncture, so that science now has a better understanding of it. The Vegatest method registers the changes in resistance of an electric flow in the acupuncture points located in the fingers

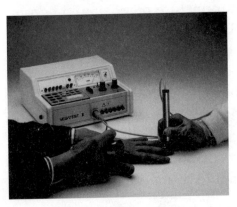

and the toes when certain substances in glass tubes are placed in a series circuit. Its central unit is an amplifier of the measurements which transforms the skin's conducting capacity into an optic and acoustic signal (an indicating needle). In practice, the patient takes a silver-plated cylinder with one hand and places the other on a table in order to measure the point. This measurement is carried out with the pressure pencil, thus closing off the circuit as shown in the picture.

Thus, a small measuring flow of current of 10 u.s., which is conducted from the tips of the fingers and toes, passing through different complex pathways through the body and leaving through the cylindrical electrode to the amplifier. Any alteration will be marked by the indicating needle and the acoustic signal. Electrically, it is a Wheatstone bridge circuit (a standard circuit of compared resistances). The principal indicator of electricity is the so-called "control of disorder," which registers any alteration in the measurement in accordance with the substance inserted into the circuit (the panel on the apparatus), indicating a higher or lower register according to the substance used. If a poison is inserted, then the apparatus can always be expected to give a low figure. For example, hepatic dysfunction can be detected if a homeopathic tube containing liver tissue is placed in the panel and the same point is measured once more. If there is a low register, then this indicates hepatic dysfunction. It is known that the acupuncture point is electrically negative with respect to the skin around it. The positive extreme of the circuit is placed on the point, and as opposite charges cancel themselves out, the electromagnetic force of the acupuncture point should become balanced, which is measured by the Vegatest. To this end, the electromagnetic force of the point, which acts as a battery, must be constantly recharged, for if this were not so, the Vegatest indicator would begin to drop. It is assumed that the recharging of the acupuncture point is produced by a flow of energy of biophotons that circulate in the meridian itself. The amount of electric tension at a specific point reflects the level of energy of the organ associated to its meridian.

The diagnosis carried out by the Vegatest can be explained through the phenomenon of resonance. The phenomenon of resonance occurs when a period of vibration is produced similar to the one previously created. For example, if we have two violins that are separate from each other and tuned to the same pitch, when the strings of one of them are touched, they will begin to vibrate and send out the sound of a note and the other violin will receive this wave and send out the same sound.

(a) *Measurement of Menstrual Blood*

This procedure consisted of comparing menstrual blood with normal blood from the veins, to show that menstrual blood has a "toxic" influence on the man's organism, unlike blood from the veins. The lymph point was measured ensuring that the Vegatest gave a stable value, that is, that the initial measurement was kept constant at 80 u.s., before a tube was placed in the panel. Then blood from the veins was extracted from the arm and placed in a glass tube. Menstrual blood was also extracted directly from the vagina with a syringe (without a needle), which was then emptied into another glass tube. After this, the tube with menstrual blood was placed in the panel and the lymph point was measured, giving an average value of 25 u.s. The same was done with the tube that contained blood from the veins, distilled water, and chlorine (a substance which is toxic for the organism).

The averages of the values obtained were significantly different between the different substances, being 80 u.s. for blood from the veins and distilled water and 25 u.s. for the chlorine, and for the menstrual blood. This procedure was applied to 30 women. The results are illustrated in Table 1 and Graph 1.

The experiment of planting magnetized seeds separately during menstruation and outside of menstruation was also carried out. A neutral group of non-magnetized seeds were left apart. In this way we wished to corroborate the results obtained in the former experiment. Wheat seeds that had been magnetized for 7 days were chosen and placed in the hands for 5 minutes per day. Before planting, they were measured with the Vegatest placed in small glass flasks and following the same procedure used for measuring blood.

It was found that the seeds that had been magnetized during menstruation gave a value of 20 u.s., similar to that given by menstrual blood. Then the seeds that had been magnetized outside of the menstrual period were measured, giving a value of 70 u.s., similar to that of the neutral (non-magnetized) seeds. All the seeds were planted and compared during the development process, and there was a noticeable difference in growth structure between those magnetized during the menstrual period and those magnetized outside the menstrual period. The former (the menstrual ones) developed late and the latter (non-menstrual ones) grew faster and stronger. The neutral seeds developed normally. The three groups of seeds received the same care as far as water, light, and environmental temperature are concerned.

(b) Measurement of Energy Loss with Masturbation

The experiment, consisting of measuring a group of 10 men who practiced masturbation over a period of 2 days, was divided into three stages. In the first stage (in the morning) a point related to the circulation and sex meridian was measured, as well as a point related to the kidneys. The kidney point was chosen because the kidneys produce most of the energy that supplies the sexual center, according to traditional Chinese acupuncture theory.

In the second stage, the patient then returned two hours after having masturbated, and the same measurement was carried out. Finally, he came the following day, also in the morning, at the same time as the first measurement was taken, and the procedure of the two first measurements was repeated. During the three stages of measurement, the therapist wore surgical gloves with the aim of electrically isolating himself from the patient, thus ensuring that measurements were not altered. The results are shown in Graph 2.

(c) Measurement of Electromagnetic Energy of the Anus

Our aim in this experiment was to show that the energy radiated by the anus is also of a "toxic" nature to the organism, by comparing the value of a suppository before and after having been inserted in the anus. In this regard, the lymph point was measured without using a tube, registering a value of 80 u.s., then the uncharged suppository was inserted in a tube, also giving a value of 80 u.s. Then, the patient was asked to keep the suppository inserted for 15 minutes, in order to charge it with the radiation given off by the anus. Then the tube was placed in the panel and gave an average value of 30 u.s. This same procedure was carried out on 5 men and 5 women, all giving the same result, which is shown in Table 4 and Graph 4.

(d) Measurement of Seeds Magnetized with Feelings of Rage

A group of 30 people was used for this measurement, each of whom was given a handful of seeds. They held them in their hands (unwrapped) and magnetized them for 7 days, 5 minutes per day, with a feeling of rage. Once this stage had been completed, the lymph point was measured. First, the point was measured with neutral seeds (non-magnetized ones), which gave an average value of 80 u.s., and then the same point was measured with the seeds that had been magnetized with feelings of rage, which gave an average value of 40 u.s., which is shown in Table 5.

In order to understand the different experiments that were carried out, one should recall what was said in Chapter 1, in which we analyzed the fact that the human body is permanently sending out electromagnetic energy through its different physiological processes, and that the quality and quantity of this energy depend on factors such as the environment, food, and the individual's psychic and emotional states. In this case, this is why the energy that is issued by the hands has the energetic characteristics of the emotion that is voluntarily being transmitted to the seeds.

4. Results of the Experiment

The results obtained from the different experiments are shown in detail in the tables given below, together with their respective graphs.

Table 1   Comparison of Blood from the Veins/Menstrual Blood

Sample Number	Point Measured	Initial Value	Blood from Veins	Menstrual Blood	Distilled Water	Chlorine
1	1	80	80	23	80	37
2	1	80	80	24	75	20
3	1	80	60	24	55	20
4	1	80	70	20	72	22
5	1	80	70	16	75	15
6	1	80	78	27	80	19
7	1	80	70	28	72	24
8	1	80	75	25	80	30
9	1	80	75	26	80	25
10	1	80	80	22	80	20
11	1	80	75	22	80	25
12	1	80	75	25	80	26
13	1	80	75	20	80	15
14	1	80	78	22	80	30
15	1	80	78	22	78	18
16	1	80	80	24	80	22
17	1	80	80	26	80	22
18	1	80	75	20	80	16
19	1	80	70	22	70	25
20	1	80	80	24	80	22
21	1	80	80	17	80	25
22	1	80	80	22	40	20
23	1	80	75	20	80	20
24	1	80	80	20	80	35
25	1	80	80	25	80	30
26	1	80	80	22	80	35
27	1	80	80	25	80	17
28	1	80	80	25	80	22
29	1	80	78	26	75	20

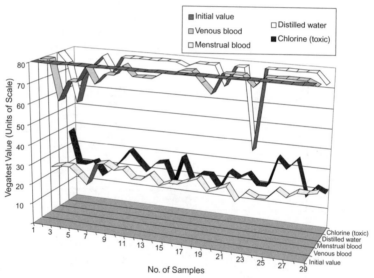

Graph No. 1:
Menstrual blood as compared to venous blood

Table 2   Comparative Results Between Masturbation and Sexual Intercourse, Measured on Point 15 (Circulation and Sex)

Sample Number	Point Measured	Initial Value	Value 2 Hours after Masturbation	Value 24 Hours after Masturbation	Value after Sexual Intercourse
1	15	80	29	24	80
2	15	80	38	36	89
3	15	80	43	41	79
4	15	80	41	30	91
5	15	80	40	34	84
6	15	80	50	26	78
7	15	80	47	32	74
8	15	80	50	30	81
9	15	80	40	32	80
10	15	80	44	37	80

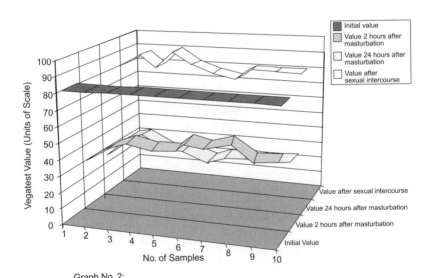

Graph No. 2:
Comparison between masturbation and
natural sexual intercourse (Point 15)

Table 3   Comparative Results Between Masturbation and Sexual Intercourse as Measured on Point 2 (Kidney)

Sample Number	Point Measured	Initial Value	Value 2 Hours after Masturbation	Value 24 Hours after Masturbation	Value after Sexual Intercourse
1	2	80	30	15	80
2	2	80	28	22	84
3	2	80	19	20	85
4	2	80	48	30	83
5	2	80	30	30	85
6	2	80	33	36	82
7	2	80	43	31	73
8	2	80	20	15	84
9	2	80	35	32	82
10	2	80	48	39	85

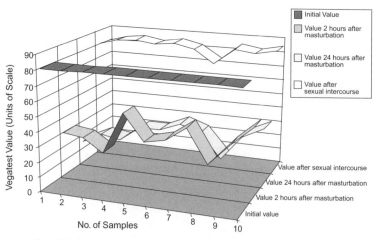

Graph No. 3:
Comparison between masturbation and
natural sexual intercourse (Point 2)

Table 4   Measurement in the Anus

Sample Number	Point Measured	Value Prior to Inserting Suppository in the Anus	Value after Inserting Suppository in the Anus
1	1	80	40
2	1	80	35
3	1	80	40
4	1	80	42
5	1	80	70
6	1	80	32
7	1	80	30
8	1	80	32
9	1	80	35
10	1	80	30

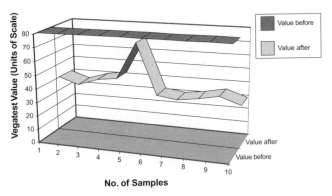

Graph No. 4:
Comparison of the electric charge in a suppository
before and after being inserted in the anus

Table 5   Measurements of the Seeds

Sample Number	Point Measured	Seed Value Prior to Magnetization	Seed Value after Magnetization
1	1	80	34
2	1	80	45
3	1	80	75
4	1	80	45
5	1	80	45
6	1	80	50
7	1	80	45
8	1	80	50
9	1	80	45
10	1	80	25
11	1	80	25
12	1	80	40
13	1	80	42
14	1	80	25
15	1	80	45
16	1	80	40
17	1	80	40
18	1	80	25
19	1	80	30
20	1	80	30
21	1	80	35
22	1	80	33
23	1	80	32
24	1	80	30
25	1	80	45
26	1	80	40
27	1	80	40
28	1	80	40
29	1	80	25
30	1	80	25

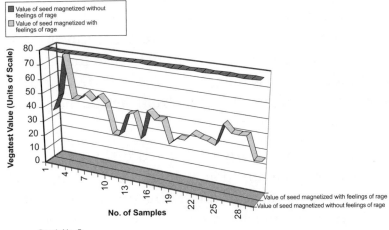

Graph No. 5:
Comparison of seeds magnetized with feelings
of rage and without feelings of rage

5. Discussion of the Results

From the results expressed in the preceding chapter, we can generally see that there exists a "noxious or toxic" component for the organism of the individual himself, and for those who interact with the individual during the menstrual period, when experiencing feelings of rage, and during anal intercourse. In the case of masturbation, one detects a notable diminishing of electromagnetic energy from the person under study.

As one can expect, the values registered by Vegatest were low, experiencing, on average, a decrease of 60 percent with respect to the initial value. This happened when the measured substances were noxious for the organism.

In Graph 1, one can see that the blood from the veins and the distilled water have a similar value, close to the initial value of 80 u.s. On the other hand, the curve of the menstrual blood is similar to that of chlorine, registering a much lower value, showing that the menstrual blood is harmful at the energetic level (because it has a frequency in the range in which illnesses are produced), in the sense that it alters our field of biophotons, leading us to get sick. This result shows us that coitus during the menstrual period has a noxious effect on man's organism.

Graphs 2 and 3 clearly show the drop in value that occurs in the two acupuncture points 15 and 2 after masturbation, and also reveal an increase in the energy of these points after normal sexual relations. Graph 2 shows that the curve corresponding to 2 hours after masturbation reveals a decrease of 47.25 percent with respect to the initial value and a decrease of 59.75 percent after 24 hours. Graph 3 shows a variation of 57.5 percent with respect to the initial value and a variation of 66.3 percent, 24 hours after. The same does not happen upon having normal sexual relations, since, in this case, an exchange of energy is produced, increasing by 2.8 percent with respect to the initial value in the first point and by 2 percent in the other.

In Graph 4, we can see that the curve obtained with the value of the suppository introduced into the anus is much lower than the initial one, thus demonstrating the harmful nature of anal coitus.

Graph 5 shows us that the curve corresponding to the seeds magnetized with feelings of rage have a lower value than the curve of the neutral seeds. This result shows us that an emotional state such as rage is also noxious, as much for the organism that generates the rage as for the surrounding environment.

WORKS CONSULTED

Nahas, Gabriel G., *Keep Off the Grass* (Paul S. Eriksson Publisher, 1990).

The Analysis of Cannabinoids in Biological Fluids (U.S.A.: National Institute of Drug Abuse, 1982).

Marijuana, Research Findings (U.S.A.: National Institute of Drug Abuse, 1980).

Testing Drugs for Physical Dependence Potential and Abuse Liability (U.S.A.: National Institute of Drug Abuse, 1984).

BIBLIOGRAPHY

Barnothy, Madeleine, *Biological Effects of Magnetic Fields,* Vol. 1 and 2 (New York: Plenum Press, 1969).

Becker, Robert, and Gary Selden, *The Body Electric* (New York: William Morrow, 1985).

Dumitrescu, Ion, and Julian Kenyon, *Electrographic Imaging in Medicine & Biology* (Great Britain: Neville Spearman Limited, 1983).

Eisberg, Robert, and Robert Resnick, *Física Cuántica* (Mexico: Limusa Publishers, 1983).

Guerrero, Alberto, and Sánchez Orto, *Electrotécnica* (Madrid: McGraw-Hill Publishers, 1994).

Kenyon, Julian, *Medicina siglo XXI* (Norma Group Publishers, 1993).

Kervran, Louis, *Las Transmutaciones Biológicas y la Fisica Moderna* (Barcelona: Sirio Publishers, 1988).

Pischinger, Albert, *Matrix and Matrix Regulation* (Brussels: Haug International, 1991).

Pomeranz, Bruce, and Gabriel Stux, *Scientific Bases of Acupuncture* (Berlin: Springer-Verlag, 1989).

Popp, Fritz Albert, *Biophotonen* (Heidelberg: Verlag fur Medizin, 1976).

Popp, Fritz Albert, Ulrich Warnke, Herbert Konig, and Walter Peschka, *Electromagnetic Bio-Information* (Munich: Urban & Schwarzenberg, 1989)

Prelat, Carlos, *El Mundo de las Vibraciones y de los Sonidos* (Argentina: Espasa Calpe, 1951).

Schrodinger, Erwin, *Ciencia y Humanismo* (Barcelona: Tusquets, 1985).

Schrodinger, Erwin, *Mente y Materia* (Barcelona: Tusquets, 1985).

Volkenshtein, M. V., *Biofísica* (Moscow: Mir Publishers, 1985).

Wilber, Kent, *Cuestiones cuánticas* (Barcelona: Kairós, 1994).

Zoll, Stuart, *The Bridge between Acupuncture and Modern Bio-Energetic Medicine* (Brussels: Haug International, 1993).

Other books published by John Baines can be ordered through the publisher:

- The Secret Science
  ISBN 1-882692-01-2 ....$8.95

- The Stellar Man
  ISBN 0-87542-026-5 ....$9.95

- The Science of Love
  ISBN 1-882692-00-4 ....$12.95

- HypsoConsciousness
  ISBN 1-882692-02-0 ....$9.95

- Morals for the 21st Century
  ISBN 1-882692-03-9 ....$18.95

Books are also available in Spanish, Bulgarian, Russian, Italian, Latvian, German, and Portuguese.

Use this page for ordering:
THE JOHN BAINES COLLECTION
P.O. Box 8556, F.D.R. Station
New York, NY 10150
JBI@bway.net

Please send me the above title(s). I am enclosing a check for $ _____.
(Please add $3.20 shipping for 1-4 titles within the USA and $12.00 for shipping outside of the USA.)

We also accept MasterCard, Visa, and American Express:
Card Number: _____
Expiration Date: _____
Signature: _____

Mr/Mrs/Ms: _____
Address: _____
City/State/Zip: _____

*Prices and availability subject to change without notice.